Praise f

'A brilliant and revelatory work of modern historical investigation, throwing new light on the French Resistance and the complex world of secret intelligence. Written with remarkable insight, understanding and empathy – a triumph.'

William Boyd

'An incredible story brilliantly told. Marnham has created an utterly gripping story of wartime espionage, deception, double-crossing and terrible betrayal that drew me in from the outset. A stunning work of investigation, research and scholarship.'

James Holland

'It is beautifully written, minutely observed . . . full of underhand trickery . . . in every sense of the word an intriguing book.'

Roger Boyes, *The Times*

'*War in the Shadows* is a melange of *Le Grand Meaulnes* and *The Spy Who Came in from the Cold*. It is unforgettable.'

Ferdinand Mount, *TLS*, Books of the Year

'A masterly analysis, impeccably presented.'

Allan Mallinson, *Spectator*

'Fascinating . . . Marnham has a vast and scholarly knowledge of this often treacherous world.'

Caroline Moorehead, *Literary Review*

'Patrick Marnham is one of our very best writers on France.'

Antony Beevor

Other Books by Patrick Marnham

Road to Katmandu
Fantastic Invasion: Dispatches from Contemporary Africa
Lourdes, A Modern Pilgrimage
The Private Eye Story: the first 21 years
So Far from God: A Journey to Central America
Trail of Havoc: In the Steps of Lord Lucan
Crime and the Académie Française: Dispatches from Paris
The Man Who Wasn't Maigret: A Portrait of Georges Simenon
Dreaming with His Eyes Open: A Life of Diego Rivera
The Death of Jean Moulin: Biography of a Ghost
Wild Mary: The Life of Mary Wesley
Snake Dance: Journeys Beneath a Nuclear Sky
Darling Pol: Letters of Mary Wesley and Eric Siepmann 1944–1967 (ed.)

WAR IN THE SHADOWS

*Resistance, Deception and Betrayal
in Occupied France*

Patrick Marnham

ONEWORLD

A Oneworld Book

First published in the United Kingdom, the Republic of Ireland
and North America by Oneworld Publications, 2020
This paperback edition published 2021

ISBN 978-0-86154-058-7
eISBN 978-1-78607-810-0

Typeset by Hewer Text UK Ltd, Edinburgh
Printed and bound in Great Britain by Clays Ltd, Elcograf S.p.A.

Oneworld Publications
10 Bloomsbury Street, London, WC1B 3SR, England

For
Anne-Marie de Bernard
Yvonne Rudellat
Nesta Cox

History is not what actually happened but what the surviving evidence says happened. If the evidence can be hidden and the secrets kept, then history will record an inaccurate version.

SIR DICK WHITE
Director General MI5, 1952–6; Chief SIS, 1956–68

Contents

Foreword

On a summer's day in 1943 in occupied France, German security police delivered a double blow to the French Resistance. In the Sologne, in central France, on the morning of 21 June, they struck at PROSPER, the largest resistance network formed by SOE in readiness for the national insurrection that was planned to accompany the D-Day landings. More than 300 members of the network were arrested. Many were tortured and deported, others were shot. And in a separate police operation on the same afternoon, in the southern city of Lyons, a resistance courier who had been persuaded to collaborate with the Germans led a Gestapo raiding party to a secret meeting where they arrested 'Max', the political head of the French Resistance.

'Max' was the field name of Jean Moulin, a senior civil servant who had been sent into Occupied France as the delegate of General de Gaulle. His arrest came one month after he had united the resistance movement behind de Gaulle.

In a biography of 'Max', originally entitled *The Death of Jean Moulin: Biography of a Ghost*, which was reissued in 2015 as *Armies of the Night*, I suggested that two senior members of the Resistance, who were then still alive, may have been partly responsible for what happened. Though I mentioned the Sologne in passing, I made no connection between the two police operations since they appeared to me to be coincidental. But shortly after the publication of *The Death of Jean Moulin* I received an anonymous letter suggesting that my solution was wrong, and that the key to the mystery lay in uncovering the link between those two disasters. The writer described himself as 'the Ghost'.

Unknown to the anonymous letter writer, I had known some of the people who had been members of PROSPER quite well and had stayed in their house many years before. What follows is the account of a quest to discover what really happened when my friends in the Sologne were arrested, and whether there was anything in the suggestion that their downfall was linked to the arrest of 'Max'.

The clues offered by 'the Ghost' led me into an increasingly complex labyrinth of calculation, deception and betrayal. It was an underworld of dead ends and false leads that characterised the warfare of secret intelligence. In that war allies were prepared to obstruct each other's work, while enemies combined in the struggle to control the most dangerous weapon of all – a knowledge of the simple truth.

Somewhere in those dark corridors I hoped to find the thread that would lead out of the labyrinth, and explain how my friends and hundreds of other resisters had been trapped.

FRANCE OCCUPIED BY AXIS POWERS

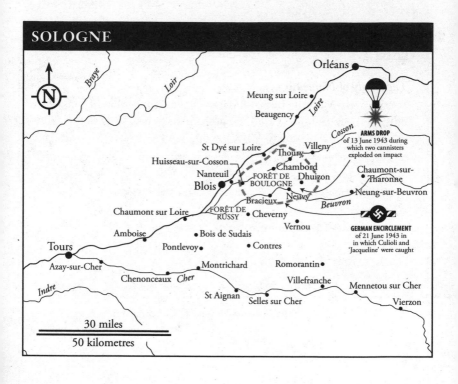

SOLOGNE

Braye

Loir

Loire

Orléans

Meung sur Loire

Beaugency

Cosson

ARMS DROP
of 13 June 1943 during
which two cannisters
exploded on impact

St Dyé sur Loire

Villeny

Thoury

Huisseau-sur-Cosson

Chambord

Chaumont-sur-
Tharonne

Nanteuil

Dhuizon

FORÊT DE
BOULOGNE

Blois

Neuvy

Neung-sur-Beuvron

Bracieux

Beuvron

FORÊT DE
RUSSY

Cheverny

Chaumont sur Loire

GERMAN ENCIRCLEMENT
of 21 June 1943 in
in which Culioli and
'Jacqueline' were caught

Vernou

Amboise

Bois de Sudais

Pontlevoy

Contres

Tours

Azay-sur-Cher

Romorantin

Chenonceaux   Cher

Montrichard

Villefranche

Mennetou sur Cher

St Aignan

Selles sur Cher

Vierzon

Indre

30 miles

50 kilometres

List of Principal Characters

Escaped POW
Corporal Charles Carter (Military Police, 4th Batt. Seaforth Highlanders)

Nanteuil Post-war
Owen (known as 'Oscar') Watson; first post-war student, m. Moune
    Gardnor-Beard 1954
Robert Cleland (regular visitor from Kentucky)
Suzanne (cook in the 1960s)
Françoise (niece of Suzanne, maid in the 1960s)
Camille (butler, husband of Suzanne)
Jean (gardener in the 1960's)

PARTS II AND III

THE RESISTANCE IN THE SOLOGNE AND TOURAINE

Network Adolphe
Marcel Buhler
Pierre Culioli (tax inspector)
André Brasseur
René Bouton (Romorantin, owner of garage and cycle shop)
Dr Francis Cortambert (vet)
Roger Couffrant (shopkeeper)
Thérèse Couffrant
Georges Duchet (owner of garage)
Georges Fermé
Albert Le Meur (hotelier at Chambord)
Julien Nadau (area manager in Contres for the electrical supply company)
Raymonde Nadau (hairdresser, wife of Julien)
Gerard Oury

Other resisters in Touraine
Maurice Lequeux (Meung-sur-Loire)
Marguerite Flamencourt

Hospital in Blois
Dr Luzuy
Dr Brun
M. Drussy

Gendarmes and Prefecture
Sergeant Jacquet
Pierre Théry

BRITISH INTELLIGENCE IN LONDON

SIS (MI6) – the Secret Intelligence Service
Sir Stewart Menzies – C (Chief)
Colonel Claude Dansey (Vice chief – director of operations)
Lieutenant Commander Kenneth Cohen (Z man) (codename 'Clam')
Commander 'Biffy' Dunderdale (SIS French specialist)

MI5 – the Security Service
Sir David Petrie 'DG' (Director General)
Guy Liddell (director of B division: counter-espionage)
Dick White (deputy director of B division: post-war head of both MI5
    and SIS)
Major Geoffrey Wethered (B1b – intelligence analysis)

Deception Agencies
LCS (London Controlling Section): Colonel John Bevan
W (Wireless) Board: Menzies, Liddell and three directors of service
    intelligence
XX Committee: John Masterman, T.A. Robertson, Frank Foley

TWIST: T.A. Robertson, Frank Foley, Anthony Blunt

SOE

Sir Frank Nelson (Z man) (CD, head of SOE, 1940–2)
Major General Colin Gubbins (CD 1942–5)
Harry Sporborg (deputy head of SOE)
Air Commodore Boyle (director of intelligence – ex-W board)
Commander John Senter, RNVR (director of security; ex-MI5)
Leo Marks (coding officer)
André Simon (also in SIS)

F section (in London)
Colonel Maurice Buckmaster
Major Nicolas Bodington (probably in SIS)
Vera Atkins

F section agents in France
PROSPER (aka PHYSICIAN in London)
Major Francis Suttill DSO ('Prosper')
Major Gilbert Norman ('Archambaud') (radio operator)
Andrée Borrel ('Denise')
Raymond Flower
Marcel Clech (radio operator)
Yvonne Rudellat ('Jacqueline')
Pierre Raynaud DSO
Frank Pickersgill
Ken Macalister (radio operator)
Henri Déricourt (air movements officer)
Jack Agazarian (radio operator)
Noor Inayat Khan (radio operator)
Marcel Rousset (radio operator)
Edouard Montfort Wilkinson ('Monsieur Alexandre')

———

France Antelme
Henri Frager ('Louba')

Local resisters in Paris
Armel Guerne ('Gaspard')
Nicolas Laurent
Maude Laurent
Germaine Tambour (ex-CARTE – 'Annette')
Roger Bardet (Gestapo collaborator)
Yvonne Wilkinson ('Madame Alexandre')

André Girard (leader of CARTE)
Maurice Dufour (ex-PAT line; probable SIS agent in London)

BCRA (in London)
Colonel Passy (André Dewavrin, head of Gaullist intelligence – the BCRA)
Captain Roger Wybot (head of BCRA security)
Jean-Louis Crémieux-Brilhac (secretary of Gaullist propaganda in London)

PART IV

THE GERMANS

German Intelligence Services – in Berlin
Ernst Kaltenbrunner, head of the RSHA
Horst Kopkow (*Obersturmbannführer* – SS Lieut. Colonel)

In Paris
SS General Karl Oberg
Sipo–SD (Sicherheitsdienst)
Dr Helmut Knochen (*Standartenführer* – SS Colonel)
Karl Boemelburg (*Sturmbannführer* – SS Major, head of the Gestapo)
Josef Kieffer
Josef Goetz (radio expert)
Karl Langer
Heinrich Meiners (interpreter)

In Blois
Ludwig Bauer (nicknamed 'Gestapo Bauer')
Mona Reimeringer (nicknamed 'Mona-la-Blonde')

In Lyons
SS Lieutenant Klaus Barbie
Robert Moog ('K30')
Jean Multon (ex-Resistance, collaborator)

Abwehr (Military Intelligence) in Paris
Hugo Bleicher ('Colonel Heinrich' – expert spy catcher)

––––––

Colonel Hippe (Army garrison commander in Blois)

––––––

The Resistance in Lyons
Emanuel d'Astier de la Vigerie (leader of *Libération*)
Jean-Pierre Levy (leader of *Franc-Tireur*)
Henri Frenay (leader of *Combat*)
Lucie 'Aubrac' (married to Raymond Samuel)
Pierre Bénouville (*Combat* – ex-*Cagoule*)
Antoinette Sachs (courier for 'Max'; sister of Colonel Groussard's mistress)

––––––

Berty Albrecht (*Combat*)
Lieutenant General Charles Delestraint (regular soldier, 'Vidal')

Arrested in Caluire
Jean Moulin ('Corporal Mercier', 'Jacques Martel', 'Rex', 'Max')
Raymond Samuel, 'Aubrac' ('Claude Ermelin', 'F. Vallet', senior
    member of *Libération*)
Captain Henri Aubry (*Combat*)
René Hardy ('Didot') (*Combat*, head of '*Resistance Fe*r')
Colonel Albert Lacaze (*France d'Abord*)
Bruno Larat (BCRA/RF – air movements officer)
André Lassagne (*Libération*)

Lieutenant Colonel Schwartzfeld (*France d'Abord*)
Dr Frédéric Dugoujon, resident of Caluire
Marguerite Brossier (Dr Dugoujon's housekeeper)

PART V

Colonel Dansey's contacts in Geneva and Berne
Victor Farrell (Z man) (SIS station chief in Geneva)
Colonel Georges Groussard (ex-*Cagoule*, based in Geneva; SIS contact
    with Vichy intelligence; associate of Victor Farrell)
Edmée Delettraz (Groussard agent in France; Gestapo double agent)

US Intelligence Services in Switzerland
Allen Dulles (head of OSS, Berne)

A Note on *Noms de Guerre*, the BCRA and SOE(RF)

Within SOE agents were given an Operational name, always and only used in communications from London, a code name correctly called a 'Field' name, used within the network in France, and a 'Cover' name which went with a false identity and complete back story and appeared on the agent's ID cards. The cover name could be changed as frequently as needed. Throughout this book field names (e.g. 'Prosper' or 'Archambaud') are given using single quotation marks.

F. section 'circuits' (or networks) were usually named after occupations – VENTRILOQUIST, SCIENTIST, LIONTAMER, etc., and appear in capital letters. Unusually, Francis Suttill's field name – 'Prosper' – became that of his circuit and I have used PROSPER throughout, even though its correct name was PHYSICIAN.

The BCRA used a similar system for agents' code names, e.g. Jean Moulin was known as 'Corporal Mercier' in London, as 'Rex' on his first mission and as 'Max' on his final mission. His last ID (cover name) before his arrest was 'Jacques Martel'. Raymond Samuel used the field name 'Aubrac' and had a succession of cover names: 'François Vallet', 'Claude Ermelin', etc. Like other resistance leaders he changed his surname after the liberation to his wartime field name.

French Resistance units (e.g. *Combat*, *Libération*), appear in italics. They were differentiated by the zone in which they were formed. In the northern Occupied Zone the *réseaux* (networks) were necessarily secret and usually paramilitary from the start. In the unoccupied Vichy Zone the three principal resistance movements (*Libération*, *Combat* and *Franc-Tireur*) were secretive rather than secret and were at first more concerned with political opposition and propaganda.

The relationship between the BCRA (the Gaullist intelligence service established in London in 1940) and SOE(RF) (the independent section of SOE which worked exclusively for the Free French) was complicated by joint command. Most of RF's agents were French and their orders were drawn up by French staff officers, but could be vetoed by British commanders, although this was unusual.

Initially RF was set up as a means to isolate SOE(F), the original French section, from any French penetration. This intention was clearly described in a memo circulated within F section in October 1940 by Sir Frank Nelson, the first head of F (see pp. 63–4).

The officer in charge of the 'special separate watertight sub-section' [i.e. RF] '. . . would work outside this office and never visit it. The whole of our HQ organisation and its field organisation would be entirely concealed from the French'.

This absurd precaution was soon abandoned. The Gaullists quickly discovered the existence of F section and imposed their own ban on any dealings with it. The rivalry between F and RF for resources and funds continued throughout the war. Nonetheless, individual RF section officers frequently visited or worked in Baker Street, F section's HQ.

In practice RF became the operational arm and travel agency for Free French agents working in and out of France. Its officers always had excellent relations with SIS (see p. 228). Indeed, relations were so close that Hugh Verity, commander of RAF 161 squadron, which flew the agents in and out of occupied territory, listed all RF operations as SIS (see K.G. Robertson (ed.), *War, Resistance and Intelligence*, pp. 169–84).

Chronology

	Nanteuil	Historical Events	Jean Moulin and de Gaulle
1939	Last English student leaves Nanteuil on 31 August		
3 Sep		Britain and France declare war on Germany	
1940			
10 May		German forces attack Holland, Belgium and France	
3 Jun		Last of 371,000 British and French troops evacuated from Dunkirk	
12 Jun		10,000 men of the 51st Highland Division surrender at St Valery-en-Caux. Captain Bradford taken prisoner	
14 Jun	*L'Exode* – Thousands of Parisian refugees reach Blois on foot		
15–16 Jun	Blois is bombed and evacuated		
17 Jun	Souris decides to leave Nanteuil and seek refuge in the south of France	Marshal Pétain broadcasts his first message to the nation: 'The battle is over'	

	Nanteuil	Historical Events	Jean Moulin and de Gaulle
18 Jun			From London, Charles de Gaulle launches his appeal for 'resistance'
20–1 Jun	Last French troops withdraw from Blois		Jean Moulin, the prefect of Chartres, surrenders the city.
21 Jun		Armistice imposed by Germany is signed by Pétain	
24 Jun	Souris and family return home.		
	Souris marries Count Pierre de Bernard de la Fosse later that week		
3–4 Jul		Royal Navy destroys French fleet at Mers-el-Kebir. 3,000 French sailors die	General de Gaulle is tried *in absentia* by Vichy court and convicted of desertion
7–9 Jul	Bradford reaches Nanteuil and then escapes into the Vichy Zone		
16 Jul		Churchill creates SOE to 'set Europe ablaze'. SOE(F) established to work in France	
Autumn	In the Sologne, Souris starts to smuggle fugitives into the Vichy Zone	SIS starts determined campaign to undermine SOE	
1941			
May	In the Sologne hundreds of resisters, from all backgrounds, begin to organise	SOE finally manages to parachute first agent into France	
July			General de Gaulle launches public attack on British alliance
October			Jean Moulin reaches London to join de Gaulle
November	In Blois, SOE emissary gives codeword 'Urbain 26' to Souris		

	Nanteuil	Historical Events	Jean Moulin and de Gaulle
1942			
2 Jan			Jean Moulin – parachuted back as de Gaulle's emissary – starts 'Mission Rex'
February		RAF 161 Squadron begins regular Lysander flights into France	
June	In Tours, Raymond Flower sets up first SOE circuit	Brig. Colin Gubbins takes command of SOE and cuts off dependence on SIS	
August	'Jacqueline' (Yvonne Rudellat), SOE courier, reaches Tours and joins Flower		Nicolas Bodington validates importance of bogus anti-Gaullist network, CARTE
September	Pierre Culioli, tax inspector, leader of local resistance, contacts Flower		PWE's anti-Gaullist radio station starts broadcasting to France from London
2 Oct	Francis Suttill of SOE(F) founds PROSPER and starts to build his circuit in Paris with veterans of CARTE in central France		
31 Oct	Major Gilbert Norman, 'Archambaud', wireless operator, joins PROSPER		
4 Nov		At El Alamein, British 8th Army defeats Rommel's *Afrika Corps*	
8 Nov		Operation Torch: 100,000 allied troops land in N. Africa	De Gaulle not briefed about allied plans to invade French territory
November	German police obtain membership list of CARTE	Soviet troops trap German 6th Army outside Stalingrad	

	Nanteuil	Historical Events	Jean Moulin and de Gaulle
December			Churchill tells Parliament, in secret session, that de Gaulle is untrustworthy

1943

	Nanteuil	Historical Events	Jean Moulin and de Gaulle
January	Major Norman arrives at Nanteuil and gives the password, 'Urbain 26'.		
24 Jan		At Casablanca, Churchill and Roosevelt commit to Sicily landings in 1943	
29 Jan		LCS deception staff prepare plans for fictional landings in France in 1943	
31 Jan		Field Marshal Paulus surrenders German 6th Army at Stalingrad	
February	In Tours, Raymond Flower attempts to poison Pierre Culioli	Soviet forces push Germans back and liberate Kharkov	
	Culioli and 'Jacqueline' abandon Flower and join PROSPER	Hitler transfers 36 divisions from western to eastern front	
	In Sologne, Culioli builds up paramilitary network called *Réseau Adolphe*		
	'Jacqueline' and Culioli lead successful sabotage campaign, blowing up trains, etc.		
9 Feb		Churchill approves LCS plans for fictional landings in France in autumn	
		Churchill assures Soviet ambassador that real landings will take place	

	Nanteuil	Historical Events	Jean Moulin and de Gaulle
14 Feb			Jean Moulin arrives in London to receive new orders from de Gaulle
3 Mar			Churchill bans de Gaulle from leaving UK
4 Mar			Jean Moulin ('Max') and General Delestraint ('Vidal') meet General Alan Brooke
10 Mar			General Brooke tells 'Max' and 'Vidal' that autumn landings still possible
11 Mar		Churchill tells Stalin that a Second Front in 1943 now improbable	
12 Mar		von Manstein retakes Kharkov destroying 52 Soviet divisions	
19 Mar			Max' and 'Vidal' return to France
11 Apr		von Manstein signals that he is ready to start Kursk offensive	
		At Bletchley Park, German plans are decoded and passed on to Stalin	
13 Apr		Churchill confirms genuine landings in France in 1943 no longer possible	
14 Apr		Churchill minutes: 'Stalin not be informed' that 2nd Front is now cancelled	
15 Apr		News reaches London from Katyn: at least 8,000 Polish officers murdered by Soviets. British government accepts Soviet denials of guilt, knowing they are false	

	Nanteuil	Historical Events	Jean Moulin and de Gaulle
15 May	'Prosper' arrives in London for briefing by Colonel Buckmaster, head of F section		
20 May	'Prosper' is flown back to France, convinced that the 2nd Front is imminent		
May	In Sologne sabotage ops. are suspended and replaced by arms deliveries		
June	Massive increase in parachute deliveries to *Adolphe*		
14 Jun	'Prosper' refuses request by exhausted resisters for a break in deliveries		
19 Jun			Churchill instructs SOE to destroy de Gaulle's control of the Resistance. SOE and War Cabinet refuse
20 Jun	Gestapo, alerted by frequent RAF operations, lay an ambush near Nanteuil		
21 Jun	Gestapo arrest Culioli and 'Jacqueline' after car chase, and break *Adolphe*		In Lyons, Gestapo arrest Jean Moulin and seven Resistance commanders. De Gaulle's command of military resistance in France is destroyed.
22 Jun	At Nanteuil, Moune and Betty sink 'Archambaud's' w/t set in the Cosson		
24 Jun	In Paris, Gestapo arrest 'Prosper' and 'Archambaud'		Lyons Gestapo identify 'Max' as Jean Moulin
27 Jun	Major Norman accepts Gestapo pact offering protection to PROSPER members who surrender		
1 Jul	In Sologne, Gestapo start to round up hundreds of resisters with aid of Culioli		

	Nanteuil	Historical Events	Jean Moulin and de Gaulle
8 Jul			Death of Jean Moulin in German custody on train to Berlin at Metz
16 Jul			De Gaulle orders BCRA to break contact with SIS
23 Jul	Major Bodington to Paris with Jacques Agazarian w/t operator. They are escorted by double agent Henri Déricourt. Gestapo are aware of their arrival		
25 Jul	Agazarian is sent into a Gestapo trap. Bodington is not arrested		
16 Aug	Bodington leaves France unharmed		
September	Gestapo arrest Souris and Pierre		
1944			
29 Jan	Souris deported to Ravensbrück		
27 Apr	Pierre deported to Buchenwald		
6 Jun		D-Day landings	
16 Aug	Blois liberated. *Épuration* in the Sologne		
25 Aug			Liberation of Paris. De Gaulle assumes power
1945			
29 Apr	Pierre is repatriated		
April	'Jacqueline' dies in Belsen		
7 May		VE Day	
12 Jul	Souris is repatriated via Sweden		
6–9 Aug		Atom bombs dropped on Hiroshima and Nagasaki	

	Nanteuil	Historical Events	Jean Moulin and de Gaulle
15 Aug		VJ Day	
1946	First post-war English student, Owen Watson, arrives – March		De Gaulle leaves power and enters political wilderness
1947	First Culioli trial – September		
1948	Trial of Henri Déricourt. He is acquitted on evidence of Nicolas Bodington		
	Resistance survivors become convinced they were betrayed in London		
1949	Pierre Culioli is acquitted of treason at his second trial in March		
Oct			General de Gaulle dines at Nanteuil
1954	Marriage of Moune and Owen Watson		
1958	*Double Webs* by J.O. Fuller connects Henri Déricourt with deception operation		De Gaulle returns to power
1959	Pierre de Bernard dies		
1971	Souris dies on 16 February		
1972	Moune closes the language school after 50 years and moves out of Nanteuil		

Glossary

Abwehr	German military intelligence
Action Française	Nationalist and monarchist movement, frequently anti-Semitic
AMGOT	Allied Military Government in Occupied Territories
BCRA	*Bureau Central de Renseignement et d'Action* – Gaullist intelligence service based in London
Cagoule	'the Hood' – derisive nickname for the CSAR, a 1930s pro-fascist terrorist conspiracy
CFLN	French Committee of National Liberation, formed in Algiers in June 1943 under the joint leadership of General Giraud and General de Gaulle
CIGS	Chief of the Imperial General Staff
CNR	*Conseil National de la Résistance* – National Resistance Council, established by Jean Moulin in Paris in May 1943
Combat	Large right-wing resistance movement that organised the Secret Army
DGSS	Director General Security Service (MI5)
Épuration	'Purification' – the post-liberation butchery of French collaborators and innocent suspects
Exode	'Exodus' – mass panic and flight from German forces, May–June 1940
Feldgendarmerie	German military police
Franc-Tireur	Centre-left southern Resistance movement
France d'Abord	Small Lyons-based Resistance network
Front National	'Non-partisan' front organisation for the Communist resistance. Political arm of the FTP-MOI

FFI	*Forces françaises de l'intérieur* (resistance units theoretically under orders of the French army after the Liberation)
FTP–MOI	*Francs-tireurs et partisans – Main d'oeuvre immigrée*: armed Communist resistance
Gestapo	*Geheime Staatspolizei* (Nazi state political police); 2,000 men in France; a department of the Sipo-SD
Gestapo française	French volunteer auxiliaries; 8,000 strong
Groupes francs	Armed resistance commandos
Hudson	Long-range armed aircraft; could carry up to nine passengers
Libération	Leading left-wing resistance movement, under Communist influence
LCS	London Controlling Section: body charged with overall control of wartime strategic deception
LRC	London Reception Centre – screening centre for incoming aliens, run by MI5, based in south London at Royal Victoria Patriotic School
Lysander	Light aircraft, flown solo, capable of carrying two to four passengers
MI5	British Security Service
MI6	See SIS
Milice	French paramilitary pro-Nazi militia, formed to fight the Resistance
NKVD	Soviet Secret Service (previously GPU, subsequently KGB)
OKW	*Oberkommando der Wehrmacht* – Combined General Staff
OSS	Office of Strategic Services (US Intelligence, later CIA)
PCF	*Parti Communiste Français* – French Communist Party
PWE	Political Warfare Executive – wartime agency responsible for 'black' propaganda
RSHA	*Reichssicherheitshauptamt* – supreme Reich Security Service
SD	*Sicherheitsdienst* – internal security service of the SS (qv)
Sipo–SD	RSHA agency in France: fusion of Reich security police and the SD (qv)
SIS	British Secret Intelligence Service (also known as MI6)

SOE	Special Operations Executive: independent secret agency charged with mounting sabotage and subversion in occupied Europe
SOE(F)	French section of SOE run by Maurice Buckmaster
SOE(RF)	Gaullist French section, run by 'Colonel Passy'
SS	*Schutzstaffel*, 'guard detachment' – Hitler's elite security force
STO	*Service du travail obligatoire* – Vichy government forced labour programme, compelling Frenchmen to work in Germany
TWIST	Sub-committee of the LCS (qv) responsible for executing deception operations and disinformation through double agents
W Board	Top-secret wartime committee charged with implementing strategic deception operations authorised by the LCS (qv)
W/T	Wireless transmission set, or operator
XX Committee	The 'Twenty' or 'Double-Cross' committee: sub-committee of W Board (qv) – dominated by officers of MI5. Controlled German spy system in Great Britain
Z organisation	Parallel secret service based initially in Switzerland, recruited and run by Claude Dansey, vice-chief of SIS

Introduction

An Anonymous Letter

The letter was posted in London, twenty years ago. The postmark is blurred but one can just make out the details. The date was the first, or possibly the eleventh, of September. The time of the collection was 7.15 p.m. The postal district looks like London W2. The author's identity was never revealed.

> Dear Mr Marnham,
> I feel I must write to congratulate you on your book *The Death of Jean Moulin: Biography of a Ghost*. I've read it carefully (not difficult as the writing is so elegantly accessible), and must tell you that I think it is a very fine piece of work indeed. It's a relief to read history from the pen of a barrister because it seems that, unlike historians, those trained in law know something about asking the right questions. Historians are not trained, as lawyers are, to look over the edge – it's not their fault, perhaps, but it makes for tiresome mistakes and, in most cases, a dull read . . .

The letter continued over more than sixteen closely typed pages of A4. The flattering introduction was succeeded by a mocking tone that gave way to a skilfully constructed, taunting commentary that was irritating and intriguing at the same time.

> Yes, your book is a very fine piece of work, but, naturally, not perfect . . . If only, I kept thinking as I turned the pages, Mr Marnham had pushed himself the tiniest bit harder . . . how very exciting this biography would have been . . . You had the facts, but the truth regrettably escaped you for want of a little focus and a smidgen more imaginative reflection . . .

The first rule with anonymous letters is to ignore them entirely, screw them up and throw them away. But the normal human reaction is to wonder who sent them. (*'Smidgen' is an interesting word, not much used nowadays, at least not much used in southern England, possibly of Scottish origin?*) This leads to the next step, which is to pick the letter out of the bin and study it closely. In the case of this letter, which was posted about three months after the publication of my biography of Jean Moulin in 2000, I first followed the best advice. Having glanced through the text and admired both the typing and the style, and seen that it contained very little precise information, I put it aside as a malicious curiosity. There was one unexpected detail. It had been posted to an address where we went for holidays, which was never used for correspondence. I returned to work and forgot about the letter.

Then something quite unexpected happened.

We had recently moved back to England after many years in France, but I still had my office in Paris and spent a week there every month. It was a solitary life, sleeping on a camp bed in the one-room office, writing or researching by day and reading half the night, the only diversion being the choice of where to go for supper. One evening I returned to our old *quartier*. There was a new bistro to try, near a bar where they dimly remembered my face. After supper I walked back to my office down the street where we had lived for so many years. The light in the concierge's *loge* was still on so I knocked at the familiar door.

We exchanged family news – 'such a long time since you dropped by' – and Madame Alves said that she had been thinking of me because although she had long since stopped keeping my post, there was a package in the box that she had not yet thrown away. And – of course – it was another intervention from my unidentified critic.

This time his communication was in a jiffy bag. Posted in London, three months after the first – and at least four months before I, by the purest chance, received it – the second package contained a paperback book, a minidisc, a postcard showing a street scene in the city where I was born, a blurred black-and-white snapshot of two small girls playing in a park on a sunny day in what looked like London in the 1950s, and a handsome Christmas card, published by the Medici Society, showing a Filippino Lippi study of *The Madonna and Child*. There was no letter this time, and nothing to confirm that this message came from the same person, except for a similarity in the block capitals employed on the envelope. Then I found some scraps of typed paper in the bottom of the bag. The first letter had terminated in mid-sentence on the sixteenth page. Pasted together these fragments formed what would have been page 17. It had been ripped up, apparently carelessly. But when the jigsaw puzzle of pieces was laid out, it became apparent that the fragments were intended to reveal and conceal at the same time. The torn paragraphs concentrated on one detail of the story I had told in *The Death of Jean Moulin*.

I never knocked on that door again, and that evening was the last occasion I saw Madame Alves. At the time I thought it rather poignant that the final letter she kept for me should have contained no more than a random collection of incoherent bric-à-brac. Back in my office, faced with another solitary night on the camp bed, I hunted around for the first letter. There had been something feline about its style that made me wonder whether it was actually written by a woman – perhaps one of those dry, brittle, clever old ladies who clustered together in bedsitters in north Oxford and had once worked at Bletchley Park. But the writer described himself as 'a very, very old man', and women do not have a monopoly of the feline. Eventually the fact that he had bothered to contact me again, this time at an address I had left over a decade earlier, struck me as so unusual that I reread the first letter.

The meeting at which Jean Moulin was betrayed had been held at a doctor's house in Caluire, a suburb of Lyons, After the war there was an official investigation into the affair and a resister called René Hardy was tried, twice, and twice acquitted – although very widely regarded as guilty. But in *The Death of Jean Moulin* I suggested that two other resistance commanders should have been investigated: they were a Communist engineer called Raymond Aubrac and a far-right journalist called Pierre Bénouville. It seemed clear that they both knew much more about the event than they had ever admitted, and they still had questions to answer. This was the solution that my anonymous critic rejected.

On page 2 of the letter 'the Ghost', or 'X', let's call him 'Major X', made a disobliging reference to Professor M.R.D. Foot, the official historian of SOE, noting that I had 'rightly and crisply dismissed' his eulogy of Jean Moulin, whose code name had been 'Max'. In other passages the writer hinted that he himself had been working in British Intelligence in London during the war and that he had known several of the characters involved in the drama of Jean Moulin's arrest in Caluire. The Gestapo officer in Lyons who arrested Jean Moulin, a brutal individual called Klaus Barbie, was under the orders of *Sturmbannführer* Karl Boemelburg, who was based in Paris. Boemelburg was the head of counter-espionage for the *Sicherheitsdienst*, the security service of the SS – known as the 'SD'. Major X seemed to have some esteem for Boemelburg. He referred to him as 'Karl', and to his son as 'Rolfe', and suggested that Boemelburg had only joined the Nazi Party because of a 'profound loathing of communism' and that by 'his heroic silence' at the end of the war he had saved his friends from the vengeful death squads of the *épuration*, the 'purification' or purge. These friends of Boemelburg's apparently included Marshal Pétain, the head of state who surrendered France in 1940 and asked the French to collaborate with the Nazis.

Later in the letter 'X' referred to *Obersturmbannführer* Horst Kopkow, the SS officer based in Berlin who was Boemelburg's direct superior. Kopkow, he said, had survived the war and been employed by the CIA in East Berlin.

This seemed to be new information. Previously I had understood that Kopkow had been interrogated by MI5 for four years after the war and sheltered from war crimes trials, despite the fact that he had ordered the killing of hundreds of British agents and servicemen and should have been hanged as a war criminal. The reason for Kopkow's immunity was the knowledge he had gained during the war by successfully penetrating Soviet intelligence. In 1948, when MI5 misled war crimes investigators with the claim that Kopkow was dead, he had in fact been handed on to SIS.[1] 'Major X' was suggesting that Kopkow was subsequently passed on again, to the CIA, which was unsurprising – but at least supported the notion that 'Major X', as a bona fide veteran, had private information about British Intelligence.

There were other passages suggesting that the Major was not a man of the left. He objected to the 'post-war indoctrinated idea that all-Nazis-were-unthinking-sadists' and the 'baby-gobbling Germans' approach to history, and he seemed to approve of my suspicions about Raymond Samuel, better known as the Communist resistance activist Raymond Aubrac. In my life of Jean Moulin, I had suggested that Aubrac knew more about the circumstances of his leader's betrayal than he had so far admitted. The Major seized on this suggestion.

Aubrac . . . Now there's a wily one to be sure. I hadn't realised he was still alive – why, he must be nearly as old as I am. Isn't he the very model of discretion? Isn't he the very devil of irony, with the spectacles tilted just so, and the twinkle in the eye at just the right moment? Isn't he the very essence of letting you know he knows but saying absolutely nothing which has not been distilled in repetition over and over throughout the last generation? They really did break the mould there. How very much I would like to see that man again. A man in a million, *parfait* in all but the last degree.

In February 1944, Aubrac, on the run from the Gestapo with his wife and child, had been picked up from a bog in the Jura and flown to England by the RAF. The only time that a British intelligence officer was likely to have encountered Aubrac during the war would have been at his subsequent debriefing in London, when MI5 – Aubrac said later – had given him quite a hard time.[2]

However, 'X' had an even lower opinion of Henri Frenay, Aubrac's bitter political opponent and the leader of the right-wing resistance group *Combat*. He described Frenay as 'jealous' and 'inferior' to Moulin, and referred mockingly to his rank, and to his 'genius, courage and modesty'. One thing was quite clear; the Major venerated Jean Moulin, who he described as 'the greatest man born in two millennia'. That description certainly seemed to be the work of a fantasist.

But 'X' made another point in his letter, a less romantic and more practical point, that made me pause before throwing both letters away. The one clear reason he gave to justify his assertion that my book had failed to solve the mystery of his hero's death referred to events in a different part of France on the day of Moulin's arrest. This was the collapse of PHYSICIAN, known in France as PROSPER,* which was the largest SOE circuit in France. Its destruction began early on the morning of 21 June 1943 in the central Sologne region.

Many reasons have been pondered for PROSPER's demise . . . [wrote the Major] and the chain reaction [it] effected throughout other networks, both French and British: none of them, alas, has been correct . . . In order to detect the real culprit, you need . . . to research

---

* For an explanation of network names and *noms de guerre* see the note on p. xxiii.

laterally (and seek material) relating to the specific operations and
London briefing of 'Prosper' [the field name of Major Francis Suttill,
leader of the PROSPER circuit] that spring and early summer of '43
– and then ask each one of these carefully catalogued facts, the question why . . .

That was all that X had decided to impart in the way of useable leads.
The rest of his letter offered an infuriating trail of obscure and apparently irrelevant clues, a random jumble of names and events that made
no sense.

The curious goings on at Cliveden . . . The Ordre Martiniste-
Synarchique, the frankly weird Otto Rahn, the conference room at
Rastenburg, a man called Stuelpnagel and the history of the cross of
Lorraine . . . the feast day of John the Baptist – there now I've virtu-
ally handed it to you on a plate . . . The jewel in the crown is there,
most definitely, waiting to be found.

It took me some time to overcome my irritation with the condescending
tone he favoured, and with the relish he betrayed in his own anonymity.

Will you forgive me for supplying neither my name nor my address?
You don't know who I am, you don't know where I am . . . It's pleasing to offer you the position of 'ghost' . . .

It seemed unlikely that he did possess unpublished information about
the activities of British intelligence agencies in occupied France during
the wartime period. And I would probably have left the question unde-
cided had it not been for one detail that even the Major could not have
known. Among the first friends I had ever made in France were three
former members of the Sologne Resistance. The family lived near
Blois and about twelve years before I received the Major's letter, on
holiday in that region, I had opened the local paper and found a familiar face.

La Nouvelle République, 3 Mai 1989
On nous prie d'annoncer le décès de Madame Muriel Watson, née
Gardnor-Beard, survenu le 1er mai, à la suite d'une cruelle maladie. La

cérémonie religieuse sera célébrée en l'église de Huisseau-sur-Cosson, le vendredi 5 mai à 10.30. Selon sa volonté, elle sera incinérée.

Beneath the photograph of Madame Watson there was a second notice which, translated, read:

The Association of Wartime Deportees, the Union of Volunteer Resistance Fighters of the Loir-et-Cher and Veterans of the Buckmaster-Adolphe Network are sad to announce the death of Madame Muriel Watson. The funeral will take place on Friday at the church of Huisseau-sur-Cosson. Rendezvous for the colour party, with flags, at the church at 10.15.

She was sixty-six. We always called her 'Moune'. Thirty years earlier, in her home, the house by the river, she had taught me French.

———

Memory is an unreliable guide, but sometimes an experience is so vivid that it lives on clearly in the mind. At Moune's funeral the colour party was formed by a group of old men, all rather short, in dark suits wearing rows of large medals. I had a blurred impression of berets, medals and moustaches. They were parading to honour a woman who had never been decorated. There was a bugler, and a Union flag among the Tricolours, and one of the wreaths was from RAF 161 Squadron marked, '*A Notre Amie*'.

Moune's coffin was incredibly heavy. I was told later that it had, for some reason, been lined with lead. During the funeral Mass in the twelfth-century church of Huisseau-sur-Cosson an older woman, quite stout, who I had not met before, sat down beside me and collapsed sobbing as the service neared its end. She was the only person who accompanied the coffin to the crematorium; her name was Marinette. Many years before she had been the bridesmaid at Moune's wedding and had apparently caused a stir by kissing the bride passionately on the steps of the *mairie*.

The coffin and Marinette were driven away, the guard of honour dispersed and some of us moved to the family home for a funeral lunch. It was a very hot day and at the end of the meal there was a curious incident. A sudden roaring noise rattled the windows, a shadow darkened the ground outside and looking up we could see a large propeller plane with RAF markings flying very low over the park. It might have been a ghost plane from the Second World War. The aircraft circled, the shadow raced across the ground again, the pilot climbed and dipped his wings in salute, and was gone. One of the French said: 'You see the English do not forget . . .'

Then 'Bubby', a friend of the family, who had also been in the Resistance, added 'Well, now at least we know how we were betrayed.' For some reason the anonymous letter took me back to that sad, hot afternoon and to that precise moment, the rather dry comment made by the woman who had been Moune's resistance colleague and lifelong friend. Could there possibly be some connection between Moune's *Buckmaster-Adolphe* network and Jean Moulin?

At the time I brushed the ambiguous remark aside. Leaving the funeral party, hiding my feelings, I walked across the lawn to the far side of the house. The river still flowed past the terrace, beneath what I still thought of as my window, and the water still splashed over the weir. And a memory returned of that time when I had first met Moune . . . during the summer of '62.

PART I

THE HOUSE BY THE RIVER

I

Summer of '62 – The Lost Domain

I am looking for something still more mysterious: for the path
you read about in books, the old lane choked with undergrowth
whose entrance the weary prince could not discover . . . As
you brush aside a tangle of branches you suddenly catch a
glimpse of a dark tunnel of green at the far end of which there
is a tiny aperture of light.

from *The Lost Domain*
(*Le Grand Meaulnes*) by Alain-Fournier[1]

It was towards the end of April that I first saw the house by the river. It stood some distance below the road behind a line of tall trees, the grey slate roof of a large house just visible and before it the narrow river, glinting in the light of evening. A stone bridge led across the stream to the entrance of a park which was closed off by heavy iron gates. This was the house that would become part of my life, first a place of friendship, then a pleasant memory. Until the day, many years later, when I received an anonymous letter offering the solution to a mystery – and a clue that led me back over the years, to that house – and the summer of '62.

————

The summer of 1962 had not gone quite as expected. In London, in April, my father had handed me a road map of France, an envelope containing some French banknotes and a set of car keys. He said that he had cancelled my plans to join an archaeological dig in Greece ('far too hot at this time of year') and arranged for me to learn French instead. I was between school and university and was now to spend some months with a family in the Touraine. He had never met these people. As far as he knew they did not speak English. There was an address inside the envelope. He wrote out some directions on how to reach the house from Blois. Blois was on the map. The journey should take two days he said. I was to find a hotel on the way for the first night. A GB sign had been attached to the car which he would not need again until the autumn. I made it clear that I was displeased by this rearrangement, but to no avail. My room in this house was ready. I was expected to arrive during the course of the week.

The first day had passed quite smoothly. I drove to Folkestone and took the car ferry to Boulogne. In the late afternoon I passed through Moitié Brulé and then Neufchatel. There were no motorways at that time. If you wanted to cross France you took the *route nationale* and followed the signposts from town to town.

Even today I am surprised by my father's decision. I had held a driving licence for barely six months, I had never 'driven on the right' and, since I was travelling alone, overtaking lorries involved leaning across the empty passenger seat and craning round the moving obstruction – while keeping one hand on the wheel of the Austin Mini and one foot on the accelerator, hoping by this contortion to catch a glimpse of the road ahead. Not that there was much danger of a collision with oncoming traffic. The towns and villages of northern France were linked by a system of straight, empty highways that ran directly through the centre of almost every settlement. There was little sign of the people who lived in these villages. Sometimes a bent figure in a dark grey or black dress would appear on the pavement and regard the car, unsmiling, apparently resentful of the brief intrusion. I had been told that if the women were dressed in black, they were widows. There seemed to be a high number of widows in northern France.

At some point I must have taken a wrong turn because I found I was no longer heading for Rouen but for somewhere called 'Dreux'. It looked as dreary as it sounded. The land on either side of the road flattened out, the horizon retreated, the villages and farmhouses vanished. It was as though I was crossing an uninhabited plain, a desert of unripened corn. I began to wonder if there would be any hotels before night fell.

And then towards evening a shape appeared in the extreme distance, two spires and a grey roof, very far away. I stopped the car and pulled over between the poplar trees, not realising that this was the emblematic view, the pilgrims' first sight of the cathedral at Chartres.

There was a hotel in the main square large enough to have its own dining room and next morning I crossed the *place* and for the first time entered that vast stone tank and found myself immersed in the blue-stained air, plunged into an underwater light so thick that you felt you were swimming through it, as though over seven hundred years it had solidified with the weight of dead piety and vanished generations – the better to protect the vision of its creators. A bell tinkled in the depths and on a distant side altar a huddle formed, the black dresses and grey scarves once again, the first Mass of the morning. Back on the road I dawdled, looking for a picnic site outside Châteaudun and distractions in Vendôme.

By mid-afternoon I had reached Blois, which was already a mythical place in my mind. There was the liquid sound of the spoken name, and its mediaeval history. The Counts of Blois had played an important part in the dynastic struggles of England and France during the twelfth and thirteenth centuries, which I had studied for several years at school. Here, not trusting my father's directions, I stopped to ask the way.

The instructions I received led me out of the city and across the bridge over the Loire, the longest river in France. It rises in the southern mountains, near the Mediterranean, runs north and then, at Orléans, turns abruptly south-west and sets off for the Atlantic. The area enclosed by the river's elbow, which I now entered, is the Sologne, a region of forests and *étangs*, or shallow lakes, that was for centuries the hunting ground of the kings of France. On the edge of the forest, in yet another deserted village, I came to the house by the river. The grey iron gates were closed and there was a sign by the enamel bell-pull – '*Attention: chien méchant*'. Since the bell was broken I pushed the gates open rather cautiously and prepared to meet the dog. This turned out to be an affectionate young boxer, not *méchant* at all, and by the time I had parked the car an elderly woman had emerged from the house to greet me. She was rather stout with a functional hair-style that looked as though it had been sheared rather than cut, and she was not dressed in black but in a practical sort of flowery smock with a rather faded pattern. She wore thick, rimless spectacles, I am not sure why since she always looked at one over the top of the lenses. 'Hello,' she said, 'I'm Nanny. I'm just pouring tea. It's the only time that you and I are allowed to speak English.'

On that first visit I stayed for three months and I returned many times in the years that followed. I was always given the same room on the second floor, the Green Room, the only bedroom with windows overlooking both the river and the park. On the night of my arrival I fell asleep for the first time to the murmur of the water sweeping over the weir. Early next morning I was woken by the reflections rippling across the ceiling. From the terrace below my window came the scratching of a rake across the gravel. Before breakfast there was a knock on my door and a girl from the village entered carrying a large pitcher of hot water which she set down beside a washbasin. This happened every morning. I do not recall any conversation during this ritual. '*Bonjour, m'sieu*', '*Bonjour, Françoise.*' That was the limit of our relationship throughout my visit. From the washstand by the window, where I shaved, I could see a groom exercising a tall chestnut hunter on a long rein in the shade of the trees that surrounded the paddock. There was no noise during this performance. The horse moved quite silently. It could have been an optical illusion from a more leisurely past.

Downstairs I found breakfast waiting in the empty dining room: coffee, fresh bread, butter and apricot jam. Suzanne, the cook, served the butter in small portions. She regarded butter for breakfast as a wild extravagance and thought that the English guests consumed far too much of it. She had grown up in the village and spent her entire life there. She had started out as a maid. The war and the poverty that followed were still fresh in her memory. She was not the only person in the house who considered that wasting food was a criminal shame.

I had breakfast alone for the first two weeks, no other students had arrived. Some company was provided by the two stags' heads that dominated the dining room, mounted high on the wall on either side of the marble fireplace. I was to spend a great deal of time with those two heads. Their gentle faces were curiously alive, patient and watchful. Something in their non-committal expression – a glint of reproach in their yellow glass eyes – suggested that they noticed and remembered far more than they were prepared to say. A lot was left unsaid in that house. Our hostess had a powerful personality and very little small talk. Her chief recreation was hunting. In winter, she hunted stag and wild boar through the forest, riding side-saddle to hounds.

There were two framed photographs in the dining room, on the mantelpiece above the open fireplace. One – rather blurred – showed a pretty woman with delicate features who was half-smiling at the camera. She had dark hair with a prominent grey streak. We were told that during the war they had known her by her code name which was 'Jacqueline' and that she had been a resistance agent sent from London who had often been in the house and who had died at German hands. The other photograph was that of an army officer in uniform. It was signed, but even without reading the signature I recognised the face of Charles de Gaulle. He still looked quite young, a wartime portrait. Apparently, after the war, he had called on this family and dined at this table.

Four years before, as an old man, he had become the president of France.

———

Nanny was apologetic about the absence of other students during those first two weeks. A young man called 'Ranulph' something – it sounded like 'Vines' – had left two days before my arrival, after a stay of only three weeks. Gilly had made a tour of inspection with her father, who was our military attaché at the Paris embassy, but he had switched her to another family – the Frobervilles in Blois. Gaya, Louise, Emma and Miss Scrymgeour-Wedderburn from Fife had preferred to stay during the previous winter's hunting season. 'Theodora Brinckman' sounded vaguely familiar, but she too had departed, as had Zoe and Emmeline. It seemed to be an awful lot of departures. Nanny said there had also been several last-minute cancellations. 'I don't know why,' she said. 'All the trouble has been in Paris. It's always quiet in Blois.' 'Trouble, Nanny?' That sounded interesting. 'Yes. Some people panicked in the *métro* and got crushed. But that was in February. There's been nothing since.'

Nanny was not really doing justice to the situation. France was in fact, though I was quite unaware of it, on the verge of civil war. Eventually, after two weeks I was joined by Angela and Elizabeth, and two weeks after that by Neil, on his way from Nairobi to join the Grenadier Guards.

The house and the park bordered the north bank of the river. There was a sunny terrace beside the house, overlooking the mill stream, but most of the park was wooded with oaks, chestnuts and sycamores. Some way into the wood the riverbank overlooked a deep pool into which we could dive on hot afternoons. A six-foot man could sink to the bottom with his arm stretched above his head and only his fingertips would be visible. That was how we measured the depth – 'three metres'. It was quiet on the river when we were not swimming, and I used to watch the fat water voles plopping into the stream and crossing to and from their burrows on either bank. And there were *vipères* in the park, quite large, and not to be confused with English adders. In summer they came down to the river to doze – or watch for voles. Nanny said they were to be avoided. She seemed to be rather more concerned about the dog stepping on one than she was about us. Away from the river, at the top of the park, there was a walled garden where I would sit and read in the evening.

During those months at the château the hours spent in the garden were my favourite time of day. There is nowhere as peaceful as a walled garden on a cool evening after a hot day. It was a classic French *potager*, large enough to produce all the vegetables and fruit and herbs needed by the house. The soil was sandy, as it was in the asparagus fields outside the park. There was a rabbit run in one corner and a deep stone well near the centre. During the daytime the garden was the domain of Jean, a young-looking man, dark-skinned, from the *Midi*. This made him a complete foreigner as far as the villagers were concerned. Jean always wore a beret. He even wore it in bed. I knew this because one afternoon, bored and curious, I explored the series of lumber rooms at the end of my corridor, behind the door leading to the back stairs. One of these rooms turned out to be Jean's bedroom where he was taking a siesta. He was up early and worked through the heat of the day. It was his rake that could be heard on the gravel in the early morning. But by evening, for an hour or so before supper, I had the *potager* to myself. I would take a book with me, there was a bench on one of the walks and a low stone wall that rimmed the well. Curious red beetles, larger than ladybirds, ran along the sandy paths and socialised like ants.

At about 8 o'clock Suzanne would tell Nanny that dinner was ready, and Nanny would summon us to the table by ringing the bell that was attached to the wall above the kitchen door.

———

Dinner was served by Camille, an amiably tipsy butler, who poured a dark red wine from a heavy decanter. It was local wine, sour and thick, so thick that it left a purple stain on the glass. Camille's last duty was to close the shutters just as it grew dark. He would do this from outside the house. Before we left the table his face would appear at each window in turn, then disappear behind the shutters, then reappear at the next window, and so on as he worked his way around. For some reason this performance never failed to delight the family. It was a ritual, a comical Grace after Meals. As the butler, still in his white jacket, appeared, and disappeared, and reappeared, his progress was followed carefully by an attentive audience, and he would look back silently through the windows while a slow smile replaced his usual discreet 'on duty' expression. He did not understand this talent to amuse, but he assumed it as just another of his duties and he beamed back through the glass, 'Now you see me, now you don't.' He had worked in the house all his life. His wife ran the kitchen, their son brought his schoolbooks to the family to be corrected. He had been on duty that night after the war when General de Gaulle came to dinner, a proximity that had made his hands tremble so much that the serving spoons rattled in the dishes as he carried them round.

Sometimes, after dinner, we played bridge in the *salon* with our hostess and an elderly cousin, Madame Denisane, a volatile and raucous presence with a glass eye. I was once asked to carry a tea tray to her room and there she was, sitting up in bed with a dark hole in her face. The Eye watched me from the table beside her. If there was no bridge we would just sit in the dark on the terrace above the river and listen to the arias being played on a wind-up gramophone by an older guest, a gentleman from Frankfort, Kentucky, who had been coming to the house for ten years. Between the arias we could hear a different music, the booming of an amplified bass echoing from the café on the hill on the other side of the river. Up there, *les jeunes* from the village were having a party. No doubt they were jiving to Johnny Hallyday or locked into '*un slow*' with Françoise Hardy. Perhaps our Françoise was enjoying an evening off? Nobody suggested that we might like to join them.

The old gentleman from Kentucky spent much of the summer alone in his room with his history books, re-fighting the American Civil War and working out how the South could have won. There was something about him that was reminiscent of the short-sighted cartoon character 'Mister Magoo'. His name was Robert R. Cleland and he always wore a nylon drip-dry shirt, a bow tie and a belt to keep his trousers up. The bow tie stayed in place on the hottest of days. He had very formal manners and seemed to understand French but spoke it very little. We soon noticed that any progressive or liberal opinion expressed at the table disturbed him. He would flush with anger and look quite put out.

This reaction was all the encouragement that some of the younger visitors needed. As Mr Cleland fell silent, turned pink and looked at his plate, his tormentors became bolder. He started to drum his fingers on the table, and I recall his hands, which were well manicured, and his fingernails, which had a sort of opaque, pearly tinge as they twitched on the tablecloth. Meanwhile we would be reminiscing about the horrors of slavery and the great men who had abolished it or enquiring about the progress of the Civil Rights Movement in the South. Our hostess watched this disgraceful performance without intervening, her slight smile suggesting that she may even have been hoping for some dramatic explosion to enliven the usual course of dinner.

Mr Cleland was a great favourite with Nanny and would drive her into Blois in his tiny, rear-engine Renault 4CV. He drove very slowly, quite oblivious to the hooting from the infuriated motorists in the queues that built up behind him. As he trundled over the Pont Jacques-Gabriel, the great eighteenth-century bridge that crosses the river into the city, and drivers, shouting abuse and shaking their fists, started to overtake him on the downward slope, he turned to Nanny, who was sitting very low in her seat by then, and said, 'That's the great thing about coming back so many times, Nanny. Everybody knows me and wants to say Hello!'

––––––

The house was called Château Nanteuil and it belonged to an old lady, Madame de Bernard, who lived there with Nanny and with her daughter Muriel, always known as 'Moune'. She had another daughter called Betty, who was married with young children and lived in Blois. Madame de Bernard walked slowly, stood erect and wore wonderfully elegant clothes. According to Nanny, Madame as a young woman had been dressed by Patou, the Parisian couturier, to show off his clothes. She was still very slim, and she always chose grey or black skirts – she had been widowed twice – with white linen shirts, thick, dark stockings, and shoes like espadrilles, but with a higher heel and an open toe. 'Madame', as we called her, spoke a lisping French with a beautiful intonation that was almost flirtatious. She spoke very quietly except when angry. She had a fierce temper, sparked without warning over trivial matters, and a strong face that seemed accustomed to suffering. Her sharp tongue and her uncompromising opinions gave her – as her daughter once explained – '*un caractère entier*'. She had a big birdcage on the balcony of her bedroom in which she kept wild songbirds. Most of the day she was with her dog, the playful young boxer that she called 'Karim'. The dog's chief amusement was to chase cats. Nanny said that boxers could easily catch and kill cats. Madame frequently used a word that caused me some embarrassment in years to come since I did not realise that if you wanted to describe something as 'disgusting' you did not normally say 'dégueulasse'. She used this word (which evokes throwing up) to describe anything she disapproved of, from the weather to a politician she disliked.

Occasionally, when Moune was busy elsewhere, Madame would drive us to visit one of the local châteaux, but she never joined in the visit. Nanny warned us that if she encountered German tourists – people she always referred to as '*Boches*' – there would be '*un incident*'. She did not tolerate the presence of Germans in France. For her the war was not over. Since her childhood, Germany had been the enemy and so it always would be – an attitude that seemed rather extreme to her students. For Madame de Bernard the enemy was not the Nazi Party – '*les Hitleriens*' – but the Germans. There had been no Nazis in 1870 when France was humiliated by Bismarck and lost Alsace and Lorraine. There had been no Nazis in 1914, when the Triple Alliance collapsed and northern France was overrun and occupied for four years by the same enemy, and one by one the young men she had danced with were killed. She had replaced them with an Englishman, a man whose ill health had only allowed them seventeen years together and left her with two children and an English nanny. By the time the Germans came back for the third visit in 1940, Madame de Bernard was confident that she could recognise the enemy.

I remember Madame de Bernard's appearance very well, probably because for three months I spent two hours with her every morning, learning French. These lessons started with the correction of my written work and I could watch her hands as they held the pencil, her fingers were swollen and twisted and there was a blue mark on her wrist, like a stain or a faded tattoo, which was ugly and out of character. It seemed to trouble her and she scratched it so that the skin went red. Most of the lesson was spent in reading aloud or just talking. She asked me about

French writers I liked and discovered that I had read Alain-Fournier's *Le Grand Meaulnes*, but in translation as *The Lost Domain*. I asked if he had written other books and she said that he had died young, 'missing in action', fighting in the French infantry in the first weeks of the Great War. The greatest French writer – she announced this without further discussion – was Victor Hugo, who had spent time in Blois. His father, the General, had lived in the rue du Foix. She gave me a poem of Hugo's to translate, '*L'Aiglon*', with its refrain, '*L'avenir, l'avenir, l'avenir c'est a moi!*'.

I enjoyed spending time with 'Madame', as we always called her. She had an inner strength that was all the more impressive for being unasserted, and her quiet amusement at my Catholic and reactionary opinions laid the foundations of our friendship. I was intrigued because although she was old and broken she seemed oblivious to this and was clearly accustomed to male admiration and quite at home with it. At some point that summer someone mentioned that Madame had been arrested by the Gestapo during the war and deported to a concentration camp. This information did at least explain the mark on her wrist, but we knew nothing of the reality of life in a Nazi camp and we could sense that it was not a subject anyone was going to discuss.

Once Nanny said, 'You should have seen her before the war in her hunting costume. She was so beautiful.' And Moune added, 'Yes, and she had a wonderful figure. She never bothered with a diet – apart from the war.' Many years later the barrister Jeremy Hutchinson, who had been at Nanteuil before the war, when he was eighteen, told me – he was ninety-nine at the time and lived for another two years – that he distinctly remembered Madame de Bernard from the pre-war days as 'rather attractive'.

Often in the afternoon there would be an expedition to visit one of the great 'Châteaux de la Loire'. The one château Madame never took us to see was Chaumont. She said that there was nothing in it and that it was best seen from across the river. But I later discovered that she had a family connection with Chaumont. Perhaps she found the idea of watching us queue to gain admission too painful.

Sometimes on our excursions we left the road and drove through the forest along straight beaten tracks that linked distant clearings. These forest ways had not been cut for the convenience of picnic parties. They were there so that riders could follow the hounds as they raced through the tangled undergrowth in pursuit of boar or deer. Away from the track there was little to be seen. The forest was impenetrable. In the summer of 1944 more than a thousand escaped allied prisoners of war were able to hide in one of these forests for months, within half a mile of a German army barracks, completely safe from discovery.

Madame de Bernard was a reckless driver and off the road she handled her Simca saloon as though she was following hounds. With a carload of students she would bolt along a ride and then, without pausing, plunge across the main road and back between the trees on the far side. There was one straight track through the Forêt de Russy that joined two forest clearings by crossing two main roads in succession. We made that journey more than once. On the far side of the *route nationale* our hostess would glance round at her passengers with an enquiring smile. Had we enjoyed that? There seemed to be another side to her mind. Was she slightly mad? Or in a dream? Or just indifferent to consequences?

On two occasions when I was with her Madame de Bernard was stopped while driving on the highway by police motorcycle patrols. When this happened she treated the gendarmes with open contempt. Her papers were produced from her handbag with a disdainful flick of the wrist. There was no eye contact. After checking her identity, the officers waved her on with a respectful salute. At the time I assumed that she just felt above such mundane inconvenience. Now I wonder whether even the uniforms of the French police reminded her of the Germans and of the time when they had worked together during the war.

We had none of these picturesque incidents when out with her daughter. There was no trace of the past about 'Moune', who conducted the informal afternoon lessons. Moune looked younger than her thirty-nine years. She had olive skin, black hair, very dark brown eyes and a mischievous smile. She had very small feet. As a child her mother had called her 'my gypsy'. She laughed easily and she seemed to enjoy our company. She did not live in the past. She was interested in jazz, photography, black tobacco cigarettes and cats, and she was writing a novel. She had misspent her post-war years in Paris on the Left Bank, having a wonderful time. Now she lived in a converted stable block on the opposite side of the courtyard. She generally dressed in trousers and a blue labourer's jacket, unless her mother was entertaining one of their 'château friends', in which case, much to our surprise, she changed into a pretty shirt and a skirt and even put on some make-up. Moune had married one of the English students after the war. He was called Owen Watson, although Nanny and Moune always called him 'Oscar'. They were separated but remained friends and he lived nearby.

She worried about her students becoming bored and was always trying to think up new diversions. She would take us to the *Cinéclub* in Blois in the evenings to watch *La Grande Illusion* or *Accroche-toi! Il y a du vent*. After which we would drive back through the heat of the night, with the windows down and insects smacking against the windscreen of her ancient Peugeot, which we nicknamed '*le camion*' (the truck). Once, in tribute to *Le Grand Meaulnes,* we set off together to find the original site of 'the Lost Domain', deciding that it was probably Villesavin, then a private house in a poor state of repair. Alain-Fournier had adapted the liquid place names of his childhood – 'La Chapelle d'Angillon', 'Epineuil-le-Fleuriel' – to situate the characters in his novel. The imaginary home village of Augustin Meaulnes was 'La Ferté-d'Angillon'. The verbal music of his haunted vision rang out every time I consulted the Michelin map. Later I discovered that the man who had refashioned that landscape into a legend had not exactly gone 'missing in action'. Henri Fournier had been killed on the Meuse in the first weeks of the Great War when his infantry company, still wearing the blue tunics, red trousers and black képis of the nineteenth century, and led by an incompetent '*illuminé*', had attacked an enemy ambulance detachment. The German unit that wiped them out in a furious counter-attack did for Fournier at the age of twenty-seven and immortalised his name, just as his only book immortalised the France that died in the war that killed him.

On one rainy day Moune cancelled all lessons and took us on a long expedition to trace the source of the Cosson. This ended in a downpour in a swamp on the far side of the Sologne, trying to enjoy damp sandwiches, near a village called Vannes. The source of our private river turned out to be an unmarked patch of sodden turf, surrounded by barbed wire.

─────

Often in the afternoons, looking for amusement, I would drive into Blois. Lafontaine had praised its beauty, describing how the city stood on opposing hills, with the château on one side and the cathedral on the other, church and state confronting each other, with the intervening streets rising like the tiers of an amphitheatre. The Château of Blois was a site of national importance. It was here that Catherine de Medici was reputed to have stored her phials of poison in a secret cupboard; you could still see the cupboard. And in 1588 it was the scene of the murder of the Duc de Guise. Guise, a giant of a man and a rival to Henri III, was set upon by twenty assassins, eight armed with daggers and twelve with swords. Alone, he fought for his life, and it took the assassins several minutes to finish him off. While they worked the King hid behind a curtain, and two priests, installed for the occasion, observed the assault and prayed for its success.

But the chief glory of Blois was not the Château. It was the Loire, the great silver *fleuve* that drifted past its quays, bringing wealth and distinction and joining it to the litany of Loire cities – Nevers, Orléans, Amboise, Tours and Saumur. There was a long English connection. Young men had been coming to Blois since the start of the Grand Tour, to learn fencing and the language and to hunt in the forests to the south. In 1826 a different sort of Englishman, uninterested in fencing – a rough-looking character with the air of *un paysan*, according to Delacroix – travelled upstream along the Loire and passed through the city. Joseph Turner called one of his watercolours *The Bridge of Blois: Fog Clearing*. (The French title, '*Dissipation du brouillard*' is more evocative of the scene.) It was painted in October, when the mushrooms appear in the forest and the stags start to bellow, and a mist covers the Loire. That smoky light is present throughout the year. One can see the course of the water reflected in the sky above it from miles away, as one approaches across the northern plain.

Beyond the *salon* at Nanteuil there was a deserted billiard room that served as a library. Most of the books were in French, but in a battered copy of Herbert Read's *Life of Wordsworth* I learnt, to my surprise, that two years after the Revolution, in 1791, the poet had travelled to Orléans in order to learn French and had fallen in love with his teacher, a girl from Blois.

When Annette Vallon left Orléans to return home, Wordsworth followed her to Blois, where her father was a respected surgeon. They lived together for a year and she gave birth to their daughter. Then Wordsworth, in a panic about the growing Reign of Terror or intending to prepare the way for Annette to join him in England, returned to London – only to be cut off from the girl with whom he was deeply in love by the war that had been declared between England and France. When peace returned nine years had passed. Wordsworth saw Annette and his daughter again, but it was too late. All feeling was dead. Remorse – the healing knife – had cut deeper than the wound. Annette's hopes of a reconciliation were deceived. After one brief meeting Wordsworth abandoned her and she died in poverty. Her death certificate read: '*Marie Anne Vallon, dite William*'. It was a story of passionate attraction that ended in betrayal. Wordsworth, according to Herbert Read, never recovered from this misadventure. His work suffered, and the damage lay across his psyche 'like bleached bones on the level sands'.

———

We reinvent the past from what is left of the memories we have lost. I would give a lot to be back in that house again, in the summer of '62. Not because I wish to relive my life but simply to re-experience the moment, to sip Nanny's tea, watch the light changing in the wood-panelled dining room, follow those first stilted attempts at making conversation, smell the musky, brown waters that flowed past the house like a constant friend. I would like to touch the lives of those characters, three women, a mystery to me then, so familiar to me now that all three are dead. Above all, of course, I would want to ask the questions that I would have asked if only I had known then what I have since discovered about their carefully concealed world.

In the summer of '62 people hardly spoke of the war. But in the house by the river they hardly spoke of the present either. While Madame de Bernard was teaching us French, France was disintegrating into armed rebellion, and the old man whose signed photo was on the dining-room mantelpiece was at the heart of all the trouble.

The country was bitterly divided on the question of Algerian independence and President de Gaulle had already survived the first in a series of attempted assassinations. A military coup led by paratroop officers in Algeria, who were planning to drop on Paris, had been cancelled at the last minute when one of the four rebel generals lost his nerve. A second general, on the run from the police, was caught and sentenced to life imprisonment for treason. Then supporters of the rebel generals, members of the revolutionary OAS ('the Organisation of the Secret Army'), started to carry out bomb attacks in Paris. Supporters of the Algerians living in the city had marched in protest and eight men were trapped by the police and crushed to death at the entrance to an underground station, the Métro Charonne. This was the incident Nanny had referred to. 'Panic,' said the police. 'Murder,' said the survivors.

A third rebel general was caught and sentenced to death and on the following day French troops shot dead forty-seven Arab nationalists in the streets of Algiers. One week before my father handed me the car keys, the leader of the OAS coup, General Salan, was tracked down, arrested and sent for trial before the 'Haut Tribunal Militaire'. Pending trial, he was being held in the prison of La Santé in Paris.

The government fell, and the country's political and social stability seemed to be on the point of dissolution, but not a word of this was spoken at the dinner table in Nanteuil. Mr Cleland continued his peaceful researches into an imaginary outcome of the American Civil War while listening to *La Traviata* in the dusk. Camille continued to doze through the afternoon in the woodpile in the disused squash court, with a litre of *gros rouge*. The dog Karim continued to add drama to our day by chasing and nearly catching Moune's beloved cats.

In the evening, while Madame was teaching us bridge, in French, naturally, Nanny would tune in to the BBC news on her solid wooden wartime wireless set, but one day – unusually – she turned it on in the afternoon and for the only time I can remember the reality of life in France broke into our peaceful retreat. Suddenly we could hear the noise of *'un manif'* – a demonstration in the capital – a sound I can recall to this day. Thousands of OAS supporters were gathering in the streets outside La Santé Prison to show their solidarity with General Salan. They were beating out a Morse-style rhythm on hundreds of car horns – 'Dot-dot-dot . . . Dash-dash . . . Dot-dot-dot . . . Dash-dash': *'Al-gé-rie . . . Fran ÇAISE . . . Al-gé-rie . . . Fran ÇAISE'*. Later in the day this was followed by a counter-demonstration with a different rhythm on the horns: Dot-dot-dot – Dot-Dot-DOT . . . *'O-A-S – AS-SAS-SIN'*. Dot-dot-dot . . . *'O-A-S'*, Dot-Dot-DOT . . . *'AS-SAS-SIN'*. It was the electrifying theatre of the Paris streets.

Madame de Bernard made no comment on these events. But as she listened to the wireless she must have recalled a February day in 1934 when she had left Nanteuil and taken the train to Paris to join an even more violent *'manifestation'* that attempted to storm the National Assembly, overthrow the Republic and restore the monarchy. On that occasion the police shot fourteen of the demonstrators dead.

On 23 May, in the third week of my visit, General Salan was tried and found guilty. The punishment was life imprisonment instead of the expected death sentence. The military judges had responded to the strength of popular feeling, the power of the car horns beating out their tunes in the street. Right verdict, wrong sentence. President de Gaulle was so angry that he promptly abolished the 'Haut Tribunal Militaire'. On 1 June a new military court was set up with a new president, General Edgard de Larminat. As a young man Larminat, like de Gaulle, had been wounded at Verdun. In 1941 he had been condemned to death by Vichy, like de Gaulle, for rallying to the Free French. On 1 July, worn out by the conflict of loyalties, Edgard de Larminat committed suicide. A number of criminal trials for conspiracy then had to be abandoned when other judges declined to condemn officers who were obviously guilty.

And all the while the four English students, oblivious to these events, continued their studies. It must have amused the ladies of the house. As the armed struggle continued, we remained absorbed in the adventures of Catherine de Medici, Joan of Arc and Richard the Lionheart – whose tomb we admired when Moune took us to the Abbey of Fontevraud. Coming out of the abbey, dazed by the afternoon sun, I found that my car had disappeared. It reappeared out of the haze fifty metres away on the opposite side of the street. It had been locked when left and it was still locked when I rediscovered it neatly parked outside a shady bar. A large customer in a grubby white vest emerged, leaving his drink on the counter, and explained that he had moved it. He had simply lifted the rear bumper, so eliminating the handbrake, and wheeled it down the road. Why? To save me from a parking fine and to win a bet. Minis were a novelty in France in those days.

Meanwhile outside Paris a paratroop legionnaire – a veteran of Dien Bien Phu – who had led an OAS assassination commando in Algiers, was executed in the Fort d'Ivry. Three officers refused to command the twelve-man firing squad and when the order was given to fire, eleven of the firing squad aimed wide. The officer in command then emptied his pistol into the wounded paratrooper. The condemned man still refused to die so a second loaded pistol had to be found. The whole business took fifteen minutes.[2]

———

Towards the end of the summer Moune started to organise picnics on the banks of the Loire and dances with students from neighbouring châteaux and generally did everything she could to cut down the rate of cancellations. Always popular was a visit to Madame de Sallier du Pin, the widow of a general, who had a splendid villa on the heights to the east of the city, with a swimming pool in the garden. At lunchtime before one such visit, I asked Madame de Bernard whether her friend had a picture of 'Jacqueline' on her mantelpiece. This question, raising the possibility of Madame de Sallier du Pin as a member of the Resistance, caused considerable amusement. It must have reminded Madame de Bernard that 'les jeunes anglais' of 1962 had no more idea of wartime reality than we had of events in Paris. Perhaps it was part of our charm.

Or perhaps not. In the last week of my visit Moune decided to broaden my education. She showed me the work she had been doing for a forthcoming exhibition that was designed to raise money for the survivors of the wartime deportations. She had a selection of photographs that shocked me, of the *Aufseherinnen*, the female guards at Ravensbrück who were tried at Nuremburg and subsequently executed. They were pictured on the day of their arrest, staring down the camera, still in SS uniform and the arrogance of their power. They had names like 'Dorothea', 'Luise' or 'Carmen' and were described as 'Punishment block leader' or – ominously – 'Nurse'. They were the sort of portraits that it is hard to forget. As it happened these women had been sentenced to death by an English judge. In my innocence this detail strengthened a sense of post-war comradeship between English visitors and the house: '*Nanteuil-Londres, Même Combat.*'

All those people, the friends I made that summer, are dead now and their world has died with them. There is precious little left of their Sologne. The forests have been flattened by 'leisure parks' and golf courses or crushed by motorways. But in 1962 this world was still governed by its past. I remember one day walking by the river where it bordered the village beyond the gates and finding a field where a tractor had tipped over the bank and fallen into the stream. The farmer, probably drunk, who had managed this feat had hitched one of his big carthorses to the machine and was encouraging the animal to pull. He was yelling and lashing it with a long carter's whip, and the horse was straining as hard as it could, but the tractor did not move. It was a brutal scene, something out of Zola, the man cursing, the beast responding with all its strength, while the whip cracked and nothing happened. There was something futile in the scene as well. The machine that had replaced the animal – the machine that was in the process of rendering the animal extinct – itself useless, immobile, silent. The man in charge incapable of finding a solution, apart from lashing his horse.

Horses are long gone from the village and any whips that remain will have become exhibits in some 'Museum of Rural Life'. And there aren't many farmers left in the village either; it's become a dormitory suburb of the city and most of the asparagus fields are covered with second homes. But when I first knew Nanteuil little had apparently changed in the fifteen years since the war. Little had changed for much longer than that.

Shortly after I left for England, on 22 August, another terrorist commando, this time led by an air-force officer, machine-gunned the president's car outside Paris and very nearly killed both de Gaulle and his wife. The incident later became the inspiration for the book and the film *The Day of the Jackal*. The leader of the commando, Lieutenant Colonel Jean-Marie Bastien-Thiry, was arrested, tried and sentenced to death. He was a Catholic and a former Gaullist. The president declined to exercise his power of clemency and 2,000 policemen guarded the Fort d'Ivry on the morning Bastien-Thiry, holding his rosary, faced a firing squad. The execution took place shortly after the verdict, before an appeal could be lodged.

When I drove out through the gates of Nanteuil at the end of the summer, as I thought for the last time, I had no idea of the role that the friendships I had made would play in my life. Wordsworth, with promises to keep, left Blois confident that he would shortly return, and never came back. I left the house by the river with no intention of coming back and returned again and again. Neither of us had any sense of the lessons we would learn about loyalty and betrayal, about illusion and reality.

I wrote to Madame de Bernard from England to thank her for her hospitality. The arrival of the letter, Neil later told me, caused a memorable explosion at the lunch table, due to some reference I had made to having a haircut before I met my father. Back in Bembridge, as French army officers plotted to assassinate their head of state, the '60s were edging into sight.

2

The Visitors' Book

The book records that 'Nita Cox' arrived at Nanteuil on 18
September 1925. The departure date was never filled in . . .

Souris de Bernard's maiden name had been Anne-Marie Denisane. She and Nesta Cox were of the same generation, both born in the last years of the reign of Queen Victoria. They grew up in countries that were hereditary rivals and they had no common language, yet they chose to spend the greater part of their lives together and soon after meeting became the closest of friends.

Anne-Marie Denisane had been born in the Sologne in 1894, in the medieval château of Savonnière, at Ouchamps, near Amboise. Her wealthy family circle included professional soldiers and artists. Her father, Raoul Denisane, was a well-known painter. He redecorated the Savonnière in the neo-Gothic style and corresponded with Maupassant, who dedicated a short story to him – '*Le Verrou*', written in 1882. Anne-Marie's mother, Yvonne, was a glass-manufacturing heiress and a descendant of Baron Vacher de Tournemine, who had fought with Napoleon and commanded a division in the post-Napoleonic army. His daughter Emilie, Anne-Marie's grandmother, had danced with the Prince Imperial. And her grandmother's sister, Great-Aunt Marie, had married the Marquis de Perrigny, an attaché at the court of Napoleon III.

Nesta Cox had been born in 1899, in Brandon, Suffolk, and christened 'Ellen'. Her mother was Eliza Cox, née Butters, who described herself as 'a furrier'. The father's name is left blank on the birth certificate, but Nanny always identified him as George Cox, a furniture remover. She may never have lived in her father's house and when she was asked in later life if she wished to contact her father's family, she replied most emphatically that she did not.

Anne-Marie's father, Raoul Denisane, eventually inherited a considerable fortune and was able to purchase the Savonnière from Marie de Perrigny, his wife's great-aunt. But in 1902, when Anne-Marie was eight, Raoul Denisane died, leaving four young children. His widow decided to remarry, and her second husband was a neighbour, Ludovic Des Chesnes, who was a royalist, a sportsman and the mayor of Valaire. Ludo Des Chesnes shared a hunting pack with Prince Amédée de Broglie, who owned the nearby Château de Chaumont. For Anne-Marie it was a magical childhood in the enchanted playground of the Sologne. She was taught forest lore – where to look for mushrooms, where to dig for truffles, when to listen for *le brame du cerf* – the night-time roaring of the stags.

She learned what to do when you got lost in the forest; she learned that moss grows on the west side of trees, to light a cigarette if you wanted to watch the wind, to shout downwind if you wanted to be heard, to trust your horse if you did not know which way to turn, and to notice when the horse quickened its pace because it meant that you had passed the middle of the forest and were on the way home.

Nesta Cox's mother died when she was three years old – she had a vague memory of having seen her in a hospital bed – and she was taken in by a Miss Chamberlain, with whom she lived for about ten years. One day Miss Chamberlain fell ill and Nesta was put into an Anglican school at Farnham where she was known as 'Rose'. By this time she had acquired the de facto status of an orphan. 'Rose' Cox's school records, which she kept for the rest of her life in two small suitcases at the back of her bedroom cupboard, do not provide much evidence of an academic education. Her four 'star registers' do not contain any stars, but the purpose of her schooling was to provide her with some simple way of earning a living. She was prepared for the St John's Ambulance examination in first aid, she was taken on nature walks to learn about wildlife and botany, and she was taught how to transform a box into a baby's bed. She was clearly intended for a children's nurse.

———

A flavour of the grown-up life watched by Anne-Marie Denisane when she was a little girl is given by an engraved silver plate attached to the wooden mount of a hunting trophy – a stag's head – that Anne-Marie kept for the rest of her life. Translated it reads:

Found near la Ferme Neuve in the Forest of Sudais, killed in the Loire at Rilly.

In attendance – Prince de Broglie, Mlle de Broglie, Prince Albert de Broglie, Count de Beaucorps, Baron de Cassin, Viscount de Thoisy, Count de Marcé, the Marquis de Chauvelin.

By car – Marchioness de Perrigny with my wife Paulette and the children, Monsieur Lebaudy.

Dispatched by Count de Beaucorps.

The honours to M. Lebaudy

2 October 1902

Of this hunting party, Albert de Broglie was the son of a French prime minister, while the Prince de Broglie's younger brother won the Nobel Prize for Physics. Mr Lebaudy, who was given the honours – an expensive present for the recipient – was an influential politician and racehorse owner. Anne-Marie, aged eight, would have been one of the children in the car. She was the youngest of Ludo Des Chesnes's stepchildren and seems to have been one of his favourites. He invented her lifelong nickname, '*Souris*' (Mouse), because she was small and quick. And he infected her with his passion for hunting.

The only drama that Nesta (now 'Rose') Cox recalled from the Farnham years, when she was growing up, occurred after an outing to the cinema. The girls, with a party of boys from the associated boys' orphanage, had been sent to watch a silent documentary film called *Soldiers of the Queen*. It was set in South Africa during the Boer War, and one scene showed a suspected spy being hanged from a lamp post. On returning to the orphanage some of the little boys responded to this new art form by imitating it – and hanged one of their classmates. In later life Nanny could not recall what the final outcome had been, but the school closed down that summer on the outbreak of war. Miss Cox, once again called 'Nesta', the name she kept for the rest of her life, needed another home. Since she now knew how to sew and crochet, as well as how to knit, she was placed in a clergyman's family, in Cricklewood, north London, as a mother's help. She was aged fifteen.

Politically, Anne-Marie Denisane's family circle, as the engraved plate on the hunting trophy confirms, was nationalist, Catholic and royalist. It was also Anglophobe, regarding England as the enemy of France following the incident at Fashoda in 1898. There a small French military expedition was forced to withdraw from the Sudan by a much larger British force, a confrontation that led to nationalists in both countries calling for war. But when war eventually came, the French royalists, perhaps rather to their surprise, found themselves on the same side as '*les Anglais*'.

War was declared just before Souris' twentieth birthday and its impact is recorded in the collection of prayer cards that she kept in her missal for the rest of her life. There is one for each casualty.

> *Jacques-Etienne Benoist de Laumont*, aged 23, Sergeant in the 66th Infantry, near Arras, 25 September 1915, *Mort pour la France*
>
> His 73-year-old father, *Baron Benoist de Laumont*, retired cavalry officer, died of grief five days later
>
> *Sous-Lieutenant Georges Valette*, former pupil of the Collège Stanislas, 16 December 1915, *Mort pour la France*
>
> *Charles de Fontenay*, aged 26, poet and painter, leading his men in attack, 10 January 1916, *Mort pour la France*
>
> *Etienne de Fontenay*, aged 23, leading his men in attack, 25 September 1916, *Mort pour la France*
>
> *André Bonnafont*, aged 33, artist, pilot, 25 October 1916, *Mort pour la France*

Etienne de Fontenay and André Bonnafont probably died at Verdun. The phrase 'Died for France' has been the response in a patriotic litany at national memorial services ever since. For Souris the consequence of the war was that when it ended in November 1918 she was still, at the age of twenty-four, unmarried. One year later she met an Englishman who was six years older than she was. His life had been spared because he had not been well enough to fight.

For Nesta Cox the move to Cricklewood took her close to the same frontline. Cricklewood was the site of the Handley Page aircraft factory and there were regular daytime bombing raids by Zeppelin – during which Nesta and the four children she cared for were supposed to take shelter in the cellar. But since the cellar was damp and dirty, and Nesta had always been frightened of the dark, she preferred to crawl under the kitchen table with the children. One night, with the children in bed, Nesta watched a Zeppelin burn to pieces in the sky above the city. The women working in the Handley Page factory ran into the street to cheer and dance in celebration, but Nesta could only think of 'the poor men who were burning alive in their machine'.

Shortly before the Armistice in November 1918, she moved to her second family, that of a Mrs Ireland who lived at Barton Mills in Suffolk. For Nesta it was the start of a connection that was to last for the rest of her life. For it was while she was at Barton Mills that she met Mrs Ireland's brother, Billy Gardnor-Beard, a young man with a private income and poor health, who was accompanied by his new fiancée, a shy young Frenchwoman with a chic wardrobe called Anne-Marie Denisane, known to her friends as 'Souris'.

William Gardnor-Beard, always known as 'Billy', came from a family of iron masters but due to his fragile health he had been brought up in Switzerland and he spoke excellent French. He was sent to Eton and Trinity College, Cambridge, and on leaving university he started to tutor young men from his old school or his old college and take them on study parties travelling in France. Most were intended for the army or the diplomatic service. Then in 1919, having booked his party into a terrible hotel near Chaumont, Billy was advised to move to a nearby country house, La Gendronnière, where a family called Tabarly took in 'les paying-guests'. The Tabarlys were cousins of Souris, and she happened to be staying with them. Shortly afterwards Billy and Souris became engaged. They were married on 3 February 1921 at Candé-sur-Loire.

It was in October of the same year that Nesta, from now on known in this account as Nanny, left Mrs Ireland and sailed for Colombo aboard the SS *Lancashire*, of the Bibby Line. She had found new employment with her third family, the Fosters. Mrs Foster lived with her husband, a major of Marines, and their two young children in Ceylon.

The four years she spent in Ceylon were the first great adventure of Nanny's life. The Fosters lived in a splendid bungalow overlooking the city, with access to a private beach, and Nanny and the children were driven around in a white Rolls-Royce. The Prince of Wales, later Edward VIII, came to Ceylon on an official visit and one evening Nanny overheard some naval officers discussing his behaviour. The prince had abandoned the official programme as well as the residence prepared for him. He had demanded different quarters, where he had installed his mistress, an American woman called Barbara, and where he was apparently spending much of his time practising on the drums. He had also demanded the use of a battleship, HMS *Renown*, in which to circle Ceylon. Worse, the Marine band of the *Renown* had been instructed by the prince to stop playing military music and play jazz tunes instead. The officers had agreed that the visit was damaging to naval discipline; the prince would never make a good king.

Nanny left Ceylon in the summer of 1925. The Foster children had outgrown her, but she had kept in touch with Mrs Ireland, who told her that Billy Gardnor-Beard, now married to his shy French fiancée, was looking for an English nanny.

———

The union of William Gardnor-Beard and Souris Denisane had not been popular with either family. Souris' mother and aunts were disconcerted that she had chosen to marry a physically frail language tutor who was '*très gentleman*' but of no particular distinction and not even French, while the Gardnor-Beards were no better pleased that Billy had proposed to a shy French girl who spoke very little English. Billy and Souris brushed these objections aside and chose to settle in France. Billy had independent means and he decided to give Souris a splendid wedding present, a country house with an enclosed park, bordering the River Cosson. They would make their lives in the forest region where Souris had grown up.

The Gardnor-Beards spent their honeymoon at the fashionable seaside resort of Arcachon, near Bordeaux, and one day, while out walking with her husband, Souris happened to cross the path of a woman she recognised. She was called Henriette Caillaux and she was the wife of a prominent politician and former minister. Madame Caillaux had become a notorious figure in France in 1914 when she called on the editor of the newspaper *Le Figaro*, in his office, and shot him dead with six bullets from a .32 Browning automatic. She had been upset by the threatened publication of the love letters her husband had written to her when they were both married to somebody else. Thanks to *Le Figaro*, their pre-marital affair had become a national scandal. Facing a murder charge Henriette Caillaux had pleaded 'crime passionel' and to general astonishment been acquitted. Then in 1918 her husband, Joseph Caillaux, who had made himself extremely unpopular during the war years by his vigorous pro-German lobbying and his efforts to negotiate peace, was imprisoned on charges of high treason. For Souris, who had arrived on honeymoon with her '*caractère entier*' intact, Henriette Caillaux was the wife of a man who was popularly known as 'the national defeatist', a traitor who had encouraged the enemy and caused the deaths of many French soldiers. So Souris confronted her in the street, abused her and slapped her twice across the face. 'La Caillaux' took refuge in a nearby bakery, where, to cover her confusion, she bought every pot of jam in the shop. The police were called and Souris' new and bewildered husband was comforted by the inspector who, on learning that he was dealing with an Englishman on his honeymoon, just shook his head saying, '*Mon pauvre monsieur . . . mon pauvre monsieur*'.

Château Nanteuil, when Billy bought it in 1921 for 100,000 francs, was in a sorry state. It had been unoccupied for seven years and saplings were growing right up to the front door. The village boys had taken to climbing over the garden wall to steal the fruit; they also used the glass-house for catapult practice. The property dated back to the eighteenth century. In 1810 it had been purchased by one of Napoleon's tax inspectors. In 1859 it passed to the Vicomte de Broc, a descendant of the military governor of both Brittany and Alsace under the *Ancien Régime*. While living at Nanteuil the Vicomte was obliged to fight a duel in the park. The next proprietor, a sharp operator called Edgar Begé, seems to have acquired title by marrying the Vicomte's widow, and may even have been the victorious opponent in the duel. Nanny, who took a close interest in the history of the house, had a low opinion of Monsieur Begé and sometimes referred to him as '*une vieille fripouille*' (a real scoundrel). The house passed through several more hands and was eventually acquired by a Madame Jacob. When she sold it to Billy Gardnor-Beard she tried at the last minute to raise the purchase price by inventing a rival bidder. The trick failed and Billy set about making the place habitable. He cleared the grounds, turned the orangery into a fives court, and levelled part of the kitchen garden to make a tennis court. He constructed a small boathouse on the riverbank and erected a diving board beside a deep pool in midstream. He also designed a central heating system that cost the same as the house and was driven by a huge engine that he installed under the back steps. Souris helped to decorate the house with some mementoes from a childhood spent in the neo-Gothic surroundings of La Savonnière. They included a portrait painted by her father of a lady in crinoline – this was Marie de Perrigny, her great-aunt – and two splendid stags' heads, one of them being the beast killed in the Loire on 2 October 1902.

At Nanteuil, Souris was still living to some extent in her enchanted playground, surrounded by her childhood circle of friends. There were six horses in the stable, and she could continue to pursue her passion for hunting. A year after their marriage, on 28 June 1922, she gave birth to a daughter, Muriel, always known as 'Moune'. Souris and Billy Gardnor-Beard spoke French together, but Billy also wanted his children to speak English and so an English nanny was hired to run the nursery. Souris did not get on with the first and a succession of English nannies came and went. Then in the summer of 1925 Souris was pregnant again and with the hunting season opening on the feast day of St Hubert, 3 November, there would be no one to supervise three-year-old Moune and Betty, the new baby. Billy's English family learnt that the girl who had formerly been employed as a nanny by Billy's sister was on the way home from a position in Ceylon, and might be available.

As a wedding present Billy had received a leather-bound Visitors' Book, with marbled endpapers and gold edging. The first entry, for Souris' brother Bernard, is dated 12 March 1922. The book records, in Billy's hand, that 'Nita Cox' arrived at Nanteuil on 18 September 1925. The departure date was never filled in.

Many years later Nanny remembered that on arriving at Nanteuil she did not unpack her bags for a month. She did not take to the abrupt manners of Madame Gardnor-Beard, she did not speak a word of French, she was irritated by the resident nursery maid, she discovered that she was in a line of English nannies who had come and gone in short order – and she resolved to do the same before Christmas. But then two strong characters began to develop mutual respect and somehow found a way to work with each other. The nursery maid was dismissed, and Nanny was able to concentrate on the baby. With the opening of the hunting season Madame Gardnor-Beard spent less and less time with the children. Nanny established her area of authority and began to construct an entirely original means of communicating with the villagers of Nanteuil. And the changing cast of young English visitors, many equally at a loss in French, provided her with welcome company.

———

At some point during that long-lost summer of '62, bored of playing Yves Montand 45s on the record player, I discovered Billy Gardnor-Beard's original Visitors' Book. It told the story of the house and the chain of friendship formed with generations of young Englishmen. It was a story of summer tennis tournaments, bathing parties, stag hunting in the winter, dances in the neighbouring châteaux, a country-house weekend that had stretched over two decades and only ended with the war. The book still exists. Now battered and worn, it records the comings and goings over sixty-two years and 130 pages. Occasionally there is a French visitor, or even a woman, but most of those who stayed at Nanteuil between the two world wars were from the same class and background as Billy Gardnor-Beard's original pupils. The names, addresses, schools and clubs listed in the pages of the 1920s and '30s evoke a world of influence and privilege whose time has passed, and read almost like a parody of that England, one that might have inspired Betjeman, or Waugh – or P.G. Wodehouse.

They came from the Cavalry Club, or Hermanus, Cape Province, the Athenaeum or Chester Square. There were residents of Pont Street and Eaton Place and arrivals from the Forest Office of Lahore, Punjab. Boys came from Stowe, Marlborough, Ampleforth and Haileybury, Eton and Winchester and Stukeley Hall, Huntingdon. A Baring, or a Profumo, is followed by a Howard of Castle Howard and Michael Portman from '22 Portman Square, London W'. 1932 was one of the busier years, with a crowd that included Bill Bradford, Christopher Mount, Dick Seaman and Robert Cecil from Southbourne who was on his way to Cambridge, where he would join his childhood friend Donald Maclean. Both were bound for the Foreign Office. At Nanteuil they were all charged a guinea a day, plus extras – which might include a doctor's visit, or the hefty tip required by the huntsman if they attended the Cheverny hunt and were honoured with a severed deer's foot. The future novelist, Anthony Powell, aged seventeen, danced to the same ritual in the rival but less fashionable establishment of Madame de la Rive, some miles downriver, an experience which he later revisited in *A Question of Upbringing*.

Despite her marriage to an Englishman, Souris remained politically *engagé*. She was still a supporter of *Action Française*, whose founder Charles Maurras had famously described Germany as 'France's Public Enemy No. 1' and England as 'France's Public Enemy No. 1b'. And her brother, Jacques, worked in the movement's Paris office. It was the decade when the framework of the Third Republic began to break up. The two most extreme political movements, *Action Française* and the *Parti Communiste Français* (PCF) were also the most dynamic, and the moderate centre became a punctured void. On 6 February 1934, with France on the verge of political collapse. Souris went up to Paris and attended the violent demonstration in the Champs-Elysées that had been summoned by *Action Française*, with the intention of storming the National Assembly.

In England as well, anti-Communist nationalism was on the rise. Captain Archibald Ramsay's 'Right Club' was building an influential group of supporters; its membership list – Sir Peter Agnew MP, Lord Semphill, Lord Redesdale and the 5th Duke of Wellington – echoed the roll call at Nanteuil. 'Right Club' members would sing 'Land of Hope and Glory' with different words ('Land of Dope and Jewry . . .') and Captain Ramsay warned his followers that anti-Nazism was a Jewish plot, and would lead to 'a Jews' war'.

There is no evidence that Billy Gardnor-Beard was remotely interested in politics but at Nanteuil his daughter Muriel, aged twelve, had become strongly attracted to the Nazi Party. As a child, Moune had loved writing plays, dressing-up and wearing homemade uniforms. Asked if this was because she admired Nazi efficiency she pointed out that she had 'never been an admirer of efficiency'. It was the romantic side – of torches, songs, marches, uniforms and rhythms (what she called 'boots and drums') – that had attracted her attention. Her heroines were the film maker Leni Riefenstahl and the aviator and stunt pilot Hanna Reitsch, and they made the Nazis seem glamorous. But the Spanish Civil War broke out in 1936 when she was fourteen and she became a strong supporter of the Republican cause. She had never been to either Spain or Germany. They were just places she could visit by listening to the wireless, and her enthusiasm for Nazism ended abruptly with the invasion of Czechoslovakia in 1938.

A tolerance of 'Nazi efficiency' outside Germany in the 1930s was widespread throughout Europe. Dick Seaman, who had first visited in 1930 when he was only seventeen and still a pupil at Rugby, became a regular visitor. He went up to Cambridge, to Billy's old college, Trinity, where he made a close study of fast cars, and on going down he decided to become a full-time racing driver. At Nanteuil, Billy allowed him to construct an inspection pit in the coach house. In 1937 R.J.B. Seaman, much against his mother's wishes, signed for Mercedes-Benz, and in the following year won the German Grand Prix on the famously dangerous Nürburgring. On the victory podium Seaman (who was not a political animal) gave the Hitler salute. A delighted Führer declared that 'Herr Seaman' was his favourite racing driver.

Another regular visitor was a slightly older student called Berenger Colborne Bradford, always known as 'Bill' – although not at Nanteuil since his name was entered by Billy Gardnor-Beard in the Visitors' Book as another 'Billy'. While Bill Bradford was staying there, Souris – who generally rode alone – was thrown by her horse in the Forest of Russy. Fortunately, one of the English students, also riding alone, saw her horse with empty saddle heading for Cheverny. He collected the stray and hurried back to Nanteuil. Nanny organised a rescue party and she and Bradford found Souris lying in a clearing in the forest. Bradford would make a return visit in 1932.

As the girls grew up, in the fourteen years that separated Nanny's arrival and the outbreak of war, she became a central figure in the family, as much a part of it as the parents or the children. Billy Gardnor-Beard died in March 1938. He had been unwell for years. One of the young men in residence when he was dying was called Valerian Wellesley. Years later he unexpectedly became the 8th Duke of Wellington and looked back on his months at Nanteuil as 'a particularly happy period' in his life. He remembered that Nanny had 'contributed enormously to the enjoyment of all there and took a lot of the sweat out of the rather boring French lessons that we had to put up with from Mr Gardnor-Beard – poor man . . .'. Nanny, who had a remarkable memory, always recalled that Valerian Wellesley had been a gentle boy who was unusually fond of animals. He stayed for nearly six months and while he was there he looked after a doe that had become a household pet and built a little pond in the deer's enclosure. He took charge of the rabbit warren and made a tumbledown dovecote beside the Cosson, which was populated by rats and owls, into one of his favourite places.

Following Billy's death there was an increase in the number of French visitors, but Souris somehow kept the teaching going and there were ten English pupils in 1939. The last of them left the château on 31 August, a week after the publication of the Nazi-Soviet Pact and three days before the outbreak of war. On 25 June, Dick Seaman, who had become the leading racing driver of the day, had overturned his Mercedes on a wet track at Spa while leading in the Belgian Grand Prix. The car hit a tree and burst into flames. Seaman suffered third degree burns and died shortly afterwards. He had married a German girl six months earlier − disappointing his mother once again. By then Bill Bradford had joined a Highland regiment, the Black Watch. And Valerian Wellesley, a junior officer in the Royal Horse Guards who was so devoted to animals, had been ordered to shoot his squadron's horses. An order had come through to mechanise the Household Cavalry.

———

The Visitors' Book records that brief interlude between the two brutal episodes that destroyed the most powerful empire the world had seen, as well as the confident assumptions shared by the young men who stayed at Nanteuil.

3

The Fugitive

On 11 June, under mortar fire and running out of ammunition, Captain Bradford's sergeant went quite mad and shot and killed his own sergeant-major . . .[1]

War came to Nanteuil gradually; for eight months nothing happened. With the disappearance of the English in September 1939, French names start to appear in the Visitors' Book. Among them is 'Comte Tony de Vibraye of Cheverny', one of Souris' hunting friends, and the Comtesse Lagallarde – who was Souris' sister Paulette – always known as 'Tante Frigidaire' by Moune and Betty, though never to her face. Another frequent visitor does not appear in the Visitors' Book at any time, although he moved into Nanteuil in 1939 and made his home there until he died. This was Pierre de Bernard, the owner of Beaumont, a neighbouring château. He was an old friend and admirer of Souris, and as Billy Gardnor-Beard lay dying he told Nanny that he hoped Souris would marry Pierre when he was gone.

The 1939–40 hunting season was not a success. With five million Frenchmen under arms it was no longer possible to keep the Cheverny hunt going and some of the hounds were lodged in the kennels at Nanteuil, where they remained for much of the war. For eight months the allied armies in Belgium and France stood idle, despite the fact that they outnumbered the German forces which were heavily engaged in the defeat and occupation of Poland. In April 1940, after eight months of this 'Phoney War', Germany invaded Denmark and Norway and on 10 May attacked Holland, Belgium and France. The Dutch army surrendered after four days.

On 16 May a family of Belgian refugees reached Nanteuil and asked for shelter. Souris took them in and they stayed for a month. In the

Visitors' Book they were recorded as '*M. et Madame A. Van Delf et ses enfants*'. They had stories of being shot up by German planes – one of their party had been machine-gunned and killed on the road, but their arrival did not trigger any panic. The Belgian surrender, when it came on 28 May, was regarded as a setback. But the French army still stood between the Sologne and the enemy and most people expected that a stand would be made on the River Marne, as in 1914, and Paris would be defended. Then, in the following six days, 371,000 British and French troops had to be evacuated from Dunkirk.

Among those left behind, and still attempting to halt the blitzkrieg, was Captain B.C. Bradford of the 1st Black Watch, part of the 51st (Highland) Division. The paths of Dick Seaman and Bill Bradford, which had crossed briefly at Nanteuil, had diverged sharply in the years that followed. When Bradford left Nanteuil he went to Sandhurst, and in 1932 he joined his regiment. But before doing so he returned to Nanteuil, again in the company of Dick Seaman, who had gone up to Cambridge. While Seaman found fame, racing to his death on behalf of Mercedes-Benz, Bradford pursued a military career. In April 1940 his battalion had been ordered to take up position under French command in eastern France, some miles in front of the French artillery forts known as the Maginot Line.

After the evacuation of Dunkirk, the Battle of France turned into a rout. Many French units were still resisting the German advance, but their efforts were hampered by the absence of effective central command. Caught up in the rout, the 1st Black Watch were ordered to move away from or back towards the enemy in a chaotic and circular progress that lasted for two weeks. Corporal Charles Carter of the Royal Military Police, attached to the 4th Battalion Seaforth Highlanders, recalled that the Highland Division held the enemy for a week in the Abbeville area before being overwhelmed and forced to retreat to the coast. By the time they had been driven back towards the little fishing port of St Valéry-en-Caux, where they were told the Navy would take them off, the Black Watch and the Seaforth Highlanders were short of rations, out of water, frustrated, exhausted and disorganised. They were surrounded by a huge body of leaderless French soldiers and were taking heavy casualties. On 11 June, with the company under mortar and machine-gun fire and running out of ammunition, Bradford's sergeant 'went quite mad'[2] and shot and killed his own sergeant-major.

Early on 12 June the 51st Division, by now surrounded, was ordered to enter the little port and await evacuation by the Royal Navy. As they were doing so German units broke through the perimeter and started to shell the town and the cliffs above the beach. Corporal Carter, standing on the quayside, was wounded by shellfire. He tried to make his way to the beach by sheltering under the 300-foot chalk cliffs. Below the cliffs, which reminded Charles Carter of Dover, there were scenes of panic. Hundreds of men, mostly French, who were descending the cliffs on ropes, came under fire from German machine gunners and snipers. On the beach, leaderless mobs were preventing the evacuation of the wounded and breaking up the Navy's lifeboats. The beachmaster requested British infantry to defend the boats and a 2nd Lieutenant of the Duke of Wellington's regiment ordered his men to fix bayonets and charge; they killed a French colonel and about fifty other ranks.[3] Other British officers who were loading the wounded had to hold the French troops off with hand grenades. Bradford, meanwhile, by now effectively in command of what was left of his battalion, was still fighting on the perimeter, attempting to hold back the Panzers with rifles and machine guns. The Naval evacuation was called off that morning and at 10 a.m. Captain Bradford received the order to surrender.

General Erwin Rommel, commanding 7th Panzer Division, received the surrender of the Highland Division from Major General Victor Fortune, and the Highlanders, still 10,000 strong, became prisoners of war. Bradford and Carter, with the rest of the division, were 'herded like sheep behind the German tanks'. Charles Carter's bitterness increased 'because far out to sea could be seen ships of the Royal Navy, which had been standing by in the hope of taking us to England'. As they were marched off

we saw the Nazi war machine in action. It made me realise how hope-lessly we were outnumbered and insufficiently equipped to face such an enemy at the time. They had tanks, these deeply stretching as far as the eye could see, and worked in fine cooperation with the Luftwaffe, the infantry following up behind the tanks . . .[4]

Rommel wrote to his wife describing the 'special joy' he felt at receiving the surrender of this British division, and of how the French people, who seemed so happy that their war was over, had started to offer flowers to his tank crews as the 7th Panzer Division pressed on.[5]

————

The stench of defeat reached Blois two days later, on 14 June, when the first wave of French refugees, fleeing before the oncoming German armies, choked the streets of the city. The decision by the French government to abandon Paris late on the evening of 10 June, and leave it as an open city, had come without warning and caused a mass exodus. The roads and pavements leading south out of the city were totally blocked over a distance of five kilometres.

The prime minister Paul Reynaud, who left at midnight accompanied by the new Under-Secretary of State for Defence, a youthful brigadier general named Charles de Gaulle, took eight hours to reach Orléans, a destination that was normally less than three hours away. On the following day Reynaud and de Gaulle left Orléans and drove through Blois to Tours where the government announced that a stand would be made on the River Loire. The citizens of Paris, tracking their government, crammed into Blois with one idea in mind. They were determined to force their way onto the Pont Jacques Gabriel, in the centre of the city, the bridge that led to the regions of France that would now be protected by the new front line. As they did so German units were already attacking Orléans, fifty-seven kilometres to the east.

On the night of 13 to 14 June, Orléans was bombed and set alight and on the following morning the population began to evacuate the city to take refuge in the Sologne. The French army, defending a key position on the new front line, retreated during the course of the day, blowing up the road bridge across the Loire behind them. By the evening of Saturday, 15 June Orléans was deserted and burning furiously. It remained alight for another nine days, until firemen from Paris arrived to rescue what was left. During those nine days Orléans was completely ransacked by gangs of looters from Paris who followed in the wake of the German army, as well as by local opportunists. When they had finished ransacking an undamaged house the looters set fire to it to conceal their activities.

Having finished with Orléans, the German bombers moved downriver and attacked Blois at 2 a.m. on the morning of 15 June. The city was still defended by a scratch collection of French units. On that day the municipal institutions began to withdraw from the battleground to join the exodus. Shops and cafés closed, and the hospitals started to move their patients. A decision was taken to evacuate the prison – but on foot as no vehicles remained to transport the prisoners. The majority of those released promptly absconded and looting of abandoned shops broke out shortly afterwards. The municipal lunatic asylum was also evacuated. The procession through the normally locked asylum gates made a strange sight. A hundred of the resident patients walked out, accompanied by their nurses, the warders, the gatekeeper and the gardener. Those patients well enough to understand instructions helped to push the asylum handcarts which were loaded with medicine, medical records and food. After several days the cortège arrived at the lunatic asylum of Châteauroux, 100 kilometres to the south, where a headcount confirmed that a number of patients, including several of the more dangerous cases, had gone missing en route.[6]

By 16 June, German forces had worked their way down river as far as Meung-sur-Loire and were only thirty-five kilometres away from Blois – so the police, the fire brigade and the staff of the departmental prefecture withdrew across the bridge. By then heavy bombing had set most of the buildings in the centre of town on fire. Five hundred houses were destroyed, and the *hôtel de ville* was burnt to the ground. At the station, trains packed with refugees were bombed and machine-gunned from the air. A wild rumour (which was quite untrue) spread through the region that Italian planes had joined the battle.

―――

Meanwhile at the château, Madame Gardnor-Beard, her two daughters and Nanny were digging in. No one had thought that it would take the 'Boches' only a month to get from the Dutch frontier to the Champs-Elysées, but despite the fact that the bombing and shelling were getting closer, Nanteuil still seemed a lot safer than the world outside. Souris was confident that, whatever happened, Nanteuil would be fine and she managed to maintain a calm atmosphere. This lasted until 10 June when her niece Victoire Boutard, the daughter of 'Tante Frigidaire', joined the Paris exodus and drove into the courtyard crying, 'Pontoise [to the west of Paris] is in flames.' This unnecessarily dramatic behaviour undid all Souris' good work. She told Victoire to stop spreading alarm, but the harm was done, and the drama panicked Marie-Louise, the cook (who was also Souris' god-daughter).

On 14 June enemy planes flew over the château and machine-gunned the refugees passing on the main road. Souris with her children, the servants and her guests left the house and took refuge in the old icehouse in the park. At one point, while they were still under attack, Nanny left the icehouse and returned to the kitchen to make a cup of tea. That night a woman from the village came up to the château to say that the *garde champêtre* (local constable) had received orders that the village was to be evacuated and most of the villagers left, as did the residents of Huisseau, led by the mayor. Monsieur and Madame Van Delf and their children departed on 16 June, remembering to sign the Visitors' Book before they rejoined the panic-stricken columns on the road south. But Souris, contrary as ever, refused to join them. Abandoning her beloved house to the mercy of looters and enemy soldiers was the last thing she wanted to do. However, the departure of the Van Delfs further demoralised the servants who had been looking after them. That night, while attempting to get some rest in the icehouse, Souris was approached by Marie-Louise and the two maids, all of whom had husbands absent in the army. 'I could not face my husband if anything happened to his son,' said the cook. It was at midday on the following day, 17 June, that Marshal Pétain, who had succeeded Paul Reynaud as prime minister on the previous evening, made his first broadcast to the French people. He announced that the battle was over and declared that the time had come to stop fighting. He had already contacted Berlin asking for terms of surrender. And so that afternoon the Gardnor-Beards joined the exodus. As Souris, Nanny and the children drove out of the courtyard, in a procession of three cars, the terrifying noise of war was clearly audible, and they all feared that they would never see Nanteuil again.

There were three drivers – Souris, Pierre and Victoire. Pierre de Bernard led the way in a small black Peugeot 202. His passengers were Betty, Suzanne the maid, Suzanne's daughter and Marguerite, the second maid. He was followed by Victoire in a grey 202 with her mother, Paulette, a baby called Bertrand – who was Paulette's grandson and Victoire's nephew – and the countess's elderly maid. Last came Souris in a big Ford V8, towing a double horsebox. In the car she had Nanny, Moune, Marie-Louise, her son Guy, and Winkie, Moune's cat. The horsebox contained Monsieur de Bernard's luxurious American mattress with metal springs, his silver dressing case, a considerable amount of cash, table linen, bed linen and his shotguns. The gardener, Gerard, stayed behind to guard the house.

Because the roads were so crowded and the traffic was so chaotic, Souris worried that the two smaller cars might move faster than the Ford, and it would be difficult to find them again. Moune remembered that it was possible to keep in touch with the second Peugeot because, even if one could no longer see the little car through the crush, the baby was making so much noise. Victoire, who had an exuberant personality – attributed to her partly Spanish blood – and who was dressed patriotically in a short blue skirt, a white shirt and a red turban, with white driving gloves, frequently leapt from her car to direct the traffic. This irritated Souris, who hardly spoke. She was close to tears of rage at the French military collapse. Nanny sat beside her, with instructions to haul on the handbrake when requested as the weight of the double horsebox was a problem when descending hills.

Heading for Clermont-Ferrand, in the Massif Central, hundreds of kilometres to the south, they eventually reached Romorantin, twenty-five kilometres away. Pierre said that Pétain's call for an armistice was not a peace treaty, and so they pressed on, not realising that German units had already cut the route south some miles ahead. They entered Mennetou-sur-Cher down a steep hill, at the foot of which Pierre pulled up to ask Souris where they were to go next. 'I don't know . . . or care,' she cried. 'I can't stop,' and with Nanny hauling on the handbrake the Ford and the horsebox careered on.

Behind them some French units were still fighting. That night – two weeks after the Royal Navy had withdrawn from Dunkirk – the last French troops holding Blois fell back, still fighting, across the bridge, and the first German soldiers entered the city, which appeared to be defenceless. Only 200 immobile residents of an old people's home remained to face the enemy, accompanied by the nuns who looked after them.

Intending to secure the Pont Gabriel, which was still intact, the armoured cars of the German advance guard set out across the bridge, but as they reached the central arch they came under heavy fire and two arches of the bridge were blown up. The battle of Blois continued for another two days, with Moroccan troops driving back a night-time German attack made in inflatable boats. Then on 20 June the last French defenders pulled out, to avoid being cut off by a much stronger enemy force that had succeeded in crossing the Loire higher upstream. That same afternoon, in Paris, French Communists, who had sought and received permission from the German authorities to start republishing their party newspaper, *L'Humanité*, prepared the first edition. They were following the party line which – with a logic worthy of Captain Ramsay – had identified the war as 'a capitalist plot' and decided that the working class should keep out of it.

Meanwhile in Chartres, 100 kilometres to the north, the prefect, Jean Moulin, who had disobeyed orders and remained at his post in order to protect the town from looters, surrendered it to the general commanding the *Wehrmacht*'s 8th Infantry Division. Almost all of Chartres' 23,000 citizens had fled, as had the police, the mayor, the bishop and the fire brigade. The prefect, with two dozen nuns, four priests and a freemason were the only responsible figures left. The Germans had shot a number of Senegalese prisoners of war and ordered Jean Moulin to sign a false statement identifying them as rapists and murderers. When he refused to cooperate he was beaten for seven hours. Feeling that he was at the end of his strength, Jean Moulin cut his throat to avoid giving in, and narrowly escaped death. The armistice was signed two days later.

———

The family party from Nanteuil had spent their first two nights as refugees sleeping in the cars and on the following day, 19 June, they continued on the road to Châteauroux. It took them four hours to travel eight kilometres and Souris ran out of patience. She decided to leave the main road and seek shelter in a field. They took the next turning, found a deserted barn and stayed there for a week. Life in the field was organised on a suitably formal level. On their first evening an unknown French general, speaking from London on the BBC, broadcast to the nation, contradicting Pétain, the new head of state, and lighting 'the flame of French resistance'. But none of those sheltering in the barn outside Châteauroux heard Charles de Gaulle's speech. Souris and Pierre – who was known as Bébert by the children – changed for dinner, and the maids wore clean blue muslin aprons to serve them. The food mainly consisted of rice, jam and some of the chickens they found in the barn. After dinner the whole party lay down on piles of straw and slept, except for Souris and Pierre who shared the American mattress.

When the Germans started to put up roadblocks around Châteauroux, Souris decided that the time had come to return home. So on 24 June they packed up and headed back to Nanteuil, which now lay in the Occupied Zone, forty kilometres north of the demarcation line. On the empty roads the journey that had taken over two days took two and a half hours and when they drove into the courtyard they found that the château had been wrecked. The electricity and the water had been cut off. The cellar had been ransacked. Clothes and books had been stolen. Their personal belongings and broken glass were scattered around. Both French and German troops had passed through, but Gerard the gardener said that it was the French who had caused most damage. The German looters were a medical unit and several spoke English. They had taken English books from the library, and a coin collection, as well as the family gramophone and records.

In Huisseau-sur-Cosson the mayor had returned and so Souris and Pierre, with Nanny as their witness, were able to marry. Madame Gardnor-Beard became the Comtesse de Bernard de la Fosse. Within days, two companies of German soldiers had arrived at Nanteuil to pitch tents and occupy the park. The senior officers moved into the English students' bedrooms, the junior officers slept on the dining-room floor. Nanny and the girls resumed family life, in so far as it was possible to do so in these unusual circumstances, and Souris went back to work. Earlier in the year she had started to volunteer for the Red Cross. There was a Red Cross depot in Blois and those who worked for it were given a permanent pass to cross the German police barriers set up on the Pont Gabriel. She found that her first task was to supervise those who were packing up food parcels for two million French prisoners of war.

———

Under the leadership of Marshal Pétain, hero of Verdun, France's humiliation was complete and any visible traces of the Anglo-French alliance were obliterated by the end of the year. Souris' circle of friends welcomed the Marshal's programme. Launched with the call to surrender, it was approved on 10 July by the majority of elected deputies, who voted themselves out of office and accorded the 84-year-old Pétain 'full powers' over the country's executive, parliament and constitution. The Third Republic was dead, to be succeeded by '*l'Etat Français*' and there was widespread popular support for Pétain and relief that the fighting was over. This went with the equally widespread feeling against 'the English', who had become the scapegoats for defeat, having 'abandoned the struggle' and 'gone home'.

For Souris the national mood presented an obvious dilemma. Still widely known in the neighbourhood, despite her remarriage, as 'Madame Gardnor-Beard', with two English daughters and an English nanny in the household, furious and ashamed of the French military collapse, she was at the same time isolated in her circle of friends by her total opposition to Pétain's call to surrender. In the weeks that followed her return to Nanteuil things went from bad to worse. On 21 June French delegates had been summoned to meet Hitler in a forest near Compiègne in northern France, where they were informed of the terms of the armistice. The French armed forces would be disarmed. The world's third-largest battle fleet would be given up with scarcely a shot fired. In the Occupied Zone the French administration would be under the orders of the German military authorities. The costs of the Occupation would be paid by France. The industrial and agricultural produce of France would be placed at the disposition of Germany.

Then on 3 July matters became even more serious. A French naval squadron anchored in the Algerian port of Mers-el-Kebir was shelled by a British naval squadron, having refused to surrender or sail for a neutral port, and 1,300 French sailors lost their lives.

On the same day at Nanteuil the miller, whose watermill adjoined the château, walked into the kitchen in a state of anxiety and asked to see the countess. When Souris returned home from working at the Red Cross that evening the miller told her that he had spent several hours fending off a suspicious-looking character speaking very bad French, who was demanding to see her. In the miller's opinion he was, by his appearance, quite obviously an Englishman. Souris and Pierre walked through the château gates, over the Roman bridge and up the lane, where Souris saw a man loitering by a hedge pretending to pick berries, and recognised the badly disguised figure of an old friend she had always known as 'Billy'.

———

Bill Bradford had been marched off from St Valéry-en-Caux on 12 June with the rest of the Highland Division. The men had no water and no shelter. If they fell out through exhaustion, they were moved on at bayonet point. Bradford spent the first night lying on slushy ground, under a farm cart, sharing a blanket and a greatcoat with a fellow officer. He had nightmares, imagining that he was still fighting, and he kept waking and ordering his companion to get up and do something. There were brutal incidents along the line of march. In one overnight camp Bradford carried some water to a group of thirsty soldiers who had just limped in; a guard knocked him down with a rifle blow and the water was poured away in front of the thirsty men. As they marched north the French population became friendlier, bringing them water and food, and Bradford became more and more determined to escape.

Charles Carter recalled that they were marched twenty-five to thirty-five kilometres a day. They spent the nights in *Lagers* – overnight prison camps specially set up for their reception. 'Usually there were trees around these camps with machine-gun nests fixed in them. We were given one meal per day consisting of black bread and about one pint of soya beans but our privations were such that combined with the fatigue of long marching, soldiers were fainting all along the line . . .'[7] At one point a German officer alleged that his camera had been stolen and told the prisoners that they would be kept without food and water for two days if it was not returned. 'It was not returned,' remembered Carter, 'and the punishment was imposed as he said.'

On 19 June, as the column neared Lille, two senior officers known to Bradford managed to get away. Bradford had been invited to join them but had decided that they were too old and slow to make it.* Later that day he too slipped away during a rest break and hid in a nearby wood. The first person he asked for help turned out to be a Polish miner who provided him with a suit of clothes that was too small – but was better than his uniform, which he buried.

At first he made for Boulogne, hoping to find a boat that he could steal on the coast, but this proved to be a bad idea; the coastal region was heavily secured and he was stopped and questioned by German patrols on several occasions. He claimed to be Belgian, hoping that this would explain his peculiar French. On 24 June he gave up looking for a boat and started the long trek south through France. All along the way he

---

* He discovered much later that they had managed to get back to London within six weeks.

was helped by the country people, often the *maire* or the *curé* who invariably recognised him as English, and who, even when they were frightened, gave him food or shelter. In one small village the mayor allowed him to stay the night despite the fact that a German officer had put a gun to his head earlier in the week, suspecting the mayor, correctly, of helping another fugitive. Occasionally Bradford met up with other escaping soldiers and they would exchange information. He was told repeatedly that the River Loire was the demarcation line, and he thought that if he could cross it, he would be safe and the way would lie clear to Spain. He had not been in touch with the Gardnor-Beards for several years, but he hoped that since their English household was south of the Loire they might still be in residence.

Making about twenty miles a day he drew close to the river on 5 July. That evening, looking south, he would have seen the course of the waters reflected in the brighter sky above, long before the river itself became visible. But it was also on 5 July that he learnt from another fugitive that the far bank was not after all in the Unoccupied Zone. His informant, a swimming instructor in civilian life, told him that the river was extremely dangerous if one was not an expert swimmer and that it would be essential to find a boat. On the evening of 6 July, Bradford paid a boy and a young man to row him across in a small fishing punt, though the current was very strong and the river, which was hundreds of yards wide, was in spate. On the far bank he spent the night in a barn belonging to a very poor family whose kitchen, full of cats and chickens, was 'indescribably filthy'. In the morning, without a proper map, he set off to find Nanteuil.

He had no very clear memory of where the château stood but thought that he could find his way there from Chambord. Both his visits had overlapped with the hunting season and he had got to know his way around the Forest of Boulogne. He reached Nanteuil in the early afternoon. 'I had hoped that Nanteuil was too small to be occupied,' he wrote later,

> but as I turned down the hill, I saw German troops on the bridge . . .
> I saw German flags at the château gates and lorries parked in the drive,
> I turned into the mill, which joined it . . . and I asked [the miller] to
> get in touch with Madame G-B and ask her to meet me here. He said
> he would but that there were German officers in the house, and he

wanted me to return in half-an-hour. I walked up to the top of the
village and hung about.[8]

When Bill Bradford saw 'Madame' walking towards him up the lane
with a man he did not recognise, he was 'overjoyed'. She introduced her
ancien élève to her new husband (they had been married the week before),
then she found him a bed with an old Spanish couple where he could
stay in safety and told him to meet her on the following morning in the
clearing in the Forest of Russy where her horse had thrown her ten
years before. That night Bradford slept 'awfully well' and next morning
had 'a good breakfast of bread and *café-au-lait* – really good coffee'.

On the following morning he found the clearing without difficulty
and at 11 o'clock the Bernards brought him maps, clothes, a razor and a
toothbrush, food and money. Souris invited him back to the château,
but Bradford decided that it would be too dangerous for the family as
someone in the village was bound to talk. If he were caught he was
confident that he faced nothing worse than a prison camp, whereas
Souris and Bébert and other members of the family could easily have
been shot. In the late afternoon the Bernards returned with Nanny,
Victoire and the girls – as well as a bicycle. Nanny brought a thermos of
her precious tea and they had a picnic in the same clearing. 'It was awful
fun seeing them again and we had a most cheerful tea party,' wrote
Bradford. 'Madame kept saying, "*Pauvre Billy*, I never thought to see
you like this." In the middle of our picnic some Germans came past, but
they paid no attention to us. Monsieur de B . . . gave me his brother's
address near Clermont-Ferrand to make for. They again pressed me to
come and stay for a few days.'[9] It was entirely characteristic of Souris,
the widow of an Englishman, with two English daughters and employing an English nanny, and with German troops quartered in her park, to
have invited a fugitive British officer to spend a few days in her house.

Bradford spent one more night with the Spaniards, who were kind
but nervous, and then, on a bicycle at last, resumed his journey south.
Later that day he managed to avoid German patrols and swam across the
River Cher into the Vichy Zone, where he was arrested and imprisoned
by the French authorities. He escaped again and after many adventures
eventually arrived home on 11 July 1941, just over a year after leaving
Nanteuil. His journey had taken him across France, over the Pyrenées

into Spain (where he was twice turned back by Franco's police), across the Mediterranean from Marseilles to Algeria, then back to Gibraltar which he reached by re-crossing the sea in an open boat. On his return to London he was debriefed by Military Intelligence and provided a detailed account of his movements.

Bradford returned to his regiment in time to fight at El Alamein and Sicily. He landed on Omaha Beach on 6 June 1944, and took part in the advance through Normandy, Belgium and Holland. He was wounded three times and ended the war as Lieutenant Colonel Bradford DSO and Bar, MBE, MC, in command of the 5th Battalion Black Watch as they crossed the Rhine into Germany. After the war he made one more visit to Nanteuil, on his honeymoon in 1951, when he was briefly reunited with Souris and Nanny. He died in 1996, aged eighty-three, a man whose life exemplified everything that the marriage of Souris Denisane and Billy Gardnor-Beard, the love and devotion of Nanny, and the long years of friendship between the family and the *jeunes anglais* of Château Nanteuil was intended to foster and defend.

Following Bradford's departure word was passed in the district that Madame de Bernard was the person to turn to if fugitive soldiers arrived in the area; and Captain Bradford became the first in a procession of British servicemen she helped on their way.

His visit set Souris on a new path. When Bill Bradford pedalled off towards the south, the memories he took with him, and the world he had briefly revived, vanished like an apparition. The chance that had brought him back to the house by the river had changed her life for ever.

PART II

A CHILDISH AND DEADLY GAME

4

'Setting Whitehall Ablaze'

*The idea is to allow the Gestapo and the de Gaulle staff to
think that we are cooperating 100 per cent with each other –
whereas in truth the whole of our organisation will be entirely
concealed from the French.*

Sir Frank Nelson, CD (Chief) of SOE

In Whitehall, in the summer of 1940, it was widely believed that the
speed of the German victory had been greatly assisted by the activities
of saboteurs behind the lines. The Nazi government had engaged in
subversion before the war in the Balkans and Austria, and in Spain the
spectre of the original 'Fifth Column' had aided Franco's forces to take
Madrid. In France a violent terrorist movement of the extreme right –
la Cagoule – had been at work, and there was compelling evidence that,
following the outbreak of war, French Communist agents had done
what they could to sabotage their own government's war effort.[1] So, on
16 July 1940, six weeks after Dunkirk, with the Battle of Britain going
badly, Winston Churchill decided that he too needed a 'Fifth Column'.
He appointed Hugh Dalton, the Minister of Economic Warfare, as
chairman of a new organisation that would take the battle to the enemy,
conduct irregular warfare and 'Set Europe Ablaze'.* This body would
specialise in sabotage and subversion and would eventually be called the
Special Operations Executive (SOE). Its invention as a separate agency
may well have been one of the least inspired of Churchill's wartime
brainwaves.

---

* Churchill may never have used this phrase. The source is Hugh Dalton quoting a
private conversation.

As early as 1938, Admiral Sir Hugh Sinclair, C (chief) of SIS,* had requested permission to expand his service's capacity for subversive warfare. In September of that year SIS had set up Section IX, later known as D Section (D for destruction) and had planned a campaign of sabotage in Germany using native Communists. 'Moral' sabotage, that is black propaganda, was circulated through a whispering campaign, by using known, often Jewish, opponents of the regime. At the same time the War Office set up a parallel organisation known as MI(R) which specialised in research into the use of irregular forces. D Section and MI(R) then proceeded to engage in a briskly fought turf war as to which should enjoy pre-eminence. Despite this distraction SIS had succeeded in launching a number of overseas operations before September 1939.[2]

The creation of a third secret agency dedicated to subversive warfare reignited the turf war, and it was said by those opposed to the birth of SOE that the new organisation was mainly notable for 'setting Whitehall ablaze'. Wars, the leaders of SIS pointed out, were not won by sabotage but by intelligence, and intelligence gathering depended on spying. Sabotage and spying did not go together. Spies had to remain invisible; saboteurs were bound to draw attention to themselves. But the protection Churchill had offered SOE – by endowing it with an independent cabinet minister – ensured its survival. And in the initial engagement with SIS, SOE appeared to emerge victorious. In October 1940 the infant body secured its own offices. D Section of SIS and MI(R) from the War Office were effectively transferred to SOE; and SOE acquired a monopoly of action in subversive warfare. SIS did however retain the capacity to undermine or redirect the new agency's activities. It controlled all SOE's wireless communication with its agents in the field. In addition, the first CD – the title of SOE's executive director – was Sir Frank Nelson, who had previously worked in France and Switzerland for Claude Dansey, who was effectively the deputy director of SIS.[3]

The existence of SOE remained 'most secret' throughout the war and when dealing with other departments it used an alias. W.J.M. Mackenzie, author of the official history of SOE,[4] identified seven of these aliases, and there may have been more. The one ministry to which SOE could never be traced was of course its own, the Ministry for

---

* SIS, the Secret Intelligence Service, popularly known as MI6. Sir Stewart Menzies succeeded Sinclair in 1939.

Economic Warfare, and the identity of CD and other senior officers, such as CD's deputy, Sir Charles Hambro – Churchill's merchant banker – and Brigadier Colin Gubbins, head of operations, was also a military secret. Not even SOE's field agents were told its name, and they sometimes referred to it as 'the Thing'.* [5]

Shortly after it was set up, SOE (like the defunct D Section of SIS)[6] was divided into twenty-three country sections. The section responsible for France was known as SOE(F), and in 1941 it came under the command of Major, later Colonel, Maurice Buckmaster, who in peacetime had been the manager of a Ford motor factory in France.

In the early years of the war the most reliable way into occupied France was by sea, and this means (usually operated by Royal Navy fast gunboats) was controlled by SIS. Its contacts with French military intelligence had become temporarily redundant with the French surrender. Instead, seeking intelligence, it started to land its own agents on French beaches immediately after Dunkirk in June 1940 and this continued for the rest of the year. But as an offensive organisation SOE also needed to use the cross-Channel route in order to land raiding parties and cargoes of arms and explosives as well as agents.[7] Its mission was clear. Internal resistance was to be organised in order to prepare a Secret Army to support the eventual D-Day landings. This objective made its representatives even more unwelcome from SIS's point of view.

Between October 1940 and August 1941 SIS infiltrated fifty-seven agents into France.[8] Meanwhile SOE(F) failed to land a single agent by the end of 1940.[9] Between February 1942 and October 1943, SOE again failed to land or take off a single agent in northern or western France by sea, once again blocked by SIS.[10] In May 1941 SOE(F) managed to deliver its first agent, by parachute. He was a Frenchman and he dropped near Châteauroux in the Vichy Zone.[11] By then, in an effort to get around the cross-Channel problem, F section had devised its own sea route via Gibraltar using adapted fishing boats, but this process was slow and inefficient.

During all this time the Intelligence Service was operating dozens of

---

* In Whitehall the agency's opponents called it 'the Mob' or 'the Racket'. Meanwhile, London taxi drivers pulling up at 64 Baker Street would call out cheerfully – 'Spy HQ!'

its own agents in France, infiltrating them by air or by the fast sea route. Whereas a great deal is now known about the activities of SOE agents in France, relatively little has been published about the agents of SIS, and what little has emerged has often been found in French sources. So anyone studying the activities of SOE in France has to accept that, however much one may discover about the agency, there was operating in the same country at the same time and for the same higher command, an invisible army of SIS agents, most of whose triumphs, disasters and unavowable activities remain off the historical record.

Throughout 1941 and 1942 SIS steadily hindered F section's attempts to land agents in France. SOE's supply problems were partially solved in August 1941, when the RAF formed 138 Squadron, which started to carry out regular parachute drops for F section. Then in February 1942 another new formation, 161 Squadron, was equipped with seven Lysander light aircraft, capable of carrying two passengers and operating by moonlight on rough ground and very short runways. Three months later SOE acquired a new CD. Dansey's man Frank Nelson resigned and was succeeded by his deputy, the old Etonian banker Charles Hambro. Since Hambro was also a director of the Bank of England and chairman of the Great Western Railway he gave less time to his SOE responsibilities than his predecessor and relied heavily on the new deputy CD, a professional soldier, Brigadier Colin Gubbins. Gubbins became the effective head of SOE and his first move was to implement an agreement whereby SOE acquired an independent radio communications system, with its own transmitter. So, on 1 June 1942,[12] Claude Dansey lost his ability to monitor SOE's wireless traffic.[13] Gubbins also organised an independent forgery service, thus rendering SOE's operations even more secure.

Just after Gubbins was promoted, SOE received a new and more precise directive from the Chiefs of Staff. Its task now was 'to build up and equip paramilitary organisations in the areas of projected operations while taking care to avoid premature risings. The task of patriot forces would be to cut enemy communications of all kinds and prevent the arrival of enemy reinforcements during the initial assault, envisaged for 1943.'[14]

For SOE the prospects looked brighter. But from Dansey's point of view all was not lost. He had already infiltrated another of his men into the most important section in SOE. This was Nicolas Bodington, a peacetime Reuters correspondent in Paris who had been desperate to join SIS. Dansey had found a better use for him and on 18 December 1940[15] Bodington became deputy head of as SOE(F). Major Bodington was very highly regarded in F section but, as will be seen in due course, his activities were not always to its advantage.

———

From early days F section's task had been complicated by the fact that it had a twin – RF section, which was partly under the orders of the man who on 28 June 1940 had been recognised by the British government as the leader in London of the 'Free French' – those French citizens who were prepared to continue the fight on the allied side – Charles de Gaulle.

'General de Gaulle, saviour of his country' was another invention of Mr Churchill's. The general had arrived in London after flying from Bordeaux in mid-afternoon on 17 June 1940 and was taken to Downing Street where he found the prime minister enjoying an afternoon siesta in a deckchair on the lawn. De Gaulle was a career soldier who, as commander of an armoured division, had led two successful counter-attacks in northern France between 17 and 31 May, driving back the Panzers and taking 500 prisoners.[16] After the second engagement, in front of Abbeville, his hard-pressed troops had been relieved by the 51st Highland Division, led as he remembered by 'General Fortune, newly arrived in France . . . *toute gaillarde et pimpante*' (hearty and fresh). Churchill knew of these exploits when he welcomed his unexpected visitor.[17] De Gaulle still held the temporary rank of brigadier-general, although he had left France and flown to England in defiance of his orders and without warning his wife. When he walked into the garden of No. 10 he did not have a penny to his name. Churchill was delighted to see him. Speaking on French radio Marshal Pétain had just announced his decision to surrender, and the newly promoted brigadier at once demanded a right of reply. Churchill saw the point of this insolent reaction and arranged for him to broadcast on the BBC on the following day. In France millions of people (including the family of Nanteuil) were still on the road, fleeing from the German army, and very few heard the broadcast. But it became the foundation of the Gaullist legend. The text read, it was later said, as though it had been written by a sleepwalker.

The leaders who for a number of years have been at the head of our armed forces have formed a government . . . This government, alleging that our armies have been defeated, has contacted the enemy and requested a ceasefire . . .

It was the German tanks, planes and tactics that overwhelmed us and which so much surprised our leaders that they have brought us to the point where we are today.

But has the last word been said? Must all hope disappear? Is this defeat final? No! . . .

Believe me . . . when I say that nothing is lost for France. The same means by which we have been conquered can one day bring us victory. For France is not alone. She is not alone! . . . She has a vast empire behind her. She can stand beside the British Empire which controls the sea and continues the struggle . . .

This war is a world war . . . Struck down today by mechanised force, we can in the future conquer through a greater mechanised force . . .

I, General de Gaulle, currently in London, invite French officers and soldiers, engineers and skilled workers who find themselves on British soil, with or without their arms . . . to contact me.

Whatever happens the flame of French resistance must not be extinguished and will not be extinguished! Tomorrow, like today, I will speak to you on the wireless from London.[18]

The final words of de Gaulle's '*Appel de 18 Juin*' came as a surprise to his producers at the BBC, who did not recall inviting him to speak on the following day.[19] The promised sequel was not broadcast, and the French Embassy, loyal to Marshal Pétain, refused to have anything to do with him.

The speech included key phrases – 'France is not alone', spoken three times in succession – and the key word, there from the very start of de Gaulle's political career, Resistance, '. . . *the flame of French resistance*'. It did not include the other celebrated phrase – '*France has lost a battle, but France has not lost the war*' which appeared, in French, on a poster that was pasted up on walls all over London on the first weekend in August. This ended '*Vive la France!*' and was followed by the signature '*C. De Gaulle*' with the address of his office, which he was already describing as his 'Headquarters, 4 Carlton Gardens, London SW1'. At this time he had attracted approximately fifty followers. His personal appeal in Glasgow on 29 June to a gathering of 6,000 of the 30,000[20] French servicemen who had been evacuated through England from Dunkirk or Norway, and who were still awaiting repatriation, was a failure. After listening to his address they decided in overwhelming numbers to return to France. On 4 July a French military tribunal sentenced Brigadier General de Gaulle to four years in prison for desertion and rebellion, and on 7 July, when he held his first rally of 'Free French' troops in the Olympia exhibition hall in London, only 500 men turned up. This half-battalion was the total of those men in uniform and still prepared to fight, out of the 94 divisions[21] that had defied the *Wehrmacht* three months earlier.

De Gaulle's original broadcast was not recorded by the BBC, but parts of the text were read out on the BBC's French service several times during the days that followed.[22] Unfortunately few heard it even then, since most people did not possess a radio set.[23] One Parisian who did eventually hear the '*appel*' said that it sounded like some obscure and noisy ruffian making a violent attack on the armistice and 'the old Marshal', while offering his listeners an unattractive choice between 'servility and treason'.[24] And one elderly lady listener told the writer Léon Werth that the English were 'egoists and traitors and that General de Gaulle was *un prétentieux*' (rather too full of himself). Most people first became familiar with the name 'de Gaulle' from the Vichy press reports of his court martial (and his eventual sentence to death).[25]

Meanwhile, the condemned brigadier general – established in London with British government recognition, and undaunted by the death sentence – assumed that he would thenceforth be in charge of all allied intelligence operations relevant to France. This assumption was officially encouraged – but silently knocked on the head. It was in order to give the appearance of full cooperation that the Gaullist intelligence service, the *Bureau Central de Renseignements et d'Action* (BCRA) had, at the suggestion of SIS, been allotted the subsidiary country section known as SOE(RF).

But the real situation was explained on 11 October by Sir Frank Nelson in an internal memo on the plan to set up RF, which revealed the level of distrust existing at that time:

The ideal is to allow the Gestapo and the de Gaulle Staff to think that we are cooperating 100% with each other – whereas in truth, whilst I should wish you to have the friendliest day-to-day relationship and liaison with the de Gaulle people, I should wish you at the same time to tell them nothing of our innermost and most confidential plans, and above all, such bases as you may establish in France must be our bases and known only to us . . .[26]

He added that the officer in charge of the 'special separate watertight sub-section' (i.e. RF)

would work outside this office and never visit it. The whole of our HQ organisation and its field organisation would be entirely concealed from the French . . .[27]

De Gaulle strongly objected to even the official cooperation offered by SOE and resented the existence of any British intelligence structure in wartime France. He particularly objected to F's recruitment of French nationals. In his view all French nationals outside France should be under his orders. The objective for de Gaulle was quite simply to close F section down. He himself refused to make any distinction between SOE, SIS and MI5, which he regarded as three pestilential manifestations of British interference in French affairs. Colonel 'Passy' (the *nom de guerre* of André Dewavrin, head of the BCRA) and his senior colleagues generally preferred to deal with '*l'Intelligence Service*' (i.e. SIS), and were largely indifferent to, and frequently unaware of, critical distinctions between SIS and SOE(F), which they usually referred to as '*Buckmaster*', after its irritating commanding officer. In his memoirs Colonel Passy mentioned the frequent quarrels the BCRA had with F section officers and complained about the frequency with which Major Maurice Buckmaster complicated or obstructed RF's operations.[28]

Colonel Passy's relations with SIS, on the other hand, were excellent, and he regarded Claude Dansey, the operational director of SIS, as a reliable friend.[29] In SOE(F) Passy and Dansey had identified a common enemy.

———

All this time, in occupied France, oblivious to the existence of SOE and the robust civil war being waged within British Intelligence, stubborn and courageous individuals had begun to fight back. The rank and file members of the French Resistance, known in London as 'local agents', were the backbone of the movement. Without them, the professionally formed members of F section could have accomplished very little. Between 1941 and 1944, SOE(F) eventually succeeded in sending over 400 agents into France, including fifty-three women. Acting alone, such a limited number of individuals could have accomplished practically nothing to disrupt the occupying forces or to weaken German defences when the invasion came, however skilful their work. But with the support and protection they received from 'local agents', F section's half-battalion became an army. In 2002 one SOE veteran, Francis Cammaerts, who won the DSO for his courage and efficiency, said that he and his SOE comrades were risking their skins, but they were trained volunteers and had chosen to face the dangers of the job, whereas 'for the French it was their homes, their families, their children that they stood to lose. They stood to lose everything.'[30]

The instinctive purpose of these untrained volunteers was to prepare a secret army to support the eventual allied landings. They knew next to nothing of the bigger picture, but were increasingly inspired by BBC radio broadcasts that referred to a previously obscure French general with an unusually evocative name.

5

The Swamps and the Forest

*Resistance . . . A movement of unconquered people in a
conquered country.*[1]

Hugh Trevor-Roper

*Resistance . . . An underworld of frightening insecurity,
where one slip, a discarded scrap of paper, falling asleep on an
overnight train, forgetting the name of a school he had never
attended in a town he had never seen, could lead to arrest,
torture and death . . .*

Jacques Baumel

For Souris it began as a game, what one resistance leader remembered as
'a childish and deadly game'.* The assistance she had offered to Bill
Bradford was a gesture made to an old friend. The British fugitives
whom she now started to help were total strangers. They may have
helped to heal her damaged pride. And the risk was exciting – like riding
side-saddle to hounds.

The Resistance in France began quite independently of either
British Intelligence or the BCRA. From the start the French Resistance
was driven by either ideology or patriotism, it was structurally divided
between those who fought for their 'tribe', *la patrie*, and those – in
Michael Howard's distinction – who fought for their ideals, in this
case Soviet Communism.[2] The natural focus of ideological resistance
should have been the PCF (*Parti communiste français*). But after the

---

* Emmanuel d'Astier, leader of the left-wing resistance movement, *Libération*.

Nazi-Soviet Pact of August 1939 the Communists followed a neutral line. The PCF's leadership maintained correct relations with the German military authorities, and the party newspaper called for fraternisation with the occupying forces rather than resistance. If individual Communists wanted to engage in active resistance they had to break ranks with the party. From June 1940 to June 1941 most remained inactive.

It was the patriotic impulse that was responsible for the earliest forms of resistance. It included people of no firm political convictions, demobilised soldiers, trade union organisers and academics, as well as many, like Souris, whose sympathies were with the hard right. Apart from the militants of *Action Française* there were freelance royalists and former members of the *Cagoule* – the pro-fascist terrorist conspiracy that had tried to overthrow the Third Republic in 1937. When the Jewish medical student and future neurosurgeon José Aboulker organised 'republican' armed resistance to the collaboration regime in the Vichy-governed colony of Algeria, his first recruits were monarchists from the anti-Semitic right. The word that united the first resisters was the word repeated in his first broadcast by Charles de Gaulle – '*Non*'. The one thing they could not accept was surrender. In Paris a group of anthropologists at the Musée de l'Homme formed an underground political movement, an intellectual resistance. They already had access to a printing press and they began by distributing broadsheets and tracts. For many, this was the way into the Resistance. It started quietly enough with a leafleting operation.

In July 1941 one such operation was organised by young Catholics in the department of the Loir-et-Cher. The leaflets attacked the authority of the Vichy regime. Shortly afterwards eleven young men and women were arrested by French gendarmes, tried by a French court in Orléans, and sentenced to between three and five years in a French prison. One of them was named André Murzeau. He lived at St Dyé-sur-Loire, a few miles upstream from Nanteuil. Ten months later, during another leafleting operation in Romorantin, a German military policeman was shot and killed. In reprisal the German authorities decided to execute ten hostages, the standard tariff for the death of a German soldier. Among those chosen for execution was Murzeau. He obtained permission to write a last letter. It was dated Tuesday, 5 May 1942.

My dear Maman,

It will greatly upset you to learn that they are going to shoot me this morning. Yes, it's true, yesterday at about 3.30 pm the Germans came for six of us, for the business at Romorantin. Well it's now 5.30 am and at 7.40, kneeling in front of 12 guns, I will give up my soul to God, hoping for some favour after 9 months of suffering in prison. As you can see, my hand is not trembling, and you can be proud of me. You can say to all my friends that I die as a true Frenchman, and as a man [. . .]

Now for my last will. A pity, as I am only 22! But there it is. For you, for Mémère [Granny] and for Janine, don't squabble too much, think of me sometimes, of Murzeau, son of Emmanuel Murzeau and Pupil of the Nation [*pupille de la nation* – i.e. child of a father killed in war], I die as he did. Let's all be proud of that.

All the comrades with me here are just as strong. What I would like you to do is to bring my body back to St Dyé as soon as possible, and at the funeral I want no wreaths, and none on my tomb either, just flowers, lots of flowers, and also a simple wooden cross [. . .]

When I think that I will never see you again it breaks my heart and causes indescribable pain. Well, I give you all my heart, my dear maman, so take it, keep it safe, before it is cut to pieces by the Mauser bullets.

They are just bringing us the traditional last cigarette. Well, I'm only 22, it's a pity that I could not live out my life, but what I did live was beautiful! It's true that I was hoping to make it more beautiful one day. I hoped too much.

Give my love to my friends, to all my friends [. . .] Tell them that I die as a man, and my mates in Blois, and my boss, and to little Jean-Claude at Saint-Dyé. Say farewell from me [. . .]

So I reach the end, my dear maman and I send you all the kisses that my heart possesses, and to granny too, and to my little Janine. Luckily for me I was arrested before I could marry, so that's one widow the less. I am smoking my last cigarette, so adieu to everyone. Maman, kiss my name, where I have signed it, your lips will be on mine.

Your son who loves you and who dies as a Frenchman,
Dédé.

Vive la France Libre! Take courage my friends.[3]

So, at a time when political leafleting could lead to the firing squad, Madame Murzeau's neighbour, a woman still best known as 'Madame Gardnor-Beard' – the widow of an Englishman and the mother of two English children – set out on her new, criminal career.

———

At first, following the departure of Bill Bradford, life at Nanteuil resumed some sort of normality. There was a new resident, an uninvited guest who had arrived in the courtyard on foot. He said that his name was 'Père Bel' and that he was Jewish. His wife was German, and they had a daughter, but he had been forced to flee Paris to avoid arrest and he had abandoned his garden supply shop. He asked if he could stay, and said he was a skilled nurseryman so he was given a little cabin in the stable courtyard, always known as the *basse-cour*, and he stayed for four years, taking over the walled garden and transforming it, filling it with fruit and vegetables. His peach trees produced excellent yellow peaches and Nanny was able to exchange these with a neighbour for melons, while Suzanne managed to make peach jam without having to use sugar – sugar being rationed to two lumps per person per day.

Nanny continued to live at the château undisturbed. She was protected at Madame de Bernard's request by the *mairie* of Huisseau-sur-Cosson, which omitted her name from the register of aliens. Even before the war the French police were listing all resident aliens, by department and by commune. During the Occupation the prefect of the department of the Loir-et-Cher had to answer to the German army commander in Blois, at the *kommandantur*. Had '*Nesta Cox – ressortissante anglaise*' (English national) been registered by the *Surveillance des étrangers* at the prefecture, she would almost certainly have been deported. When rare enquiries were made about it Souris always described Nanny as 'an English orphan who helps in the house'.

Nanny may also have been protected to some extent by the German soldiers billeted in the park, since they never reported her presence. The soldiers became a regular presence, although the units changed from time to time. A mounted troop arrived and released their horses in the park. These men had covered waggons and told the girls that they were en route to the Russian front. Relations remained mostly 'correct'. At the beginning of the Occupation, in an attempt to win the sympathy of the population, German forces were under strict orders to behave politely towards the French. Once, Moune nearly caused serious trouble by photographing some officers from behind the curtains on the first floor of the château. Fortunately, she was not caught. There was one unpleasant incident. Souris, who according to Nanny 'always spoiled Betty', had arranged for a dovecote to be made so that Betty could breed fantailed pigeons. The birds cooed all night which kept some of the soldiers awake and in the morning they shot the entire flock, claiming that they could have been used as carrier pigeons. This upset the girls and angered Nanny, who is said to have served the soldiers their usual soup that evening, but on flat plates.

———

Souris was a natural rebel but not a natural outlaw and in starting her resistance work she realised that she had to be particularly cautious. Her position with the Red Cross in Blois meant that she had a permanent pass to move in and out of the city, so crossing the Loire, with its formidable German police controls, was no problem for her. But unlike the academics at the Musée de l'Homme in Paris she had no 'group' to work with. Souris' family support group consisted of the people who signed the Visitors' Book after the English had left. These people, the counts and countesses, the visitors from the 16th arrondissement, were not naturally Anglophiles, let alone resisters. Moune called them 'the château people' and remarked that very few of them had anything to do with resistance. Souris learnt this lesson early. Among the first friends she approached for help was Philippe de Vibraye, the owner of Cheverny, and master of the Cheverny hunt. The marquis and his family were frequent visitors to Nanteuil, and his thousands of acres of woodland and *étangs* offered the ideal refuge. Monsieur de Vibraye turned down her request out of hand. He was appalled to hear that Souris was supporting 'that Judeo-Freemasonic-Communist' as he described General de Gaulle. Like so many of the château people, including Pierre de Bernard's brother Henri, and Souris' own brother Jacques, he was *Maurrassien* and *Pétainiste*. 'I suppose he would rather fill his bathtubs with noodles than weapons,' was Souris' comment to Nanny, when she returned from Cheverny empty-handed.

Souris' work was spontaneous and intuitive. And she started on her own. Once she left her enemy-occupied house she was not on friendly territory. The company of her fellow countrymen could be even more hazardous than that of the occupying forces. When Bill Bradford was debriefed on his return to London he noted that, 'In occupied France, people are willing to take great risks to help the British. In unoccupied France, I should say that 80 per cent are pro-British but are not willing to take so much risk to help.'[4] His experience of occupied France was partly formed by the welcome he had received at Nanteuil, but it was generally twelve months out of date. As time passed and the ruthless nature of German military rule became clear, the strength of neutralism increased, and the spirit of 'collaboration' – as required by Marshal Pétain – became widely acceptable. Resistance therefore grew more dangerous. In the words of one Sologne history, 'the earliest Resistance pioneers, very few of whom survived, had to struggle in difficult conditions against not just the occupying forces, but also against the spirit of defeatism, which developed into *attentisme*, the "wait and see" attitude that was adopted by so many members of the shattered population.'[5] For too many, the price of resistance was to have your life destroyed.

———

The first steps into this underworld were often taken through friendship, or by chance. A throwaway remark in a café or a resentful comment about the Occupation or the presence of German troops, could lead to the recognition of a kindred spirit. In Souris' case it came through her friendship with a neighbour, Marcel Buhler, a veteran of Verdun, who had come across a camouflaged German munitions dump north of Blois. He brought a plan of the site and a map reference to Souris who took it to Paris and handed it on to another neighbour, Philippe de Tristan, whose wife was American and therefore still a neutral. The information reached London and they eventually received an acknowledgement of its safe arrival.[6]

One day, while Souris was packing parcels for French POWs in her office in the Château of Blois, she was approached by a curious-looking man who introduced himself as Pierre Culioli, a returned prisoner of war. She recognised his name because she had been involved in the petition for his release on compassionate grounds following the death of his wife, who had been killed during the German advance. Culioli told her, in quite a loud voice, that he wanted to get to England and asked for her help. Souris did not like the look of him. Apart from his tactless manner he had an unreassuring air, he was too intense, and he wore a ridiculous little 'Adolf Hitler' moustache. He could easily have been an agent provocateur, so she told him that she could nothing for him, and he left.

She felt more confident when she worked with people she already knew and one of her first recruits came through her love of horses. The vet at Bracieux, Francis Cortambert, was a friend of hers, and he told her that he had a school friend called Albert Le Meur who was a former naval officer. Le Meur owned the hotel at Chambord and he too wanted to fight back. Gradually, by word of mouth and by selecting people they trusted, they made contact with other loosely organised outposts throughout the Sologne and along the River Cher, at Mur, Villefranche, Selles, Châtres and Saint-Loup. In Pontlevoy, Souris recruited a second hotel keeper, Marcel Thénot, and he was joined by his father, Alfred, who was in his seventies. He was a poacher and the oldest member of the group. There was also a gamekeeper, Auguste Cordelet, who lived well away from Alfred Thénot, and then she contacted the wine merchant of St-Aignan, André Gatignon. One of the most useful recruits was Julien Nadau of Contres. He was the area manager for the electrical supply company that served many of the Sologne communes, and his wife Raymonde ran a hairdresser's that was ideal cover for a dead letter box. Nadau was a freemason, like several other members of *Adolphe*. At some point another poacher, Théo Bertin, joined up.

Before long Souris contacted one of the largest groups, based around the town of Romorantin and started by a garage owner, René Bouton, and by Roger Couffrant, the father of six children, who with his wife Thérèse owned an electrical goods shop.

Unlike Souris, the *Solognots* were natural born outlaws and had been since long before the wartime Occupation. For centuries the marshy wastelands they inhabited had been a breeding ground for fevers and by the time of the Revolution, which did nothing for the Sologne, life expectancy at birth was twenty years and many families were enduring a brief existence in mouldy shelters made from reeds. A miraculous change occurred in the middle of the nineteenth century, when Parisians embraced the Romantic movement and wealthy members of the bourgeoisie were inspired to descend on the sodden wilderness, buy it up and construct hunting lodges. Within thirty years more than three hundred châteaux had been constructed amid the swamps and forests of the

Sologne, each surrounded by a suitably large estate. Among these new arrivals was the wealthy artist, and friend of Maupassant, Raoul Denisane. The infested bogs were drained, fields were planted with crops and vines, cooks, maids, coachmen, gamekeepers, huntsmen, boatmen and gardeners were employed, and even poachers flourished. Life became easier, but the community retained its independent spirit and its separate habit of mind. This was fertile soil in 1940 for the formation of conspiracies, groups of a few dozen men and women who were drawn haphazardly into a secret and ill-assorted association of patriots with only one conviction in common: a loathing for the country's Vichy government and a refusal to accept that for France the war was over.

For the early resisters of the Sologne, who took such immense risks and who were challenging the occupying forces on a regular basis, the rhythm of their work was unpredictable and its significance a mystery. They had very little idea who they were even working for. An individual man or woman who decided one day that enough was enough had to invent an entirely new way of life. Jacques Baumel, a medical student in Marseilles known as '*Z'oreilles*' (from '*les Oreilles*' – he had big ears), had adventurous friends. When he agreed to join them he was given forty-eight hours to say goodbye to a well-planned, professional existence before he disappeared into an underworld of frightening insecurity, a world for which he was completely unprepared, where his opponents were highly trained professionals, where he endured daily exhaustion and fear and where one slip – a discarded scrap of paper, falling asleep on an overnight train, forgetting the name of a school he had never attended in a town he had never seen – could lead to arrest, torture and death. But Baumel was selected to become a paid, full-time resister, protected by a false identity and living in the shadows, 'underground'. For the amateur part-timers of the Sologne the choice was even more precarious. They lived in broad daylight under their real identities at their usual addresses, hiding in plain sight, available for arrest at any time the authorities cared to call.

To help evaders who had reached Nanteuil to safety in the Unoccupied Zone, Souris had to find a way across the demarcation line that ran along the River Cher; this was the southern border of her *département* and was only thirty miles away. At St Aignan-sur-Cher there were several small islands in the middle of the river and the frontier ran through the property of the former prime minister, Joseph Paul-Boncour, which was on one of these islands. It was sometimes possible by calling on him to start the visit in the Occupied Zone and terminate it on the other side. Among those who had used this route in both directions in 1940 and 1941 was Jean Moulin, when he was crossing in and out of the northern zone in his search for resistance groups. He was now the ex-prefect of Chartres, having been fired by the Vichy government. A similar passage was possible, but rarely used, through the Château of Chenonceaux, a structure built on a bridge across the Cher. The principal entrance was in the Occupied Zone but there was a rear exit on the southern bank. Souris, however, found a more original method. German controls at the authorised crossing points were strict, but as a friend said after the war, 'She was very clever. She got people away by burying them.'

Dressing up and amateur dramatics had always played a lively part in the family life of Nanteuil. Realising that a funeral party was liable to be treated with a certain measure of respect, Souris would arrange a funeral service in the Vichy Zone, hire a hearse, place a fugitive airman in the coffin and cast other evaders as undertakers; she herself sometimes played the part of the grieving widow. A death certificate was obtained from a sympathetic doctor in Blois, a booking was made with a co-operative *curé* in Valençay or Châteauroux, prior permission was sought for an *ausweis* and the military bureaucrats at the control post stamped the party through.

Souris was a freelance smuggler. She was never supported by the famous escape lines, the PAT line or the COMET line, run by the agents of MI9, who were responsible for organising escape from France, and since she had German troops on the premises Nanteuil would not have been a suitable station on such a line anyway.

———

In October 1941, working through Gibraltar, SOE began to build up its force of operational agents in central France and one of these agents, a native French speaker, approached Souris de Bernard in November of that year in the Red Cross office in Blois and asked her if she was prepared to help the British. Since Bill Bradford had reached England in July of that year and had made a detailed report to Military Intelligence, it seems possible that SOE had obtained the Nanteuil address and Souris' name from the young officer who had been a friend of Nanteuil since

1930. But at this time Souris was given no more than a code word, 'Urbain 26', and told that she would be contacted later. Nearly a year passed and then 'one day', as Nanny remembered, 'a man on a bicycle arrived at Nanteuil'. It was 29 January 1943.[7]

'He was a young man,' Nanny recalled, 'with a dark moustache wearing a green suit. Suzanne saw him first, because he walked into the kitchen when she was preparing tripe for lunch. He spoke French, but Suzanne was suspicious. She thought he looked like an Englishman. She came and told me that there was an escaped prisoner who was asking to see Madame de Bernard. Madame had gone out and I was cross with the man. I was worried about Moune and Betty, so I told him that if he was trying to get out of France he had come to the wrong place and he should leave Nanteuil. Because the service that smuggled them out of France was organised elsewhere. I thought he was an airman who had been shot down, but he told me that he wanted to see Madame about something else. So I told him he could wait. When Madame returned she said the same thing. "I can't have you here, go to Blois."'[8] And then the visitor said, 'Urbain 26.'

The man in the green suit identified himself as 'Archambaud'; his real name was Major Gilbert Norman. He was British, but he had been raised in Brittany and – unlike far too many SOE agents – he spoke French fluently with the correct accent. 'He stayed for lunch,' Nanny continued. 'He had a suitcase on the back of his bicycle, and it was full of toilet rolls. That was his cover story – he was a toilet roll salesman. But at the bottom of the case he had these important papers for Madame. They meant that from then on we were part of a *Réseau Buckmaster*.'* Norman had been sent as a reinforcement for Major Francis Suttill, whose field name was 'Prosper'. Suttill was a remarkable man, the son of an English father and a French mother, who had been brought up in Lille and educated by Jesuits in England before passing the Baccalauréat

---

* *Réseaux Buckmaster* is the term that has been used in France since 1945 for SOE(F) networks. Major Norman was the radio operator of an F section circuit, known in London as PHYSICIAN and in France as PROSPER, which was to become for a time the largest SOE circuit in France. In London the *Réseau Adolphe* was regarded as one of PHYSICIAN/PROSPER's sub-circuits. It remained nameless and unidentified in F section records, despite its ninety-two listed members in the Romorantin district alone. Its anonymous and untrained resisters were referred to simply as 'local agents'. As such they were generally graded as 'of unknown reliability'.

in France. He had read law at both the University of Lille and London University and had then been called to the Bar by Lincoln's Inn.[9] He had been recruited by SOE because of his fluent French, under the impression that he was being trained as a commando.

Nanny's post-war account of Gilbert Norman was rather brief. 'He enjoyed the tripe,' she said. 'And then he went back to Paris that evening. I think his train left at about 9 o'clock.'

6

A Network Called *Adolphe*

'Gestapo Bauer' was a small, thin man who habitually wore riding breeches. He was well known in Blois, and widely feared. Also well known and widely feared was his interpreter, a native of Alsace . . . nicknamed 'Mona-la-Blonde'. She took part in the beatings handed out to prisoners and was regarded as more violent than some of the men.

The writer Gilles Perrault was a schoolboy living in the 5th arrondissement in Paris in 1942 and his mother was in the Resistance. After the war he published a vivid description of the impact made on the imagination of a twelve-year-old boy by the arrival of an SOE agent in the household. For Gilles, the mysterious 'Alexandre' was one of his new best friends.[1]

In time of peace 'Alexandre', Edouard Montfort Wilkinson, always known as 'Teddy', was an Anglo-French sales manager living in Angers. In 1940 Wilkinson, who had trained as a professional pilot, travelled to England and joined the RAF but since he spoke better French than English, he was recruited into SOE. In June 1942 he was given the field name of 'Alexandre' and parachuted into France where he built up and ran the PRIVET circuit. He based himself in Angers, where his wife Yvonne, who was running a boarding house, became the network's secretary. Edouard Wilkinson travelled frequently to Paris and while there usually stayed with the Perraults who lived in the Avenue de l'Observatoire. As *'l'agent anglais'* he arrived, in the opinion of Gilles, with all the prestige of one whose country had stood alone and confronted the all-powerful *Wehrmacht* and whose Spitfire pilots had made mincemeat of Reichsmarschall Goering's Messerschmitts. This was particularly impressive for the boy since the Luftwaffe's French headquarters were in the Senate building just across the Luxembourg Gardens, opposite his apartment, and the Reichsmarschall frequently stayed there when he was in Paris.

For Gilles and his school friends a British secret agent was a member of the legendary 'Intelligence Service'. As such he made the men of the Gestapo look like brutal *parvenus*. He descended from the sky on silken cords like an archangel. He proved his identity by inviting the French family to select any phrase they liked, which he would then arrange for the BBC to broadcast to the whole of France. He could be a drunk, a lecher or a bag of nerves, nobody cared. He was 'the man from London' who had chosen them, out of all the nondescript families in France, to play an active part in the allied cause.

When Edouard Montfort Wilkinson joined the Perrault family at the dinner table, Gilles saw a tall thin man with a friendly expression, grey eyes and a light moustache who frequently smoked a pipe and who looked like a cartoon impression of an elegant English gentleman. He did not look the sort of person who would start waving his hands around when he talked; he was the essence of sangfroid, he spoke quietly, in impeccable French, but he made one mistake. When pronouncing an English name, like Birmingham, he pronounced it . . . *à l'anglaise*!

Wilkinson had been educated at the Lycée Henri IV, as had Gilles' father. As a boy Wilkinson, like Gilles, had spent his summer holidays in Brittany. Wilkinson told the Perraults that when he was in their apartment in the Avenue de l'Observatoire he felt 'completely safe'. They gave him a haven behind closed shutters, a family life, evenings spent at a supper table where the conversation was punctuated by the laughter of children. Wilkinson had old-fashioned manners and told them stories of some of his adventures. One night he arrived late and, 'not wanting to disturb the concierge', climbed into the Jardins de l'Observatoire and spent the night in an air-raid shelter! On another occasion he was caught out on the wrong side of Paris by the curfew and took refuge in the nearest hotel. There was no one at the reception desk and, finding himself locked in without a room, he passed the night in an armchair in the lobby. In the morning he woke to find a man in a raincoat standing beside him, so Wilkinson gave him a cheerful '*bonjour*'. The stranger grunted. Then a second guest walked in and the two men exchanged the Hitler salute. He had spent the night in a German police section house!

With such a man fighting for France, the boy knew for a certainty, even in the darkest days, that victory would one day be theirs.

———

The first attempt to organise an SOE network in what the official historian M.R.D. Foot has called 'the middle Loire' had come in June 1942 with the arrival in Tours of a British officer, Raymond Flower.[2] His task was to establish a network, codenamed MONKEYPUZZLE, that was intended to become the main entry point for F section agents into northern France.[3] Their objective was to raise and train a 'Secret Army' and while awaiting the allied landings to make life as uncomfortable as possible for the occupying German forces. Unfortunately, Flower does not seem to have been well suited to the work of an SOE agent. Foot described him as 'brave and cheerful enough, but undistinguished for security sense or forethought'.[4] This brief apology hardly does justice to Flower's performance.

His first decision was to move his headquarters. He was supposed to base himself in Le Mans but decided that this would be inadvisable since he was known in the city, having worked there in the hotel trade before the war. He therefore moved 100 kilometres south, to Tours, and remained dormant while awaiting the arrival of a radio operator. This unauthorised move left a large gap in F section's coverage of northern France. While waiting for support Flower did recruit one local agent, a French tax inspector who had approached him and whom he agreed to employ. This was Pierre Culioli, the man previously rebuffed by Souris when he had approached her in Blois. Flower's radio operator, a Breton named Marcel Clech, eventually arrived by parachute but instead of being galvanised by this development Flower became convinced that German detector vans were tracking him, and banned all transmissions. Then SOE further complicated his life by sending him a second agent, Yvonne Rudellat ('Jacqueline') – the first woman that SOE had landed in France – who had been instructed to act as his courier. She was a native-born Frenchwoman of forty-five, mother of a grown-up child, who had lived most of her adult life in London and she was extremely energetic. Flower was still lying low, a situation that 'Jacqueline' could not abide. Flower resented her arrival, took a strong dislike to her and declined to find her a safe house, so she had to fend for herself.

Flower was asked to identify fields in the Touraine which would be suitable for parachute dropping zones, as SOE had plans to increase its presence in the area with the arrival of 'Prosper'. Culioli quickly found an excellent dropping ground north of the park of Chambord, on family land known as Bois-Renard – and Flower attended the first drop on 23/24 September 1942, but the operation turned into a fiasco. First Flower failed to set up the landing lights, then he placed them in the wrong pattern. The aircraft departed and Flower, deciding that the plane must have been German, abandoned his colleagues in a hurry and set off for a safe house. He then refused to have anything more to do with the operation and Culioli had to take over on the following night and receive the two women agents who were parachuted in. One of them was a young Frenchwoman called Andrée Borrel. She had been assigned to work with 'Prosper' as his courier,[5] so she left the Touraine and headed for Paris.

Flower then told Culioli that 'Jacqueline' was a useless fool and possibly a German double agent and seems to have attempted to get her arrested by dumping a suitcase containing a revolver, a radio and a code book in her unlocked bedroom, despite the fact that he knew her landlord lived on the premises and was taking a close interest in her. Culioli was not impressed and banned Flower from attending any more operations on landing grounds that he had found. Flower did not appreciate being banned by an amateur who was supposed to be under his command. He decided to eliminate Culioli and asked London to send him a lethal pill so that he could administer it to one of his local agents. Baker Street obliged and the pill was carried out to France by Major Norman, when he arrived by parachute at the beginning of November. It was in a package labelled for Flower's personal attention. Norman, unaware of its contents, actually passed the package on to Culioli and asked him to deliver it. Culioli duly handed it to Flower, but Flower then refused to administer the poison personally and asked Marcel Clech to slip the pill into Culioli's food. The radio operator declined, as did a number of other resisters, so Flower – by now part of the PROSPER network – raised the matter with 'Prosper' in person, Major Francis Suttill, who had been dropped 'blind' (without a reception committee) on 2 October 1942. Suttill already knew Culioli; they had been in contact soon after his arrival.[6] He advised Flower to have Culioli summoned to London if he was concerned about him. Flower did nothing about this and the farcical and hazardous situation was only brought to an end in March 1943, when Flower himself was recalled.

As PROSPER established itself on the Loire, SIS continued its parallel and incompatible operations throughout France, landing its agents by sea and air. Hugh Verity, the commanding officer of 161 Squadron, estimated that throughout the war 'at least 100 pick-ups were completed for SIS compared with about 80 for SOE'.[7] But these intelligence gathering operations remained hidden from the saboteurs of F section. Raymond Flower's problem was that he distrusted everyone. Left to himself, as might have happened had he been an SIS field agent, searching in secrecy for information, he might have been a brilliant success. But he was not a team leader, and long before Flower's recall Culioli had given up on him and had applied to work with 'Archambaud' (Gilbert Norman) instead.

At Nanteuil, Major Norman became a regular guest. He was supposed to use his field name when contacting other resisters, or the cover name that was on his identity papers. In fact, he soon told the Bernards his real name, and it was as 'Gilbert' that he became generally known throughout the Sologne. He often lunched at the house and was served coffee by Moune or Betty, who may have shared some of Gilles Perrault's excitement at the presence of an agent from London.[8] One evening Nanny showed him her photograph album – a selection of the boys who had come to Nanteuil before the war. One was called 'Brody'. One side of his face was paralysed but despite this handicap he had joined the army; Gilbert said that he recognised him and told Nanny that Brody had been his colonel in Egypt.

Shortly after that Gilbert arrived at Nanteuil with 'a French recruit' who claimed to know Souris. It was the man with the little 'Hitler' moustache, and he was working closely with a London agent called 'Jacqueline'.

———

The great days of the *Réseau Adolphe* coincided with the arrival of 'Jacqueline'. She and Culioli established themselves as a couple in Contres, and she became a regular visitor to Nanteuil. Yvonne Rudellat had lived for so long in London that she had lost her original French accent and spoke with an unusual accent in both languages. This worried Souris when they first met, and Nanny was asked to take her aside and find out what she actually knew about England. Nanny interviewed her in the bathroom while she was having a bath – the noise of the taps drowned the sound of spoken English – and soon realised that 'Jacqueline' knew London very well. 'Jacqueline' and Souris became great friends. Souris never knew her real name. She only knew her by her field name and her cover name, which by the time she reached Nanteuil was 'Jacqueline Leclaire'. Describing her after the war Souris wrote:

> Physically she was small and lively, her hair changing colour according to circumstances, her eyes very black and striking with their luminosity and depth: her intelligence and will-power were reflected in them. Her laugh – she wrinkled her nose in a droll manner – was attractive and catching. For this woman, who played with death all the time, was as gay as a child . . .[9]

'Jacqueline' was the first female saboteur sent from London to work in the Sologne and quickly became a local character among the resisters. After the war the hairdresser of Contres, Raymonde Nadau, recalled that she had frequently dyed 'Jacqueline's' grey hair in different colours to change her disguise, while her client taught Raymonde's three-year-old daughter to sing 'Tipperary' and other patriotic English songs.[10] And she recalled 'Jacqueline's' light-hearted approach to danger. Once when Culioli was out in the forest awaiting an arms drop very close to their hideout, a party of German boar hunters arrived just as the aircraft began to pass backwards and forwards, low over the house. Discovery seemed certain so 'Jacqueline' started to wire up her refuge, preparing to destroy it when the Germans broke in. Then Raymonde called with a basket full of cakes and spiced bread, so 'Jacqueline' decided to eat all the cakes first as she did not want to 'die on a diet'. When Culioli returned, the house was still standing but the basket was empty.

By the beginning of 1943 *Adolphe* had grown considerably and although there was no formal structure Souris estimated that it could call on about 300 resisters. None of them had code names and none were living underground. Their only protection was personal trust, and the natural discretion of neighbours who knew when not to ask questions. Now, with the arrival of trained SOE agents, the Sologne

Resistance became directly involved in subversive warfare. Their initial duty was to interrupt enemy transport and signals.[11] The Bernards were not trained to take part in sabotage and armed attacks, they left that work to Culioli and 'Jacqueline', but they were heavily engaged in the reception and sheltering of agents who arrived either by parachute or via Lysander or Hudson light aircraft, and the Nanteuil resisters also specialised in the reception and concealment of parachuted arms and supplies.

Souris was the driving force of the household. Her husband, Pierre – unlike most of his friends – seems to have been happy to become involved but may not have had much choice. Privately he may have been as disconcerted as Billy Gardnor-Beard had been on the pavement in Arcachon in 1921. Whatever the truth, Pierre, or 'Bébert', showed no particular talent for the work.

On one occasion he had been asked by Culioli to transport some parachuted arms. Accompanied by Souris, he had driven the Peugeot, which had been converted to run off charcoal, to a distant farm. There Culioli packed a consignment of grenades, sub-machine guns, ammunition and plastic explosive into empty tea chests labelled by the Red Cross as 'jam', 'corned beef', or 'pickled cucumbers' and when these had been loaded into the Peugeot, Bébert and Souris set off for the chosen hiding place, which was the Red Cross depot inside the Château of Blois. After half an hour the Peugeot came to a halt in the middle of Mont, near the Forest of Boulogne. Bébert sent Souris to find a mechanic and stayed by the car guarding his cargo and brooding on his bad luck. Then he noticed that the charcoal reservoir was empty. Once it had been refilled they could drive on to Blois. Using Souris' pass they were able to get through the German army checkpoint on the bridge without being searched, and arrived at the depot – where the arms were stacked beside genuine food stores due to be sent to the prisoners of war.

Another problem, as Nanny remembered, was that 'Monsieur de Bernard' was not just absent-minded, he was 'far too talkative'. As a result, Souris withheld a lot of information from him. Nanny, on the other hand, was the soul of dissimulation. She was once asked if life had not been very difficult for her, an Englishwoman, living with German officers in the house. 'Oh no,' she said. 'They were no trouble . . . *as long as you polished their boots.*' When she was not polishing their boots she was acting as the group's listening post. She had hidden her big, wooden wireless set in the back of the bedroom cupboard and she tuned in to the BBC News every evening, in itself a serious offence. Later she listened out for the *avis*, the coded messages dropped into regular broadcasts at 7.30. If they were re-broadcast at 9.15 p.m. on the World Service,[12] it meant the operation was going ahead. Fielding these messages was dangerous enough, but Souris also agreed to allow Gilbert to leave a radio transmitter at Nanteuil, although the Vichy government had passed a law in August 1942 imposing the death penalty on anyone found in possession of a transmitter.

In as far as it was possible Nanny and Souris took care to keep their activities secret from the rest of the household, and in particular from Moune and Betty. But the girls soon guessed what was going on. In old age Betty described those years. 'We sometimes overheard conversations by chance. And we noticed when they went out in the evenings and did not return until the early morning,' she said. 'And we also knew that Nanny had a wireless set hidden in her bedroom.'[13] The refrain from Kipling's poem 'A Smuggler's Song' – *Watch the wall my darling while the gentlemen go by* – would have seemed very familiar to them.

———

The first '*parachutage*' organised by the Nanteuil team was not a great success. It was shortly after the arrival of 'Prosper' in the area. Things got off to a bad start when Nanny received a coded instruction, '*Les sauterelles sont venues par milliers*' (The locusts are arriving in their thousands) and repeated it to Souris, in Bébert's hearing.

'Monsieur de Bernard couldn't keep his mouth shut,' said Nanny. 'He picked up the telephone and immediately passed this message on to a friend. Without thinking for a moment that the Germans might be listening in. If Madame de Bernard had been holding a revolver I think she would have shot him on the spot, she was in such a temper.'*[14]

———

* The telephone was a particularly risky form of communication. All calls had to pass through the local exchange where they were connected manually by an operator who invariably passed the time by listening in. At Nanteuil the wooden instrument was screwed into the wall at the foot of the main staircase and telephone conversations echoed along all three floors of the house. The same instrument was still in use in 1962.

The locusts' message alerted the *réseau* to a forthcoming parachute drop and when it reached Gilbert Norman he asked Marcel Buhler to help him identify a suitable field. Souris suggested a district north of the Loire; Gilbert and Buhler chose a field on the edge of the road from Blois to Châteaudun which they codenamed 'Malakof'. The leader of the reception committee was to be Captain Buhler.

But on the night in question, 9/10 February 1943, Buhler failed to hear the radio message and the planes had to return fully laden to London. The operation was rearranged for the 13th. This time Buhler heard the message but failed to assemble a reception committee, so the planes returned to London fully laden once more. At this point London lost patience with Buhler and an agent was sent from Paris to take command, a Swiss national called Armel Guerne. Guerne, a poet in pre-war life, stayed at the château and sent one of his team, a man who was – as Nanny later recalled – 'extremely fat', to look at 'Malakof'. This man returned saying that as a DZ (dropping zone) it was useless. There was open ground for as far as the eye could see, there was no shelter to hide the containers and there was a German observation post about 200 metres away. So the third operation was cancelled and Gilbert received an order from London forbidding him to use Buhler for parachute drops again.

The 'Malakof' misadventure led to the Bernards' first encounter with their commanding officer, 'Prosper', in person. It took place at 'Jacqueline's' safe house outside Contres. There was a blazing row, 'Prosper' blaming Buhler and the Bernards for their incompetence. This was rather unfair on Souris since the 'Malakof' site had actually been selected by Buhler and Gilbert. Souris, who knew nothing about dropping zones, had merely indicated the general locality as a possibility because it was so sparsely inhabited. Hoping to make up the quarrel, the Bernards then invited 'Prosper', who was with 'Jacqueline', to have lunch with them in Cour-Cheverny. The choice of a restaurant in Cour-Cheverny could not have been chance. It would have delighted Souris to entertain two British 'terrorists' at the Marquis de Vibraye's château gates.

After lunch Souris arranged for 'Prosper' to meet Philippe de Tristan. Tristan, who had been the means of passing information about the German arms dump to London in 1941, agreed to the meeting, but not at his house, the Château d'Herbault. It took place on the edge of a marsh bordering his estate, and Tristan told 'Prosper' that he thought it was too early to launch a national resistance movement and advised him to limit his operations. 'Prosper' paid no attention to this advice and seems subsequently to have had some reservations about the Culioli group's willingness to follow his instructions.[15] But there were good reasons for Tristan's caution, one of which was the recent arrival in Blois of a significant reinforcement for the German police.

Among those who had signed the Nanteuil Visitors' Book in that month of February 1943 was Souris' cousin, Christian Tabarly, who had given his address as 'Le Cavalier, Blois'. This was not entirely correct, since 'Le Cavalier', his splendid house on a summit in the town overlooking the river, had been requisitioned and Christian Tabarly had been evicted. 'Le Cavalier' was now occupied by the Gestapo; its senior officer was a Munich policeman called Ludwig Bauer.[16] Bauer, known locally as 'Gestapo Bauer', was a small, thin man who habitually wore riding breeches. He was well known in town, and widely feared. Also well known and widely feared was his interpreter, a native of Alsace, Mona Reimeringer, nicknamed 'Mona-la-Blonde'. She took part in the beatings handed out to prisoners and was regarded as more violent than some of the men. Her brother, Franz Reimeringer, was a prominent associate of the Orléans Gestapo. Bauer had also occupied two other houses near the villa, one of which, 'Les Tilleuls' ('The Limes'), stood behind high railings and was used as a prison.

———

In early 1943 Culioli and 'Jacqueline', by this time posing as man and wife, left Contres and moved into an isolated cottage called 'Le Cercle' in the middle of the Sologne. From there they trained saboteurs, directed sabotage operations and organised the reception and stockpiling of the weapons, ammunition and explosives that were dropped by night on zones that Culioli selected. In their absence the cottage was always booby-trapped with high explosives. Quite quickly Culioli promoted himself into a dominant position. He was supposed to be acting under Gilbert's direction, but Gilbert's visits were becoming less frequent. As Suttill's radio operator he moved throughout the rapidly growing area of Paris and central France that was covered by the PROSPER network.

Meanwhile in Paris, 'Prosper' himself was finding life increasingly complicated. One of the first contacts he had been given in October 1942 had been Germaine Tambour – formerly a member of a southern resistance group called CARTE – whose Paris address became known to the *Abwehr* in November. Germaine Tambour became a key member of 'Prosper's' Paris operation. But in April she and her sister were arrested by the Gestapo, and 'Prosper' tried to ransom them. This ill-judged initiative, possibly an early sign that stress was beginning to overwhelm 'Prosper', was not a success. The German policemen who had been paid to set them free kept the one million francs but failed to deliver the Tambours. Instead they photographed 'Prosper' himself at the broken rendezvous.

Following this rebuff 'Prosper' dumped a 'cumbersome remnant' of Germaine Tambour's circle, a man called Valentin Rey, on the *Réseau Adolphe*. Souris, having been introduced to Rey and knowing nothing about him, arranged for him to rent a farm at Fontaine-en-Sologne. Rey had run a garage before the war and once installed on the farm he started to deal in tyres on the black market and 'to behave more like a gangster than a hero'.[17] Culioli, who had already seen off the SOE officer Flower, made short work of Rey. After the war he explained how he went about it. In order to get rid of Rey he set up a parallel organisation into which he recruited the Bernards and their entire group. 'Within eight days I had everything organised and the Blois group, with its subsidiaries in Chambord, Bracieux, Montrichard and so on was up and running. Valentin Rey was definitely excluded,' Culioli said.[18] But he executed this coup without informing either 'Prosper' or Gilbert.

Under the increasingly dominant Culioli, the Sologne Resistance got into its stride, undertaking a vigorous programme of sabotage. According to the French historian Paul Guillaume the *réseau* was responsible for a long string of armed attacks on German targets. This is supported by an SOE progress report of 15 March.[19] On 10 March Culioli and 'Jacqueline', working with Julien Nadau, the electrical company's area manager, blew up two high-tension lines in one night. Using cyclists as scouts they avoided the frequent German police roadblocks and drove the explosives to remote spots crossed by the high-tension lines in the heart of the Sologne, near Vernou and Chaumont-sur-Tharonne. Once the attacks had been successfully carried out they retired, to spend a comfortable night in a hotel at Pontlevoy, near Amboise.[20]

Shortly afterwards three troop trains were derailed near Blois resulting in 43 German dead and 110 wounded; the city was put under curfew and the cinemas were closed for a week but – unusually – no reprisal killings followed. A large electrical transformer station near Tours was destroyed after the RAF had carried out an unsuccessful attack. A supply train heading for the Eastern Front was set on fire, a sugar refinery and its storage tanks were destroyed, a railway bridge was blown up and there were numerous further attacks on rolling stock. Most of these operations took place in the first three months of the year. Nanteuil was at the centre of much of this activity, and Culioli, 'Jacqueline' and Major Norman all used the house regularly as a base.

But one day, following Christian Tabarly's visit in the spring of 1943, Souris and Bébert were called in by the mayor of Blois, Monsieur Drussy,[21] whom they hardly knew. When they walked into his office he took the telephone off the hook, locked the door and started to whisper. He said that the *Boches* knew about their activities and had placed them 'at the centre of the spider's web'. He strongly advised them to leave Nanteuil without delay.[22] The Bernards considered Mr Drussy's behaviour a bit theatrical. They returned home and talked it over, then decided to stay 'for family reasons'. They had Nanny to think of, as well as their teenage girls.

On 9 March, jubilant at his network's progress, 'Prosper' sent a report to Baker Street claiming that he and Norman were now ready to receive an airborne division each. 'Hurry up with the Landings,' he added. 'We could all do with *un petit congé* [a brief holiday].[23] Plans were made to feed and fuel 40,000 men who would be dropped between Meung-sur-Loire and Mer.[24] Two months later, on 14 May, Francis Suttill left on a short visit to London. He had been in the field for just over seven months and PROSPER had grown into an unusually large and wide-ranging organisation that included a number of Communist cells in the Paris region. His flight was organised by SOE's air movements officer, a French military pilot named Henri Déricourt, who escorted him to a Lysander that touched down near Azay-sur-Cher. The recall was made at his own request. 'Prosper' was becoming increasingly uneasy about security. He feared that his network might have been penetrated by a German agent.

7

Dreaming Up a Second Front

*The operation had one serious disadvantage. What would be
the effect of this deception operation on the French Resistance,
the Secret Army that was being armed and trained to support
the real landings when they eventually took place? . . . It was
impossible to tell the Maquis what we were doing.*[1]

Lieutenant General Sir Frederick Morgan,
Chief of Staff, Supreme Allied Command

In his letter linking PROSPER and Jean Moulin the Major had referred
to '*what was brewing in the cabinet war rooms and in MI6* [SIS]' in the spring
and summer of 1943. This was a critical period of the war, but its
complications had started to develop in the previous year.

On 4 November 1942 at El Alamein in Egypt the British 8th Army
defeated Rommel's *Afrika Korps* and forced it into retreat, and on 8
November the Allies launched Operation Torch, landing 100,000 troops
in North Africa. In response, German forces were withdrawn from the
Eastern Front to occupy the southern Vichy Zone of France and a large
number of German aircraft were diverted from Russia to Tunisia to
support Rommel's retreat.[2]

These Anglo-American victories preceded the Soviet army's success
on 20 November, when it encircled the 6th German Army at Stalingrad.
On 29 November Winston Churchill, in optimistic mood, minuted the
Chiefs of Staff, outlining his plans for the 'Second Front' that would be
formed by allied landings on the northern coast of France. He suggested
a target date of 12 July 1943. General Sir Alan Brooke, the head of the
army and chairman of the Chiefs of Staff Committee, taking – as was
his habit – a more practical view, wrote in his diary that he had been

examining 'the PM's most recent ideas for a re-entry into the Continent in 1943 . . . He never faces realities. At one moment we are reducing our forces, and the next we are invading the Continent with vast armies for which there is no hope of finding the shipping.'

On 9 December Brooke returned to the subject, writing, 'We are going to have great difficulties in getting out of Winston's promise to Stalin, namely the establishment of a Western Front in 1943! Stalin seems to be banking on it and Clark Kerr* fears a possible peace between Hitler and Stalin if we disappoint the latter.'

A second Nazi–Soviet pact would have spelt disaster for the Allies, since it would have freed 180 German divisions to invade England. Nor was such a betrayal merely a figment of the ambassador's imagination. Churchill and Roosevelt had initially encouraged Stalin to think that they might be able to open a second front in 1941. Nothing happened, and Stalin had made discreet enquiries about the possibility of a separate peace with Germany in October of that year – when German forces were approaching Moscow.[3] And for as long as the German armies were advancing into Soviet territory Stalin kept this option open.[4]

Further plans for a second front were discussed in 1942 and in July of that year Stalin was still hoping that they would be implemented. 'I must say in the most emphatic manner,' he wrote to Churchill, 'that the Soviet Government cannot acquiesce in the postponement of a second front until 1943.'[5] By August, after meeting Churchill in Moscow, he realised that he was to be disappointed once again, and his tone hardened. 'The refusal of the British government to open a second front in Europe in 1942 inflicts a mortal blow to the whole of Soviet public opinion,' he wrote on 13 August, '. . . and prejudices the plan of the Soviet Command.'[6] By October Stalin – still toying with the possibility of a separate peace[7] – was projecting his own tentative duplicity onto Churchill, expressing fears that the British prime minister was deliberately postponing the second front in order to see the Soviet Union defeated, so that he could subsequently come to terms with Hitler.[8]

After Operation Torch, Churchill attempted to persuade Stalin that this *was* the second front and that it had been as effective in dispersing German military strength as a landing in France would have been; but to little effect. Churchill and Roosevelt therefore decided that a

---

*British ambassador in Moscow.

tripartite conference was necessary and invited Stalin to join them in Morocco in January. Stalin, preoccupied with the critical situation in Stalingrad, declined, and the central decision taken without him at the Casablanca Conference by Roosevelt and Churchill – to go ahead with landings in Sicily in the summer of 1943 – ensured that landings in northern France would not take place that year.[9] There was an allied shipping crisis, a chronic shortage of assault craft and escort vessels. The postponement of the second front until 1944 was the most significant consequence of the decisions taken at Casablanca. This development was not immediately explained to Stalin, but he smelt a rat.

'Sicily,' he wrote, '*cannot* replace the Second Front in France,' and 'It is extremely important to deliver the blow from the West in the spring and early summer, and not to postpone it until the second half of the year.'[10] Stalin was demanding a force of fifty to sixty allied divisions in France by the spring of 1943[11] to force the German general staff to increase the number of divisions in France under Field Marshal von Rundstedt's command from forty-five. Churchill, well aware of the real situation, tried to brush aside the implications for further delay on more than one occasion. Even before Casablanca, on 29 December, he had asked the chiefs of staff to examine the possibility of concurrent landings in Sicily and France in 1943. The Chiefs of Staff advised him on 5 January that this would be quite impossible,[12] and further advised him that even one landing in northern or western Europe would have to be limited to a maximum of four divisions. Despite this advice, on 24 January Churchill and Roosevelt, presumably with Stalin's sensitivities in mind, added a commitment in the final Casablanca agreement to mount Operation Sledgehammer. There would be some form of cross-Channel attack, short of an invasion, and it would take place in August 1943.[13]

On 29 January 1943 the Chiefs of Staff, evidently unimpressed by the possibilities of Operation Sledgehammer, turned to the London Controlling Section (LCS). The LCS, which had been established under deep cover in 1941, had overall control of the numerous deception bodies established in London during the war. It was attached to the War Cabinet and was situated in the Central War Rooms. From 21 May 1942 its director, Colonel J.H. Bevan, whose official title was Controlling Officer, had direct access to Churchill when he required it.[14] His regular deception team worked with liaison officers from other secret agencies including MI5 and SIS.

On this occasion Colonel Bevan was instructed to prepare as a matter of urgency general strategic deception plans for three amphibious operations against the French coast. If there were to be no actual landings in France in 1943, designed to provoke a diversion of German divisions from the Eastern Front, the same result might be achieved by a deception operation. Genuine landings could be replaced by imaginary operations. These plans were to include real raids to provoke real air battles, an imaginary bridgehead on either side of Boulogne, and imaginary landings of a larger force on the Cotentin Peninsula in Normandy on 1 August. The plans, drawn up by the LCS, were approved by the Chiefs of Staff on 9 February. The imaginary bridgehead was the most important component of the operation.[15] In the event of Operation Sledgehammer being cancelled, tactics for dealing with Stalin's anger on learning of the failure of his democratic allies to attack the Reich from the west yet again, would need to be in place.

On the same day, 9 February, Winston Churchill, meeting with Ivan Maisky, the Soviet ambassador, in London, and continuing his game of bluff, said – in an apparent reference to Sledgehammer – that 'at some time in August or September . . . a landing operation will be carried out across the Channel in France'.[16] Maisky did not believe him.

Meanwhile, on the Eastern Front, General Friedrich Paulus, having refused to accept Hitler's invitation to commit suicide – despite being promoted to Field Marshal – and without food or ammunition, had surrendered his 6th Army on 31 January, and the relief of Stalingrad had been followed by a succession of Red Army advances that drove German forces back from the River Don and, by 16 February, included the retaking of Rostov and Kharkov. But the war on the Eastern Front was very far from won. To strengthen the German lines and reverse the Soviet advance Hitler ordered seven divisions to be transferred from France to the East[17] – a move that once again underlined the Anglo-American failure to open a second front – and by 28 February Field Marshal von Manstein had contained the Soviet 'winter offensive' and launched his counter-attack. By 12 March the 4th Panzer Army, including the SS 'Das Reich' Panzer division newly arrived from France,[18] had retaken Kharkov and destroyed fifty-two Soviet divisions. Three days later Stalin complained that thirty-six more German divisions had been transferred from the west.[19] On 11 April von Manstein signalled to

Hitler that he was now ready to launch a major counter-offensive, designed to destroy the Red Army's armoured capacity, at Kursk.[20]

The successful German counter-attack at Kharkov on 12 March, in the continuing absence of a second front, marked a very dangerous moment in the Anglo-American-Soviet alliance. In London, on 14 March, Ambassador Maisky noted that popular anger in Russia against the continuing Anglo-American failure to open a Western Front was growing.[21] Matters did not improve when Stalin, on the same day, digested another telegram from Churchill in which the prime minister mentioned that the cross-Channel operation 'envisaged for August' would not take place unless Nazi Germany had become significantly weaker by then.[22]

In reality it was the allied merchant fleet that was becoming significantly weaker. The Battle of the Atlantic was going badly. In two days U-boats had sunk twenty British merchantmen and there were so few ships available that Churchill was obliged to cancel the March supply convoy to Archangel, causing Stalin further distress. Then, at a staff conference on 13 April, General Brooke finally managed to knock Churchill's unrealistic hopes on the head. He told the prime minister that the landing craft intended for a cross-Channel operation in 1943 would have to be sent to North Africa and used for the Sicily landings instead. Churchill accepted this change of plan and added that it would now be necessary to inform the War Cabinet that Operation Sledgehammer was a dead duck.[23]

On the same day that Sledgehammer was formally cancelled, 15 April, news arrived of a further complication for London–Moscow relations. The German general staff announced that a mass grave had been discovered in a forest near Smolensk called Katyn; it contained the bodies of more than 8,000 Polish officers. It was known that these officers had been interned by the Soviet army in the autumn of 1939, following the Soviet invasion of Poland, but nothing had been heard from them since. On examination it turned out that most had been shot in the back of the neck.

As soon as he heard the news General Sikorski, the exiled commander-in-chief of Polish forces, called on Churchill, who told him that although the German announcement was probably true, nothing should be done to provoke Stalin. Sikorski ignored this advice and protested publicly about the discovery, accusing the Soviet government of responsibility. In response Stalin broke off relations with the Polish government. Churchill then met Maisky and told him that he did *not* believe the German version of the story,[24] although he was aware that 'everything can happen in war'. Churchill attempted to mediate between the Soviets and the Poles by urging Stalin to liberate the 40,000 Polish soldiers still being held in the Soviet Union so that they could join the allied armies in the west. At the same time he assured Stalin that he would see to it that the Polish press in London would be subjected to 'proper discipline'.[25] In line with the overwhelming strategic priority – allied unity – the need to conciliate Stalin limited the British government's reaction to the dreadful news from Katyn.* Sir Owen O'Malley, British ambassador to the Sikorski government, noted: 'We have in fact used the good name of England . . . to cover up a massacre.'[26]

On 14 April Churchill minuted that *he did not propose to inform Stalin of this development* [i.e. the cancellation of Sledgehammer] *until later in the year* [my emphasis]. Instead, 'powerful camouflage and cover operations should continue . . . in order to pin the enemy to the French coast *and so as not to discourage our Russian allies*'.[27] So at this initial stage, Stalin, like the OKW (*Oberkommando der Wehrmacht*, the German General Staff) was to be deceived. In April 1943 'deception' was the major weapon at Churchill's disposal in his battle to keep Stalin in the war.

———

In his official history, *British Intelligence in the Second World War: Vol. V Strategic Deception* (by some way the slimmest volume in the series), Professor Michael Howard wrote that 'the decisions reached at Casablanca in January 1943 imposed heavy tasks on the deception staffs'. Colonel Bevan was an intelligence officer with 'vast responsibilities'. He worked closely with the War Cabinet Office, the Joint Intelligence Sub-Committee, the Political Warfare Executive, the Special Operations Executive and the Secret Intelligence Service (SIS). He also worked closely with the W board, a committee that, according to Professor Howard, operated in total secrecy, reported to no one and was responsible to no one. Among other duties it operated double agents. The double agents were run by a sub-committee, the XX (or 'Double-Cross') Committee, under the supervision of MI5.[28]

---

* Soviet responsibility for the murder of a total of 26,000 Polish officers was finally acknowledged in 1990. The crime had been proposed by Beria and endorsed by the Politburo on 5 March 1940.

By the summer of 1943 the responsibility for pinning down German forces in north-western Europe and preventing reinforcements from being sent to the eastern front or the Mediterranean, rested 'overwhelmingly' with Bevan and his colleagues on the deception staff.[29] Bevan operated in secret and with the necessary degree of ruthlessness. On being appointed he had received a directive which instructed him to keep in touch with both SOE and SIS; it also stated that his work was not 'limited to strategic deception alone'. It was 'to include any matter calculated to mystify or mislead the enemy wherever military advantage may be so gained'.[30] His powers, in time of war and in the field of deception, were theoretically unlimited. But he had no executive authority. He was there to plan, coordinate and supervise.

———

Following Casablanca, a new body had been set up – COSSAC (Chief of Staff, Supreme Allied Commander); this was the embryo of the Supreme Allied Command in Europe. There was no Supreme Allied Commander, as General Eisenhower had not yet been appointed, but this non-existent supremo already had a chief of staff, Lieutenant General Sir Frederick Morgan, whose primary responsibility was to prepare plans for D-Day in 1944. On 26 April 1943, he received one of his first instructions. COSSAC was ordered to develop 'an elaborate camouflage and deception scheme *extending over the whole of the summer* with a view to pinning the enemy in the West and keeping alive the expectation of large-scale cross-Channel operations in 1943'.[31] One deception mechanism was known as 'controlled leakage' or 'Special Means'. COSSAC favoured this method and naturally decided that the appropriate agency to supervise the passage of information to the enemy through controlled leakage was the LCS. The deception plans already laid by the LCS in February were now given the code name Cockade. Their purpose was to contain German forces in north-western Europe, preventing them from being used elsewhere. Writing after the war General Morgan recalled that by the spring of 1943 the enemy appeared to be 'on the defensive in the East . . . (and we) had to convince them that danger threatening from Great Britain was at least as great'.[32]

The centrepiece of this attempt was a sub-section of Cockade, Operation Starkey, an imaginary assault on the Pas de Calais, with D-Day as 8 September 1943. This would include a mock invasion in which a real fleet of landing craft 'would approach within a few miles of the French coast'.[33] And it included real air battles in which potential losses were estimated at 340 aircraft.[34] In order to deceive the enemy, the lives of over 300 allied pilots would, if necessary, be sacrificed. A means had to be found to mislead German Intelligence and leak news of this imaginary September assault to the OKW. By May 1943 Operation Cockade was under way.

———

For a deception operation to have any chance of success it was sometimes necessary for it to deceive those engaged in it as well as the enemy. In this case, as General Morgan wrote: 'The operation had one serious foreseeable disadvantage . . . We did not want to give the impression that we had actually attempted invasion and failed . . . [yet] it was impossible to tell the Maquis what we were doing . . . *What would be the effect of this deception operation on the French Resistance, the Secret Army that was being armed and trained to support the real landings when they eventually took place?*' [my italics].

It was at this delicate moment, on 15 May, that Major Suttill ('Prosper') arrived on his flying visit to London and lunched with Colonel Buckmaster in the SOE canteen in Baker Street. 'Prosper' and the head of F section held five further meetings before his departure for France on 20 May.[35] Suttill had originally requested these meetings because of his growing concern about the reliability of one of his colleagues, F section's air movements officer, Henri Déricourt. While in London he had told his commanders that he no longer trusted Déricourt; and he refused to be flown back to a reception organised by him. He opted to return by parachute, to a reception organised by Pierre Culioli, even though on his previous parachute jump he had injured his leg quite badly. Although there is no record of the specific briefings given to 'Prosper' in London in May 1943, we do know that when he returned to France it was with a new conviction in mind – that the long-awaited allied landings were imminent.

Meanwhile in London, throughout the spring and early summer of 1943, another inter-allied political problem was bubbling away in the background; Churchill and Roosevelt's growing exasperation with General de Gaulle.

8

'That Jeanne d'Arc in Trousers'

I am looking for some bishops to burn him . . .
> Winston Churchill, of General
> de Gaulle, February 1943

For the first twelve months following his arrival in June 1940, the reputation of Charles de Gaulle as a trustworthy ally grew steadily. Having survived the initial disasters of Mers-el-Kebir and Dakar, he started to impose his national vision by sheer force of character and political intelligence. For listeners in France the name 'de Gaulle' had a symbolic ring. It was an appropriate name for a national leader, the name of France in Roman times. And this general spoke from the freedom of London, capital of the only European country that was still defying Hitler.

At first de Gaulle had Churchill's unqualified support. He was provided with funds and the means to build up his own secretariat. The formation of his own intelligence service, the BCRA, was followed by the establishment of SOE(RF), the rival service to F section. The prime minister wrote in February 1941, 'I think de Gaulle is the best Frenchman now in the arena, and I want him taken care of as much as possible.'[1] However, as de Gaulle grew in stature some in the British government, and the prime minister in particular, began to worry that they had unleashed a force they could not control.

The first time the allied leadership, in attempting to manage de Gaulle, considered 'locking him up' came in July 1941. De Gaulle, in Syria, at the head of an Anglo-French army that was overwhelming local Vichy French forces, disobeyed his instructions and started to undermine an armistice agreement. When he was reproved, he responded by threatening to withdraw all Free French forces from British command. On his way back to

London from Damascus, de Gaulle gave an interview to an American reporter suggesting that Britain had done a tacit deal with Hitler over Vichy, since Pétain's government made France secure for the Germans and also kept the French fleet out of the naval war against Britain. The United States was still neutral at that time and Churchill was appalled by this public disloyalty. He took his revenge by banning de Gaulle from broadcasting for two months.[2] The incident turned some very influential members of the War Cabinet and the Chiefs of Staff Committee against de Gaulle for the duration. General Sir Alan Brooke, arguably the most influential member of the wartime administration after Churchill, hardly bothered to conceal his low opinion of de Gaulle. He had never taken the French leader seriously and regarded him thenceforth as a professional nuisance rather than a valuable ally.

However, on 20 October 1941, de Gaulle's position received an unexpected boost; Jean Moulin succeeded in reaching London. He had escaped from France in September, but had been held in Lisbon by British Intelligence for six weeks. Once in London the ex-prefect was vetted by Colonel Passy, given the code name 'Rex' by RF section and parachuted back into France on 2 January 1942 as the general's most important recruit. His successful return transformed de Gaulle's power base. He was no longer a voice crying in the wilderness, but the potential leader of resistance within France as well as outside it.

But as de Gaulle's power in France grew, suspicions in London about his ultimate ambitions also increased, and on several occasions he was very nearly cast aside. A promising opportunity to replace him presented itself in April 1942 with the escape from German custody of General Henri Giraud, formerly commander of France's 9th Army. Giraud had been held as a prisoner of war in the mediaeval castle of Königstein in Alsace and, at the age of sixty-three, had made a spectacular descent down the castle walls by rope. His escape had been coordinated by SOE. He was three ranks senior to de Gaulle and had become a popular French hero.[*] The foreign secretary, Anthony Eden, wrote to Churchill

---

[*] Giraud's admirers did not include Charles de Gaulle. On one occasion in Algiers in 1943, having listened once too often to his rival's account of his extraordinary feat at Königstein, de Gaulle said, 'Now why don't you tell us how you got captured?' (Philippe Ragueneau, *Humeurs et Humour du Général*, p. 66.) Giraud had been captured on 19 May 1940 when, having allowed himself to be separated from his command, he had spent the night hiding in an isolated farmhouse in northern France. He awoke to

suggesting that if Giraud could be persuaded to come to London, 'We should . . . have a real leader of the Free French movement, a man whose name and record inspires devotion among all sections of the French army and people.'[3] Churchill passed the suggestion on to Roosevelt, whose anti-Gaullism, fed by influential French exiles such as the diplomats Alexis Leger and Jean Monnet, was already incurable.

In France, through the summer of 1942, support for de Gaulle among influential members of the French Resistance continued to grow. Jean Moulin, 'Rex', was funding and uniting movements in both zones. But in London relations between de Gaulle and the War Cabinet continued to deteriorate. On 10 July Sir Alan Brooke, having lunched with de Gaulle at Claridge's, noted in his diary, 'He was in one of his better moods, but I fail to see how we are ever to make much use of him.' Four days later, on Bastille Day, the official name of the 'Free French' was changed to 'la France Combattante' – the Fighting French. This was more than symbolic. The intended implication was that de Gaulle stood at the head of all those, inside and outside France, who were opposing the defeat of 1940.[*] In August he demanded that the French High Command should be incorporated into the Allied High Command and that he personally should henceforward direct the activities of all French nationals who were preparing the liberation of France,[4] wherever they were. It was one of his many attempts to close down F section. In response, General Brooke reiterated his settled view that de Gaulle would be a military liability everywhere except in occupied France.[5]

In September, after de Gaulle had completed another disruptive tour of France's Middle Eastern colonies, Churchill summoned him to Downing Street for a further dressing-down. General Brooke, who arrived in Downing Street just as de Gaulle was leaving, commented on a 'memorable' meeting that had 'almost broken up in disorder'.[6] In fact, matters had gone so badly that de Gaulle had smashed a chair.[7] After the leader of the Fighting French had left No. 10, Churchill discovered that

---

find that his refuge had been surrounded by enemy troops and he was obliged to surrender to the field kitchen unit of a Panzer division.

[*] Two days later, on 16 July, the French police in Paris arrested 13,000 Jews and locked them into the Velodrome d'Hiver cycling stadium – thus implementing an agreement made between the Vichy government and SS General Karl Oberg concerning the accelerated deportation of Jews from France.

he was on his way to the BBC for a scheduled broadcast, so he telephoned to Broadcasting House with the instruction that if the general
departed from his script he was to be cut off in mid-sentence.[8]

In the same month a new opportunity arose to bypass de Gaulle.
SOE(F) reported that it had discovered a very large and well-organised
resistance network, based in the southern zone but extending right
across France, that was ripe for development and loyal to General
Giraud. Rumours of this organisation, CARTE, had been reaching
London for some time and in July 1942 'an experienced officer'[9] – in
fact the deputy head of F section, Major Nicolas Bodington – had
been sent out, via Gibraltar and a fishing boat to the Côte d'Azur, to
investigate. On his return he reported that CARTE was led by an artist
called André Girard who was apparently working with the Vichy
army's secret intelligence service and preparing for the day of liberation. The group had no attachment to de Gaulle, was capable of
putting between 100,000 and 300,000 men into the field at short notice
and was demanding 50,000 Sten guns and 600 radio transmitters.
Bodington's report was taken very seriously in Baker Street. The
discovery of a large resistance organisation that was primarily interested in military action rather than internal politics was a novelty.
Two tons of arms and seventy radio transmitters were swiftly
despatched.[10] An SOE liaison officer[11] was parachuted in, and CARTE
was promptly endowed with its own radio station, *Radio Patrie*, as a
rival to the Gaullist *Ici Londres*. This was operated by the PWE, the
'black propaganda' arm of British Intelligence. The first that the
BCRA knew about any of this was on 10 December, when the
Gaullists discovered that an anti-Gaullist radio station was broadcasting to France – apparently from within France, but actually from
London.[12] It had been on the air for two months entirely without the
knowledge of the BCRA, but supposedly with its agreement.[13] On 14
October Colonel Passy asked SOE why the UK government was 'trying
to block the development of the Resistance'.

However, by the end of the year it became apparent that Major
Bodington had been thoroughly misled. There was no 'phantom army'
on stand by. André Girard had at most a few hundred names and addresses
in his card index and was either a fantasist or clinically insane. Furthermore,
the arms deliveries to CARTE had served to draw German attention to
genuine resistance in the south of France. The disastrous involvement

with CARTE severely damaged Major Bodington's credibility with the BCRA,[14] but in SOE he somehow emerged with an unblemished reputation. In France the German attention attracted by Bodington's misjudgement did lasting damage. In November a CARTE courier was followed onto the Marseilles-Paris express by an *Abwehr* agent, and when the courier fell asleep his briefcase was stolen.[15] It contained the names and addresses of 200 members of CARTE, practically the entire membership. The German police cashed in this information as and when it suited them over the next eight months. Among the names discovered was that of Germaine Tambour, one of 'Prosper's' principal Paris contacts.

Bodington's calamitous misjudgement had a serious effect on the fate of hundreds of rank and file resisters. But it was not all bad news. Curiously, his misadventure never seems to have been used as ammunition against SOE by SIS. On the positive side, the arms deliveries to CARTE may have led German Intelligence to suspect that allied landings were imminent on the Riviera and so distracted attention from the preparations that were actually being made to land 100,000 British and American troops on Algerian and Moroccan beaches. Allied commanders had been extremely concerned about the risks involved in this amphibious assault. It involved transferring troops on the high seas from ships onto landing craft that had in turn been lowered from other transport ships. One American staff officer considered Operation Torch to be the riskiest operation of the entire war,[16] but it passed without a hitch.

Operation Torch was a military success but a political setback. The American commanders had hoped to take their favoured candidate, General Giraud, with them and install him in place of Admiral Darlan, the Vichy governor of the colony. Unfortunately Giraud, who was devoid of political imagination, made one of his regular tactical blunders and refused their offer on the grounds that it was insufficient, so he was left behind in Gibraltar. Then the Vichy French forces defending Algeria, instead of welcoming their 'liberators' as planned, fought back with determination. The inexperienced US troops were soon in trouble. As a result, after two days' fighting General Mark Clark, their field commander, was persuaded to negotiate with Darlan. A ceasefire was declared, and Clark agreed to recognise Darlan's continuing authority. This was done even though Darlan made it clear that he was not changing sides on allied terms. He would be an American ally but remain loyal to Marshal Pétain and Vichy France. Communist deputies in

Algeria would remain in prison, Jews would remain stateless and interned, trade union activities would still be banned. Roosevelt was delighted and the senior American general in the region, Dwight Eisenhower, warmly endorsed the Darlan regime.[17]

Meanwhile de Gaulle was once again left out in the cold. He had no prior knowledge of Operation Torch and was given no news of its progress beyond what was broadcast by the BBC or printed in the British press. Three days before the Torch landings Roosevelt had overruled Churchill's wish to inform de Gaulle of the planned invasion of Vichy French territory before it took place.[18] Churchill later regretted giving way – and with reason. The news that allied forces had invaded French territory without any French authority or assistance caused the mother of all explosions from de Gaulle. 'Well I hope the Vichy crowd drive them back into the sea! You don't enter France by breaking in,' was his first reaction.[19]

It was the low point in his career as a national leader.

———

By the end of 1942, unknown to de Gaulle, Roosevelt's low opinion of him had begun to influence his original protector. On 10 December 1942, one month after Torch, Winston Churchill addressed the House of Commons in secret session. His personal admiration was undimmed. But his patience with the politician was running out. The prime minister's remarks were considered so sensitive that they were omitted from the collection of Churchill's speeches published in 1966.*

I must now say a word about General de Gaulle . . . We have done everything in our power to help him. We finance his Movement. We have helped his operations. But we have never recognised him as representing France . . . I cannot feel that de Gaulle is France . . . France is something greater, more complex, more formidable . . .

I have tried to work as far as possible with General de Gaulle, making allowances for his many difficulties, for his temperament and for the limitations of his outlook . . . I consider that we have been in every respect faithful in the discharge of our obligations to de Gaulle, and we shall so continue to the end. However, we are now in Secret

---

* Since Churchill was dead by then and de Gaulle was the president of the French Republic, and had just taken France out of NATO, this may not be so surprising.

Session [and] the House must not be led to believe that General de Gaulle is an unfaltering friend of Britain. On the contrary I think he is one of those good Frenchmen who have a traditional antagonism engrained in French hearts by centuries of war against the English. On his way back from Syria in the summer of 1941 . . . he left a trail of anglophobia behind him . . . He gave an interview [to a Chicago newspaper] . . . in which he said . . . 'England is carrying out a war-time deal with Hitler in which Vichy serves as a go-between'.

This year in July [he] wished to visit Syria. He promised me before I agreed to facilitate his journey, which I was very well able to stop, that he would behave in a friendly and helpful manner, but no sooner did he get to Cairo than he adopted a most hectoring attitude . . . and in Syria his whole object seemed to be to foment ill-will between the British military and the Free French civil administration . . .

I continue to maintain friendly personal relations with General de Gaulle and I help him as much as I possibly can . . . All the same I could not recommend you to base all your hopes and confidence upon him, and still less to assume at this stage that it is our duty to place . . . the destiny of France in his hands.[20]

Churchill's words, like all proceedings in Secret Session, went unreported. But rumours of his comments quickly spread around London and may well have reached the ears of the BCRA. Meanwhile British public opinion, already strongly pro-Gaullist, became increasingly critical of the Washington–Darlan agreement.

———

On Christmas Eve, two weeks after that speech, the Washington–Vichy coalition, which had been generated by the limited military success of Operation Torch, was terminated when Admiral Darlan was assassinated in his office in Algiers. His executioner – a twenty-year-old resister called Fernand Bonnier – was immediately overpowered. He was tried by secret court martial by the Vichy authorities on Christmas night, and shot at dawn on Boxing Day. Bonnier had been measured for his coffin before his judges had even taken their seats.[21]

Among those blamed for this politically convenient crime were the BCRA, General Giraud, the American Secret Service (the OSS), and the Comte de Paris – pretender to the French throne.[22] Professor Jackson concludes that 'we will never know for sure' who was responsible for Darlan's death, and slightly favours the army officers loyal to General Giraud, on the grounds that he was the chief beneficiary. Jean Lacouture prefers a royalist plot.[23] It seems that, whoever was pulling the strings, Bonnier saw himself as a royalist resister acting in defence of the Fighting French. But, according to evidence provided at a symposium in Paris in 1988 by some of those who had been involved, Darlan's assassination was authorised at the highest levels in London and discreetly organised by British Intelligence. Bonnier had been recruited, trained and armed by SOE.[*]

The news that Admiral Darlan had been 'bumped off' caused jubilation in Baker Street.[24] Colonel Passy, invited for a Christmas Day lunch with Robin Brook, SOE's regional controller, was startled when his host poured him a glass of champagne and proposed a toast to 'the death of the traitor Darlan'.[25] In the previous weeks Brook had been receiving reports from SOE officers in Algeria, notably David Keswick, urging that decisive action be taken against Darlan. Under Roosevelt and Eisenhower's protection, Darlan's power was growing and Washington's ambition to redesign post-liberation Europe was becoming increasingly clear.[†]

If, as Professor Jackson says, we cannot know for sure who was responsible, we can say that the killing of Admiral Darlan was a decisive intervention in French internal affairs discussed in London at the highest levels, the ground having been laid by SOE. It was also a striking example of the ruthless character of intelligence operations at a critical stage of the war.[‡] De Gaulle was once again forced to observe events from a distance.

———

[*] Bonnier was one of a group of royalist resisters supposedly being trained as special forces for the eventual allied landings in the south of France. His SOE training officers knew that this group were plotting Darlan's assassination (see Verrier, and British Institute, *Franco–British Studies*, No. 7).

[†] Churchill had mulled over the advantages of assassinating Admiral Darlan with Desmond Morton, his intelligence adviser. Morton flew to Gibraltar on 4 December to discuss the possibilities with SIS and SOE officers on the spot. See Verrier *passim* and *Franco–British Studies*, No. 7; Gill Bennett, *Churchill's Man of Mystery: Desmond Morton and the World of Intelligence*.

[‡] The extent of British involvement remained speculative until it was revealed in a symposium of retired allied warriors held at the British Institute in Paris on 19 September 1988 (see *Franco–British Studies*, No. 7).

Meanwhile in London an additional complication in British–Gaullist relations was coming to a head. This had first arisen with the arrival in England in the spring of 1942 of two French resisters who had been working with MI9 on escape lines through occupied France. MI9 was under the ultimate direction of the deputy head of SIS, Colonel Claude Dansey, and the resisters were called Maurice Dufour and Andrée Borrel.

When Dufour disembarked from the Lisbon flying boat in March 1942 he was taken under armed escort, like all new arrivals, to the MI5 interrogation centre that had been set up in the Royal Victoria Patriotic School in Wandsworth, south London. Andrée Borrel arrived one month later. Both were passed as bona fide and both volunteered to continue fighting. They were offered the choice between working for SOE(F) or joining the Free French. Borrel joined SOE. She told MI5 that she had rejected the Gaullists because when she applied to join them, they had made it a condition that she gave them all the information she had on the organisation that she had been working with in France. When she refused, they refused to employ her. She told SOE, on the other hand, that she was perfectly willing to give them any useful information she had. On joining SOE on 5 July 1942 she signed the Official Secrets Act, although she can have had little idea what she was signing since she could not understand English.[26]

Dufour apparently hesitated before deciding and was offered a personal interview with '*le Symbole*', as the general was known by his admirers. The fact that he had been working for British Intelligence in France quickly came to light and thenceforth Dufour fell under suspicion of spying on the BCRA. On 17 May 1942 he went to de Gaulle's headquarters in Duke Street for what he was told was a routine interview. Instead he was threatened and questioned about MI9, SIS and SOE(F). When he refused to answer any questions he said that he was imprisoned in the cellar, questioned for two weeks, beaten repeatedly with a steel rod and eventually forced to sign an engagement form with the Free French.

Once Dufour had signed up with the Free French he was outside British jurisdiction. He was transferred to the French military camp at Camberley and held under arrest, pending court martial. But he managed to escape and make his way to Andrée Borrel's lodgings in London. From there he appealed for help from SOE and was handed over to MI5.[27] Normally MI5 would have handed him straight back to the French, but Dufour was sent to a safe house instead. Dufour alleged that the officer in charge of his interrogation had been Captain Roger Wybot, the head of the BCRA's counter-espionage service. He also claimed that Wybot had threatened to kidnap and rape Andrée Borrel, who was about to be parachuted back into France.*

The story told by Dufour was not an isolated incident. Following a series of cases involving allegations of torture in the Duke Street cellars, the Home Office, MI5 and the US Embassy all became involved. In January 1943, after the 'suicide' in the coal cellar of Duke Street of a man called Paul Manuel, Admiral Strang, Roosevelt's delegate in London to the allied governments in exile, who had regular dealings with Colonel Passy, referred to these cases in a letter to the US Department of State dated 13 May 1943, as the 'Duke Street atrocities'. There was evidence that Manuel, who was suspected by Wybot of being a German agent, had been murdered.

Jean-Louis Crémieux-Brilhac, editor of Passy's memoirs, described[28] the Dufour affair as 'a dishonest scheme cobbled together from various allegations' made by an inveterate liar called Dufour who had been roughed up and then charged by Captain Wybot.[29] Cremieux-Brilhac added that the whole business had been paid for by the American Secret Service and supported by the *Observer*, *Tribune* and the *Catholic Herald*, three newspapers that Colonel Passy regarded as 'hostile' to de Gaulle. (But Cremieux-Brilhac also referred to the 'brutal methods . . . [Wybot] . . . sometimes employed'.)[30]

Foot dismissed the allegations against Wybot[31] and described the Dufour case as 'an absurd tale'. Professor Jackson agrees and adds that the British government eventually apologised to de Gaulle, having realised that Dufour was either 'a fantasist or a blackmailer'. In fact, behind the scenes, the matter was settled rather differently. On 17 September a harassed Foreign Office official noted that '"C" [Sir Stewart Menzies,

---

* Wybot had formerly been a member of the personal protection squad of Marshal Pétain, under the command of a French intelligence officer called Colonel Georges Groussard. De Gaulle did not like the look of Wybot, once described as 'cold, hard, cynical . . . with light blue eyes and an impression of cruelty'. De Gaulle told Colonel Passy to get rid of him. But after a brief absence Wybot was reinstated in Duke Street (Colonel Passy, *Mémoires du Chef des Services Secrets de la France Libre*, pp. 205, 366, 410).

head of SIS] believes Dufour's story to be true', and the Foreign Office and MI5 took the same view.[32] In the summer of 1943 Dufour, advised by a very able young barrister called Patrick Devlin (later Lord Devlin, a judge of the House of Lords, now the Supreme Court), issued a writ for false imprisonment and assault against General de Gaulle, Colonel Passy and Captain Wybot. Since de Gaulle refused to acknowledge the jurisdiction of the High Court, and refused to appear in court, the case was on the verge of becoming a public scandal. It was eventually settled on the eve of D-Day with the payment of £5,000 (worth about £225,000 in 2020) to Dufour,* coupled with a signed declaration by the French authorities that Dufour was not a member of the Free French forces. He was given British residency and a job at a secret training base in Scotland. A Foreign Office official 'vouchsafed' to the court that the settlement had not been paid by the British government. This was an interesting example of official perjury, since the money came from the Secret Service vote.[33]

The Dufour affair has all the marks of Colonel Dansey, flitting silently into the daylight on one of his brief sorties out of the Whitehall undergrowth, and leaving a nasty stench behind him. It had started in July 1942, when MI5 began to have second thoughts about its policy of sending would-be resisters to Duke Street for interrogation, and it reached its climax in the spring of 1943 with the involvement of Admiral Strang.

Had Dufour been merely 'a fantasist or a blackmailer' there would have been no reason for the British government to have paid him a very large sum of money to shut him up. He could have been interned, or he could have been 'sectioned' – spending the rest of the war in a convenient asylum. One possible explanation is that the brutal Captain Wybot's suspicions were well founded. Dufour was a spy. But he was not working for the Germans. He was working for SIS. In France he had been involved with SIS 'Z' agents, as well as with MI9.[34] In both cases his activities were under the final control of Claude Dansey. French soldiers who were released from the Patriotic School† were not

---

* In his diary Guy Liddell noted that Dufour received £5,000, having demanded £10,000 and been offered £1,000.
† The Royal Victoria Patriotic School in Wandsworth, south London, was the site of MI5's LRC (London Reception Centre), which was a screening centre for aliens arriving from enemy territory.

usually recommended to join the Free French. They were encouraged
first to call on F section, which was in desperate need of native French
staff. That is where Andrée Borrel was being trained and it would have
been entirely foreseeable for her close friend Dufour to join her there.
As a battle-hardened soldier who had proved his ability in the shadowy world of resistance, he would have been tailor-made for F. But he
arrived in England as Dansey's man and he continued as such.
Unfortunately, in an attempt to impress the BCRA, Dufour over-
played his hand and claimed – falsely – to hold the *Légion d'Honneur*.[35]
This alerted Colonel Passy, who quickly suspected him of being an
SIS spy. When his mission in Duke Street went terribly wrong,
Dufour never admitted what it was, and he was eventually compen-
sated for his loyalty.

It was when the Dufour case was at its height, and causing real harm
to de Gaulle's reputation, in February 1943, that de Gaulle's emissary to
the 'Resistance of the Interior' returned to London on his second visit,
to report on his mission after thirteen months in the field.

———

Jean Moulin's second visit to London lasted for five weeks. It came at a
time when in both Africa and on the Eastern Front the military tide was
turning, but the victory was still very far from certain. The North Atlantic
and the Arctic convoys that supplied Britain, and Stalin, with oil, planes,
tanks, munitions and medical supplies, were losing ships as fast as they
could be replaced. The Soviet army was paying an appalling price for its
progress, and the initial German counter-attack after Stalingrad had been
devastating. Stalin was losing patience with British and American delays
in setting up a second front – and the landings had just been been post-
poned for another twelve months. Thanks to Enigma decrypts, von
Manstein's plans for a major counter-attack at Kursk were known in
London and details were passed from London to Moscow, but the initiative still lay with the *Wehrmacht*. Meanwhile on the Western Front, with
the success of Operation Torch, good relations with the Free French
leadership had suddenly become of first importance. But de Gaulle was
proving as truculent and insubordinate as before.

Less than ever inclined to accept Anglo-American leadership, de
Gaulle had needed considerable pressure to attend the Casablanca
Conference and meet his despised rival General Giraud, and when he did

arrive, to be greeted by Churchill and Roosevelt, he once again behaved like a prima donna. Churchill returned from Casablanca on 7 February[36] and on the following evening talking to the Soviet ambassador Ivan Maisky 'snarled, "I'm fed up with that Jeanne d'Arc in trousers."'[37] He added, '"I have been looking for some bishops to burn him."'

Meanwhile, undeterred by Churchill's hostility, de Gaulle was in the process of welcoming and re-briefing 'Corporal Mercier' (when in London Jean Moulin, like all visiting resisters, protected his real identity with a *nom de guerre*). The 'corporal' received a hero's welcome. His success in drawing together the numerous strands of French resistance under the Gaullist flag had become an invaluable weapon in de Gaulle's armoury. And he arrived in the company of Lieutenant General Charles Delestraint, the newly appointed military commander of the Secret Army.

Two days after their arrival Pierre Laval's Vichy government announced the start of the STO (*Service du travail obligatoire*), a forced labour programme imposed on all Frenchmen aged between nineteen and twenty-four. The STO – which eventually led to the deportation to Germany of about 500,000 French civilians – provoked a mass exodus of young men from their homes across France. They took to the hills, where they demanded food and shelter and ration cards[38] from the Resistance. This was a dramatic opportunity for the Free French movement to weaken Vichy's hold over the occupied population and it required an urgent response.

Jean Moulin and General Delestraint therefore requested an early meeting with the CIGS, General Sir Alan Brooke. Delestraint was the first senior officer from occupied France who sought to discuss military resistance with the British government. Furthermore, as Colonel Passy believed, Delestraint had friends among the British general staff who had a high opinion of his ability, regarding him as 'serious and dynamic'.[39] If so, they do not seem to have included General Brooke, who noted briefly in his diary for the afternoon of 2 March that he had 'come back to the WO [War Office] to meet a French general over from France who is organising secret forces in France'. Brooke's entries for the previous two days included the following: 'Marshall [General George Marshall, the US Supreme Commander] is quite hopeless and has no strategic concepts of any kind. He now proposes to waste shipping *equipping French forces which can play no part in the strategy of 1943* . . . The Americans are letting us down and we cannot find the shipping for all our enterprises.'[40]

On the following day, 3 March, Churchill refused de Gaulle's request to be allowed to tour French colonial Africa, the area of the world which he called '*mes fiefs*'.[41] In a letter to the king, the prime minister explained his ban, calling de Gaulle 'insolent' and adding, 'he is hostile to this country'. De Gaulle's response, on hearing that he had been banned from leaving the country, was to place himself under house arrest in Hampstead. This self-imposed punishment lasted for a week.[42]

During that time Sir Alan Brooke had two further meetings with 'Vidal' (General Delestraint), on 4 and 10 March, and on both these occasions 'Corporal Mercier' was also present. The Resistance leaders were desperate to take advantage of the STO crisis and to start training the thousands of fugitives who had taken refuge in the *maquis* – the uninhabited scrubland in remote areas of France. Delestraint argued for an immediate massive increase in equipment and supplies, painting a colourful picture of an army of '50,000 paratroopers already on the ground'. He had the strong impression that the CIGS was sympathetic to his appeal and an experienced member of the French delegation who had been negotiating with the British authorities for three years was struck by the sudden change in '*l'attitude britannique*'.[43] And the minutes of the second meeting included an aside that the French delegation considered significant. They were told that although the Allies did not intend to carry out major landings in France before the end of the year, they no longer excluded 'the possibility of establishing a bridgehead on French soil before the autumn of 1943'.[44] Both 'Vidal' and 'Rex' believed that their advocacy had been decisive; in fact they had been thoroughly misled.

For on 11 March, the day after 'Vidal's' second meeting with Sir Alan Brooke, Churchill wrote to Stalin, effectively dispelling all hope of a second front in 1943. The possibility of 'a bridgehead' in France in the late summer of 1943 – waved so enticingly in front of the Resistance leaders – was illusory. The only 'bridgehead' in view was the imaginary one – to be created as part of the deception operation codenamed Operation Starkey. The shipping crisis excluded any actual possibility of real landings, and the Chiefs of Staff had been aware of this since the start of the year. On 29 January they had instructed the London

Controlling Section to prepare 'urgent strategic deception plans' for 'a bridgehead on the Cotentin Peninsula' in August, and the plans had been approved, as we have seen, on 9 February.[45] But Delestraint and Moulin were unaware of these deception plans. And they left their meetings with Brooke and his staff encouraged by the conviction that the allied high command would be reconsidering the possibility of 'landings in France before the end of the summer'.[46]

When 'Corporal Mercier' and 'Vidal' were flown back to France on 19 March the former carried new instructions from de Gaulle, making him the general's representative throughout France. But he and his distinguished colleague had been enrolled, unknown to themselves, in a deception operation. In the minutes of the final meeting held with the allied high command, 'Corporal Mercier' was identified as 'a former prefect'. Jean Moulin left a note on the record stating that this breach of his personal security was *infiniment regrettable*.[47]

––––––

For his second tour of duty Jean Moulin changed his code name from 'Rex' to 'Max'. His task now was to create a formal political structure that would unite the Resistance under de Gaulle's leadership prior to the expected landings. But following his departure from London, Anglo-French relations continued on their previous rocky course. In early June the French Committee of National Liberation (CFLN) was formed in Algiers, jointly led by de Gaulle and Giraud, who had by then – following pressure from Washington – been appointed as commander-in-chief of the Free French Army. However, this new cooperative façade was misleading. Roosevelt suspected, correctly, that de Gaulle was plotting to sideline Giraud and use the CFLN as a stepping stone towards the formation of a post-war government under his own leadership. De Gaulle's long-term objective was the restoration of a united and democratic republic, able to repel any American or Soviet attempts to control it. But for Roosevelt, de Gaulle was not just a loose cannon with an incurable loathing of *les Anglos-Saxons*.[48] He was a symbol of the imperial France of the nineteenth century, a country that had been permanently destroyed in 1940, and one which had no place in Roosevelt's plans for a democratic post-war Europe. Getting rid of him was now a Washington priority.

By June the War Cabinet in London, following further pressure from President Roosevelt, was discussing whether de Gaulle should be sidelined and replaced by General Giraud. Churchill concurred with the president and made it clear that he would not hesitate to get rid of de Gaulle if necessary.[49] However the War Cabinet, marshalled by Clement Attlee and Anthony Eden, resisted this pressure. It was thought that de Gaulle's popularity in France made him indispensable; he was the unchallenged leader of organised French Resistance. Undeterred, Churchill wrote to Lord Selborne, the minister responsible for SOE, on 19 June[50] urging him to 'take the direction of French resistance . . . out of the hands of de Gaulle and his satellites'.[51] SOE was to be used, if Churchill had his way, to eliminate de Gaulle from future allied plans. But Lord Selborne, too, demurred and did nothing.

Churchill once described his method of running the war as 'compliance with my wishes after reasonable discussion'.[52] When Lord Selborne and the War Cabinet declined to cooperate, the prime minister would have been obliged to find other means of enforcing 'compliance' with his wishes. In this situation he had several options. Churchill exercised one of those on 30 June, by cancelling the British government's commitment to finance the Resistance via the BCRA. This move was a serious threat to the organisation built by Jean Moulin, and a senior Gaullist officer had to carry eighty million francs in French banknotes in a suitcase from Algiers to London in order to make up the deficit.[53] Another of the prime minister's options was to damage de Gaulle's reputation. The BCRA concluded that an anti-Gaullist element in the British government accounted for a hostile campaign in the London press at this time, and that the same lobby had been responsible for leaking Maurice Dufour's allegations to de Gaulle's rival, General Giraud. On 2 June Giraud had written to de Gaulle accusing him of 'using the methods of the Gestapo' and suggesting that he was 'constructing a totalitarian regime' with 'the BCRA playing the role of the SS'.[54]

A third of the prime minister's options could have involved his former comrade-in-arms from the South African War, Colonel Dansey.[*]

---

[*] Dansey had known Churchill since 1900 when they had served together against the Boers in the South African Light Horse. Dansey liked to let people know this and would recall how he had once sold his brother officer a dud horse. Churchill and Dansey had a direct line of communication via the prime minister's intelligence adviser, Desmond Morton.

This possibility is suggested by a cable dated 16 July that de Gaulle, who had moved his headquarters to Algiers, sent to the head of his own secret service, Colonel Passy, who remained in London. De Gaulle noted that *l'Intelligence Service* was doing everything possible to break the link between the BCRA and '*la France Combattante*'. That being so, de Gaulle instructed the head of the BCRA to launch '*une action brutale sur Dansey*' immediately. If necessary, Passy should go so far as to break off all contact ('*allant au besoin jusqu'à rupture complète*') with British Intelligence.[55]

De Gaulle's fortunes were once again in the balance. On 21 June 'Max' had been arrested when a Resistance meeting in Caluire, a suburb of Lyons, was betrayed. By chance it was on the same day that Sir Alan Brooke, in London, made a note in his diary that reflected his true feelings: 'We must get rid of de Gaulle at the earliest possible date.'[56]

9

The Fall of PROSPER

Raynaud still had his secret agent's antennae in working order.
He was sitting in a château, beside an English nanny . . . in a
world of stags' heads, white linen, silver napkin rings and
wine decanters. And separated by a thin pane of glass from the
world he had been sent to destroy, police dogs . . . the straight
arm salutes, the guttural pleasantries, the jackboots and field
grey tunics of the men he had come to kill. The unreality of the
situation set alarm bells ringing in his mind.

When German forces first occupied France in June 1940 police activities were the responsibility of the Army, and the Nazi secret police were relatively few in number. This changed on 1 June 1942, when control of security in France was removed from the Army and handed over to an SS General, Karl Oberg. Oberg, a bald, tubby, smiling figure – previously in charge of butchering Poland – was installed with full autonomy in Paris, in the Boulevard Lannes, on the edge of the Bois de Boulogne. Oberg headed the 'Sipo-SD' which was an amalgamation of the national police force and the SD (*Sicherheitsdienst*), the internal security service of the SS.* In France the Sipo-SD were

---

* The SS (*Schutzstaffel* – protection squadron) were the Nazi elite. They formed Hitler's bodyguard and enforced the Nazi Party's racial policy. Among their other responsibilities, members of the SS directed the RSHA (*Reichssicherheitshauptamt* – Reich Security Service). This was based in Berlin and was led by Reinhard Heydrich. In May 1942 Heydrich was assassinated in Prague – during an SOE operation conducted by Czech resisters. He was succeeded as head of the RSHA by Ernst Kaltenbrunner. Kaltenbrunner, like Heydrich, was a senior officer in the SS and he reported directly to *Reichsführer* Heinrich Himmler, the head of the SS. The Sipo-SD came under the RSHA umbrella, and its takeover of police operations in France began immediately after Heydrich's assassination.

popularly known as the 'Gestapo'. In fact, the organisation was divided into seven sections (*Amts*) and 'the Gestapo' (*Geheime Staatspolizei* – secret state police) was *Amt. IV*. The other relevant section was *Amt. VI*, the SD, which was responsible for intelligence and counter-espionage. Senior officers in these two sections were invariably members of the SS.

In Paris, the operational head of the Sipo-SD was *Standartenführer* (SS Colonel) Dr Helmut Knochen. Knochen's deputy was *Sturmbannführer* (SS Major) Karl Boemelburg. Before the war Boemelburg had been a professional policeman based in Paris as Germany's delegate to Interpol. Now he became the head of Section IV, the department properly referred to as the Gestapo. He was a specialist in running double agents. Knochen and Boemelburg established their Paris headquarters in two large private houses in the fashionable 16th arrondissement, Nos. 82 and 84 Avenue Foch. For the next two years these were among the most sinister buildings in France.

The Gestapo was renowned for its brutality and sadism, in particular through the use of torture. But as time passed another technique at its disposal became notorious. This was 'NN' – '*Nacht und Nebel*' or 'Night and Fog' – a decree issued in December 1941 by Adolf Hitler. It was aimed at political opponents and 'terrorists'. If prisoners were listed as 'NN' they were to be deported to Germany and killed, without any information about their fate being released, ever. It was a punishment imposed on many resisters, and the fear it aroused became one of the Gestapo's most effective tools.

By 1943 the entire Sipo-SD in France numbered only 2,000 men. But in support they could call on approximately 8,000 French auxiliaries who had volunteered to work with them. The result was that a typical Gestapo squad announcing its arrival with shouts of '*Police allemande!*' ('German police!') would frequently contain a majority of Frenchmen. Oberg and Knochen could also call on the regular French police and on the pro-Nazi *Milice* (Militia), an armed and uniformed body of volunteer citizens formed to fight the Resistance and numbering between 3,000 and 8,000 men.[*1] Under Oberg and Knochen the Sipo-SD spread out across France and set up local *Kommandos* in

---

* It is a measure of the political divisions in France caused by the Occupation that the *Milice* achieved its highest membership *after* the D-Day landings in June 1944.

seventeen major cities. Ludwig Bauer – who ran the unit in Blois from the villa of Souris' cousin, Christian Tabarly – reported to the *Kommando* in Orléans.

———

In the late spring of 1943 sabotage operations in the Sologne died out. The military supply trains ran towards Germany unhindered and the electricity pylons remained standing. London had decided instead to build up the supply of arms. The pace of parachute drops increased. In 1941 the Sologne resisters had received one *parachutage*. Between September and December 1942 they received five, and between January and May 1943 there were nine. In the first three weeks of June twelve more drops took place. Ever greater numbers of men had to be assembled and deployed on moonlit nights to handle and transport the heavily laden steel containers out of the marshes, pools and wallows of the Sologne where they had fallen and onto horse carts which would carry them to a place of safety. Nanny remembered that, as the pace increased, the empty drums were thrown back into the marshes, although some people kept them since they were so well made – and painted them as items of decorative furniture. 'Some people even put them outside their cottage doors and stood flower-pots on top,' she recalled.

Then, on the night of 12/13 June 1943, there was an alarming incident.

Towards the end of May 1943, following Prosper's return from London, a rumour started to circulate in the Sologne that the allied invasion of France was imminent and the armed insurrection that was planned to support it had to be prepared in haste. One summer evening Nanny heard the message '*Les mousquetaires sont assis par terre*', which meant that a large parachute delivery was expected outside the village of Neuvy for the following night, the 12/13 June.

An experienced reception party was organised and the Bernards drove to the dropping zone in Georges Fermé's car with Marcel Buhler. Culioli and 'Jacqueline' also attended, as did a sizeable contingent from Chambord and Bracieux including Canard, Le Meur, Cortambert, Bernier and Deck, about twenty resisters in all.[2] The aircraft, a Halifax heavy bomber of 138 squadron, with a Polish crew, reached the DZ (dropping zone) at 1.30 a.m., flying at 500 feet, and released nine parachutes.[3] But as the first containers hit the ground there was 'a blinding glare as though from a phosphorus bomb'[4] and a terrific explosion, followed by a second explosion that was heard by Nanny at Nanteuil, seven kilometres away. Souris was blown off her feet into a swampy ditch. 'Jacqueline' panicked for a moment and, convinced that the planes had been German bombers, cried, 'Run! We've been betrayed.'

Most of the party scattered. Buhler and Fermé wanted to get into the car and drive off as there was a German army observation post just three kilometres away at Fontaines-en-Sologne, and it was obvious that they would have been alerted. Bébert objected to Buhler's suggestion. 'We are not going to leave the ladies,' he said, before disappearing into the night to hide his revolver. 'When I got back,' he said, 'the car had gone, our comrades had abandoned us in the forest, and I had lost all contact with the others.' And he still had his revolver.

In his absence Albert Le Meur heard a voice calling in the darkness and found Souris, who was trapped in the ditch. When he helped her out, she was in a filthy temper. 'See, Albert,' she said. 'Look at them. They are behaving as they did in 1940. Running away like rabbits.' Souris told Le Meur to make his way home and then set off on her own. After wading across the River Beuvron she had to hide from German motorcyclists who passed her on the road to Bauzy at a distance of about four metres. They were coming from the observation post at Fontaines to investigate the explosions. 'I made my way to Château Herbault,' she said, 'and sought refuge with friends.' These were the Tristans, Philippe and his daughter Bubby. Bubby de Tristan clearly remembered that night. She had known about the operation but had been forbidden to join it. 'I heard the explosion and I was worried for Souris, who would never let me go out at night. She said I was too young. I was looking out of my window when she appeared out of the dark. She was filthy and soaked.' Meanwhile Bébert, likewise making his way home through the night, found that his route took him past the schoolhouse at Neuvy, and since he still had his revolver he left the weapon behind a water cistern in the school washroom. When he eventually arrived at the château, Nanny was waiting up. She ran him a hot bath.

'The following morning,' Souris later recalled, 'my husband arrived to collect me.' She added, 'He was freshly shaved and changed.'* They never discovered what had caused the explosions.

———

Following the narrow escape of 12/13 June the *Solognots* decided that it was time for a break, and Culioli was asked to negotiate a pause in the parachute drops. It was clear that the explosion had drawn German attention to the region; many of the volunteers were already exhausted; a short pause in their dangerous work, until German activity had calmed down, looked like common sense. Memories differ as to whether Culioli made his request in writing or face to face, but it was in any case refused. Albert Le Meur said that he was a prime mover in the request to call a temporary halt. He said that he had been present at a meeting at the 'Le Cercle' hideout with Pierre and 'Jacqueline'. 'Prosper' also attended and Le Meur urged his leader not to underestimate the Germans. But 'Prosper' refused to call a halt. Like 'Max' and 'Vidal' (General Delestraint), he had returned from London with the conviction that the landings were imminent and had mentioned this to several members of the network. He was very tense and seems to have regarded Culioli's sensible request as a near mutiny by the *Réseau Adolphe*; accordingly he sent Culioli a written order to continue organising receptions. The rumour spread that the weapons were intended for 'at least one' division of allied paratroops that would be dropped into the Sologne before the end of the year.[5]

On the night of 15/16 June there was another delivery to Culioli, not containers this time but two more SOE agents, both Canadians, one a circuit organiser, the other a radio operator. Their names were Frank Pickersgill ('Bertrand') and Ken Macalister ('Valentin'). They were dropped on a site near the River Cher and were joined two nights later by a French sabotage instructor called Pierre Raynaud ('Alain'). All three men were sheltered by Culioli and 'Jacqueline' in 'Le Cercle', and all three were taken on the morning of 20 June to lunch with the Bernards at Nanteuil. It was a Sunday. They sat in the dining room,

———

* Pierre de Bernard was always well turned out. On the morning after the explosion, having dropped in at the schoolhouse to recover his revolver, he turned up at the Tristans' in his usual outfit of bow tie, plus-fours and highly polished shoes. He had forty pairs of highly polished shoes and his wardrobe included a grey overall which he donned for 'rough work', that is, cleaning guns – or polishing shoes.

around the table that was still there in 1962, beneath the same two stags' heads and the portrait of the Marquise de Perrigny. The conversation would have been in French as Bébert did not speak much English. Nanny was there, but not the girls. This was a working lunch.

Outside the long dining-room windows, everything carried on normally. In the park, in the sunshine, off-duty German soldiers came and went. Inside the château the resisters laid their plans. Culioli had received an instruction from 'Prosper' to take the new arrivals up to Paris so that they could hand over the information and equipment they were carrying and he could brief them before they moved on. Culioli, 'Jacqueline' and the three newly arrived agents were to take the train to Paris together on the following morning. But after lunch the plan changed.

It changed because one of the eight resisters sitting around the dining-room table, Pierre Raynaud, still had his secret agent's antennae in working order. Raynaud was a young officer in the French army, a soldier who had retrained as a saboteur and unarmed killer. He had been parachuted back into his own country two nights before. Now he was sitting in a château, beside an English nanny, being entertained by a count and countess, in a world of stags' heads, white linen, silver napkin rings and wine decanters. And separated by a thin pane of glass from the world he had been sent to destroy, police dogs, an anti-aircraft gun beneath the trees, the straight arm salutes, the guttural pleasantries, the jackboots and field grey tunics of the men he had come to kill. The unreality of the situation must have set alarm bells ringing in his mind. Furthermore, he was appalled by the Canadians' attempts to speak French.

After lunch he announced that he had decided to travel on alone. Souris drove him to Blois to catch the Paris train that afternoon. It was one of the best decisions Raynaud[*][6] ever made. Even Nanny considered Ken Macalister's accent to be 'quite dreadful'.

Before leaving Nanteuil that day, 'Jacqueline' said that she missed reading in English and asked if she could borrow a book from the library and Souris lent her a copy of *The Life of the Bee* by Maeterlinck. It bore the Nanteuil book plate – '*Ex-libris – Château Nanteuil*'.

———

* For his work as a sabotage instructor in the Jura over the following twelve months with Francis Cammaerts, Pierre Raynaud was awarded the DSO.

In France as a whole the delivery of arms to the Resistance was heavily reduced in the first part of 1943. This was to avoid the danger of a premature uprising provoked by the imposition of the STO (*Service du travail obligatoire*). On 10 March de Gaulle, urged on by 'Max', had written to Churchill demanding the means to support and arm the new recruits, estimated to number 50,000, as they joined the Secret Army. This letter received no reply until 22 March – three days after 'Max's' departure – when Churchill urged de Gaulle to stand down the Secret Army in order to avoid the danger of the massacre that would result if a general insurrection broke out before the landings.[7] Despite this instruction, throughout the month of June, arms deliveries to PROSPER continued at a growing pace. As the French historian Olivier Wieviorka has pointed out,[8] this was in strong contrast to the lack of arms deliveries elsewhere.

There were six arms drops on the 14 and 15 June and fourteen further drops later in the month. Not all were into the Sologne.[9] But between 12 and 21 June, Culioli's group received the astonishing total of 120 containers.[10] Georges Fermé's network received fifteen containers near Montrichard early on the morning of 21 June. On the same night another drop took place at Villeny, quite close to Neuvy where the two containers had exploded the week before. It was received by members of the Romorantin Resistance led by Roger Couffrant and shortly after dawn a lorry arrived at the DZ to transport this delivery to 'Le Cercle' for temporary storage.[11]

As was easily predictable all this activity, and the explosions of 12/13 June, had attracted German attention. The senior officer in Blois, Colonel Hippe, enjoyed a reputation in the city for being a decent man.[12] Oddly enough, his headquarters had been set up in the ornate cavalry barracks named after 'Maurice de Saxe', a German general who became a Marshal of France under Louis XV. It was Colonel Hippe who had omitted to order reprisal executions after the death of forty-three German soldiers in a Resistance attack outside the city – a very unusual omission in 1943. Now he was contacted by a Luftwaffe colonel who was 'intrigued by the almost nightly flights of English planes over the area'.[13] So Colonel Hippe ordered a military cordon to be set up at 3 a.m. on the morning of 21 June around Neuvy, site of the exploding containers. It was a major operation. The cordon encircled the communes of Bracieux, Huisseau, Chambord, Thoury, Neuvy and Dhuizon.[14] The troops manning it were from a Luftwaffe battalion, a mixture of young recruits and elderly territorials directed by *Feldgendarmes* (military police), but they were backed up by the Blois Gestapo.

The headquarters of the operation was outside Bracieux. Comte de Tristan's house, the Château d'Herbault, where Souris had taken refuge after being blown into the ditch, was requisitioned for the day. Early that morning Roger Couffrant's lorry, loaded with the arms recovered from Villeny, and on its way to 'Le Cercle', drove into this trap. He and his men were arrested and taken to Blois. An hour or so later Culioli set off with 'Jacqueline' and the two Canadians to drive to Beaugency, where they would board the Paris train. They left without waiting for the safe arrival of Couffrant's lorry. After the war Culioli said, 'I set out despite the fact that none of my reception leaders had reported on the night's operations.'[15]

The road from 'Le Cercle' to Beaugency lay straight through the German military cordon. Culioli's car was waved past one roadblock but stopped at a second outside Dhuizon, where the Canadians were ordered out and marched into the little town. Two soldiers got into the car and ordered Culioli to drive to the *mairie*. The road was lined with troops. Inside the *mairie* the resisters were questioned by the Gestapo. Culioli and 'Jacqueline' were told to join the queue and while they were waiting Culioli, whose briefcase contained numerous compromising documents, managed to conceal it behind a chair.[16] After questioning, 'Monsieur et Madame' were allowed to go. But the Canadians were still waiting their turn and Culioli was unable to recover his briefcase. Back in the car he started the engine. Shortly afterwards a soldier came running out of the *mairie* and ordered them back inside. Culioli let out the clutch and set off at top speed on the road to Neuvy and Bracieux.

The underpowered Citroën was pursued by two German police Fords. After the war Culioli wondered whether he should have tried to escape by leaving the main road and driving onto one of the forest tracks, some of which he knew well. Looking at his route today it is clear that the only chance he would have had to do so would have been in Neuvy, five kilometres from Dhuizon, where he might have been far enough ahead to take a right turn off the D18 in the centre of town without being seen. This would have led him into the Forest of Boulogne. There the forest rides might have saved him.

In the event, the chase did not last long. After racing through Neuvy the police were close enough to open fire and outside Bracieux the

Citroën was faced with another military roadblock. Culioli tried to force his way through it but a bullet shattered his windscreen and another hit 'Jacqueline' in the head. She slumped against him and he thought she was dead. The car swerved off the road and bounced against the stone wall of a cottage belonging to 'la Mère Loulou'. Culioli was thrown out and promptly beaten up by his pursuers. Although badly shaken by the crash he fought back so hard that one of them had to calm him with a pistol shot through the leg.[17] 'Jacqueline', unconscious, was taken under guard to a hospital in Blois. Culioli was given first aid at the Luftwaffe field hospital in Blois and then locked in one of Ludwig Bauer's underground cells at 'Les Tilleuls'.

Back in Dhuizon, where the Canadians' attempts to speak French had aroused immediate suspicion, the briefcase had been discovered. In the Citroën's boot the police found the equipment and documents that the Canadians had carried from London. There were two radio transmitters, six new 'crystals' for setting new wavelengths, and correspondence for 'Prosper' and his principal lieutenants, 'Archambaud' and 'Denise'. The messages were addressed to each agent by his or her field name,[18] but SOE staff in London had written the names, addresses and new passwords for other members of the PROSPER network in English and sometimes 'in clear'. However, no immediate connection was made by the German authorities between the arrest of the four British agents outside Dhuizon and the lorryload of arms being driven around the countryside earlier that morning by a group of French *paysans*.

—————

Oddly enough, Ludwig Bauer was not in Blois on 20/21 June, even though he knew that the military dragnet would be in operation that night. It is possible that he had been sent to Lyons to support that city's *Kommando*, a much bigger unit, which was preparing to break into a meeting of senior resistance leaders also scheduled for 21 June.[19] The Lyons Gestapo had requested and received reinforcements for the raid.[20]

It was only when Bauer returned to Blois on 23 June and examined the contents of the car boot that the full significance of the Sologne arrests became apparent. On the same day the Germans had captured a significant quantity of arms, and the party that had received that arms, as well as two British agents and two of their French colleagues. Pierre Culioli said that his interrogation took place at Orléans and that it was carried out while he was lying on a stretcher. Bauer processed Culioli with the assistance of Wolbrandt, the deputy head of the Orléans SD,[21] and of 'Mona-la-Blonde'. According to Mona Reimeringer, who was also Bauer's mistress, Culioli, who was in pain from his wound, told his interrogators that he 'hated the Germans but that he hated the English more, since they had tried to poison him' and he offered to provide information if his life and that of his 'wife' (that is, 'Jacqueline') were spared. Bauer's response to this story, according to Reimeringer, was 'You couldn't make this up'.[22]

Having gone through the documents that Culioli was carrying, Bauer telephoned Sipo-SD headquarters in Paris and Kieffer* told him to drive Culioli up to the capital at once. They reached the Avenue Foch just before midnight.

Shortly after their arrival a Gestapo raiding party drove to an address at 75 Boulevard Lannes.[23] The house was frequently used by 'Archambaud' (Gilbert Norman) and was known as one of his addresses. It belonged to a French couple, the Laurents, and was well chosen as it had a second entrance on the Avenue Henri-Martin. 'Denise' (Andrée Borrel), who was having an affair with Norman, was spending the night there too. The two SOE officers had dined earlier that evening in Montparnasse with another member of the network, Armel Guerne.

'Archambaud' was by this time regarded as a security risk by some of his French colleagues. A few days earlier one of them, a liaison officer, had complained to 'Prosper' about this situation. The resister said that 'Prosper', 'Denise' and 'Archambaud' were drawing attention to them-selves by appearing in public together far too often – and spending too much money. 'Archambaud' in particular, he said, was very imprudent. 'Prosper' brushed the criticism aside. He explained that 'Archambaud' was very tired so he was sending him away for a rest.[24]

At 00.15, when the Gestapo rang the bell at 75 Boulevard Lannes, 'Archambaud' and 'Denise' were working on a pile of false papers spread out on the dining-room table. Nicolas and Maude Laurent had undressed and were going to bed, but 'Archambaud' called out, asking Laurent to answer the door, so Nicolas assumed that they were expecting someone. When the Gestapo burst past him they met no resistance. On the dining-room table they found dozens of blank identity cards, photographs and

---

* *Sturmbannführer* Josef Kieffer, Boemelburg's deputy.

a list of addresses, as well as a collection of *kommandantur* stamps being used to verify the papers. The four resisters were taken the short distance to the Avenue Foch and Kieffer's men went on to another address in the rue de Mazagran, off the Grands Boulevards in central Paris. There they arrested the concierge, Madame Fevre, and placed her in a back room.

———

Francis Suttill ('Prosper') had spent the previous night in Trie-Château, near Beauvais, attending an aborted parachute drop. Before he returned to Paris he was told that Culioli had missed the third rendezvous. He said to one colleague that he was seriously worried but was not free to tell her why. Another resister remembered that Suttill had previously confided that he was really concerned about the network's security. 'There are hard blows coming,' he had said, 'and they're coming from London.'[25]

On arriving back in Paris on the morning of 24 June, Suttill attended one meeting and then returned to his lodgings, a room at 18 rue de Mazagran which he had moved into only five days before.[26] In *Shadows in the Fog* his son, Francis J. Suttill, described what happened next. 'There were German agents in his room as well as on the stairs above and below him . . . It seems he put up quite a fight as the concierge reported that when he was taken away it was clear that he had been not only ill-treated but also disfigured, and his room was left in great disorder.'[27] Suttill was then taken to the Avenue Foch, at which point the Gestapo doors close, and we can be certain of little more.

———

News of the arrest of Roger Couffrant, 'Jacqueline' and Pierre Culioli quickly spread through the Sologne. Apart from the disruption caused by the German roadblocks there had been the spectacular car chase through Neuvy and the aggressive questioning that had taken place in the *mairie*. Bubby de Tristan drove to Nanteuil to warn the Bernards and tell them that Pierre and 'Jacqueline' had been arrested and that both had been shot. Souris and the count set off by car that afternoon and drove around the district warning their contacts. In Romorantin they discovered that Roger Couffrant had not returned from the operation of the previous night and was presumed to be in German custody. They also asked the garage owner, Georges Duchet, who knew the way to 'Le Cercle', to wait until nightfall and then recover their copy of *The Life of the Bee*. He went there at dawn the next day to clean the place out.

That night, having burnt bundles of resistance literature and their stock of parachute silk, which Nanny had been collecting to make into dresses for the girls, the Bernards prepared to bury a wireless transmitter left behind by Gilbert Norman and some weapons that belonged to 'Jacqueline'. Then Nanny remembered some advice she had heard on her wireless; it was better not to bury compromising material for fear of German tracker dogs. But Souris knew how to fool hounds. They waited until everyone working in the house had gone to bed and then, having packed the transmitter into a sealed waterproof cover, Moune and Betty took their canoe, paddled up the Cosson and lowered the transmitter into a pool in the deepest part of the river, the spot where the water was three metres deep, just below the diving board that Billy Gardnor-Beard had made for the English students before the war. The girls moved through the dark as silently as possible. Nanteuil, like the rest of the country, had greatly changed since the arrival of Bill Bradford in the summer of 1940, and after three years of Occupation they no longer knew whether or not they could trust the family living in the mill.

On the following morning they heard that Culioli was in German custody and that 'Jacqueline' had been taken to the Hotel Dieu, the principal hospital in Blois. Souris decided that an attempt must be made to rescue her.

———

The doctor looking after 'Jacqueline' was Doctor Luzuy, who was *Pétainiste* and a former member of *Action Française*. He was also Souris' family doctor. On the following day he called Souris to his surgery and told her that he was caring for an Englishwoman who was gravely ill; she had a bullet in her head and she had been trepanned during an emergency operation. Souris, blunt as usual, told him to keep 'Jacqueline' in his care by any means for as long as possible and 'trepan her a second time if necessary'. From then on the medical staff at the hospital did what they could to help. 'Jacqueline' was in a private side-room connected with one of the wards; there was a sentry posted outside her door, but he never entered her room. The Gestapo called regularly, intending to interrogate 'Jacqueline', so an alarm system was set up in reception and whenever they arrived at the front entrance of the hospital a bell rang in the ward and the doctor on duty gave her a pentothal injection. By the time the Germans reached the ward she appeared to be in a coma.

While a plan was being prepared Valentin Rey made another appearance. He made the mistake of approaching Marcel Buhler and saying, 'I know everything.' Souris said that he was warned that if he said a word about the escape plan, he would be *descendu* (rubbed out), 'so he said nothing'. Meanwhile at the hospital others had been drawn in. In addition to Dr Luzuy, the hospital director, there was Drussy, the almoner – a brother of the mayor, and Allart and Doctor Brun. Some of the nurses, who were nuns, had become part of the conspiracy, and it was one of the nuns who gave Souris the information she needed to plan a rescue bid.

The Hotel Dieu is a handsome eighteenth-century building that is attached to the abbey church of Saint-Nicolas. A mediaeval door connects the two buildings, but in 1943 it had not been used for many years. The nun found the heavy iron key to this door and Souris gave it to Albert Le Meur, who had it copied. The plan was to wait until 'Jacqueline' was well enough to walk, and then at night dress her in a religious habit and walk her past the guard, through the ward, through the unlocked door and into the church. Bébert would be ready outside the church and would drive her a short distance to where she would change cars and be driven five miles downstream to Chouzy. There another conspirator would be ready to row her across the Loire. On the opposite bank Le Meur would be waiting to drive her to a safe house. The plan had to be executed as quickly as possible, before a German military doctor was sent to check on 'Jacqueline's' condition.

To alert 'Jacqueline', Dr Brun murmured, 'Your friend with the two daughters is thinking of you.' She did not react, but he could see that she had understood the message. As the day approached Souris was informed by another member of the *réseau*, the gendarme Sergeant Jacquet, that if he was warned in time he would make sure that none of the gendarmes on duty would intervene. But he strongly advised against the attempt as he had noticed the presence of men in raincoats around the hospital who appeared to be keeping watch. They were either German police or French auxiliaries.

Whether Souris' desperate plan would have worked will never be known as 'Jacqueline' was removed from Blois and driven to Orléans by Ludwig Bauer on the morning of the chosen day. By that time, the consequences of the German ambush were being felt all over the Sologne as the Gestapo, who had somehow acquired a great deal of information about the *Réseau Adolphe*, or 'sub-section South Touraine' as it was known in London, had started to carry out dozens of arrests.

———

For the first ten days following Culioli's arrest, life in the Sologne had continued normally. The Bernards, having warned as many people as they could, returned to Nanteuil. Some of the resisters who had fled from their homes returned. At first, all they could be certain of was that Roger Couffrant had been caught with a lorryload of weapons and that the Gestapo had arrested Pierre and 'Jacqueline'. There were no more visits from 'Prosper' or 'Archambaud', no more messengers from Paris, no more night-time parachute deliveries or moonlit flights by allied aircraft at 500 feet. Even the landings by Lysander or Hudson, the delivery or recovery of agents, became infrequent. A Lysander operation organised for the same night, 20/21 June, near Amboise failed because SOE's air movements officer failed to provide reception on the ground. There was no reception on the following night either, but on the third night – the last night of the June moon – Déricourt turned up and the operation succeeded, delivering an F section agent and a French army officer. However, the Gestapo were waiting and the officer was promptly arrested.[28] In the following month only one operation was flown into the Sologne, landing in a field near Azay-sur-Cher. It had to be run over two nights as Déricourt once again missed his first rendezvous.

By then the Germans were reaping the fruits of 21 June.

———

The Gestapo began to move through the Sologne on 1 July. In Meung-sur-Loire, on the north bank of the Loire, they seized Maurice Lequeux, who had been appointed *chef du secteur* by 'Prosper' some months before. Then they raided the 'Hotel le Grand St Michel' at Chambord. Here Albert Le Meur tried to escape when he saw the German police. He was shot in the head and then taken to Orléans with his brother and both their wives. The Gestapo told him that they knew he was concealing fourteen parachuted containers. Later that morning the German police arrived in Romorantin searching for Roger Couffrant. When they asked his wife where her husband was she said that she had no idea since he had been arrested two weeks earlier. With the assistance of French gendarmes Couffrant was then traced to the prison in Blois and brought back to Romorantin. He was asked to confirm that 'the man who sells bicycles', René Bouton, was the 'London letter box' of his network (which he was). Couffrant stuck to the story he had been telling since his lorry was stopped and searched outside Dhuizon early on the morning of 21 June. He was not a resister, he had no 'network' – he had merely been asked to go to a farm and pick up a delivery by a man he had never met before, apart from which he had no idea what 'a London letter box' was.

The senior Gestapo officer, Karl Langer of the Paris SD, then showed Couffrant a letter written to him by Pierre Culioli. In this letter Culioli apologised for identifying him and said that he was only doing so because they had underestimated the enemy, who knew all about their activities. In consequence an agreement or 'pact' had been made by their commanders in Paris under which the lives of the resisters would be spared and their families would not be troubled so long as they surrendered all their weapons. Culioli asked Couffrant to cooperate by revealing where all the arms were hidden and ensuring that any booby traps in place were first removed. Karl Langer told Couffrant that he had a shopping list of thirty containers.

Later on the same day Langer and his men raided the houses of Julien Nadau at Contres, of Auguste Cordelet at Chaumont-sur-Loire (twenty-five containers) and of André Gatignon at St Aignan (twenty containers). In each case they presented a similar letter from Culioli, with details of the parachute operations, maps of the dropping zones and in some cases a list of the places where arms were hidden. The arrests continued throughout July and August with the same scene being played out in village after village, resisters being identified and told to come forward and surrender all their weapons. Culioli did not have to write any more letters. Langer decided it would be quicker if his prisoner appeared in person. With his leg still in bandages, and turning gangrenous, Culioli was driven through the Sologne so that he could spread news of 'the pact' directly. After a while Culioli was replaced and the Gestapo were accompanied by a British officer who the resisters recognised as 'Archambaud', Major Gilbert Norman. For a number of days men and women all over the Sologne who had risked their lives to fight for their country were treated to the sight of a British officer, one of their commanders, working with the Gestapo to dismantle their entire network.

The initial wave of arrests was carried out correctly. The 'pact' was apparently observed and some of those arrested were released shortly afterwards and sent home. But in the third week of July, by which time most of the weapons had been recovered, Gestapo tactics changed.[29] The men who had been released were rearrested, their families were threatened, and more than a hundred resisters were deported to concentration camps, where many were either executed or died from mistreatment. By 6 July 1943, three days after the arms searches began at Chambord and Romorantin, 'Gestapo' Bauer told the Blois police that the SD in Paris considered that the operation in the Sologne on 21 June had led to 'the most important discovery of arms and agents to have been made in France since the start of the Occupation'.[30]

Dr Knochen, who took the credit for the operation, claimed that it had led to the arrest of the entire general staff of the English intelligence service in France. In a post-war statement he added:

Up until May 1943 my service had never succeeded in finding a resistance organisation that was in direct contact with London. Berlin told us at this time that there was such a group in France, similar to one that we had already discovered in Holland. I immediately alerted SD branches all over France. *Amt*. IVe led by Kieffer of the Sipo-SD, was ordered to find it. Kieffer subsequently arrested the English resistance command in the Bvd. Flandrin [the Laurents' apartment in the Boulevard Lannes].[31]

Knochen's statement also linked operations in the Loire and Lyons, where German security forces had enjoyed a second major success on the same day. On the afternoon of 21 June, in a suburb of Lyons, they had arrested Jean Moulin, General de Gaulle's emissary to the French Resistance and effectively its political leader.

'I know,' Knochen continued, 'that an important personage who had come from London was arrested by chance during this operation. The RSHA in Berlin immediately sent an official to interrogate those arrested. This became a very important affair. We were able to carry out arrests in Lyons and other cities over 100 kilometres from Paris. Due to the importance of the matter Berlin sent two additional radio tracking teams which were deployed between Lyons, Marseilles and Toulouse'.[32]

In Berlin in June 1943 Hitler greeted news of the Gestapo success with enthusiasm. He was persuaded that allied invasion plans had suffered a setback,[33] and he required to be kept in close touch with developments in what was known as 'the French section affair'. His commander-in-chief in the West, stationed in Paris, Field Marshal von Rundstedt, recorded 'an increasing danger to German troops'[34] and remained convinced that an invasion of France in 1943 was likely.

———

With the breaking of PROSPER, almost all resistance activity in the Sologne ceased, and German police operations also came to an end. It seemed that Souris and Bébert had escaped detection and they felt confident enough to welcome friends from the 8th and 16th arrondissements of Paris, whose names appear in the Visitors' Book for August. They would never have signed their names if there had been any sense that the family was in danger. The Bernards did not respond when a young man called 'de Maldan' came to the Red Cross office when Souris was on duty and told her that he was transmitting an order 'from Paris' that she and Bébert should leave immediately. She never found out who this man was, or who had sent him.[35]

When their old friend Marcel Buhler was arrested, Souris and Bébert still stood their ground, and even when another friend, Doctor Roy, told them that a waiter at the 'Tour Eiffel', a café in Vienne (Blois) had overheard French Gestapo agents saying, 'After Buhler it will be the turn of Monsieur and Madame de Bernard,' they decided to carry on as usual.

The weather in August was fine. Moune had a new camera and started to make a collection of portraits of friends, mixed up with holiday snaps. There are photographs in the family album of friends sunbathing on the grass outside the château; a good-looking young man called Pierre Théry, in a bow tie, at a picnic at Mont on 1 August; Betty in a summer frock with her hair down; and Moune herself posing with a flirtatious friend, Marinette. There was another picnic on the banks of the Loire on 18 August. Pierre Théry is there again with his skinny younger brother Serge, the latter posing in bathing trunks and with long hair. On 10 August there was another opportunity: the Ford V8 was wheeled out of the barn where it had been concealed for three years, covered in dust. It was washed and polished until it sparkled in the sunlight, once more Bébert's pride and joy. A tranquil family summer recorded in a rather conventional way by a better than average photographer.*

On 24 August it was Betty's birthday. Moune piled all her sister's cards and presents onto a chair outside the front entrance and surrounded them with flowers – dahlias and roses – and Betty washed her hair, put on a pretty summer dress and posed beside the arrangement. At eighteen her childhood had come to an end.

Another page in the album, August slides into September. On 6 September another picnic. Betty takes a slightly out of focus shot – Nanny, Souris, Moune, a capacious leather picnic hamper with silver service and Peter, Nanny's Skye terrier, in the long grass under a birch tree. In the foreground, in front of the hamper, Bébert, resting on one elbow, in bow tie and well-polished two-tone golfing shoes, appears to be examining some insects through a magnifying glass.

The Gestapo came for him three days later.

————

Before leaving with Bébert the Gestapo ransacked the château, found a commercial radio set and took it to pieces, removed all the money he had in his desk and thoroughly searched the cellars under the stables. As they took him away they told him he would be home by Saturday. He was trembling visibly. At Blois, in their headquarters in 'Le Cavalier', before the interrogation started, the officer in charge offered him a glass of Benedictine. A sealed bottle was opened, and three glasses were poured out, for the German officer, the interpreter and Bébert. And to reassure him the German officer and the female interpreter tasted it first. 'Make yourself at home, Count,' said Ludwig Bauer. Bébert did not mention that he was already at home – since they were drinking in a house that belonged to his wife's cousin.

Saturday came and went; a week passed. On 16 September Souris, who was desperately worried, received a visit from two friends, Bubby

———

* See illustration section.

de Tristan and Huguette Burin des Roziers. They held a council of war. Nothing had been heard of Bébert since his arrest, and they agreed that the best thing to do was for Souris to go to Blois, to 'Le Cavalier', to enquire. Before her mother set out Moune took her photograph, sitting in the sunshine on the grass with her friends, in front of the château. Later Souris described what happened next . . .

Accompanied by my brother-in-law,[36] who was more or less *Pétainiste*, I went to the Gestapo office in Blois to obtain permission to see my husband. They sent us on to Orléans saying, 'Your husband will be released.' In Orléans we first went to see Monsieur Bussière [the prefect] who provided an interpreter to go with us to the Gestapo. After some time in the waiting room I was asked to go up to the second floor alone. There were two German officers, one civilian and a very pretty female interpreter. She was the one who said, 'Would you like to sit down? Madame, we have received an order from Paris to arrest you.'

PART III

SETTLING SCORES

10

The Purge

*Yes, she slept with a Boche . . . But why shave her head? She
would just as soon have slept with a Yank.*

Mother of a girl seized by a
gang of 'resistance' thugs[1]

When Henri de Bernard returned to Nanteuil with the news that Souris
had been arrested, Nanny packed a suitcase for her and on the following
day Moune drove into Orléans. But she was not allowed to see her
mother, whose interrogation had begun. Hopes that Souris might be
released after questioning were disappointed and so, for the next two
years, Nanny found herself running Nanteuil. Her first problem was
how to feed the household. With both her employers in prison and their
bank accounts frozen, she had no money. It was no longer possible to
pay the cook or the maids or the gardener, but they all refused to leave
and worked for the next two years without wages.

The *potager* was still flourishing under the direction of 'le Père Bel', but
it could not supply everything. There was, for instance, no coffee. Most
people brewed a coffee substitute made from grilled acorns which gave
Nanny a stomach ache. Then Suzanne started to make 'coffee' from fine-
ground barley, which was so good that people sometimes mistook it for
the real thing. 'Tea', brewed from grilled and shredded carrots, was less
successful – according to Nanny '*un breuvage infecte*' (a filthy brew).
Wartime village life went on. Sometimes, when collecting eggs in the
Basse-Cour, Nanny would overhear the voice of la Mère Michot, who
lived on the other side of the wall, arguing with her daughter Madeleine.
Madeleine was regarded in the village as 'a good-time girl' because she
had a German soldier boyfriend. The dispute usually ended with Mère

Michot yelling, '*Retourne, donc, à ton boche!*' (Alright! Go back to your *Boche*!). Mère Michot drank like a fish. One day she either fell or jumped into the Cosson. Her skirts filled up with air and kept her afloat, much to the amusement of her neighbours, who gathered on the bank to enjoy the spectacle. Eventually her grandson managed to pull her out.

Camille made excellent rabbit pâté and Nanny wanted to send some to Souris while she was still in the prison at Orléans. But Camille's recipe needed pork fat. A couple living at the other end of the village, Monsieur et Madame C, owned more than the usual amount of land and kept two cows, chickens and rabbits, as well as pigs and a horse and cart. They did good business at the weekly market in Blois, but they were mean. Since Nanny also kept rabbits in the *basse-cour*, she called on Madame C and offered her a breeding doe in exchange for some pork fat, explaining why she wanted it. Madame C agreed, but then said that she required a sea fish in addition – though she knew that this was impossible to obtain. Nanny was furious as she had seen Madame C put six sugar lumps into her son's cup of chocolate, though the daily ration was two.

One day they were alarmed to hear that there were plans to requisition Nanteuil to accommodate Reichsmarschall Hermann Goering, who had decided to visit Chambord. He had discovered that paintings from the Louvre had been stored there for the duration. However, after investigation, the German authorities determined that Nanteuil was too cold for the Reichsmarschall. Goering was eventually lodged in the Château of Chambord, where a curator from the Louvre called Schommer, who was a cousin of Souris', and who spoke fluent German, had been directed to distract him. In Goering's place a convent of nuns was quartered on Nanteuil. Six nuns with their two aged servants and the twenty-two pensioners they cared for installed themselves in a house with only two lavatories. The dining room was once again turned into an emergency dormitory.

The nuns could pay their way and possessed a considerable stock of corn, which they stored in the *basse-cour*. They were also entitled to a generous food ration, which they sometimes shared with the house-hold. Nonetheless when they eventually departed it was a welcome relief. Following their departure Nanny was asked for her preference between the German army and the nuns. 'Give me the Germans any day,' she replied. '*Les Bonnes Soeurs, ça puent!*'

No sooner had the nuns left than two German officers arrived with an infantry company and further plans for requisition. To get rid of

them Nanny said that there was typhoid in the village, which was true
– someone had dumped a pile of manure too close to a drinking well –
and the officers promptly departed.

Throughout this time Nanny remained under the silent protection of
the *Mairie* at Huisseau-sur-Cosson. Although armed resistance appeared
to have come to a halt in the Sologne, its obstinate spirit lived on. Nanny
continued to listen to the BBC; she was no longer required to receive the
coded messages, but she was secretly very worried. She was happy to walk
Peter past the German guns, so that he could socialise with the Alsatian
guard dog, but she always carried her prayer book in her pocket. It was
the book she had been given by her orphanage in Farnham, marked
'Nettie'. She was all too aware that she might be arrested at any time.

And one day this disaster happened to one of her friends. For there
was a second English spinster living in the commune of Huisseau, Miss
Hilda Meal. Miss Meal had first been seen in the district when she cycled
into the courtyard of Nanteuil on a brand-new bicycle in 1940, shortly
before the arrival of the Germans. She explained that she had been
working at the British Embassy in Paris but when the embassy was evacuated to Bordeaux she had somehow become separated from her
colleagues and so, having recently met a Frenchman who had given her
the keys to a two-room cottage in Huisseau, she intended to occupy it
for the duration. Nanny and Miss Meal became friends and saw each
other regularly, until the day when Miss Meal was summoned to
Gestapo headquarters in Blois. Someone in Huisseau had denounced
her as a spy on the grounds that she was regularly sending letters to
addresses abroad, sometimes to Jersey (which was occupied, like France)
but also to neutral Sweden.

The Gestapo decided that these letters must be in code and locked
her up for several months. After she was released, Nanny discovered
that she had been asking her gaolers why they 'had arrested her and not
Nanny Cox of Nanteuil'. Miss Meal explained that she had only done
this because she was bored and wanted company, which Nanny did not
think was sufficient excuse.

———

Nanny worried all the time about the girls, who paid no attention either to
her or to the curfew if there was news of *une soirée* (a party). They would
walk home in the dark through the fields, confident that they could avoid

German patrols. Betty had fallen for Pierre Théry, the young man Moune had photographed among the bathing party on 18 August on the banks of the Loire. He was the son of an evacuee docker of good Communist stock from Dunkirk, and he worked at the prefecture in Blois, where he forged identity papers for the Resistance. His younger brother, Serge, had been taken on by the Cheverny estate. The Marquis de Vibraye's steward, Monsieur de Berthier, was anxious to keep young men of the district out of trouble, so he employed them as loggers. This tactic did not always work. A tree could be felled across a ride to prevent the occupying forces from using it – a trick that infuriated the Germans and sometimes led to reprisals. On one occasion, seeking revenge, soldiers ordered a group of students travelling from Paris to Blois off the train and shot them beside the tracks.

Also working in the prefecture was Moune, who noticed that the anonymous letters denouncing 'traitors' or 'terrorists' had grown to such a flood that the German police no longer bothered to open them. They went straight into the bin.

This situation lasted for a year, as France waited for its liberation. The ominous yellow postcard, dated 29 January 1944 and posted from the prison at Compiègne, arrived with its cryptic message – 'Anne-Marie de Bernard, departed leaving no address'; in other words, deported. It was this news, and the conviction that she would probably never see her mother again, that led Moune to resume Souris' work in the Resistance. On 23 March, Pierre Théry was arrested by the Gestapo. He was deported and died in Dachau the following May. By the time a second card had arrived, dated 27 April, with news of Bébert's departure, Moune was acting as a courier for a small resistance group in Blois. Her job at the prefecture meant that she had a permanent pass to cross in and out of the city, an invaluable advantage for a courier. She had made contact with the group through Dr Brun, who had once helped her mother to work out an escape plan for 'Jacqueline', and who was still working in Blois, at the prison.[2] They were part of a much larger, Communist-led movement known as the *Front National*. Resistance had returned to the Sologne, this time without the assistance of SOE, and the RAF had resumed its parachute drops. Everyone knew that D-Day could not be far away, and the resisters were preparing to support it.

———

On 6 June 1944 came news of the landings in Normandy, and shortly afterwards fighting broke out across the Loir-et-Cher. Nanny had a clear memory of the day when the war returned. It was when the railway bridge over the Loire at La Chaussée-St Victor was destroyed by the RAF. She saw the bombers in formation flying quite low over the château, which must have been taken as a landmark, and shortly afterwards she heard the explosions. The five bombers returned, still in formation, and circled over the house again before returning to base. It was 11 June.

On the previous day there had been an incident near La Ferté St Aubin. German troops had surrounded a small farmhouse in the *étangs* that housed a party of students. Their identity cards were in order and they had no weapons. Nonetheless, fifteen of the party, which included schoolboys, were arrested and deported. The remainder, forty-two of them, were immediately shot in the back of the neck with semi-automatic rifles. Their identity papers were then burnt and their valuables were removed. The oldest, Pascal de Brunhoff, was twenty. He had set out five days earlier, on 6 June, from Paris to cycle to the Sologne with two friends, excited by the long-awaited news from Normandy.[3] Recording this event, the journalist Jean Galtier-Boissière, who had just heard of the massacre at Oradour-sur-Glane which had taken place on the same day, noted that these atrocities recalled the Napoleonic Wars, in particular the war in Spain. To shut the population of the village in the church then set light to it and shoot anyone who tried to escape was a traditional procedure of soldiers on campaign, so traditional that it could have been set out in the recruiting handbook, next to the section on how to salute.

As the fighting approached Nanteuil, German reprisals became more frequent. The resisters, now known as *Forces françaises de l'intérieur* (FFI), had reformed and were camped out in the Forests of Russy and Boulogne. Attacks on German outposts and retreating troops started on 10 August and continued for two weeks. On 18 August an unknown sniper took a shot at a German convoy near Huisseau, so the soldiers seized the first man they met, Charles Velly, who was fifty-eight and had nothing to do with the attack, beat him up and then shot him dead. Three days later German units counter-attacked the FTP (Communist) *maquis* which had barricaded the roads around the Château of Chambord. Their commander, Major Leye, led his men on a punitive expedition that resulted in more than thirty civilian deaths. To celebrate this success the major decided to burn down the château, which still sheltered many of the treasures of the Louvre. Monsieur Schommer managed to calm him down. On their way back to barracks his men passed a boy of seventeen, Jean Pommepuy, who was working in the fields outside Huisseau, and demanded his papers. Since he was in his shirt sleeves, and his jacket was out of reach, he could not produce any papers – so they shot him too.

The Germans had reason to be nervous. On 28 August fourteen German soldiers who had surrendered to an FFI unit led by a self-appointed officer operating under a *nom de guerre*, 'Capitaine Brasseur', were shot, instead of being made prisoners of war. Their bodies were discovered one month later, in a marsh in the commune of Theillay. Blois, with the US Army at its gates, was officially liberated by the FFI on 16 August. When the resisters entered the Grand Hotel, final residence of Colonel Huppe, the *Feldkommandant*, they found his sabre, his pipe and his tobacco pouch abandoned in his bedroom.[4]

Victoire's brother-in-law, Jacques Boutard, serving with the 2nd Armoured Division of General Leclerc, was killed on 24 August in the Vallée de la Chevreuse, outside Paris. That evening his comrades entered the city and reached the *Hôtel de Ville*. Unknown to Victoire, her husband Pierre Boutard, deported for resistance, had died ten days earlier in a German concentration camp.

————

But the German retreat did nothing to bring peace to France. In cities such as Lyons there was a complete breakdown of law and order.

Three men were lynched in the Place Bellecour on the day of liberation, and hundreds of others were summarily tried and shot. Bodies were fished out of both the rivers that run through Lyons, the Rhône and the Saône – seven on 14 September, five more three days later. Most had been shot. One woman's feet were tied to a car bumper. In the turmoil of liberation men and women accused of collaboration were rounded up by armed gangs of 'resisters' and brought into the city's *hôtel de ville*, fifty at a time. They had often been beaten up, their clothes ripped off, and the women had shaven heads. Charles Dagostini, a regional *Milice* commander who had hunted down hundreds of *maquisards* was brought in with his mistress, 'the pitiless Maud', niece of a pre-war senator. Dagostini's trial lasted fifteen minutes. Both he and his mistress were shot.[5] A total of twenty-two women were executed after some form of trial.[6]

In the first days of freedom anarchy reigned. An avalanche of anonymous denunciations poured into the *hôtel de ville* – this time from the

The house by the river

Above: Nanteuil, 1962.

Right: The water mill on the river Cosson at Nanteuil, 1962.

Anne-Marie Gardnor-Beard, known as Souris, with her two children, Moune (*standing*) and Betty, c. 1927.

FRÉDÉRIC THÉRY

Four Sologne resisters and one collaborator

Francis Suttill
('Prosper').

Gilbert Norman
('Archambaud').

Yvonne Rudellat
('Jacqueline').

Pierre Culioli
('Adolphe').

Mona Reimeringer, known to the people
of Blois as 'Mona la Blonde'.

Nanteuil during the Occupation

FRÉDÉRIC THÉRY

German officers at the front door of Nanteuil, with Count and Countess de Bernard. Photograph taken by Moune from a first-floor window of the château.

FRÉDÉRIC THÉRY

Picnic by the Loire, 18 August 1943: Moune (*third from left*); Pierre Théry (*foreground in white robe*), who forged ID cards for the Resistance. He was arrested, deported and died in Dachau. Betty married his younger brother, Serge (*seated beside Moune*).

Before the Gestapo called

Top: Nanny, Peter (the dog), Souris, Moune and Pierre de Bernard – picnic, 6 September 1943.

Centre: Souris (*left*), Bubby de Tristan and (*right*) Huguette Burin des Roziers in the garden at Nanteuil, 16 September 1943, after Pierre's arrest on 9 September and immediately before Souris's arrest.

Left: Moune, c. 1945.

Survivors and casualties

Henri Déricourt,
SOE (F), air movements
officer.

Nicolas Bodington deputy head
of SOE(F) and SIS mole.

Jack Agazarian,
SOE radio operator.

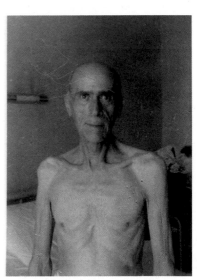

Pierre de Bernard, after his return
from Buchenwald.

The meeting at Caluire

The House of Dr Dugoujon, Lyons.

Jean Moulin, de Gaulle's delegate to the French Resistance.

Raymond Aubrac.

Klaus Barbie.

The Z network at war

Claude Dansey.

Colonel Groussard, SIS agent in Geneva.

Pierre Bénouville, Groussard contact and leader of *Combat* in Lyons.

Edmée Delletraz (Groussard agent in France, Gestapo double-agent).

After the war

FRÉDÉRIC THÉRY

Above: M. Burlot (*left*), Souris, and Pierre Sudreau, mayor of Blois, early 1950s.

Right: Moune and Owen Watson (known as Oscar) at Dieppe, 1950s.

Souris, Nanny, and three English students at Nanteuil, 1964.

other side. The poison pens that had betrayed resisters were now listing alleged collaborators. Five days after the liberation of the city the newly appointed republican commissioner, or governor, Yves Farge, was obliged to announce that he would pay no further attention to unsigned information. In scenes that recalled the Revolutionary Terror, the courts martial sitting in St Paul's Prison started to hold disorderly public hearings where members of the audience would shout out denunciations of each other. Commissioner Farge noted that a growing number of *voyous* (thugs) were now wearing FFI uniforms, and that '*certificats de résistance*' were being handed out too easily.

In fact, much of the great post-war purge was fuelled by the need of those who had collaborated to cover up their activities. It was natural that the *Milice* and their accomplices should be hunted down without mercy, but the first victims of the purge were often women who were charged with '*relations intimes avec l'ennemi*'. The men who had denounced Jews for money were often the same as those who now established their patriotism by banding together to humiliate and shave the heads of women.[7] Women selected for this treatment were shaved in public on platforms, lined up and mocked, branded with swastikas and paraded around the streets as a decorative addition to the general euphoria; some onlookers were reminded of the rituals of public execution, a practice that had only been abolished in France in 1939. In Paris, near the Luxembourg Gardens, four women were shaved in the street, their hair dropped in the gutter. Then they were marched through the *quartier*, their 'wild eyes and clammy faces' reminding one onlooker of the expression he had once seen on a man being led to the guillotine.[8] In the suburb of Villeurbanne the popular jubilation was brought to an abrupt halt when the German army briefly reappeared, in force. The partisans hurriedly retreated and the shaven women were unexpectedly rescued.[9]

In Lyons, ninety-nine of these women were eventually charged and eighteen were imprisoned by military tribunals or the regular criminal courts. Another forty-one were punished with the confiscation of all their property. The mother of one victim protested. 'Yes, she slept with a *boche*. But why shave her head? She would just as soon have slept with a Yank.' A local newspaper carried an indignant announcement from 'the Women of the Resistance'. This was a protest against 'certain forms of welcome being offered' to the soldiers of the liberating armies. 'The friendly and fraternal welcome due to our liberators should not pass the limits of *la bonne tenue* (good behaviour) . . . the scandalous attitude of certain *françaises* could give our allies a false idea of the French woman . . . Because the soldiers are not German such behaviour is not infamous, but its moral value is highly doubtful.'[10] In the carnival of liberty and death such appeals were frequently ignored.

———

And life in the villages of the Sologne could be just as frightening. Less than twenty years before the summer of '62, the woods and lakes that formed the enchanted landscape of *Le Grand Meaulnes* became the scene of summary executions and random brutality.

As the German retreat gathered pace, undisciplined gangs wearing FFI armbands and claiming to be in the Resistance, some being very late arrivals, started to roam through the Sologne looking for targets. In Nanteuil, Suzanne's niece, Françoise, then aged three – and too small to carry shaving water up to the Green Room – was hidden in the cellar of her father's house in the village street and told to make no noise. She can remember looking through the cellar grating and seeing men's boots as they marched down the street, not knowing whether they were Germans or 'FiFi'. Nanny had a low opinion of the FFI in general. She said that they were supposed to be trained fighters taking on the enemy, but since there were no experienced men available to train them they were undisciplined and dangerous. Betty, who had followed her mother into the Red Cross in Blois, reported that one day, as she was crossing the Loire in the temporary ferry that had replaced the Pont Gabriel – which had once again been blown up, this time by German army engineers – a 'FiFi' who was concealing a revolver in his trousers accidentally pulled the trigger and shot another FiFi in the backside.

Many 'FiFi' had played no part in the Resistance which had been far too dangerous, but this did not inhibit them from joining it as soon as the Germans had left. The *épuration* came through the gates of Nanteuil with a band of young locals wearing armbands who arrived at the château and appropriated M. de Bernard's little Citroën car, as well as all the charcoal that was used for heating the kitchen stove. Nanny sought out two FFI who claimed to be officers and complained about the theft.

'Perhaps you would prefer to have the Germans back?' remarked one of them sarcastically. 'I would prefer to have neither the Germans nor the FFI,' replied Nanny. 'But at least when the Germans removed our property they left requisition orders. The two young men who removed the car left no papers. And as far as I can see they just use it for driving the village girls around.' Shortly afterwards the Citroën and the sacks of charcoal were returned.

———

One day 'le Père Bel' decided that enough was enough and it was time to return to Paris. He was given an old pram from which he fashioned a little cart. On the following morning, he loaded up his few belongings and set off through the gates of the *basse-cour*, down through the village and over the bridge, and they never saw him again. Eventually Betty received a letter in which he said that he had arrived in the department of the Allier. They were never sure whether he had said that he was in the Allier to conceal the fact that he had returned to Paris, or whether he said that he was returning to Paris to conceal the fact that he was heading for the south of France. He gave no news of his German wife, or of their daughter. No sooner had he walked through the gates than a suggestion started to circulate in the village, riddled as it was with fear and suspicion, that it had been 'le Père Bel' who had denounced Monsieur and Madame de Bernard. Nanny did not believe a word of it.

The killings continued.

Pierre de Vomécourt, a distinguished F section agent, known locally as Commandant St Paul, 'authorised' the execution of Pierre Debiez, a *milicien* who had been captured by Baron de Vomécourt's FFI. The sentence was carried out on 16 July. A fellow *milicien* was executed at the same time and their bodies were eventually discovered ten months later in the commune of Theillay. Also recovered were the remains of a certain Alice Courtois, dumped in the same *étang* – formerly a favourite picnic spot for Moune, Betty and their friends – for crimes unknown.[11]

A working knowledge of German was a dangerous accomplishment in occupied France. Many of those who acted as interpreters were first drawn into the task simply because they responded to a request to help a neighbour. Fernand Bertrand, a Belgian citizen who had acted as an interpreter at the *Feldkommandantur* of Romorantin was seized by unidentified FiFi at La Ferté-Imbault on 27 August and shot on the same day. The usual practice was followed. The body was concealed in a swamp and only discovered months later.

A Lithuanian woman, identity unknown, who was said to be a frequent visitor at the *Feldkommandantur* of Blois, was executed with her husband by a FiFi firing squad at the cemetery gates of Selommes on 25 July. The men who shot Simon Malesa, a Polish agricultural labourer, on 28 July as he slept in his bed at Villemarin, and who managed in addition to kill his six-year-old son who was asleep beside him, also omitted to identify themselves.

On 10 August Elise Chauveau, a shopkeeper of Santenay, was shot dead with her daughter by four '*inconnus*' while her husband was on duty with the telephone company. Her son was able to flee. She had been accused of 'black-market dealings with the Germans', but her death caused widespread indignation since she was not regarded as being at all 'Germanophile'. None of the four men who carried out this killing were ever identified.

Gustave Moreau, a grain merchant and mayor of Villefrancoeur, was attacked before the Germans had even left, on 30 June. He lived near the ill-fated DZ identified by the Bernards as 'Malakof'. A group of 'armed men' broke into his house and fired seven shots but he escaped with minor injuries through a rear window. In February 1945 he was sentenced to eight years '*dégradation nationale*' (loss of civil rights) for his war record and three months after that he was shot and killed in the street by a former FiFi called 'Persillet', who had identified him as 'a notorious collaborator'.

And then, at St Claude de Diray, a few miles from Nanteuil, a married couple who were known to have sold some goat's cheese to German soldiers were accused by the FFI of supplying the enemy with information. They were seized, tortured, tied up with barbed wire and thrown into a deep pool in the nearest convenient river. Nobody knew what had become of them, until their bodies resurfaced weeks later. The spot chosen by their killers was on the banks of the Cosson, beside a dark spinney where the German soldiers had kept their hostages. It was half a mile upstream from the walled garden of the château. People who know its history still avoid it today. Moune used her contacts at the prefecture to take charge of the couple's eleven-year-old daughter and find a home for her.

Eventually, terror degenerated into farce. On 13 December, as a French regiment in the Vosges mountains overlooking Alsace surrendered to a German infantry counter-attack, and final preparations were made for the last German push in the Ardennes, parachutists dropping through the moonlight from a low-flying aircraft were once again seen over the Sologne and eight *Waffen SS* landed north of St-Aignan. One was injured on landing, so the assault party split up; three sheltered in a barn with the injured man while the other four boarded the last bus to Blois. Gendarmes who had surrounded the barn quickly arrested two of the four SS inside. A third took a suicide pill and a fourth escaped, never to be seen again. The four SS on the bus never reached Blois as they too were arrested en route at St-Gerard. The wounded man was sent to hospital and his eventual fate is not recorded. Of the five SS who were fit for trial, four were sentenced to death by the Military Court in Orléans and shot on 3 February 1945. The remaining SS, who was nineteen years old, was released by the Orléans court and sent to a prison camp. The incident was widely reported, a Lyons newspaper seeing it as evidence of a growing Nazi Fifth Column.

On 29 April 1945 Moune and Betty heard that Bébert, looking like a living skeleton, had returned to Paris from Buchenwald. He reached Nanteuil on an unusually hot spring day. Nanny remembered that he was a bag of bones. She wrapped him in an overcoat that almost went round him twice. He had pneumonia and was shivering violently so, despite the heat, she lit a roaring fire in the dining room and sat him in front of it. Then Dr Luzuy arrived and drove him to hospital. The doctor, who had trepanned 'Jacqueline' two years earlier, said Pierre would die unless they could get some penicillin. He eventually managed to get enough from London to treat several other patients as well.

But survivors of Ravensbrück repeatedly told the girls that their mother had died. The wait for official confirmation lasted several weeks. Then, on the evening of 12 July 1945, Nanny switched on the radio and tuned in to the BBC, which was playing 'We'll Gather Lilacs in the Spring Again'. She retuned to the French station broadcasting the latest list of returning deportees. Anne-Marie de Bernard's name was the third 'B' on the list. She had been rescued from Ravensbrück by the Swedish Red Cross and treated for typhus. But since – like so many other patients – she was expected to die, they had withheld news of her liberation.[12]

Bubby de Tristan travelled up to Paris to meet the train at the Gare de l'Est and bring her home. Dr Luzuy taught Nanny how to give Souris and Pierre vitamin injections, which was not easy, Nanny remembered, 'as there was nothing to put the needle in, just bone'.[13] It was nearly a year before the Bernards felt well enough to take in any English guests.

————

A few months after the war had ended, Nanny met Madame C out walking in the fields. She was in tears because her neighbours had been very cruel to her. Her husband had recently died and she had heard them saying, 'He must have died from all that overeating – when other people were starving to death.' 'It was true, in a way,' said Nanny. 'They wanted for nothing, but they would give nothing. Obviously, I couldn't tell her what I really thought.'

On one of the long summer evenings of 1945, with the family reunited around Souris on the terrace, somebody wondered what had happened to Major Norman's radio transmitter. A party was formed, Betty dived into the pool beneath her father's diving board and located the sodden package. It was dragged up the bank, unpacked and switched on. To general amazement there was a crackling sound and then the lights came on. It still worked!

'Well of course it works,' sniffed Nanny. 'It was made in England.'

II

The Jurors of Honour

'There was no question of convicting Déricourt after Bodington's evidence,' Colonel Mercier, one of the prosecutors said later. 'We received the clear impression that the British government would, for whatever reason, have seen this as a hostile act.'[1]

Of the 301 men and women deported from the Loir-et-Cher during the Occupation, 166 were never seen again.[2] Among them were the ninety-three members of the Sologne Resistance who died in the camps[3] following the collapse of PROSPER. Many others suffered an early death from the after-effects.*

The country to which they returned was heavily marked by the years of pillage and defeat. Factories were bombed out, road bridges were broken, the railway tracks were littered with the rusting detritus of blown-up trains. The windows of the food shops were empty, and butter, milk and sugar were often impossible to obtain. Hot water was a rarity and the lights went out every day at regular intervals.[4]

Approximately 200,000 children had been fathered by German servicemen during the Occupation – an average rate of 137 a day – which helps to explain why, despite the French Resistance, a posting to France was considered to be a welcome break in a German soldier's war.

---

* These figures do not include the scores of PROSPER members arrested in Normandy and the Paris region during the summer of 1943. Some were shot while trying to escape or executed on arrest; many of those deported died after the war as a result of their mistreatment. An exact total has never been established.

When Marcel Braun – the jeweller who had specialised in forging ID cards for PROSPER and other networks – returned from deportation, he found that the French Gestapo agent who had arrested him was living in the 16th arrondissement at 114 Quai Louis Blériot, a luxurious apartment with a view over the Seine. Braun denounced Hans Alma to the police – who advised him to drop his complaint.[5] No matter how many witnesses Marcel Braun produced, it would be a waste of time; Alma was now working for allied intelligence and was well protected. Short of taking the law into his own hands, Braun had to forgo his revenge.

Victor Dojlida was not so easily dissuaded. He had joined the Resistance in Nancy at the age of sixteen, taking part in sabotage operations and armed attacks until he was arrested by the *Brigade Spéciale* of the French police, charged with terrorism and Communism and handed over to the Gestapo. He was condemned to death by a military tribunal, but the sentence was commuted to deportation in view of his age – he was seventeen – and he was sent to Dachau. On his return to France he tracked down the French judge, a man called 'Chiny', who had passed his file to the Gestapo, and beat him up. Then he traced the policeman who had turned his mother's house upside down and attacked him in public. Victor Dojlida was sentenced to one month's prison for these assaults, after which he went back to his wartime trade of armed robbery, concentrating on the houses of former collaborators. This activity earned him a sentence of twenty years' hard labour in April 1948. Shortly after he had served this sentence he was rearrested and charged with two further armed robberies, which he always denied committing, and given a further twenty years. The prosecutor who secured this second conviction informed him that he had 'not forgotten the attack on Judge Chiny'. Victor Dojlida was finally released at the age of sixty-four, having spent forty-three years of his life either in German concentration camps or French prisons. He said that for him the war came to an end in 1989.

The official status of Resistance veterans was that of decorated heroes who had saved the honour of France, but that image suited some better than others. François Marcantoni was a young man who had been one of the boldest members of his *maquis* in Provence. He had been born in 1920 in a small village in Corsica. Following his father's death when he was aged eight, his mother moved to the mainland, to the port of

Toulon, where he eventually found work in the naval dockyards. When German forces occupied the Vichy Zone in November 1942, and the French authorities scuttled seventy-five warships in Toulon docks to prevent them from falling into German hands, the dockers were forced to work under German command. In 1943 Marcantoni joined the Resistance and became a specialist in the theft of arms, explosives and vehicles and the destruction of railway tracks and trains. Following a night attack on a defended position he was captured, tortured and deported, but he survived the war and was decorated with the *Croix de Guerre* and the Resistance Medal.

Despite these distinctions he too decided to carry on with his wartime trade. His enemy, the *Police Nationale*, was unchanged. His years as an unwashed fugitive had given him a craving for expensive suits, silk shirts and fine cigars. He used his resistance skills to attack French banks rather than German armouries. He opened a nightclub and used it as cover for a lucrative business smuggling black-market goods. For him the Occupation never ended, and the Resistance never stood down. He needed the same qualities for both peace and war – courage, a cool head, a capacity for meticulous planning, quick wits, a talent for deception and a ruthless contempt for established authority. Suspected at various times of murder, contract killings and living off prostitution, and repeatedly imprisoned, he died like an officer and a gentleman at the age of ninety, his wartime record earning him the right to a private room in Val-de-Grace, the military hospital in central Paris.

———

As the newly installed provisional government slowly regained control of the country, the lawless violence of the *épuration* was succeeded by a second wave of score-settling, this time carried out through the courts. In the Sologne this process was notably embittered, driven by the anger of the returning resisters, many of whom were convinced that they had been betrayed by their own countrymen. For some of these men and women the nightmare of 'Night and Fog' was to be succeeded by an ordeal that could lead them straight back to the execution yard, this time before a French firing squad.

One of the first public inquiries into what had happened to the *Réseau Adolphe* in the summer of 1943 was not a legal trial but a '*tribunal d'honneur*', held in this case at the request of the accused.

Roger Couffrant, the Resistance *chef de secteur* of Romorantin, and the first man to fall into the trap on 21 June 1943 when he drove his lorryload of arms straight into the German army's roadblock, had returned to Romorantin from the Mauthausen slave labour camp to find the little town alive with rumours and accusations, many concerning him. He demanded an inquiry and the tribunal assembled on 27 July in the 'Café de Square' of Romorantin, in the centre of town. Georges Duchet, who had cleared out 'Le Cercle' after 'Jacqueline's' arrest, presided over the jury. His twenty-one fellow jurors included the mayor of Romorantin and five women.[6]

Couffrant was asked to explain why he had toured the Sologne in July 1943 in the company of a Gestapo officer, Karl Langer, identifying members of *Adolphe* and instructing them to give up their weapons. In his defence he said that everything that had happened had been a consequence of events in Paris which he had been unaware of at the time – that is, 'the arrest of our leadership and the confessions that followed'. He had been informed by colleagues that the Gestapo had secured

a list of the principal leaders of our *réseau*, they knew all the dropping zones, the location and number of our arms dumps and had read many of the messages we had received . . . In view of the exact information they already possessed I decided to take steps to avoid the searches, mass arrests and reprisals that would have fallen on the general population, and I took full responsibility for our sabotage operations.[7]

He had one defence witness, Pierre Culioli, who confirmed that Couffrant had been acting on a written order to save the lives of those already arrested and to prevent further arrests.

The tribunal delivered its verdict on the same day. It passed a motion of total confidence in Couffrant and rebuked those in Romorantin who had been circulating malicious rumours that had been started by 'people who were badly informed' and who were 'exploiting the understandable grief of the widow of one deportee'.[8] Roger Couffrant announced that he was resigning from all his public functions in order to be free to reply to the numerous attacks that had been aimed at him. In the event he faced a further trial before a military tribunal, which acquitted him, and he was not troubled again. But his account of what had happened did nothing to calm public feeling in the Sologne.

Since Pierre Culioli had admitted sending a written order to Couffrant telling him to dismantle the *réseau* and cooperate with the Gestapo, he was the next to be investigated. On his return from Buchenwald he was arrested and held in Fresnes Prison near Paris (the prison that a year previously had been used by the Gestapo). From there he wrote a letter to a friend denouncing the reckless and cynical behaviour of a third deportee, Maurice Lequeux, the *chef régional* of the Resistance of Meung-sur-Loire. Lequeux had been a controversial figure in his home town for some years. In June 1941, while working as a shop assistant in Meung, he had written to Marshal Pétain asking for a position as a *fonctionnaire*. He was promptly appointed as a police inspector, working in the *Service Economique*, and after five months, in November 1941, he succeeded in getting himself nominated as *contrôleur du ravitaillement*. This was a powerful position since it meant that he regulated food supplies and 'investigated' – in other words controlled – the black market. He carried out this role so aggressively that he succeeded in making himself universally hated.[9] He prosecuted smallholders who produced a little butter and milk while at the same time on his own account raising pigs and cows to supply his brother-in-law's hotel. He was suspended by the Vichy government in August 1942 and dismissed from his post in November. There was no evidence that he had taken part in any resistance activities before 11 November 1942, when German forces occupied the Vichy Zone.

But when he did join the Resistance, Lequeux proved very effective and 'Prosper' – unaware of his local reputation – promoted him to the rank of *chef du secteur* for Orléans, Blois and the north Loiret in May 1943. Culioli's letter suggested that Lequeux had continued to behave more like a black marketeer than a resister and in his eagerness to make money illegally had put other men's lives at risk. By this time Lequeux was also under arrest, in Blois Prison – which was an unexpected address for a man who had just been repatriated from Auschwitz. But on his return to Meung-sur-Loire, in place of the affectionate welcome that might have been expected, he had been denounced as a traitor by his fellow citizens, who had a number of scores to settle. The Blois Prison governor's report stated that Lequeux had been severely mistreated during the war following his arrest by the German police, that he was still suffering great pain and was in the prison hospital. A resistance *jurée d'honneur* cleared him on 4 October 1945, but a week later he was tried

by the Court of Justice in Orléans in the first of an extraordinary
sequence of post-war treason trials that, with the perspective of time,
fall into a supervised pattern.

At his first trial in 1945 Lequeux was convicted of '*intelligence* (secret
dealings) with the enemy'. He was sentenced to ten years hard labour,
loss of civil rights and confiscation of all his property for the rest of his
life, and taken back to the prison hospital in Blois to continue his
convalescence.

The case against Lequeux was that in his zeal to follow the same
instructions as Couffrant he had given up arms dumps which only he
knew about and which he could have kept concealed. He had also
volunteered information about sabotage operations and the men
involved which he had no reason to disclose. He claimed to have done
no more than Roger Couffrant and said that he had only provided
information that the Gestapo already had and which it was impossible
to deny. But the court found that he had been personally responsible for
the deportation of ten resisters, six of whom died in the camps.[10] His
trial took place at a time when many people refused to believe Culioli's
story of 'a pact with the Gestapo'. The only thing that was perfectly
clear was that Culioli, Couffrant and Lequeux had all been seen in the
company of the Gestapo, identifying resisters and ordering them to give
up their weapons. Suspicions continued to grow.

Lequeux's sentence led to a correspondence in London between MI5
and SOE. The sentence was regarded as 'extremely harsh'; it was agreed
that an appeal for help to British Intelligence that Lequeux had made,
could not be ignored. Much of the information he had been accused of
divulging could equally well have been given away by 'Archambaud'
(Major Norman). And since 'Archambaud' had been mentioned in
newspaper reports of Lequeux's trial, it was possible to make this point
to the French authorities without breaching official secrecy. Vera Atkins,
F section's intelligence officer, who was effectively third in command,
was copied into the instruction sent on 9 November 1945 to MI5's office
in Paris.

> Point out that our agent 'Gilbert' [Major Norman] is known to have
> disclosed to the SD at Avenue Foch the whereabouts of arms dumps
> etc. in the hope of saving lives of resistance members in accordance
> with the 'agreement' . . . We are morally bound to point this out to

the French . . . since he [Norman] was a British officer . . . Sound out Commissaire Pradon . . . He may advise whether any official intervention on our part would produce any result.[11]

The result was that Lequeux's appeal, in 1947, was partially successful. His sentence was reduced to two years in prison and he was released immediately with his property and civil rights restored. Predictably, the first civil right he chose to exercise was to denounce Culioli for treason.

In demanding the prosecution of Culioli he was joined by a fourth of the Sologne deportees, André Brasseur. Meanwhile a fifth deportee, Georges Duchet of Romorantin, who had presided over Couffrant's *jurée d'honneur*, accused a sixth, Gerard Oury, of being responsible for the arrest of a seventh comrade, André Lemoine. And an eighth man, René Bouton, who personally accused neither Culioli nor Lequeux, said that he had been imprisoned with a ninth resister, Jean Bordier, who also accused his *chef*, Lequeux, of betrayal. Four of these men, Brasseur, Duchet, Bouton and Oury, had been prominent members of the Romorantin Resistance, just as Lequeux had dominated the Resistance in Meung-sur-Loire. Until the summer of 1943 they had been comrades in a desperate armed conspiracy, willingly placing their lives in each other's hands. Now, still desperate, seeking to discover who had caused the disaster, they became involved in a spiral of vengeful distrust that threatened their mutual destruction and divided village communities throughout the Sologne.

———

Culioli was tried twice, on both occasions before a military tribunal. The first trial was in September 1947, before the *Deuxième Tribunal Militaire de Paris* sitting in Reuilly Barracks. Culioli said in evidence that since he had been caught in possession of papers addressed to 'Prosper' and 'Archambaud' he had been forced to admit that he knew them. But under German interrogation he had claimed that he had no means of contacting them since he had missed the third rendezvous – after which a meeting was automatically cancelled.[12] He also claimed that he had not given away the address of 'Prosper' since it had recently been changed and he did not know it. He also said that he had only been taken to Paris after the arrest of 'Prosper'. This was untrue. In fact, he had been driven from Orléans to

Paris on the night of 23 June. The court noted that he had given information without suffering any torture. He was acquitted of betraying his country but criticised for offering assistance to the Gestapo.

Culioli was not satisfied with this verdict and was eventually tried a second time, but before this could happen another national scandal broke. A new villain had emerged to be charged with responsibility for betraying the PROSPER network. His trial opened in June 1948, and the man in the dock was none other than F section's air movements officer, Flying Officer Henri Déricourt. During the course of 1945 and 1946 French prosecutors had accumulated a weight of evidence from French and British official sources suggesting that Déricourt had also been working for the Paris SD.

Henri Déricourt was a civilian pilot who had joined the French Air Force in 1939. He left France in 1942 and travelled to London. There he had been directed into the RAF, before transferring to SOE. He was allocated to F section and parachuted into France on 22 January 1943. Early in 1944 he was recommended for the DSO and he attached the ribbon to his uniform[13] although the award had never been gazetted. He was discharged and paid off on 29 August 1944 and signed a receipt for an enormous amount of money – £1,000 and 550,000 French francs (worth in total approximately £130,000 today) in recompense for his wartime service.[14] By 19 February 1945 Déricourt had returned to France and was writing to the SOE representative in Paris asking for help. He wanted protection and an automatic pistol, and he wanted his DSO. He said that he had been told by the French authorities that he was not welcome as he had belonged to a *Réseau Buckmaster*. Lieutenant Colonel Warden declined to give him a gun and advised him to try the black market or 'one of the US coloured troops'.[15]

In April 1946, Déricourt – who had started working for Air France again on the London–Paris route – appeared before Croydon Magistrates, accused of smuggling £6,000 worth (approximately £244,500) of gold, platinum and currency out of England through Croydon airport. He was defended by an expensive barrister who explained that his client was not a smuggler, he had been engaged on confidential French government business and the booty belonged to a secret state fund. The magistrates convicted him and fined him a nominal amount before deporting him – together with his gold bars and his platinum. His fine and legal costs were paid by an unknown party and in July of that year he received the *Légion d'Honneur* from the Gaullist government. But four months later, on 26 November 1946, Déricourt was arrested by the French police and remanded in custody, accused of treason and collaboration with the enemy. There was evidence that during the war he had been in regular contact with the SD in the Avenue Foch, where his controller had been Karl Boemelburg.

As a former officer in the French Air Force, Déricourt had the choice of a civil or a military tribunal. A verdict in a civil court was open to appeal by either side. The judgement of a military tribunal was final, but the death sentence was mandatory for those found guilty of treason. Déricourt chose the military tribunal.

In his defence Déricourt said that after being parachuted into France by SOE he had travelled to Paris with his wife and moved back into his pre-war address. This was an apartment in the rue Pergolèse that happened to be 300 metres away from the Gestapo headquarters in the Avenue Foch. He admitted an association with the SD and gave 2 June 1943 as the date of his first contact. He said that on that day some of his old Lufthansa friends, now in the Luftwaffe, called at his apartment and invited him out for a drink. When he got into their car he found three German strangers in plain clothes already in it. The pilots got out and the car was driven round the Bois de Boulogne while one of the German civilians, who introduced himself as 'Herr Doctor Joseph Goetz', informed him of the correct date of his arrival in France, the details of his journey to and from England and various details about the organisation of SOE, and invited him, since they knew all about him, to work for them. He was told that if he did not do so both he and his wife would be arrested. He therefore agreed to become a German double agent. He said that he had agreed to work with them as the best means of protecting the forty-eight British agents 'whose lives depended on me'. He had worked honestly for British Intelligence and had only pretended to work with the Germans. When he gave the Germans information about landing grounds, he never used those fields again. He said that he considered himself to be a prisoner of the Germans, 'a prisoner at liberty'.

Several former SD and Gestapo officers emerged from French prisons to give evidence for the prosecution. They said that they had realised that Déricourt was deceiving them but had left him at liberty as they thought he might eventually provide information about the date and location of the allied invasion. SS Colonel Helmut Knochen, the head of the Sipo-SD in France, said that he had appointed Boemelburg, Kieffer and Dr Goetz to run Déricourt, and that the accused had been known as 'Boe.48', that is a numbered agent of Boemelburg. Dr Goetz stated that SD chiefs discussed with Déricourt the orders he had received from SOE in London. And a senior *Abwehr* officer said that he believed that Déricourt had indeed given the SD vital information about arrangements being made for D-Day.

The prosecution produced evidence that Déricourt had provided the Germans with information about numerous Lysander landing grounds, the dates of forthcoming operations, the personal letters and official correspondence that SOE agents had entrusted to him for onward transmission to London and various addresses used by SOE in Paris and elsewhere. Most of the agents Déricourt had assisted were members of PROSPER, which meant that he had apparently furnished the German security police with the means to break SOE's largest French network whenever they wished to do so.

In addition, two of the Gestapo witnesses stated that Déricourt had been paid a very large sum for providing information about the arrival of SOE agents. His treachery seemed to have been proved and he was expected to face a firing squad. But at the last moment an unexpected witness was produced by the defence, Major Nicolas Bodington, described only as a 'British intelligence officer'. In his defence Déricourt had said that before he was enlisted in SOE he had been contacted by a different service that was connected to SIS.[16] Nobody believed him until Bodington gave his evidence, which saved Déricourt's life. He claimed that he had known that Déricourt was in contact with the Germans and that he had instructed Déricourt to remain in contact. Bodington was not challenged on this claim, although neither he nor his commanding officer Colonel Buckmaster had any authority to issue any such instructions. Bodington also said that he himself had spent a month in Paris in 1943 and that he had been protected by Déricourt, who could have betrayed him at any time. If he had to do it again, he said, he 'would do it with Déricourt'. This argument, that Déricourt could not have been betraying F section agents because Déricourt did not betray Bodington in Paris in July 1943, was obviously absurd. Déricourt could have earned a small fortune selling Bodington to Boemelburg, but had he done so his treachery would have been discovered by SOE and Boe.48's usefulness would have come to an end. The Gestapo would have put him out of circulation long before SOE could have reached him. However, Bodington's reasoning also passed without challenge.

'There was no question of convicting Déricourt after Bodington's evidence,' Colonel Mercier, one of the prosecutors, said later. 'We received the clear impression that the British government would, for whatever reason, have seen this as a hostile act.'[17] When Bodington left the witness box the prosecution case collapsed and the court acquitted Henri Déricourt that same day. The appearance of Major Bodington for Déricourt's defence, as well as the widely attested evidence of 'Archambaud's' collaboration with the Gestapo, led many of the survivors of PROSPER to the conclusion that the destruction of their network in June 1943 had, for whatever reason, been plotted in London.

————

The trials of Lequeux, Culioli and Déricourt were closely followed in London and there was British intervention, at various levels, in all three cases. Viewed today they resemble episodes in one and the same prosecution – a judicial manhunt in search of a scapegoat, someone who would carry the blame for the death of hundreds of members of the French Resistance. With the acquittal of Déricourt, Pierre Culioli realised that the spotlight had fallen back on him. His second trial, the last in the sequence, opened on 17 March 1949, in Metz.

This time the leader of *Adolphe* had been able to organise a more impressive defence. Dozens of resisters gave statements in his favour and many made the journey to Metz to support him, but there were also two new witnesses for the prosecution. The British interest had apparently changed sides because one witness was a former Gestapo agent whose life depended on her cooperating with allied security, and a second was supplied by SIS. SOE had been abruptly dissolved in January 1946 and the Foreign Office (that is, SIS) had become responsible for clearing up the mess created by its hasty dissolution.

Among the witnesses for the defence was Souris de Bernard. When she arrived at the courthouse in Metz she was immediately confronted by 'Mona' Reimeringer, now using her real name of Marie-Delphine

Reimeringer, *épouse* Blavot. Reimeringer arrived in Metz under police guard, not because she was under arrest but for her own protection. When Blois was liberated in August 1944 a warrant had been issued for the arrest of 'Mona-la-Blonde'. Identified as 'Alsatian' or 'Luxembourgeoise', she was described as *'assez forte'* (quite burly), about 1.65 metres tall, with brown hair dyed blonde, dark brown eyes and a heavy jaw.

The police eventually tracked her down to Paris, but by then she was under US protection, having somehow managed to make contact with American forces before they entered Blois. The sight of 'Mona-la-Blonde' – under police protection and summoned by a French prosecutor to give evidence against them – caused outrage among the Resistance veterans. Souris was furious when she walked into the waiting room and found Mona comfortably installed and surrounded by *gendarmes*. 'What is *she* doing here?' she asked. 'This is the only room that is heated,' replied the sergeant. 'Oh, so she's cold?' said Souris. 'Well put her in the freezer.' Souris continued on form throughout the day. She was an unconditional supporter of Culioli and was upset that he had been forced to seek a retrial in order to clear his name. During the recess, waiting for the court's verdict, she approached Maurice Lequeux, the original instigator of the prosecution.

'Do you know Marguerite Flamencourt and Marie de Robien?' she asked. These were two of the people who had been arrested on Lequeux's information.

'Yes,' he replied.

'They were in Ravensbrück thanks to you,' said Souris. 'This is from them.'

She then hit him hard in the face, twice. Marguerite Flamencourt and Marie de Robien had both survived deportation, but their husbands had not.[18]

Only four witnesses were called to give evidence for the second prosecution of Pierre Culioli. Two were fellow members of the network, Lequeux, his personal enemy, and Lequeux's friend, André Brasseur, co-founder of the Romorantin group. They told a familiar story. Culioli had been seen in the company of Gestapo officers touring the Sologne, calling at individual addresses and instructing the resisters to identify themselves and give up their weapons. He had assured them that if they cooperated, they and their families would be left in peace. They had done what he asked, and they had been deported or shot.

Even without Mona Reimeringer's tainted evidence the case against Culioli seemed clear. But Reimeringer's testimony opened Culioli to a far more serious accusation. She claimed that he had betrayed not only the Resistance in the Sologne but the entire PROSPER network, including its leaders in Paris. She claimed that when he was interrogated in Blois, Culioli was neither beaten nor tortured. The bullet wound in his leg had been hurting, so he had been given a good meal and medical attention. He had told 'Gestapo Bauer' that because of the attempt to poison him he was prepared to supply the names and addresses of the two commanders of the French section, and then 'the entire English and French Resistance, deprived of its leaders, will collapse'.

According to Reimeringer, Culioli was one of a group of men in the Loir-et-Cher who were either *cagoulards* or '*Croix de Feu*' (that is to say, a terrorist and a pre-war supporter of the extreme right), people who were basically anti-English, men who, as she put it, 'through hatred and cowardice betrayed the leaders of the most formidable organisation that ever existed'. (This was her post-war view of British Intelligence.) Her deposition continued, 'After an excellent meal the Corsican called Culioli was driven to Paris by Bauer to the address of Dr Knochen, the head of the Paris Gestapo.' Mona had added, 'I now work for the Americans and [with] Major Cope of the Intelligence Service who is passionately interested in the affairs of the "SOE French section".'[19]

Much of Reimeringer's evidence was hearsay at best (she had worked in Blois not Paris) and was contradicted by statements from SD officers based in the Avenue Foch; and her new loyalty to the Americans and 'the most formidable organisation that ever existed' might not have had the intended effect in a French court. Apart from which, Mona's obvious loathing of Culioli may also have worked in his favour. But it is hard to see how she could have known about the poison pill unless Culioli himself had mentioned it. And her story was partly corroborated by the fourth prosecution witness, Culioli's old enemy, Raymond Flower of SOE. In an unexpected twist the British authorities supplied evidence from a former British agent to support the story of a former Gestapo collaborator. Flower did not travel to Metz to give evidence in person, but his sworn statement was produced at the hearing. He said that Culioli had been very 'anti-English and had been impossible to work with as he wanted to know everything and control everyone'. He also said, in support of Reimeringer, that he was certain that Culioli had known the Paris address of both 'Prosper' and 'Archambaud'. Since Flower had left France three months before 'Prosper' was arrested, this last claim carried little weight. And furthermore, Flower lied. When he was asked why he had ordered poison for Culioli, he replied that it had been intended for someone else.

Culioli's defence was the familiar one; he had been acting under orders. Instead of blaming one of his former comrades he cited Major Gilbert Norman, of the Durham Light Infantry and SOE. Just as Couffrant and Lequeux had been able to show that they had received written instructions from Culioli, so he claimed to have been following the orders of 'Archambaud', who had been executed in Mauthausen on 6 September 1944.[20] And Culioli had support from many other survivors.

Pierre de Bernard said that when he was taken to Orléans for questioning he was only ever questioned about his work with Major Norman, whom he called 'Gilbert'. This had taken place before the arrival of Culioli in the Sologne and concerned events that only Gilbert knew, about which Culioli knew nothing.[21]

> The Germans told me there was no point in denying that I knew Gilbert. 'You even invited him to dinner, and he had *tripes*,' they said. This was true. 'You have a Visitors' Book at the château,' they said, 'which has been signed by many English officers.' [Gilbert Norman had seen the book and had told Nanny that he recognised some of the names.]
>
> They also accused me of a plan to bomb the arms depot at the Camp des Allées, and of the parachute drop that was coded '*Les sauterelles sont venues par milliers*'. But as for my activities with Pierre Culioli, their questions never concerned that. There was a Michelin map of the region with all the *réseau*'s arms dumps marked in red displayed in the room where I was questioned.[22]

And Souris had a similar experience. She recalled that after her arrest:

> I was locked up in a prison in the same cell as Madame Oury of Romorantin who let my husband know that I had been arrested, and through her Pierre let me know what he had said under interrogation. My first interview was perfectly polite, I denied everything. Every time I said something the Germans said, '*For a countess she is a pretty good*

liar!' But I could tell from the questions that they had a lot of evidence against Marcel Buhler. After this session I received a note from Buhler in my bread ration, 'They know everything. No point in denying it. Conceal nothing.'

At the second session I led the way and when the *chef* of the Gestapo, fat, short, probably Mersch (head of the Orléans Gestapo),* who was questioning me started shouting I said –

'Why are you shouting like that?'

He said, 'Because I am Prussian.'

'I <u>am</u> going to tell you everything,' I said. 'The other day I denied everything as I did not want to compromise a French officer [Buhler]. Today I am going to talk. But don't interrupt me . . . and don't shout.'

I was questioned for a long while about Jacqueline, Culioli and Gilbert, and on the resistance work carried out by Gilbert and Buhler before the arrival of Culioli . . . My interrogators listened with interest to the retransmission of what Buhler had already said, written on the paper in the loaf of bread, which omitted details concerning the work of Culioli and Jacqueline. This proved that the Germans were not aware of the work we did with Pierre and Jacqueline . . .

When I was in Ravensbrück [Souris continued] I met Jacqueline and she told me in confidence that there had been a bad relationship between Culioli and Major Norman. She was very critical of Norman and said that he had only been thinking of his post-war career. He had altered the messages they had sent to London, which was why they had asked for their own radio operator. But Norman had arranged for this man to be recalled 24 hours after his arrival. She was convinced that it was Norman who was responsible for our arrest because of something he had said which had shocked her profoundly. Norman had told her, 'If I am arrested I will do absolutely anything to survive without thinking about the fate of others. They will have to look after themselves.'[23]

The military tribunal reached its decision before the end of the day. As the verdict of 'not guilty' was pronounced – after a recess of seven

---

* In fact Mersch was from the Rhineland. The fat Prussian was his deputy, Wolbrandt. (See Paul Guillaume, *La Sologne au temps de l'heroisme et de la trahison*, p. 10.)

minutes – the prosecution witnesses departed at speed and scenes of wild rejoicing broke out in court. To cries of '*Vive la France!*' the presiding judge, an officer called Rosambert, who appeared to be even more emotional than the defendant's supporters, was applauded out of the building. Then Pierre Culioli with his lawyers, his witnesses and his friends moved on to the station buffet to continue their celebrations. And Judge Rosambert said that presiding over the acquittal of Culioli had been 'the honour of his life'.[24]

———

Perhaps the most amused spectator of the day's proceedings in Metz was Mona-la-Blonde. She had been present at Culioli's original interrogation in Blois, which according to him had been a great deal rougher than she had admitted. And she had already enjoyed months of fun at the resisters' expense, freewheeling through her memories and inventions and chattering on about 'Major Cope' and 'the most formidable' British Intelligence Service – almost as though someone had written her script. And all through her day in court she had enjoyed the spectacle of the remnants of the *Réseau Adolphe* struggling to work out what had hit them and accusing each other of crimes for which they could have been executed. Meanwhile she, who had worked for the Gestapo, taken part in torture, and relished the brutal mistreatment of prisoners, escaped unpunished, guarded by officers of the same French police force that had cooperated with her so frequently during her days of power.

12

Questions in Parliament

I do not think I should say what I did. I do not think Governments should admit to such matters, even if they were done in wartime.[1]

Colonel John Bevan, in 1975,
Controller of Deception 1942–5

In Blois today, in a courtyard on the banks of the Loire, there is a small Museum of the Resistance. Underfunded and ill-equipped, it is frequently closed. When open its neglected air suggests that it functions reluctantly, more as a matter of duty than of civic or national pride. Within, one has a strong sense of time moving on. The achievements of the men and women from this part of France, who fought on alone, no longer seem notable or relevant. Parties of schoolchildren pass through its rooms, incuriously.

Among the exhibits is the wireless transmitter abandoned by Major Norman at Nanteuil, the set that the girls took out in the canoe and dropped into the Cosson at dead of night. But its adventures are not recounted, and nobody today is checking to see whether it still works. This is not the usual self-confident, patriotic display. Just by the exit, on a recent visit, I found a wall display recording the number of *Solognots* resisters who had been arrested in the summer of 1943. It described them as soldiers who had died for their country, fighting a different battle to the one in which they believed they were engaged. And a poster explained in some detail that the men and women of the PROSPER network had been sacrificed in a British deception operation designed to limit allied casualties during the D-Day landings.

This was a summary statement of what has, for some time, been received opinion in France. Following the acquittal of Henri Déricourt, the wealth of evidence from the survivors of PROSPER – that Suttill and Norman had signed a 'pact of honour' with Berlin, and that a British officer had been seen touring the Sologne with the Gestapo identifying resisters and telling them to give up their arms – was repeatedly accepted in historical accounts into what had happened in the summer and autumn of 1943.[2]

In 1967 the historian Henri Noguères edited a five-volume *History of the Resistance in France: 1940–1945*: this stated quite bluntly that the PROSPER network had been 'deliberately sacrificed' by British Intelligence.[3] Part of the reason for the consensus of French opinion was that few could believe that the directors of a secret British intelligence operation could have been as incompetent as any less cynical explanation required them to have been.

The theme was subsequently taken up by other French authors and researchers. The SOE saboteur, Pierre Raynaud, who had separated himself from the two Canadians after lunching with them at Nanteuil and hearing their accents, became embittered and obsessed by the conviction that he and many other agents had been betrayed by their controllers in London. He spent years amassing a personal archive in order to prove that they had been pawns in a complex intelligence operation.[4] Another resister, Jacques Bureau, a radio operator and local agent who worked with PROSPER, was more forgiving. Although just as convinced that London knew about the SD's penetration of PROSPER, Bureau remained sanguine, arguing that theirs had been an 'honourable betrayal'. In assisting in the deception of German Intelligence they had played an essential role in the success of the D-Day landings. Those who had died so tragically had not died in vain.[5]

This was very different from London's explanation for the disaster.

———

Among those agents who remained at liberty following the arrest of 'Prosper' was a newly arrived radio operator called Noor Inayat Khan ('Madeleine'). She was a sensitive young woman who owing to her striking beauty and distinctive Indian appearance was entirely unsuitable to be a secret agent in occupied France. As a child she had been taught by her father that the worst sin she could commit was to tell a lie, a discovery that drove her code trainer, Leo Marks, to despair.[6] Her final training report described her as 'unstable and temperamental' and strongly advised against sending her into France. This was overruled by Buckmaster,[7] who commented, 'Nonsense! Makes me cross,' and decided that on the contrary her departure should be speeded up. She was delivered by Lysander early on the morning of 17 June near Angers, to a reception organised by Henri Déricourt. Four days after her arrival 'Jacqueline', Culioli and the Canadians were arrested and before Khan was able to make contact with the leadership of her network, Francis Suttill, Gilbert Norman and Andrée Borrel were all inside 84 Avenue Foch.

'Madeleine' went into hiding in Paris, having refused a direction to return to England. She remained in contact with London until she too was arrested by the Gestapo on 13 October. After the war Vera Atkins, F section's intelligence officer, mounted an investigation into the fate of the agents who had disappeared on active service. She was particularly concerned about the women agents, although they were no more protected by the rules of war than any other spy. Atkins, who spoke fluent German – she had been born in Romania in 1908, a citizen of the Austro-Hungarian Empire – was determined to disperse the lethal fog into which they had disappeared; she obtained permission to interrogate Gestapo officers, prison guards and other eyewitnesses who had been in contact with them after their arrest. Her investigation subsequently became the basis for several prosecutions for war crimes, but she never revealed most of what she discovered, possibly because it was so damaging to SOE. Vera Atkins was the first person to gain a clear insight into the extent of the German penetration of SOE, and the extent to which Baker Street had failed to protect them.[8] None of her discoveries were published. In the middle of her investigation, in January 1946, SOE was closed down. To continue her enquiries Atkins had to obtain a semi-official posting to SIS, the agency which thenceforth inherited responsibility for Britain's peacetime capacity for sabotage and undeclared warfare.

Once SOE no longer existed, its wartime existence could be acknowledged, but the picture presented in officially sanctioned accounts bore little resemblance to the facts. The first public reference, a plaque honouring the memory of the women agents who had died on active service, was unveiled in St Paul's Church in Knightsbridge in 1948. This broke the news that women agents had been sent into enemy territory, and led to a film, *Odette*, which romanticised the story of Odette Sansom, who had endured torture without betraying any information and had survived the war. In 1946, following her return from Ravensbrück, Odette Sansom was awarded the George Cross.

In 1949, Noor Inayat Khan was awarded a posthumous George Cross, and this award aroused the curiosity of a writer, Jean Overton Fuller, who had been a friend of hers and who wanted to find out exactly what her fate had been. In 1952 Fuller published *Madeleine*, an account of Khan's wartime service. In 1958, another biographer, Elizabeth Nicholas, published *Death Be Not Proud*, an investigation into the torture and brutal murder in Natzweiler concentration camp of four other female SOE agents, including Andrée Borrel. Meanwhile, in a succession of books Jean Fuller revealed that SOE(F) had dropped a number of agents directly into German hands after the SD had successfully 'played back' captured wireless sets, sometimes for months, so convincing London that they were still being properly used by their original SOE operators.

In *Double Webs*, published in 1958, Fuller drew British attention to the fact that an SOE officer, Henri Déricourt, who had been working for the Paris Gestapo, had nonetheless been put up for the DSO. The lamentable state of SOE's relations with SIS became public knowledge and some began to wonder why an enemy informer had been tolerated within the ranks of SOE. Following the French line, speculation grew that the agency might have been used by another British intelligence agency as part of a complex deception operation to mislead the German High Command about the date of the D-Day landings. A series of allegations were made concerning the collapse of PROSPER. It was suggested that London had known that Déricourt had been working for the Gestapo but had continued to send agents into his care. Between them, Jean Overton Fuller and Elizabeth Nicholas, neither of them professional historians, forced a change in government tactics. They painted a picture of astonishing incompetence among the leadership of F section and strongly suggested that a string of agents had been sacrificed, having been sent into occupied territory even after their circuits were suspected to have been blown.[9] They were joined by a third critic, the Conservative MP Irene Ward, who campaigned with a long succession of awkward questions in the House of Commons.

All these allegations were repeatedly denied but by 1958 the matter had become so sensitive that the prime minister, Harold Macmillan,

authorised an official history of SOE(F) to set the record straight –
although even the decision to commission this book remained an official
secret until it was published.

––––––

All official histories suffer from the disadvantage of government control.
But in the case of a secret service history the historian has a further
problem since he or she is dealing with a profession that is trained to be
'economical with the truth'. And yet official historians, who must be
incurable optimists, continue to produce them. And we, in the same
cheerful spirit, continue to read them. It seems, for instance, improbable, that a senior army intelligence officer whose wartime title was
Controller of Deception would ever be a reliable witness when questioned about his wartime activities. Colonel John Bevan held that position from 1942 to 1945 in an organisation that did not officially exist.
But after the war, when the existence of the London Controlling
Section (LCS) was unexpectedly made public – fifteen years after it had
been abolished – the controlling deceiver spoke some words about his
wartime service that were undoubtedly true.

'I do not think I should say what I did. I do not think Governments
should admit to such matters, even if they were done in wartime.'

He could hardly have made it any clearer. At the time of his expo-
sure, Colonel Bevan appeared to be a retired public servant with an
honourable, if rather humdrum, record of government service.
Suddenly a more interesting life was revealed. One can hear the quiet
dismay in his voice when contemplating this act of official betrayal –
and one can sympathise.

In the case of SOE(F)'s official historian, his brief was to answer the
long list of allegations, clear the air and put the history of F section on
a sound academic base. When he was appointed for this task in 1960,
M.R.D. Foot was attached to the Institute for Strategic Studies. He had
previously specialised in Gladstone and nineteenth-century Liberalism.
But he had been a wartime intelligence officer and enjoyed the full
confidence of all interested official parties. Nonetheless, he was forced
to work in strict secrecy and under conditions that made it unusually
difficult to fulfil a historian's task.

He was allowed access to the full SOE archive (or what remained of
it after it had been in SIS's care for seven years) but was not necessarily

allowed to quote from it. In an appendix on his sources he mentioned the chaotic state of the registry and lamented the fact that two post-war weeding programmes and a 'wholly accidental' fire had destroyed much of the SOE archive. He added that most messages exchanged with the field and all the training files had disappeared, as had all the circuit (or network) files, and that when F section's remaining files were divided into two groups of less important and more important papers, *it was the second group that was destroyed*. Many of the records that did survive were only available if specifically requested. In an elliptical description of other difficulties Foot hinted that his brief had obliged him to work on the assumption that SIS did not exist. He was also banned from consulting French records or talking to French historians. He was not even allowed to talk to any of the hundreds of surviving SOE staff. No one (not even his wife) was allowed to know what he was working on. If the custodians of official intelligence had wanted to make it impossible to write a professional history of SOE(F) they could hardly have done a better job.

Foot listed eleven pages of published sources but was not allowed to mention the existence of his most important unpublished source, which was *The Secret History of SOE* by William Mackenzie. (And he was not even allowed to contact the author of this in-house official history.) Mackenzie's account provided Foot with valuable guidance since it was written in the 1940s when the surviving archive was much larger; furthermore Mackenzie had been able to work under much less restrictive conditions (his work never having been designed for publication).* Finally, to make absolutely certain that Foot would produce the goods, his publishers, Her Majesty's Government, retained copyright in his work and made no commitment to publish his text. For agreeing to work in these unpromising circumstances, Foot was paid £5,000 (today's equivalent value would be about £115,000). Dame Irene Ward, who was well informed, made a fuss about this as well.[10]

SOE in France was duly published in 1966 by HMSO, the government printer, but hit an unexpected snag when it provoked a number of libel threats from some of those it was intended to immortalise. Several former SOE agents, including Odette Sansom GC, sued him and the first edition had to be withdrawn. A 'second impression',

---

* It was eventually published in 2000, after its author had died.

containing what HMSO described as 'amendments'*[11] appeared in 1968. This edition became the standard work on the subject and remains so to this day. The author wrote that his intention had been to show that 'the dead deserve honour', and in that he certainly succeeded.

In a slightly eccentric introduction, Foot, who had a finely tuned sense of English social distinctions, stated that most of the women recruited into SOE were 'of good family' and that 'Not unexpectedly the senior staff came from the English ruling class . . .' He added, 'though not on the whole from the highest quarters'.

A detailed account of the schools, universities, regiments and family backgrounds of one senior officer after another occupied a further two pages. Disconcertingly, the list of institutions bears a strong resemblance to the Visitors' Book at Nanteuil. Foot noted that one officer, a 'Major Bodington', had been admitted to Lincoln College, Oxford, but was then 'sent down' (i.e. expelled) after one year. 'One young peer of ancient lineage,' he continued, 'who was killed on the coast of Normandy in 1942' was the exception to SOE's general reliance 'on business and professional circles . . . [rather than] . . . on the landed aristocracy or gentry'. 'Few,' he added, 'came from outside the closed social circle of the pre-war public schools,' and one officer who had not attended a public school did at least belong 'to an impeccable regiment'. Such a social structure, Foot continued, 'provided widely accepted doctrines of thought and behaviour'. (The same confident, and disastrous, assertion had been made, of course, in the case of the Cambridge Spies.)

It comes as a relief when the reader is assured that there was no similar social uniformity among the agents SOE despatched to the front line – or 'the field'.

———

The real value of *SOE in France* lay in the lengthy, and frequently accurate, accounts of individual agents' courageous adventures, and it retains that value today. The first hint of its other, unstated, purpose came in Chapter Three.

———

* In unofficial histories these are normally known as 'corrections'.

At the end of the war Sir Archibald Sinclair revealed in parliament that some young women had been parachuted into France to assist resistance operations.[12] This precipitated a flurry of excited newspaper comment, and since then official revelations have been few indeed. History and journalism, like nature, abhor a vacuum; and in the vacuum of official silence no end of speculation about what might have happened to these girls has grown. The current state of the French and English press is such that some of these women have received a great deal of attention, much of it ill-informed and some of it ill-intentioned, while many others have been ignored. They will receive no special treatment below ... [but] ... a list of all of them who were sent to France on SOE's business will be found, with an indication of their fates.[13]

Foot reached the thorny topic of Henri Déricourt in chronological order and in Chapter Ten. The chapter title is 'A Run of Errors' and it is largely about the fall of PROSPER.

Dealing first with the fact that SOE's air movements officer was also working for the Paris SD, Foot wrote: 'Which side this man was "really" on has been much disputed.' He was 'entangled with' the Gestapo, and 'did what he could to serve both sides at once'. The fact that his Paris flat was next door to that of an *Abwehr* officer 'suggests complicity but cannot directly prove it'. His failure to report on Prosper's troubles in France is judged to be 'little to his credit'.[14] The fact that the Gestapo were waiting for incoming agents received by Déricourt is omitted.[15] The fact that Major Bodington claimed that SOE knew that Déricourt was 'in contact with the Germans and also how and why' is mentioned but left hanging.[16] But while Déricourt – who, even on Foot's partial admission, was clearly betraying SOE agents – is handled objectively (although there was no libel risk as he was known to have died in Laos in 1962)[17] and presented as a bit of a mystery man, the British agents he betrayed are thoroughly discredited and their downfall is presented as very much their own fault.

'Gallant men and women,' Foot wrote, 'had to be found to preach armed resistance, before an armed resistance movement could be got under way; and if they preached it under the Germans' noses in and around Paris, with the negligible security precautions which PROSPER's leaders took, they must expect trouble.'[18]

Foot describes how the leaders of PROSPER disregarded direct orders about limiting their contacts, and said that they had trusted too easily, they had spent too much time socialising with each other and doing so indiscreetly, they had become too tired to make sensible judgements and that some of them had talked too much under interrogation and torture. 'The real wonder,' he summarised, 'is not that Suttill and his friends were caught. But that it took so long for so many Germans to catch them.' Even the fact that Déricourt was lending their correspondence to the SD before flying it on to London is blamed on them for entrusting it to their air movements officer and is produced as further evidence of naivety.[19]

Foot introduces 'Prosper', Major Francis Suttill, as not being 'particular about where he made his contacts . . . Armel Guerne (his 'second in command') . . . first met him . . . at a night club in Montmartre where Suttill and Andrée Borrel were demonstrating Sten guns to an interested mixed audience'.[20] The overall portrait he paints of SOE(F)'s biggest circuit is devastating. By Foot's account it was, by June 1943, a complete shambles. Suttill, Gilbert Norman, the wireless operator, and Andrée Borrel, the courier, were 'an almost inseparable trio' and would meet in Paris 'most evenings over cards'. The source of this information is a second wireless operator, Jack Agazarian,[21] who was supposed to be keeping well clear. Later Foot mentions that Suttill did not get on with Agazarian, sent him home early and suspected him of being careless. Agazarian was unable to respond to any of these comments since he was arrested on a second mission to Paris, and then deported to Flossenbürg concentration camp where he was executed in March 1945.[22]

It was in the chapter on Henri Déricourt that Foot finally made the only reference to the matter that had provoked his entire book, that is the suggestion that PROSPER was deliberately betrayed by the British to the Germans as part of a deception operation. He introduced the subject by revealing the existence of a previously obscure and absurd rumour – which he sourced to 'private information'. 'It is said to be widely believed in France,' he wrote, 'that Suttill's circuit was deliberately betrayed by the British to the Germans; even directly by wireless to the Avenue Foch.'[23] He then rubbished his own novel suggestion (about the direct wireless contact) with an irrelevant reference to a witty remark made by the first Duke of Wellington.

Illogically, having just demolished any idea of a conspiracy, Foot ended his chapter on the PROSPER disaster by reference to the 'justified plea of necessity',[24] and with a comparison that, since it was by his own account irrelevant, reads almost as an admission. He contrasted the loss of the French resisters (that is, the torture, drawn-out suffering and eventual deaths of hundreds of untrained civilian volunteers in concentration camps) with the battlefield losses suffered by the Royal Engineers sent in to clear the D-Day beaches, where 'three-quarters of them were shot down at their work',[*25] and adds that the soldiers' sacrifice had 'received none of the notice devoted to PROSPER – partly perhaps because no women were on the spot'. He further mitigated the fall of PROSPER by comparing it to Arnhem, which he described, in another curious turn of phrase, as 'a larger, splendid disaster'.[26]

Foot rounded off the approved official version of the fall of PROSPER with a confident assertion. 'It is undoubtedly the case,' he wrote, 'that no use was made of SOE's work in France for any purposes of deception, then or later.' In his Note on Sources he had written, more prudently, ' If any papers about major strategic deceptions survive, they have not come my way.' His account remains in print as a work of reference, and his arguments denying any official intention to allow the circuit to be dismantled by the Gestapo as part of a deception operation, have passed unchallenged into many of the best subsequent accounts of SOE.[27]

––––––

In a final dismissal of the drama Foot inserted the following reflection.

The German authorities who gleefully spoke of the PROSPER arrests as 'our finest coup' spoke foolishly. Quantitatively they were right: they pulled in *several hundred earnest men and women who would have given them a great deal more trouble had they stayed at liberty*. But the crowning disaster to French resistance in midsummer 1943 was the arrest of Jean Moulin and his companions at that ill-fated house in Caluire . . . [a loss which] . . . disrupted the whole system for articulating a national uprising of the French people [and was] of far greater consequence for the allied cause.[28]

––––––

* In a subsequent book Foot amended this figure to read '75% casualties' rather than killed (*SOE: 1940–1946*, p. 73).

Major X's letter to me had suggested that there was a connection between the Gestapo operations of 21 June 1943 in Lyons and in the Sologne. The obvious place to look for such a connection is in the records of the Gestapo and in the statements made after the war by former Gestapo agents. Most of the former have been destroyed and many of the latter are naturally regarded as untrustworthy. But at least one objective police report on the Sologne operation has survived. On 6 July 1943, three days after the arms searches began at Chambord and Romorantin, the French police in Blois – as already cited – recorded that the German authorities in the city judged the arrests in the Sologne since the 21 June to be 'the most important discovery of arms and agents to have been made in France since the start of the Occupation'.[29] If a deception operation was in progress, one that was intended to give the OKW the impression that allied landings were imminent, German Intelligence was evidently sniffing at the bait.

PART IV

THE MYSTERY OF CALUIRE

13

Inside 84 Avenue Foch

You see, Maurice, I was never made for this battle. It was beyond my strength. I should have remained 'Multon, from the Poitou' and never become 'Lunel of the Resistance'. But I believe in God . . . and God will be my judge.

The resister – and collaborator – Jean Multon,
writing to his former Resistance commander,
on the eve of his execution for treason in 1946

The repeated success of the German security forces against the Resistance in France in 1943 was not due to a lucky break. It was the result of fifteen months of patient police work that had started in Holland with the capture of a single SOE wireless operator in February or March 1942. The wireless operator who had originally been captured immediately attempted to warn London that he was in enemy hands by omitting his second or 'true' identity check.* This warning was picked up, and then ignored.

In his memoirs, *Between Silk and Cyanide*, Leo Marks, SOE's coding officer, entitled his chapter on this episode 'Criminal Negligence' and Mackenzie described it as 'a debacle'.[1] Marks had an instinct that there was something terribly wrong in Holland and tried to warn the director of SOE(N), Major Blizzard,[2] but he was repeatedly brushed aside. The omission of the true check was just taken by the SOE commanders as

---

* If a wireless operator was captured his captors expected him to omit his identity check. This check, the 'bluff' check, could be surrendered to the Germans and would then be included in the message. But there was a second 'check', which was kept secret, and if this was omitted the warning would be sent anyway.

evidence of understandable carelessness. When other captured agents started sending back deliberate errors Major Blizzard put these down to bad training or garbled signals.[3]

The result was that between March 1942 and May 1943 SOE despatched forty-eight agents to Holland, of whom forty-three were dropped straight into German hands.[4] Forty of those men died, mostly by execution in Mauthausen concentration camp. All 544 containers of stores dropped at the same time to arm the Dutch secret army were also safely received by the Germans. Thanks to this long list of errors, German Military Intelligence (the *Abwehr*) acquired a bank of detailed information about the nature of the agency and its activities. Meanwhile, SOE(N) went ahead with the 'Plan for Holland'. According to this a network of resistance saboteurs was installed across the country and, supplied with 3,000 weapons, 12,000 lbs of high explosive, 800 magnetic mines and 350,000 Dutch florins, in preparation for the hour of liberation. The delivery of these supplies resulted in the loss of 11 RAF aircraft. Meanwhile the reality on the ground was that Holland's national resistance network consisted of just two men, both German. By using captured SOE radio sets the *Abwehr* directed a *Funkspiel*, a 'radio game', and reported back to Baker Street on the activities of a complex and entirely imaginary 'secret army'. At the same time they extracted more and more information from each of the forty-three parachuted agents who were welcomed in turn as soon as their boots touched the ground either by *Oberstleutnant* (Lieutenant Colonel) Giskes or by *Sonderführer* (Special Officer) Hunteman. By the spring of 1943 much of the information the *Abwehr* had acquired in Holland about SOE had been passed to the Gestapo in Paris.

———

Although the Gestapo was widely and correctly regarded as a lawless organisation, its agents were in theory required to operate within the limits of German law. The ultimate purpose of the law was to serve the interests of the Master race and to destroy lesser forms of human life.[5] In 1933 Friedrich Frick, the German Minister of the Interior, ruled that 'Law is what serves the German people. Injustice is what injures it.'[6] The law empowered the secret police to carry out arrests and to impose imprisonment without trial. And their powers were increased because they acted on the general principle that 'the law was the will of the leadership'.

The Gestapo had received one clear expression of the leadership's will in December 1941, when Hitler issued *Nacht und Nebel*. In June 1942 *Reichsführer*-SS Heinrich Himmler issued a further expression of the leadership's will in the form of a direct order legitimising the use of 'the Third Degree'. This was a synonym for torture, which could be used without specific authorisation to elicit information from saboteurs, terrorists, members of resistance movements, Communists and Jehovah's Witnesses.[7] The 'Third Degree' included torture by beating, semi-starvation, solitary confinement, sleep deprivation, suffocation, mutilation and so on. It was supposed to be medically supervised in order to prevent cases of 'accidental' death. (An 'accidental' death was a death that occurred before the maximum amount of information had been obtained.) In Paris senior officers in the Sipo-SD tended to delegate third degree interrogation to specialists, although in Lyons the SS officer in charge, Klaus Barbie, often initiated it personally, or joined in later.

The first PROSPER resister to be brought to the Avenue Foch was Pierre Culioli, who was driven there from Blois, arriving late in the evening on 23 June. He was placed in a cell and left there for several days. Later that night Major Norman and Andrée Borrel were brought in. They had been taken by surprise and neither had resisted arrest. On the other hand, when Francis Suttill was brought in on the following morning, he had already been beaten up, his hotel room having been wrecked in the struggle to detain him. Once the doors of No. 84 closed behind Suttill there are conflicting reports as to the course of events. According to the post-war statement of the Gestapo interpreter, Ernst Vogt, Suttill and Norman were separated and interrogated for forty-eight hours non-stop but were not otherwise mistreated. During that time neither agreed to talk. Another report from a captured resister[8] stated that Suttill was extensively beaten from the time of his arrival. Several accounts agree that after forty-eight hours, on 26 June, both officers were confronted with documents and information previously provided either by the *Abwehr* in Holland or by Henri Déricourt. They were told that it was useless to remain silent since the Sipo-SD knew all about their activities and had a spy in SOE's headquarters in Baker Street. They were shown maps of their landing grounds, dates of their air operations and copies of their personal correspondence, and they were given numerous details about the layout and personnel of the building in Baker Street. Both men were shattered by the discovery that the Gestapo held so much accurate information about SOE.[9]

The officer in charge of the case, Josef Kieffer, then offered the leaders of PROSPER an unusual deal. He said that if they agreed to identify all the members of their network and ordered them to surrender all their arms and explosives, he would guarantee that the resisters would be treated as prisoners of war and their families would not be harmed. This was an old trick, but what made the offer unusual was the suggestion that the deal would be authorised and documented by the RSHA in Berlin, and that a sealed copy of the agreement would be given to 'Prosper'. Again, it is not clear what happened next – there is more conflicting information – but according to a statement made by Kieffer,[10] 'Prosper' himself still refused to cooperate and was sent to Berlin for further interrogation a few days later. Norman, 'who had not the integrity of "Prosper"',[11] did agree to cooperate.[12]

As a radio operator Norman was invaluable to the Paris Gestapo because his capture meant that they could start playing the *Funkspiel* on his captured transmitter, as the *Abwehr* had done with such success in Holland. But on 24 June there was a problem. Kieffer could not start the radio game with Norman's set because his chief radio officer, Dr Josef Goetz, was in Germany on leave as his wife had just had a baby. Once Kieffer realised that he had captured a radio operator with his transmitter, complete with the latest set of crystals newly arrived from London and neatly labelled and 'in clear' (uncoded), he recalled Goetz urgently. The latter arrived back in Paris on 26 June[13] and prepared to set up the game. At first Norman does not appear to have been cooperating, because on 27 June he was still following his orders from London. In the first message sent on his transmitter Norman attempted to warn F section that he was no longer a free man. He did this by sending a signal from Avenue Foch which omitted his second or 'true' check.

What happened next has been described by Leo Marks, F section's coding officer, in *Between Silk and Cyanide*, which is one of the most vivid published accounts of life in SOE. Marks described it as 'the worst breach of security any country section had yet committed'.[14] He recalled that on 27 June, Norman – who was an unusually skilful encoder, and who had never omitted either his bluff or his true checks – sent a message with his true check omitted. Leo Marks was immediately alarmed and started to examine all Norman's previous messages to confirm his conviction that something very unusual had taken place. While he was doing this Colonel Buckmaster, without saying anything to Marks, sent an immediate reply informing Norman that he had forgotten his true check and accusing him of committing 'a serious breach of security which must not, *repeat must not*, be allowed to happen again'. When Norman, who was sitting in Avenue Foch with Kieffer at his elbow, read this message he exploded in anger. And it was then that he apparently agreed to accept 'the pact' and dismantle PROSPER.

From then on, Major Norman became something of a feature at No. 84. At least six members of the network said that they had been confronted by Norman – who usually introduced himself as 'Gilbert' – during their Gestapo interrogations. He had repeatedly urged them to cooperate as the Germans knew everything about their organisation and there was no point in withholding information. A pact had been signed, he assured them, between 'Prosper' personally* and the SD in Berlin. Provided they concealed nothing, there would be no collective punishments and those taken prisoner would not be mistreated but would be held as prisoners of war.

One resister, Germaine Tambour, who had been interrogated in front of Norman, said that he kept on prompting her and filling in details that she was trying to conceal. Norman had been seen outside the Avenue Foch working with the German police on several occasions, at least once in the company of Suttill's courier, Andrée Borrel. He had participated in arrests and had even made the tea during interrogations. The F section agent with whom Norman had parachuted into France, Roger Landes, was certain that he saw Norman in a car with the Gestapo in Bordeaux.

By April 1944 Major Norman's usefulness in No. 84 Avenue Foch was more or less exhausted. He had enjoyed a great deal of freedom and eventually took the opportunity to escape but he was seen and shot by a guard. Shortly afterwards he was deported, limping badly, on a train carrying several of the resisters he had confronted or identified. One of them, Marcel Rousset, an SOE wireless operator who had been identified by Norman after his arrest, said that on the train the major – who was on the way to execution – had 'implored his forgiveness'.[15]

---

*The only evidence of Prosper's agreement was provided by the interpreter, Ernst Vogt, in a post-war interrogation by the French security service (SHD – GR/P/16/364747).

But not every resister arrested and brought into No. 84 followed Major Norman's instructions. What happened to those who continued to protect their weapons and their comrades despite the 'pact' is illustrated by the story of the agent codenamed 'Alexandre'.

———

On the morning of 6 June 1943, Edouard Montfort Wilkinson ('Alexandre') waved goodbye to twelve-year-old Gilles Perrault and set off from the Avenue de l'Observatoire never to be seen again in the Perrault household. He was arrested shortly afterwards in the company of a Frenchwoman who had been a childhood friend and who had appealed to him for help. They met in a café near the Gare de l'Est, and the Gestapo were waiting. On the evening following Wilkinson's failure to reappear, Madame Perrault, fearing the worst, burnt the papers and other belongings he had left behind in her apartment[16] – except for his pyjamas and his toothbrush, which she gave to her elder son. Wilkinson's wife, Yvonne, who was running a boarding house in Angers, took over the leadership of their group. Her lack of training for this task is suggested by her choice of code name, 'Madame Alexandre'.

Four months later, in October, she too was arrested by the Gestapo, but she refused to talk so her interrogator confronted her with 'someone who will put you in the picture'. According to the statement Yvonne Wilkinson gave to French investigators after the war:

A stocky man with brown hair then came into the room and said – 'Madame Alexandre, I am Gilbert. We have all been caught. We have decided to give up our arms. Don't be stubborn and get your comrades shot. An agreement has been reached between the English and the Germans. If the arms are surrendered none of the resisters will be shot. Before your interrogation, you can look through the file on your case and you will see that we have been broken and that there is nothing left to hide.'

'You are frightening me,' I said.

'Madame Alexandre, you must admit everything . . .'. At this moment the Germans came back into the room.

'You have seen Monsieur Gilbert,' they said. 'He has understood that it is impossible to beat us.' Then they gave me a thick file and left me alone again to look through it. The box was marked 'ALEXANDRE – Edouard Montfort Wilkinson, officer in the RAF'.

'In this box [her statement continued] I found a photocopy of all the reports we had sent to Madame Guerne [wife of Suttill's deputy in Paris], all the photographs of the port of Nantes and the ships moored there, our list of contacts with their real names, in short everything we had sent to London by using the Buckmaster air link. When the Germans returned, they said, 'Madame Alexandre, was it perhaps you who typed those reports?' That was true, but I denied it.

Yvonne Wilkinson still refused to say where the arms of the PRIVET circuit were hidden. Her interrogation had started at 9 p.m. and it continued without a break until midday on the following day. She was then taken to the Gare Montparnasse and put on a train to Angers. There she was taken to the prison, stripped and interrogated again (nineteen times in all). Then, still naked, she was confronted with her husband who, after four months of prison and torture, was unrecognisable and unable to walk. He was carried into the room on a stretcher. She was then beaten and questioned in front of her husband, but neither of them would talk. On the following day she was allowed to get dressed and taken to the Gestapo at Nantes for further interrogation. When she still refused to talk she was taken to the hospital in Nantes where she was treated for three weeks until she was well enough to be deported. She returned from Ravensbrück after the war. Her husband, like Major Norman, was deported and hanged (possibly with piano wire rather than a rope, to prolong the ordeal) at Mauthausen in September 1944.

The arms that the Wilkinsons refused to give up were made available to resisters on D-Day.

———

In November 1942, in response to the allied landings that had taken place in Algeria and Morocco, German forces had been deployed south of the demarcation line, inside Vichy France. The distinction between the Occupied and Unoccupied Zones was maintained but became less important and the Gestapo proceeded to set up local units throughout the country. One of the largest of these units was stationed in the city of Lyons, and its headquarters was installed in the Hotel Terminus, the imposing railway hotel in the centre of the city.

The men of the Sipo-SD in Lyons were led by *Obersturmbannführer* (SS Lieutenant Colonel) Dr Werner Knab, who had served for a time on the Eastern Front. As in Paris the service was divided into six *Abteilungen* (sections). *Abt. IV*, the Gestapo, was commanded by SS Lieutenant Klaus Barbie. His number two was Ernst Floreck, who was responsible for anti-Communism and sabotage.[17] In March 1943, only four months after Barbie's arrival, a mistake made by the Resistance offered him a very handsome present.

————

In February of that year, while 'Max' was on his second visit to London, Henri Frenay, the leader of the right-wing movement *Combat*, took advantage of his absence to launch an initiative of his own. Within the Resistance Frenay's initiative became known as *l'Affaire Suisse*.

Using a contact provided by one of his recruits, Pierre Bénouville, Frenay had approached SIS in Berne with a request for direct funding. Bénouville, who was a prominent young journalist of the extreme-right, was also a survivor of the CARTE debacle. He was a pre-war *cagoulard* and an admirer of Marshal Pétain who was untroubled by Vichy's anti-Semitic laws.[18] For a time, he had acted as CARTE's liaison with SIS in Berne.[19] When CARTE collapsed Bénouville remained in contact with SIS, then used his SIS contacts as a means of entry into *Combat*.

At first the response to Frenay's approach was positive, but early in March SIS broke off the discussion. Frenay then forged a link with the newly established OSS (US Intelligence) office in Berne. This was run by Allen Dulles (later to become the first director of the CIA). Dulles was delighted to 'penetrate' the French Resistance, particularly any part of it that was seeking independence from Gaullist control,[20] and he handed over 1 million French francs* as a deposit on a supply of military information from *Combat*.[21] In accepting this money Frenay was clearly attempting to escape from 'Max's' control.

On 10 March 1943 Frenay bolstered his claim for OSS support with a seventeen-page report on the organisation of the Secret Army. This set out the operational plans of the armed resistance, as well as Frenay's analysis of the internal politics of the movement. He included an

---

* FF1,000,000 in 1943 would have been worth approximately £237,000 in 2018.

account of 'Max's' activities over the previous eighteen months, referred to the appointment of General Delestraint, and listed the orders he had received from de Gaulle. Frenay referred to the contacts he had in Switzerland and to the assistance he was receiving from the British and US embassies. He estimated that the Secret Army numbered 105,000 men but complained bitterly about London's policy of encouraging 'armed insurrection'*[22] while at the same time starving his movement of weapons and funds.[23] A copy of Frenay's letter to Allen Dulles was filed in *Combat*'s records in Lyons. But on 13 March, three days after the letter was sent, this archive was seized during a Vichy police operation and passed to Klaus Barbie in Lyons.

———

The Sipo-SD took Frenay's report at face value and were alarmed by the estimate of his organisation's size. It was sent on to Berlin where it became part of a long document, 'Report on the Secret Army in France', compiled by Ernst Kaltenbrunner, the head of the RSHA, which was submitted to Hitler.[24] Berlin's response was to instruct the Sipo-SD in France to concentrate its efforts on dismantling the 'Secret Army', and reinforcements were despatched.[25]

By then Jean Moulin had returned to France on his second mission. He arrived on 20 March, but a month passed before he learnt what Frenay had been up to. 'Max' then summoned leading representatives of the three southern movements to a meeting on 28 April and after a violent confrontation with Frenay accused him of treason and of 'stabbing de Gaulle in the back'.[26] In offering military information to the OSS, Frenay was deliberately undermining any influence de Gaulle's BCRA might have with the combined Chiefs of Staff in London – since the regular supply of accurate military information was by far the most important contribution the Resistance could make to the allied war effort at that time.

---

* In referring to London's calls for 'insurrection', Frenay may have been thinking of early rumblings – through the BBC – of Operation Starkey. Encouraged by these broadcasts the MUR, the coordinating committee of the non-Communist southern Resistance, published 'General directions for the preparation of the armed insurrection' in mid March. This call was echoed on 9 April by the underground edition of the PCF newspaper, *L'Humanité*.

'Max' was supported by the other resistance leaders and also by representatives of the Communist groups. News of the quarrel between 'tribalism' and 'ideology' spread through the Resistance. When Raymond Aubrac, a senior member of *Libération*, heard of Frenay's actions he said that 'the greatest service anyone could render the Resistance at that moment was *the elimination by any necessary means* of a certain number of elements, starting with Henri Frenay' [my emphasis].[27] 'Max' countered Frenay's bid for freedom by arranging for the promised payments by the OSS to be confirmed, but to be diverted from *Combat* to his own account.[28] Frenay's reaction was to continue on his chosen path and, with American support, to separate *Combat* from 'Max's' control. He decided that he should return to London and join Astier de la Vigerie and J.-P. Levy, the leaders of *Libération* and *Franc-Tireur* who – despite their support for 'Max' in *l'Affaire Suisse* – were demanding his recall and the dismissal of Delestraint as head of the Secret Army. The military command was a post that Frenay intended to claim for himself. At first 'Max' opposed Frenay's departure, then he supported it, possibly calculating that once Frenay had left France he would not be allowed to return.

Meanwhile, in the Hotel Terminus, *Abt. IV* was continuing its work.

———

On 12 April 1943 an *Abwehr* agent, Robert Moog, an Alsatian who spoke fluent German and French, who was known to German security police as 'K30', penetrated GILBERT, an anti-Communist resistance network based in Geneva that was controlled by SIS. Moog then followed a courier from Toulouse to Lyons, where he identified a GILBERT letter box in a laundry in the rue Béchevelin. Armed with this information he contacted the Lyons SD and was seconded to the service of Klaus Barbie. Moog set an ambush in the rue Béchevelin and when another courier arrived, Moog shot him dead. He then pocketed his papers – so providing himself with a new false identity.

On 15 May the Gestapo learnt, from a premature announcement in London (in the Gaullist newspaper, *France*), that a 'National Resistance Council' (CNR) was being formed in France. The communiqué gave some details of the CNR's structure.[29] This announcement, made for political reasons[30] and designed to strengthen de Gaulle's position at the head of *la France Combattante*, caused 'fury' in the Foreign Office, which immediately banned the BBC from making any further reference to the existence of the CNR. One US ambassador described it as de Gaulle's latest move towards a post-war 'dictatorship'.[31] The BBC ban, which lasted for several days, was clear evidence of London's opposition to 'Max's' mission.

On 24 May, Barbie acquired another useful new recruit named Jean Multon. Multon was a committed resister from Marseilles who, following his arrest, had been persuaded to abandon the Resistance and take up paid employment with the Gestapo. He had previously worked with a number of resistance leaders in the Unoccupied Zone and he immediately betrayed several of the Marseilles organisation, whose leaders issued a death notice in his favour.

On 26 May in Lyons the Gestapo arrested a woman who owned one of the six letter boxes betrayed earlier in the month; it was in the rue Bouteille and used by René Hardy. Hardy was a railway engineer and a specialist in sabotage who was a senior member of *Combat*. Following her arrest Hardy stopped using that letter box and warned his contacts that it was blown. Despite this warning, one of his colleagues in *Combat*, Henri Aubry, continued to use the letter box in the rue Bouteille for uncoded correspondence. One of the messages left there gave full details of a forthcoming meeting in Paris between René Hardy and the military commander of the Secret Army, General Charles Delestraint.[32]

On 27 May in Paris, Jean Moulin summoned the first meeting of the CNR, this political success having once again been announced in London[33] – in fact it was announced twelve days before the meeting had even taken place. Simultaneously, in Lyons, the Gestapo, which was still monitoring resistance correspondence, became aware that General de Gaulle's delegate to the French Resistance, who was also the chairman of the CNR, went by the codename 'Max'.

The next breakthrough for the Gestapo came on 8 June when Barbie despatched his two new collaborators, 'K30' (Moog) and Jean Multon, to Paris so that they could ambush the following day's meeting between General Delestraint and René Hardy. By chance Hardy (who had never received the summons to meet Delestraint) was booked into a couchette in the same carriage on the night train. Multon and Hardy recognised each other at once, but Hardy, who was going to Paris for urgent personal reasons, decided to continue his journey. The Gestapo then stopped the train at Chalon-sur-Saône and removed Hardy. Multon and

'K30' continued on to Paris where they arrested Delestraint at the meeting place outside the 'La Muette' *métro* station. Delestraint was taken to the Avenue Foch for interrogation.

Meanwhile in Chalon-sur-Saône Barbie had started to interrogate Hardy and had discovered the name and address of his young mistress and her parents – so gaining three hostages. Having acquired that information Barbie released him on 10 June. Hardy disappeared for two days before re-contacting his colleagues in *Combat*. He concealed his arrest and told them that he had jumped off the night train to Paris in order to avoid capture. Nevertheless a rumour circulated within the Lyons Resistance that Hardy had indeed been arrested by the Gestapo. On 15 June, when 'Max' learnt that Hardy was still free and had not been arrested with Delestraint, he warned his staff to avoid any contact with him.[34]

At the same time, faced with the urgent necessity to replace General Delestraint – and aware that the Gestapo were closing in – 'Max' started to assemble representatives of the leading resistance movements for a meeting in Lyons where the appointment could be made. On 19 June he instructed Aubry to find a room where they could meet two days later. The address selected was the house of a doctor who lived in the suburb of Caluire.

14

The House of Doctor Dugoujon

Barbie put his face ten centimetres away from mine. Ten centimetres! And he said, 'You were armed. Why?' It was true. I had a revolver in the drawer of my desk. I said, 'I'm a doctor. My patients pay me in cash.' This amused him. He smiled. He said, 'I know.'

Interview with Dr Frédéric
Dugoujon in Caluire, 1985

The story of Caluire is a mystery that has baffled historians of the French Resistance and all other enquirers for more than seventy-five years, and yet its outlines are not in dispute.

The five men that 'Max' summoned to discuss his proposals for replacing General Delestraint were all leading members of the armed resistance. André Lassagne, of *Libération*, was a secondary school teacher and a veteran of the Spanish Civil War. Raymond Aubrac – also of *Libération* – was a committed Communist and a civil engineer. Captain Henri Aubry, a senior staff officer in the Secret Army, was a member of the right-wing group *Combat*. Bruno Larat was the air movements officer of the BCRA. And Colonel Albert Lacaze, a retired army officer and logistics specialist, was a member of the third southern group, *France d'Abord*.

In the classic arrangement of a resistance meeting, those summoned would be given a coded message with a pick-up point, a time and a description of the liaison agent who would be their guide. They would not speak to the guide, who would lead them on foot or by public transport to a second rendezvous and then disappear. The security agent, the first person who knew the address, would then lead them to the meeting place by a circuitous route. Everyone summoned to the meeting was given a different pick-up point and a different guide. If there was an armed guard around the meeting place it would already have been discreetly deployed.

Unfortunately, André Lassagne, who was in charge of organising the meeting at Caluire, did not follow this procedure. Early on the evening of 19 June he met Aubrac and Henri Aubry to fix the arrangements. They agreed that the meeting would start at 2.15 and that the address was still to be decided. Aubry was never given the address. He was simply told to rendezvous at 1.45 p.m. on Monday at the top of the 'ficelle' – a funicular. He then left the meeting. After the war, when he had returned from Buchenwald, Lassagne stated to an official inquiry that the meeting point he had given Aubry was suitable for either one of the two houses he had in mind. In his statement Lassagne added that he had no need to take the same precautions with Raymond Aubrac. Firstly, he and Aubrac were old friends and senior members of *Libération*. Secondly, both of the two potential meeting places were in the suburb of Caluire and were already known to Aubrac. One was the house of Dr David, a cousin of Aubrac's. The other was the nearby house of Dr Dugoujon, who was an old friend of Lassagne's and well known to Aubrac. Aubrac would immediately have appreciated why Lassagne had selected Aubry's meeting point. Lassagne said that he intended to lunch with Dr Dugoujon on the following day, Sunday, and that he would decide after that lunch which address he would use. He would then telephone Aubrac with the information so that Aubrac could guide 'Max' to the selected house.

On the following morning, Sunday, Aubrac met 'Max' and they discussed strategy for the meeting. Henri Frenay, the leader of *Combat*, who was in London, was known to want the role of military commander of the Secret Army for himself, and 'Max' needed the support of Aubrac and Lassagne of *Libération* to prevent this. This was why he had decided to invite only one representative of *Combat*, Henri Aubry, to the meeting. At some point during their conversation Aubrac must have given 'Max' the time of the meeting and the location of the preliminary rendezvous – the top of the Croix-Paquet funicular – because, vitally, 'Max' did not see Aubrac again before using this rendezvous on the following morning to summon a last-minute addition to the list,

Lieutenant Colonel Emile Schwartzfeld, a radio engineer in the Army reserve and also a member of *France d'Abord*.

Before 'Max' and Aubrac parted, 'Max', characteristically, took an additional precaution. He told Aubrac that they themselves would not be meeting at the top of the funicular. Instead they would have a new preliminary meeting time and place – 1.30 at the No. 7 bus stop outside Perrache railway station, at the opposite end of Lyons. This would give them adequate time to reach the original rendezvous via the bus. Aubrac did not give 'Max' the address of Dr Dugoujon on the Sunday morning because Lassagne had not yet arranged it. Lassagne was to do that after he had lunched with Dugoujon. And that afternoon, following this lunch, Lassagne duly telephoned Aubrac and passed on the confirmed address.[1] He then told two other conspirators, Colonel Lacaze and Bruno Larat.

The first to arrive at the doctor's house on Monday 21 June was Colonel Lacaze, who was on time. Lassagne was next. He had Henri Aubry with him, as expected. But he also had an uninvited guest, another member of Aubry's *Combat* group, none other than René Hardy. Hardy had been ordered by the acting leader of the group, Pierre Bénouville, to gatecrash the meeting in order to back up Henri Aubry. It was strictly against resistance rules to bring anyone to a meeting who had not been invited; but Lassagne failed to bar Hardy from the meeting. Furthermore, when Bénouville did this he knew that Hardy had in all probability been arrested and then released by the Gestapo a few days earlier. He had questioned Hardy about this and had not been reassured by his denials,[2] but still ordered him to attend the meeting.

Bruno Larat was the fifth man to arrive.[3]

These five men then sat in the meeting room for more than forty-five minutes, waiting for the arrival of 'Max', who was to be guided to the house by Raymond Aubrac. Another basic rule of such meetings was that you never waited for longer than ten to fifteen minutes if anyone was late. But this was a critical meeting to decide on the future political and military control of the Secret Army. Aubry and Hardy could not leave the meeting without abandoning *Combat*'s chances of influencing the decision, and Lassagne could not leave while the representatives of *Combat* stayed. The three of them were yoked together by their mutual distrust. The importance of the agenda overruled their common sense.

'Max' and Aubrac, who had inexplicably dawdled on the way to the meeting, arrived at the doctor's house approximately forty-five minutes late and were then shown into the waiting room, apparently by a confused receptionist. For some reason, instead of correcting the mistake and going upstairs, they remained in the wrong room for more than five minutes, at which point the house was raided and everyone inside was arrested.

Those in the waiting room were assumed to be patients, and, with the doctor and his receptionist, were bundled into Gestapo cars and driven away. They included 'Max', Aubrac and Schwartzfeld – who had followed 'Max' and Aubrac into the waiting room. The five men in the meeting room on the first floor were treated as terrorists, beaten up and handcuffed. Since there were not enough handcuffs, one of those arrested, René Hardy, was attached by his wrist to a leather strap which was held by a guard. As he was being led to a car Hardy overpowered his guard, broke away and ran across the square outside the doctor's house. Several shots were fired after him and one appeared to hit him but he carried on running and disappeared over a low wall on the far side of the square.

All those arrested were taken to Barbie's interrogation centre in a building known as the Ecole de Santé Militaire in the Avenue Berthelot. The three resisters who had been arrested in the waiting room, Jean Moulin, Raymond Aubrac and Lieutenant Colonel Schwartzfeld, were at first treated as bona fide patients. On arrival in the Avenue Berthelot they were not made to stand facing the wall but were instead offered chairs. The genuine patients in the doctor's waiting room – all women – and the doctor's receptionist, were soon released.

The three younger men from the upper room, Lassagne, Aubry and Larat, were each suspected of being 'Max' and were subjected to brutal torture under the supervision of Klaus Barbie, the SS officer who had led the raid. Aubry and Lassagne, still handcuffed, were interrogated together. Since they refused to talk, Barbie and one of his assistants started to beat them. While this was going on, as Aubry remembered, 'a very large man with a sinister look about him'[4] came into the room and throwing a bundle of correspondence onto the desk said, in French, '"Max" is among them.' Barbie was jubilant and, in his excitement, redoubled his attacks. Aubry was beaten for three days and marched before a firing squad to face four simulated executions. By then Aubrac, who had been in Gestapo custody before, had been recognised, and this immediately placed the other two male 'patients' in the waiting room – Schwartzfeld and Jean Moulin – under suspicion. Aubrac said that after he was recognised he was severely beaten but not tortured. Eventually, on about 24 June, one of those being interrogated identified 'Max'. After the war Raymond Aubrac suggested that it had probably been Aubry.[5]

Once 'Max' had been identified, André Lassagne, Bruno Larat and Emile Schwartzfeld were transferred to Fresnes Prison near Paris and subsequently deported. Larat and Schwartzfeld died in German camps. Henri Aubry was also transferred to Paris and lodged in Boemelburg's villa at Neuilly for several months. He said that he cooperated extensively with his interrogators and was eventually released on condition that he continued to supply them with information. He made his way to North Africa instead. René Hardy, who had escaped across the square, was caught by French police on the evening of 21 June and transferred to German custody. He had a bullet wound in his arm and was held in a German military hospital from which he escaped, again, on 3 August.[6] Dr Dugoujon was held in Fresnes Prison near Paris for several months before being released. Colonel Lacaze told his interrogators that Lassagne – who was a former student of his from the Military Academy – had invited him to a meeting but that he had had no idea what it was about, and the meeting had not started before it was broken up. Lacaze was the only resister to be arrested on 21 June who had never met 'Max'. He too was released after being held in Fresnes for some months.

Alone among the resisters, Aubrac was not transferred to Fresnes. Instead Barbie kept him in Montluc Prison in Lyons until he eventually escaped in circumstances that made Hardy's get-away look banal.

———

On 24 June, when Barbie realised that the artist 'Jacques Martel' (the cover name 'Max' was using that day), was the man he was looking for, he was taken from his cell to Gestapo headquarters for his first interrogation. He faced that ordeal in the misled belief that allied landings in northern France might well be attempted within the following three months. For the Gestapo, prior knowledge of the date of the landing was the jewel in the crown, one of the most valuable pieces of information that 'Max' believed he possessed.

That evening when he was returned to the prison he was limping and had a bandage round his head. He was taken back to Gestapo HQ on the following morning, and that evening on his return he was unable to walk and was supported by two guards. He was interrogated again on the following day and, according to Barbie and an interpreter, he refused to talk at any time, he banged his head against a wall whenever he could and eventually succeeded in throwing himself over the edge of a stone stairwell. It was probably on 28 June that Barbie telephoned to Paris and reported that 'Max' could no longer be questioned. He was ordered to drive his prisoner to Paris at once. According to Barbie they reached Boemelburg's villa at 2 a.m.; two doctors were waiting to examine him. The interpreter Ernst Misselwitz said that he had to help 'Max', who was semi-conscious, into the house. He heard Boemelburg criticising Barbie for delivering a prisoner in that state.

In the following days several other people saw 'Max', now identified as 'Jean Moulin, a former prefect', in Boemelburg's villa at Neuilly. Heinrich Meiners, another interpreter working for the Gestapo, saw a prisoner with an SS guard. He could scarcely walk, he seemed to be near death and was referred to as 'Moulin'. He had a fixed expression, he was nursing his side and he looked as though he had 'melted' inside his suit which seemed to be too big for him.

Henri Aubry, who had also been transferred to Boemelburg's villa, was taken to see him early in July. Moulin was stretched out on a sofa motionless and appeared to be in a coma. Barbie was there once more, clicking his heels in front of Boemelburg, who was chain-smoking. Later André Lassagne and General Delestraint were taken to see Moulin. Lassagne said that he looked as though he had been very severely tortured and that he was more or less unrecognisable. Only his eyes seemed to be alive, and his head was bandaged. Delestraint was asked if he could confirm Moulin's identity. He replied: 'How do you expect me to recognise a man in that state?'[7]

On 7 July, Jean Moulin, accompanied by a police guard and a nurse, was driven in an ambulance to the Gare de l'Est and put on a night train to Frankfurt. On 8 July, at 2 a.m., a German army doctor, Major Beschke, issued a certificate stating that he had been called to the railway station in Metz where he had confirmed the death of a man identified as 'Jean-Pierre Moulin, prefect, born in Béziers on 20 June 1899', who had died on the train between Paris and Metz, probably as the result of a heart attack. The interpreter Misselwitz stated after the war that he had spoken to the military nurse who had accompanied 'Max' on his last journey. The nurse had told him that the body had been covered with cuts and bruises. The principal organs all showed signs of internal bleeding, and the external marks suggested blows from a club or a boot.[8] So whether or not 'Max' committed suicide, there is no doubt that he had been tortured. Barbie had broken one of the basic rules of the Third Degree – he had failed to prevent 'an accidental death'. The maximum amount of information had not been extracted.

The fact that 'Max's' arrest did not lead to any German units being diverted from the Eastern Front to defend the Atlantic Wall, is further evidence that Jean Moulin told the Gestapo nothing.

———

After the war Klaus Barbie became a notorious figure in France. He was seen as an outstandingly brutal Gestapo officer who had tortured a national hero to death. The French authorities attempted to extradite him from Germany, but he was protected by US Intelligence, which employed him as an anti-Communist specialist at a monthly salary of $1,700.[9] He was nonetheless tried twice, in his absence, by the French courts and sentenced to death for war crimes, in 1952 and 1954. Eventually, having been released by the US military, he fled from Germany to Bolivia where he was tracked down in 1972 by a French lawyer, Serge Klarsfeld – whose Jewish father had died in Auschwitz after being deported from France. In 1983 Barbie was expelled from Bolivia and flown to France to stand trial for a third time.

The third Barbie trial in 1987 attracted worldwide attention and became the occasion for a national psychodrama, a confrontation between the French nation and the fate of more than 78,000 Jews who had been deported to the Nazi death camps with the willing cooperation of the Vichy government. The charges all related to the Gestapo lieutenant's role in deporting Jewish civilians. His mistreatment of resisters was defined as a war crime rather than a 'crime against humanity', and war crimes were prescribed after twenty years under French law. Many resistance veterans found this frustrating, since it appeared to condone the tortures and collective punishments he had inflicted on them. Jean Moulin's name was never mentioned at Barbie's trial, but his ghost was a powerful presence in the city – and in the national memory.

It was the national memory and its ghostly population that had first drawn me to the story of Jean Moulin, and I approached it by following in his footsteps to the doors of the doctor's house in Caluire in 1985. I reached his house by the same route the conspirators had taken forty-two years earlier – the bus, the funicular and the tram. It was 20 July at 3.00 in the afternoon.

———

The grey stone house stood in a square, facing the plane trees, on the heights above the city, overlooking a bend in the river. The chipped paint flaked off its wooden shutters. Ivy crept up its walls and twisted through the spiked railings that sheltered it from the life of the street. Beneath the front steps a cellar door swung on a broken hinge, creaking in the breeze. Inside lived an old man and his housekeeper, locked into the secrets of a past they had shared. When you opened the gate and pulled the bell you entered a different city, a city without children, where everyone was either dead or old. The sun still shone on its walls, the specks still danced in the beams of its deserted alleys. Its floorboards still creaked under the boots of those who crossed them. In the streets around the house, the people of that city were walking once again. The doctor, who was long retired, spent much of his time with those ghosts.

In 1985, as in 1943, the front door was opened by Marguerite, now an old lady, the housekeeper who had shown 'Max' and Aubrac into the wrong room. The doctor introduced her, 'My Marguerite – so faithful, still with me today', and then suggested that we should talk in the room where he had been working when the Gestapo *kommando* broke in on 21 June.[10] Dr Dugoujon sat at his desk with his back to the window. It was a pleasant day, but the curtains were drawn, to keep out the light – or to hide the back of his neck. Sensible to take a few precautions. One never knew when the past would jump out from behind those curtains. One face in particular had returned, smiling at him from the newspapers and the television news. Smiling at him – as before. It was an ordinary-looking face belonging to an ordinary-looking little man. He wore a German uniform in the photographs, but he had spoken good French and he was called by the few people who knew him by a French name – 'Barbié', first name 'Klaus'.

The first surprise the doctor had for me was his attitude to the forthcoming trial. I had supposed that he would be in favour. In fact he was appalled by the prospect. Had the frightening little man been tried after the war, when he could have been suitably punished for the fear he had inflicted and the crimes he had committed, and sentenced to death, the doctor would not have objected. 'But,' he said 'they can't punish him now. He is an old man who is going to tell a lot of lies and go to prison, and die in comfort. He will end up in a prison hospital. He will be cared for by young men who have no idea what he was like.'

After the war Barbie had been smuggled to safety by the Americans. Now some damn fool had found him in the Andes and actually brought him back. Back to the city he terrorised. You could hear his army of ghosts at night, in the streets outside. The people who listened and looked away and said nothing. The people who remembered too much. The city was still full of them.

———

The doctor described the daily routine of life in Lyons in 1943:

> In those days, in the city, people were often hungry. It was alright in the country, they had food. But in the city some people were starving. The butchers were always shut on Tuesday and Wednesday, but if there was no meat they were closed for three weeks at a time. *There were live crows on sale in the food market, for ten francs each.* At least you did not need food coupons to get them. The ration tickets gave us half the average pre-war food allowance.*
>
> The bread ration equalled one quarter of a baguette per person each day. But when the baguette reached the house it was usually half-eaten, because the person who had gone to buy it was so hungry. And everyone accepted that. If you wanted to eat more you went to '*un Bof*' – '*Beurre, Oeufs, Fromage*', the swine who ran the black market. We had to look after ourselves, *Système D* – sort it out yourself, make do and manage. You had to know your way around.
>
> We queued for everything. If something was being sold '*sans tickets*' a queue formed immediately. You did not know what it was for until you reached the head of the queue.

---

* The daily ration was 1,150 calories and 26 grams of protein. Each adult was allowed 3.5 grams of butter and 275 grams of bread a day. Flour and rice were unavailable.

There was very little coal. The Germans took it. So people got cold, and then they fell ill. Hot water was scarce. You had to go to a communal bath house which opened when they had some wood. But there was no soap. There were no leather shoes so people wore wooden clogs. It was dreadful but you didn't live in a state of permanent anxiety – unless you were in the Resistance. Very few people were in the Resistance because very few people are made to be heroes. I was not a hero.

It is true that some of the women slept with a German. What did that matter? It didn't affect the war. Anyway, the Germans were not the worst. The *Milice* were much worse. They did the Gestapo's dirty work for them. They were local people, our neighbours . . . Killers. They stole food, they used threats. They were the scum of the earth.

———

That was how it had been until that Monday afternoon. The doctor continued:

I was working in this room, my consulting room. Just as you see it now. It was about three in the afternoon. Marguerite was showing patients into the waiting room, directly across the hall. If anyone asked for 'the special consultation', she showed them upstairs to the room above this one. I was not in the Resistance. But my friend André had asked if he could use my house for a meeting, so I said yes. I did not know who would be there.

'Max' was late. He arrived with Raymond Samuel who knew the way to this house. Samuel's cousin Fred, Dr. David, was my locum. Max had never been here so Raymond Samuel, who was called 'Aubrac' in the Resistance, showed him the way. They arrived together just before 3 p.m. but they were so late there was a muddle and they went into the waiting room. The German police arrived shortly afterwards.

I was examining a small boy who had his mother with him.[11] Then I heard a crash in the hall. I went out of my room and the first thing I saw was two enormous men, *enormous*, bursting in from the terrace. Then this little man came in, only *'un petit bonhomme'*, but with piercing eyes and swarthy. I understood at once that this was *'le chef'*. We were pushed into my waiting room and told to face the wall. Then they started searching upstairs. They did a lot of damage upstairs, breaking the furniture. They broke the leg off a Henri II table and used it as a club. André was beaten up. Then the men upstairs were handcuffed and taken outside. One of them got away. They tried to put him in the car beside Marguerite, but he punched his guard and ran across the square and jumped over the wall at the end.

In the waiting room we were questioned and searched. Most of the people there were my patients, but there were three who should have been upstairs. One of them I recognised, Raymond Samuel. Another had a *loden* coat and looked like an officer. The third one was a stranger. I could hear what he said when he was questioned. He said he was an artist called 'Jacques Martel'.[12] He showed them a letter addressed to me from a doctor in Nice.[13] Then we were all taken out and pushed into the police cars and driven down to their headquarters in the Ecole de Santé Militaire. It was about 3.30.

I was taken down to the cellars and ordered to stand facing the wall. It was about eleven that night when my turn came, and I was already exhausted in body and mind. Barbie came into my room and made me turn around. He put his face ten centimetres away from mine. *Ten centimetres!* And he said, 'You were armed. Why?' It was true. I had a revolver in the drawer of my desk. I said, 'I'm a doctor. My patients pay me in cash.' This amused him. He smiled. He said, 'I know.' Then he took me out into the corridor. There was a very pretty blonde girl there. He asked her something in German. She looked at me carefully for some time. Then she said, '*Nein*.' I don't know what he asked her, but I was very glad she had not said, '*Ja*.' I never saw Barbie again. My interrogation by the Gestapo took place later in Paris. That man shattered my life but did nothing to me personally. I speak of him without passion, except when I think of what he did to 'Max'.

'There was nothing special about Barbie. Now they say they are going to try him again. Why? The Nazis had men like him all over Europe. There must be fifty other Klauses today, living quite happily in Austria – or Spain, or South America. Nobody would remember him if it were not for what he did to 'Max'. And 'Max' will not be mentioned during the trial! So, what's the point?

And what if it all goes wrong? *What if he changes from the accused into the judge?* That man will be sitting in judgement on the Resistance! He and his lawyer will cover us with dirt. They have started already, raking up the past. They are telling people that my brother was in the *Milice* . . . *Pas commode la vieillesse, monsieur* (Old age is not easy).

'Yes,' said the doctor. 'That was what it was like. It's true that my brother was in the *Milice*. You had to be pretty thick to join them. They got him when the city was liberated, in September 1944. He was seventeen years old. Anyway, the *Milice* had nothing to do with what happened here on 21 June.'

It was 20 July 1985. The Barbie trial was still two years away. But all that the old doctor could see, beyond the drawn curtains, was the summer of '43.

———

Just over a year after the 'Caluire Affair', on 3 September 1944, Lyons was liberated by French and American forces and the settling of scores started immediately. Members of the *Milice* were hunted without mercy.

In the winter of 1944 none of those who had been deported had returned, and awareness of the reality of the death camps and of 'Night and Fog' grew slowly. In December the concentration camp in Alsace, Natzweiler-Struthof, was liberated and 'a gas chamber for killing prisoners' was discovered. Survivors had stories of forced labour in the local quarries and of vivisection being carried out on the prisoners by the camp doctors. A month later Charles Maurras, the dominant intellectual of *Action Française* was given a life sentence – convicted of 'preaching hatred of the Jews and death to the Maquis'. While two and a half million French prisoners were still being held in Germany, Winston Churchill travelled to Paris where, accompanied by General de Gaulle, he was reported to have received 'a delirious welcome'. De Gaulle had spoken of 'our old and brave ally, England . . . that saved the liberty of the world'. Meanwhile in Lyons an office to assist those who were attempting to recover the property of Jewish deportees had been opened. On 2 February 1945 the Lyons newspaper, *Le Progrès*, mentioned the large number of Jews deported to Germany, 'of whom there was no news'.

———

The third trial of Klaus Barbie, the first at which he was present, opened in 1987, but the doctor played no part in it. For six weeks a procession of dignified witnesses, survivors of the Jewish population of Lyons, described their ordeal. There were two public prosecutors, three advocates for the defence, and no fewer than forty other members of the French bar who were there to represent the individuals or associations who were suing the accused for civil damages.

The trial was not really an exercise in the application of justice. Criminal trials are usually based on police enquiries and the examination of witnesses. When a verdict is reached the evidence serves as the raw material of history. But in a curious reversal, the Barbie trial was based on published historical records, which were overwhelmingly in favour of the prosecution. History had long since convicted this SS lieutenant, and once the court had ruled that there were no legal objections to the prosecution the result was a foregone conclusion. If anything, the proceedings resembled a political show trial, with daily briefings for the world's press, photo opportunities and confrontations with witnesses outside the courthouse, and speeches on the sidelines from the Israeli ambassador, who moved around with his own security detachment. The French government justified all this on the grounds that the spectacle was not designed to administer justice but to provide an essential history lesson for the children of France. They needed to know what had been done to Jews, both citizens and aliens, during the war.

After eight weeks Barbie was convicted on seventeen counts of crimes against humanity and sentenced to life imprisonment on each count. Several of the prosecution witnesses spoke of the pleasure Barbie had taken in inflicting physical and mental pain, sometimes on children, sometimes by using his dog. My landlady in Lyons, who had been a little girl during the war, told me that she had often seen him walking this dog in the street. She said that he had generally been in civilian clothes and that the dog was a large '*berger allemand*', an Alsatian. I did not find this story entirely convincing and wondered whether she was writing herself into the transcript of an international event.

If so she was not alone, because on day nine of the hearing a farcical element intruded when the prosecution called its next witness, the director of a New York language school named 'Michel Thomas'.

Mr Thomas, who was Jewish and born in Poland, claimed to have been interrogated by Barbie on 9 February 1943, during a Gestapo raid on the UGIF (*Union Générale des Israelites de France* – a Jewish welfare centre), when eighty-six Jews were arrested and deported. Mr Thomas described himself as both a resister and a veteran of French army special forces and mentioned that he had once escaped from a *French* concentration camp. He said that Barbie had 'a smile like the angel of death' and that he had recently recognised him from a photograph in *Time* magazine that showed an asymmetry in one of his ears. He said that he had first noted this irregularity when they had come face to face at the time of his interrogation in 1943. By his own account, during that confrontation he, Michel Thomas, had outwitted Barbie, who had let him go.

Michel Thomas was the only prosecution witness to be thoroughly discredited as an impostor. Barbie's advocate Jacques Verges destroyed his credibility with one question – 'In 1943 did your Gestapo interrogator fail to notice the slight accent you possess?' Since Thomas had given his evidence in French with a marked New York accent the question caused several members of the jury to smile. It did not help that Mr Thomas appeared to be wearing a toupée. An eyewitness account had been reduced to an ego trip into past suffering – imaginary history. The chief prosecutor later eliminated Thomas's testimony, describing it as 'given in bad faith'.* The national history lesson had gone slightly astray.

Mr Thomas's brief moment of glory in Lyons in 1987 was a rather chilling reminder of the fragility of historical truth. Before his cross-examination his imaginary adventures had been part of the official international record of Nazi crimes.

———

In Fresnes Prison, in the autumn of 1943, Dr Dugoujon had been interrogated by the interpreter Heinrich Meiners. He was freed on 17 January 1944 and returned to his house in Caluire. He lived there, with Marguerite, through the liberation of Lyons, the *épuration*, the post-war treason trials and the long years of peace. He was awarded the *Médaille de la Résistance*, although he himself pointed out that he

---

* Four years before the Barbie trial opened Thomas had told a senior official of the US Department of Justice that he had been tortured for several hours by Barbie. Thomas's numerous wartime fantasies, which included the 'hunting down and arrest of major Nazi war criminals', the 'liberation of Dachau' and the 'identification of 10 million members of the Nazi Party', were eventually exposed in 2001 by the *Los Angeles Times*.

had never been a member of it, and he became a local *notable*, the mayor of Caluire, voted in by the men and women who had confided so many of their problems and secrets to him over the years. Then he was elected to the National Assembly as a member of the CDS, a small group of Christian Democrats opposed to both the Gaullists and the left. He succeeded in remaking his life and served his community honourably and with an easy conscience, until the day a French government commando squad kidnapped 'Klaus Altmann' in Bolivia and flew him back to France.

I returned to Caluire, with my book about Jean Moulin almost complete, in July 1999. The doctor's house was abandoned. Frédéric Dugoujon had long since retired and his home had been empty for three years. On the opposite side of the little square, the square across which Hardy ran so desperately, zigzagging to avoid the Gestapo bullets, there was a new block of flats and I found the doctor's name on one of the doorbells. I had a further list of questions. In particular, I wanted to ask him about the letter carried by 'Jacques Martel'. No one had been able to trace 'the doctor in Nice' who had supposedly written it, and Dr Dugoujon seemed to be the only witness to its existence. Curiously enough, 'the Ghost' had also been interested in the mysterious 'doctor in Nice'. The torn-up fragments in the second envelope I received from him had been speculating about that doctor's letter. Surely Dr Dugoujon must also have wondered about it. What did he think? Was that why 'Max' was in the waiting room? That letter would not have been much use to him if he had been sitting upstairs.

I wanted to ask Dr Dugoujon how well he spoke German,[14] and whether Marguerite was still alive, and whether she had recognised Raymond Samuel when he stepped through the door with 'Max'. How come she had shown them into the waiting room? Madame Samuel, now – as 'Lucie Aubrac' – a national celebrity and official heroine of the Resistance, claimed to have known Marguerite quite well. And Raymond Aubrac recalled speaking to her in Montluc. Without an answer to those two questions – the failure to leave the waiting room, and the Nice doctor's letter – and the possible connection between the two, the story of Caluire seemed as mysterious as ever.

I wanted to ask the doctor about his friend from student days, André Lassagne, who had returned from Flossenbürg with his health broken, an embittered man who died young. What had Lassagne said about the meeting which had overturned both their lives? And what had Lassagne said about Raymond Samuel, or Aubrac, who had escaped deportation, and who claimed not to have known where the meeting was to be held?

I had so many questions for the old doctor. I rang the bell several times but there was no answer, and I never saw him again. He died a few years later at the age of ninety-one in July 2004.

15

A Resistance Legend Is Born

*The courageous activity of Monsieur Aubrac is too well
known to require any further comment.*
BCRA interrogation – 19 February 1944

At 23.30 hours on the night of 8 February 1944 an RAF Hudson of 161
Squadron landed in a field in the Jura to pick up eight passengers. It was
an 'RF' section operation and one of the more chaotic episodes in the
squadron's experience of moonlit landings in occupied territory.

The pick-up was a second attempt, the first having failed four nights
previously because there was no one on the landing ground near
Chalon-sur-Saône. This time the field selected by RF's air movements
officer outside the village of Villevieux was practically waterlogged and
the comparatively heavy aircraft, with its five-man crew, became bogged
down immediately after landing. The pilot, Flying Officer J.R. Affleck,
stopped the engines and appealed for assistance. The passengers waiting
anxiously in the moonlight, together with a local reception committee
who were standing by to unload the cargo, succeeded in manhandling
the plane back to the take-off point, where the cargo was unloaded, the
passengers boarded, and the pilot restarted the engines.

But the Hudson was stuck once again. The tail wheel had sunk into
the mud and by the time this was freed the two main wheels had sunk in
up to the hubs. At this point a number of additional helpers arrived
from the village carrying spades. The Hudson remained attached to the
heavy clay, so oxen and horses were brought up and hitched to the fuse-
lage. Then a German aircraft flew low overhead and the rescue operation had to be interrupted. Two hours passed – instead of the routine
five or six minutes on the ground – but the oxen and horses proved

unequal to the task and the pilot began to make plans to set fire to his aircraft and head for the Pyrenées. A number of resisters then started to remove the Hudson's heavy machine guns, 'in order to lighten it', so they said, and had to be dissuaded. F/O Affleck decided to dig channels in front of the main wheels so that he could taxi onto firmer soil with the engines. This worked and the plane was reloaded, but the second take-off had to be aborted halfway down the runway due to lack of speed. Taxiing back to the start point the Hudson became bogged down for the fourth time. Once again it was freed, and Affleck calculated that he had just time for one final attempt. By now the Hudson was covered with heavy mud and had lost all its aerials, which meant that even if it did get into the air it would be unable to identify itself to British air defence. In order to give the plane the best chance Affleck decided to offload some of the passengers. Among those he bounced was the resister and future neurosurgeon José Aboulker. To remain on board he selected one RAF evader, whose Halifax bomber had crashed in November, and a married couple who were escaping from France with their young son. The man, 'under sentence of death, had been rescued from a police van by his wife and friends . . . He seemed to be a nervous wreck . . . His wife had attacked the Gestapo in the van, tommy gun in hand, when eight months pregnant . . . She just sat there in the mud.'[1]

With three adult passengers and one child, Affleck set off across the field for the third time and just before running out of grass hit a bump that knocked the Hudson into the air. It was 02.05.

F/O Affleck, flying without radio contact, managed to dodge British air defences and landed his Hudson at RAF Tempsford in Bedfordshire without further incident at 06.40. The married couple were called Aubrac. Madame Aubrac, who was now nine months pregnant, gave birth to their second child later that week, and Flying Officer John Affleck was awarded an immediate DSO. Later, looking back on the experience, Affleck recalled that his main concern had been working out how to stop the reception committee from mistakenly damaging the aircraft – when neither he nor any of his crew could speak a word of French.

———

On arrival in England Lucie Aubrac was taken to hospital to have her baby, while her husband, like all escapers from occupied Europe, was detained for debriefing under armed guard at the Royal Patriotic School in south London. His interrogation lasted two days, and he was released on 12 February. Aubrac said afterwards[2] that the British secret services 'knew a great deal' and had '*une documentation énorme*', and that their enquiry was the most detailed he had to face. He was then passed to the BCRA where he must have expected to be questioned even more thoroughly. He should have been of particular interest to the Gaullists since he was the first survivor of the raid on Caluire to reach London. But in the event, he was questioned by French Intelligence only once, and for only one hour, on 19 February, a week after his release.

Almost the first question the French investigator asked Aubrac was, 'Can you describe the role "Didot"(René Hardy) played in the Calluire [*sic*] affair?'[3] Aubrac replied that he had reached the meeting after being given a rendezvous by 'Max'. There had been a delay of half an hour and then they had taken the 33 tram to Caluire. It was on the tram that 'Max' had told him that they were going to 'the house of Dr du Goujon [*sic*]'. There, he and 'Max', with Schwartzfcld, had found themselves in the doctor's waiting room, together with five or six women. The Gestapo arrived 'a quarter of an hour later'.[*] He was held in the house for an hour and never saw 'Didot'. The doctor's maid, who was already sitting in the car when 'Didot' was pushed in beside her, said that he had got away by jostling a German guard and running across the square. She had heard shouting and some gunshots. That was the only information Aubrac had received from an eyewitness of Hardy's escape. But, surprisingly, there is no record in the BCRA report of any interest in the details of his own remarkable escape from Gestapo custody. This report by French Intelligence ended with the comment: 'The courageous activity of Monsieur Aubrac is too well known to require any further comment.'[4]

The interrogator was probably referring to the fact that within days of their arrival the Aubracs had been turned into a Resistance legend. On 24 March Lucie Aubrac's version of her husband's escape was broadcast on the BBC's French service and taken up, with additional details, by the British press.[5] The story of their adventures was eventually published in an American comic strip. Aubrac and his wife had become the instant heroes of 'the Caluire Affair'.

———

---

[*] It was actually about five minutes later.

While historians in England striving to uncover the events of the war were hindered by an official operation to conceal or – in some cases – destroy the evidence, historians in France faced an additional challenge; how to deal with the nation's reluctance to face the truth.

The history of the Occupation became an intrinsic part of French politics and remained so for more than fifty years. The PCF (French Communist Party) was foremost in turning the history of the Resistance into a self-glorifying legend, portraying the party as its dominant component, exaggerating the activities and losses of its armed body, the FTP, and going to great lengths to conceal the secret operations it had mounted under NKVD direction[6] to weaken the patriotic Resistance and undermine the influence of its democratic rivals. Among the exponents of this misleading propaganda was Raymond Samuel, who became known after the war as 'Raymond Aubrac'. In the autumn of 1944, following the liberation of Marseilles, Aubrac was appointed to the all-powerful position of Commissioner of the Republic for that city and its hinterland. For four months he was its mayor, regional prefect, police commissioner and judge. Under his leadership the region degenerated into a state of anarchy. Order was only restored in December after General de Gaulle had dismissed him. Aubrac then emerged as a militant supporter of the PCF, and one of his first initiatives was to lead the campaign demanding the prosecution of René Hardy for the betrayal of Jean Moulin.[7] He had first started to denounce his former comrade to the military prosecutors in Algiers as early as June 1944.[8]

———

There were obvious grounds for suspecting René Hardy of betrayal. There were the rumours already circulating before the meeting that he had been in Gestapo custody, which he had denied. There was the fact that he had infiltrated the meeting in the first place, against all resistance rules. There were the circumstances of his escape – that he had been the only man not to be handcuffed, that he had overpowered his guard with apparent ease, that most of the shots fired at him had missed, that the search for him had been so perfunctory, and that after being recaptured he had escaped from German custody a second time. Lucie Aubrac found all this so suspicious that she organised an attempt to poison Hardy in the German prison hospital where he was held after his recapture. She did this even before she had begun to plot the escape of her husband. Hardy was given no chance to defend himself. Instead, Madame Aubrac, acting on a surprisingly rapid conviction, and hearing that Hardy had a weakness for jam, which was generally unobtainable in the city of Lyons, made a pot of blackberry jam, laced it with cyanide, labelled it for Hardy and delivered it to the hospital gate.*

In 1945 Lucie Aubrac was contacted by Laure Moulin, the sister of Jean Moulin, who was desperately seeking information about the disappearance of her brother, and together with 'Max's' former courier Antoinette Sachs, they started to lobby for the prosecution of René Hardy. A judicial inquiry into Caluire was opened and for the first time the role played in the raid by a French Resistance double agent, Edmée Delettraz, was disclosed. Madame Delettraz had serious problems after the war. She had been an underground courier who had also worked for the Gestapo and she had betrayed a number of her fellow resisters. She needed friends and she urgently needed protection. The Communist lobby working for the conviction of René Hardy could offer both.

The trial, which opened in January 1947, became a national event that drew comparisons with the 'Dreyfus Affair'.[9] In the publicity build-up, the Communist press proclaimed Hardy's guilt on a daily basis and rehearsed the case against him. In court Madame Delettraz, the principal prosecution witness, said that she had been called to Gestapo HQ on the morning of 21 June and introduced to Hardy, who was going to attend an important resistance meeting later that day. She was instructed to wait near his rendezvous and then follow him to the meeting place, before returning to inform the Gestapo of the address. Hardy denied the allegation. And he had strong points in his defence. He had an outstanding record in the military resistance. His closest colleagues still trusted him and could not believe that he was a traitor. And he had an alibi for the time when he was supposed to have met Madame Delettraz with the Gestapo. In a brilliant performance his advocate, Maître Maurice Garçon, denounced the prosecution as a Communist plot and secured his acquittal.

---

* The jam, if it existed, never reached Hardy. Lucie Aubrac subsequently argued that Hardy's failure to eat the jam showed that he was expecting to be poisoned, which – QED – was further evidence of his guilt. History does not relate whether someone else, perhaps the infant child of a hospital porter, was poisoned instead. We have only Lucie Aubrac's word for the existence of the poisoned pot of jam.

But in 1950 a witness to Hardy's arrest on the Lyons-Paris night train on 8 June 1943 unexpectedly came forward. Hardy was tried again and Maître Garçon was called on to give a repeat performance. Asked to explain why he had lied at his first trial about being arrested by Barbie, Hardy claimed, plausibly, that it was because he thought that if other resisters heard he had been taken off the Paris train the night before the arrest of General Delestraint he would be suspected of betraying the general. He argued that if he had been a Gestapo informer Barbie would never have drawn attention to the fact by arranging for him to escape in such a spectacular manner. And he suggested that if his escape was facilitated by the Gestapo it must have been because Barbie wanted to draw attention away from the real traitor – a veiled reference to his principal persecutors, Raymond and Lucie Aubrac.

He was again given the benefit of the doubt, the military judges narrowly failing to reach the required majority. But his reputation had been destroyed, and for the rest of his otherwise obscure and embittered life René Hardy continued to deny[10] what most people believed, that he had betrayed the meeting at Caluire. He died in poverty, after a long illness, in April 1987, less than a month before the start of the Barbie trial.[11]

16

The Trial of Commissioner Aubrac

The Aubracs should remember that they spoke for those who remained silent or who had died for France. They had an absolute duty of truthful accuracy, and that if they refused to give clear answers they betrayed both history and their comrades . . .

Observation of panel of French historians, during discussion with the Aubracs, 1997[1]

The shades of this affair conceal the very depths of infamy.
Charles de Gaulle[2]

Klaus Barbie's arrival in France after being illegally extradited from Bolivia in 1983 brought the grim period of the post-war *épuration* back to life. In 1984 René Hardy published a long summary of the arguments in his favour, which attacked the reputation of the Aubracs. In reply Lucie Aubrac published another volume of her memoirs, *Ils partiront dans l'ivresse*. His book attracted little attention, hers was a resounding success.* Its publication marked the resumption of her career as a legend of the Resistance, rather as Odette Sansom in England had become the legend of SOE thirty years earlier.

In 1997, ten years after the Barbie trial, *Ils partiront dans l'ivresse* became the basis for a popular feature film directed by Claude Berri. The title was *Lucie Aubrac* and the star was Carole Bouquet. In the same year Gérard Chauvy, a Lyons historian who had written several accounts

---

* The English language edition was favourably reviewed by Professor Foot in the *Times Literary Supplement*, 11 June 1993.

of the wartime years without arousing controversy, published *Aubrac Lyon 1943*. In this work Chauvy quoted at length from a document entitled 'The last will and testament of Klaus Barbie', which had been drawn up by Barbie's lawyer, the professional troublemaker Jacques Vergès. Despite the fact that this was not a will, and was therefore a forgery, Chauvy treated it as though it was a valid historical document, arguing that whatever its legal status it gave Barbie's version of events and that it had to be considered with the same objectivity as any other historical document. In this account Barbie claimed that Raymond Aubrac had been one of his agents, and Chauvy insinuated that it was Aubrac who had betrayed the meeting at Caluire.

Nineteen veteran resisters, including Geneviève de Gaulle, defended Aubrac and responded with a public attack on Chauvy and his book, and the Aubracs successfully sued the author for libel, just as Odette had successfully sued Professor Foot. But one leading specialist, Jean Moulin's biographer Daniel Cordier, did not join in this attack. Cordier was an art dealer who had been 'Max's' secretary and radio operator in 1943. He had subsequently published a four-volume biography of Moulin based on the astonishingly detailed, unpublished wartime records he had kept in his possession. Surprisingly Cordier, who was on friendly terms with the Aubracs, not only refused to sign the resisters' public protest. He wrote a newspaper article in which he argued that Chauvy had produced a number of important and previously unpublished documents that raised questions about the Aubracs' account of events and that these questions needed to be answered.

In order to resolve the situation Raymond Aubrac then suggested that he and his wife should hold a round-table discussion with a panel of historians, a sort of latter-day 'jury of honour'. The panel was convened by the newspaper *Libération*, the meeting lasted all day and a transcript of the proceedings was published on 9 July 1997. The eight-person 'jury' selected for the investigation into the Aubracs' resistance record consisted of six specialists in the history of the Occupation, and two former resisters who were personal friends of the Aubracs. Of the six specialist historians,[*] four further identified themselves as personal

---

[*] They were François Bédarida, Jean-Pierre Azema, Henry Rousso, Laurent Douzou, Dominique Veillon and Daniel Cordier.

friends of the Aubracs. Seven of the eight members of the panel were professional academics.

Despite the presence of so many friends on the panel – had it been a real trial the jury would have been described as 'packed' – the meeting was a disaster from the Aubracs' point of view. The historians set out to answer two questions. Had Raymond Aubrac been turned into a collaborator by the Gestapo and so betrayed the meeting at Caluire, as insinuated by Chauvy? And why, over the years, had both Aubracs contradicted themselves so often in their accounts of their wartime activities?

———

The panel quickly decided that there was no evidence that the Aubracs had betrayed the meeting at Caluire and cleared them of any suspicion of treason. But since historians are obliged to seek verifiable facts that stand up to critical examination, their questioning became more and more insistent. And it quickly became clear that Lucie Aubrac was both a bona fide member of the Resistance – and a serial purveyor of invented 'facts'.

On 13 March 1943, a resistance courier called Curtil fell asleep on a train. He woke up, got off at the wrong station and was arrested at a French police control. His papers led the police to an address where they discovered Henri Frenay's report on the command structure of the Secret Army. Among those subsequently arrested was Raymond Aubrac, who was at that time the chief of staff of *Libération*, the largest left-wing resistance organisation apart from the Communist FTP.[*] Aubrac had two cover names: 'François Vallet' and 'Claude Ermelin'. These concealed his resistance field name, 'Raymond Aubrac'.[†] On

———

[*] *Libération* was heavily infiltrated by the Communist 'Front National'. And Aubrac was one of the party's most influential moles.

[†] Aubrac's real name was Raymond Samuel, but since he was Jewish it was vital that this identity should be permanently concealed. Nonetheless, he and his wife lived openly under their correct married name in their house in the Avenue Esquirol in Lyons, and Lucie, who was a history teacher at the girls' lycée in Lyons, was employed there as 'Madame Lucie Samuel'. Until November 1942 Lyons had been in the unoccupied Vichy Zone of France and the established Jewish community of the city had felt relatively safe. The synagogue and the Jewish graveyard were in regular use and the chief rabbi of Lyons continued to carry out his official duties in public, despite the Vichy regime's policy of persecution and growing anti-Semitism. With

being arrested on 15 March, 'François Vallet' claimed to be a black-market dealer in sugar, but the French police did not believe him and identified him as a regional leader of the Resistance.

Since he had been identified as a resister, Aubrac – following an agreement reached by Vichy and the German police – was sent over to the Gestapo, where he was held for twenty-four hours. He said that he was briefly questioned before being returned to the French police, who detained him on remand. After the war Lucie Aubrac claimed that in order to secure Raymond's release she had confronted the *juge d'instruction* (examining magistrate) and threatened him with death, claiming to be a personal emissary of General de Gaulle. In order to validate this improbable story Lucie claimed that she had told the *juge*, who was known to be an energetic enemy of the Resistance, that the BBC would broadcast the message *'Continuez de gravir les pentes'* (Continue to climb the slopes) that evening, that this message was duly broadcast, and that Raymond was promptly released.

It fell to Cordier to point out that no such message had ever been broadcast by the BBC. When Madame Aubrac continued to insist that it had, and advised him to check the list, Cordier replied that he had been through the entire list of BBC broadcasts which was lodged in the *Archives Nationales*, and that no such message existed. In a devastating afterthought he recalled that a similar-sounding message had been broadcast a month or so earlier, but this had been destined for Cordier himself, and had nothing to do with the Aubracs.

Subsequent discussion among the historians suggested that Aubrac had actually been given 'provisional liberty' because his barrister, a resister, had made contact with the Vichy prosecutor who was also sympathetic to the Resistance. Any meeting that might have taken place between Lucie Aubrac and the *juge* would have been irrelevant and might, had it taken place as described, have been seriously counter-productive. For a wife to introduce herself as a personal emissary of General de Gaulle when seeking the release of a husband who was claiming to be a petty tax offender would have been unhelpful to say the

---

the arrival of the Gestapo the Jewish community was at much greater risk. Among those still in the city were Aubrac's parents and his aunts and cousins. His father still maintained 'a blind trust' in Marshal Pétain and refused his son's entreaties to take refuge in Switzerland.

least. The historians thought that the *juge* had probably dismissed Lucie as a fantasist and that the radio message was never broadcast – and that the threat may not even have been made. It was an exchange that left Lucie Aubrac's reputation as a historian and as an eyewitness in shreds.

―――――

Next to be questioned was Raymond. Why, if he had been arrested and identified as a resister had he claimed for more than fifty years to have been identified as 'François Vallet', a petty trader fiddling the black market?

If a resister had passed through the hands of the Gestapo and been released, he was supposed to warn his comrades and then break contact to check that he was not being followed. If he had been identified as a resister the prudent assumption was that he had agreed to work for the Germans in order to gain his release, whether or not he was actually doing so. It was one of the main grounds for suspicion of René Hardy that for many years he had claimed that he had avoided arrest by jumping from a moving train, when in fact the Gestapo had taken him off the train to be interrogated by Klaus Barbie. Aubrac tried to persuade the jury that he had not been identified as a resister, but French police documents proved otherwise. Pressed as to why he had repeatedly claimed to have been identified as a small-time dealer in black-market sugar he had no answer – just an evasive reference to the fact that that had been his alibi when he was arrested. Aubrac's denial placed him in the same category as Hardy. Both had been in Gestapo custody; both lied about it after being released. Hardy apparently told his lie because he was afraid that he would be suspected of the betrayal of General Delestraint. Aubrac had no such excuse. When combined with Lucie Aubrac's account of her reckless (but imaginary) intervention with the *juge d'instruction*, Aubrac's claim gave the clear impression of two people who had quite a lot to hide. The husband was obscuring the fact that he had been identified as a resister and the wife was inventing a story as to why he was released.

Aubrac was then asked if, when he *was* released, he had told his comrades in *Libération* that he had been held by the Gestapo for twenty-four hours? Initially, no answer. But when pressed he stated that everyone in the Resistance had known the real reason for his arrest, including Jean Moulin. He then claimed that that was why he had been summoned to

Caluire, so that Moulin could officially appoint him as military leader for the northern zone, where he would be safer since he was listed as a resister in the southern zone. Cordier did not find this remark very convincing. The idea of sending an identified military leader to Paris – the city where the previous military commander had been arrested – so that he might avoid the Gestapo would have been original to say the least. And, as Cordier pointed out, both the German and the Vichy police had by then abolished the administrative frontier between the two zones. The police in both zones used the same record system. Furthermore, it seemed odd for 'Max' to have chosen as the successor to General Delestraint a man whose fingerprints, photograph and false identities were already in the possession of both the French and German police.

–––––

The session continued after lunch and passed on to the meeting in Caluire. François Bédarida asked Aubrac why he claimed that he had not known the address of the meeting until he was given it by 'Max', when two other resisters clearly remembered that Aubrac had been given the address two days previously? The question was of great importance. If Aubrac had known that Dr Dugoujon had agreed to host the meeting two days before it took place he would have been in a position to betray the address. He remained categorical that he had not known the address until told it by 'Max'. He was not pressed on this by the panel, although it was probably the most significant question he was asked all day. Over the years Aubrac had certainly been consistent in his replies. From his very first interrogation in the Royal Patriotic School he had stated that he did not know the address of the rendezvous until he and 'Max' had boarded the 33 tram at the top of the funicular. This put him in the improbable position of being guided to the house of a personal friend by a man who had never been there, being guided through the familiar public transport system of Caluire by a man who was unfamiliar with that suburb, and being guided to a critical meeting he had helped to organise by a man who had not been involved in planning the logistics of that meeting.[3] Aubrac's argument was that rather than contacting him, Lassagne must have contacted 'Max' to pass on the address after lunching with Dr Dugoujon on the Sunday. This raised a further implausibility. It would have been extremely difficult for Lassagne to contact 'Max' at short notice since nobody knew where

'Max' was, unless he chose to tell them.[4] Resisters did not contact 'Max' when they had something to say. They contacted his secretariat, and then 'Max' contacted them. There would have been no problem for Lassagne, on the other hand, in contacting Aubrac. They were in constant touch. And that is what Lassagne said he had done in a statement he gave to the police on 21 January 1946.[5]

In other words, it seems highly probable that Aubrac untruthfully concealed the fact that for two days he had been one of only two resisters who knew the location of the meeting in Caluire.

———

The third session of the round table was a discussion of the course of events following Aubrac's arrest in Caluire, and in particular the means by which Aubrac's spectacular escape from German custody was arranged. In her post-war memoirs, *Ils partiront dans l'ivresse*, Lucie Aubrac said that while plotting her husband's escape she called on Klaus Barbie twice, on 23 and 28 June 1943, claiming to be an unmarried young lady of good family who was pregnant by 'François Vallet' and who needed to marry him in order to save her reputation. Her purpose was to get Aubrac transferred from Montluc Prison to Gestapo HQ on a previously arranged date. A resistance commando would then attack the prison van on that day, knowing that Aubrac was on board. She said that Barbie threw her out on 28 June, having told her that 'François Vallet', the man who had made her pregnant, was actually called Aubrac and that he was a terrorist who was going to be shot.

Aubrac had attended the meeting in Caluire as 'Claude Ermelin'. But he said that while under arrest at Gestapo headquarters he had been identified as 'François Vallet' by a *Gestapiste* who had questioned him after his previous arrest in March. Since by this time the Gestapo knew that 'François Vallet' was actually Raymond Aubrac, the chief of staff of *Libération*, his importance for the Gestapo would have been clear. Aubrac told the historians that his identification as 'Aubrac' had been made after his second interrogation on 28 June, although at the second Hardy trial in 1950 he said that he had been recognised as Aubrac 'after two or three days' – that is, by 24 June at the latest.[6] Aubrac's new, later, date led to another awkward question. If he was arrested as 'Ermelin' and not identified as 'Vallet' until 28 June, why was it that Lucie Aubrac told Klaus Barbie on 23 June that she had been made pregnant by one of the men arrested at Caluire, a certain 'François Vallet'? She must have known that her husband's cover name on that day was not 'Vallet' but 'Ermelin'.

She told the historians that after Barbie had expelled her from Gestapo headquarters she had raised 350,000 francs (c. £82,935 in 2020) from *Libération*'s funds. She had passed this money to the leader of a resistance commando, the *groupes francs*. She had asked this man, Serge Ravanel, to prepare an attack on the van transporting prisoners from the prison to Gestapo headquarters. Daniel Cordier, presumably working from his own records, reminded her that she had also received 300,000 francs from central resistance funds so that she could bribe Klaus Barbie to keep her husband in Lyons, rather than sending him to Paris with the other resisters. But she flatly denied ever having received this second payment.

On the morning of the attack Serge Ravanel, leader of the commando, happened to have a high temperature from a bullet wound, so Lucie Aubrac said that she led the group herself, although this was not her normal line of work. Asked to confirm the dates of her visits to Gestapo HQ, thirteen in all, she declined to do so, saying that she could only be categoric about three of them. Her book, she said, was not history with a capital 'H', but simply the account of an interesting life. Cordier said that in that case it would have been simpler if she had just described it as fiction and called it a novel.

Lucie Aubrac replied that she was as well qualified as any historian in the room but that she was a teacher not a researcher. That meant she had to embroider her history, to bring it to life. Her life was the life of a pedagogue and a political militant; her work did not consist of tracking down a time, a name or a date. Cordier pointed out that she and her husband had a responsibility towards those who had given up their lives and who would be completely forgotten if survivors did not recall their struggle, and that she had an absolute duty of truthful accuracy. The Aubracs should remember that they spoke for those who remained silent or who had died for France, and that if they multiplied approximations, or contradicted themselves, or refused to give clear answers they betrayed both history and their comrades.

As the discussion developed its tone degenerated. Cordier was the most persistent interrogator. He insisted on the fact that the Aubracs were hiding something. He wondered whether – since the Gestapo had discovered that Aubrac was in the Resistance – Barbie had also uncovered Aubrac's real – Jewish – identity. Had that been so, Barbie could have blackmailed Aubrac by threatening to deport his parents. Aubrac continued to deny that Barbie had ever known that his real name was Samuel. Cordier asked in that case how was it that the Germans had raided the home of 'Raymond and Lucie Samuel' the day after the successful attack on the prison lorry?

Finally, there is something both frustrating and absurd about the Aubracs and the jury of historians. If the Aubracs were telling the truth, why could they not have been persuaded to give a coherent account of events? If they were not telling the truth, why were they allowed to get away with it? They had been the prime movers in destroying the life and honour of René Hardy, in accusing him of concealing the fact that he had been arrested by the Gestapo; and it looked as though they had mounted this persecution to conceal the fact that they had behaved in exactly the same way themselves. The historians said that they were not prosecutors and based their questions on documentary evidence. But most of the documents they cited had been produced during judicial enquiries. And it was a legal process that dealt briskly with another wartime fantasist called Michel Thomas. By the end of the day there seemed to be as many unanswered questions about the 'legendary' Aubracs as there had always been about the 'treacherous' René Hardy.

The published report of the *table ronde* disturbed many who read it. There was a natural sympathy for an elderly couple confronted by a jury of experts demanding answers to questions about the events of fifty years before. In the eyes of their supporters the Aubracs were not diminished. And after Lucie Aubrac died in 2007, a Paris metro station was named in her honour. Jacques Baumel, of *Combat*, was less impressed. Thinking of the achievements and tragic fate of his comrade Berty Albrecht, he found the idea that Lucie Aubrac should have come to 'incarnate the Resistance and symbolise its highest qualities to be "*un peu court*" [short of the truth]'.[7] In 1947 Charles de Gaulle, by then a private citizen reading reports of the first Hardy trial, said that 'the shades of this affair conceal the very depths of infamy'.[8]

In *The Death of Jean Moulin* I had suggested that two resisters were concealing information about Caluire. They were Pierre Bénouville, who sent Hardy to the meeting knowing that Hardy had been arrested and released by the Gestapo, and Raymond Aubrac. But by 21 June 1943 'Max' had many enemies. There was the Gestapo and there was the Vichy police. Within de Gaulle's headquarters some of the senior members of the BCRA had become increasingly critical of 'Max's' growing power. Within the Resistance the leaders of all three principal movements had travelled to England intending to ask for his recall.[9] Meanwhile two of those resistance organisations, *Combat* and *Libération*, were mutually hostile. Frenay, the leader of the former, was regarded by Max and the BCRA as a traitor for seeking secret funding from the OSS.[10] And on 4 June Raymond Aubrac was recorded as saying that 'the greatest service anyone could offer the Resistance just now would be the elimination by any necessary means of Frenay himself'.[11] 'Max' had also fallen out with the Communist FTP, having told them that the time had come to 'click their heels' and follow his instructions. In addition, he had cut off their funding.[12] The Communist 'mole' who was arrested with 'Max', Aubrac, had previously been identified by the Gestapo, had subsequently lied about this, knew where the meeting was to be held, had subsequently denied it, was the only resister not to be sent to Paris en route for deportation, and eventually escaped in sensationally improbable circumstances. Clearly the Communist resistance, like Pierre Bénouville, could be suspected of some responsibility for Caluire.

But the curious thing about the betrayal at Caluire is that it damaged all branches of the Resistance. The loss of 'Max' crippled de Gaulle's authority and undermined his overall control of the movement; the arrest of Aubrac weakened *Libération* and removed one of the best-placed of the Communist Party's moles; the deportation of Lassagne eliminated one of Aubrac's strongest supporters; the arrest of Aubry removed a leading member of *Combat*; the disappearance of Lacaze and Schwartzfeld greatly diminished the influence of *France d'Abord*. If there was a 'traitor', he does not seem to have had much time for any of them.

Which turns one's thoughts back to London – where, in Baker Street, SOE logged the fall of PROSPER as F section's worst disaster of the war, and famously, in the corridors of Broadway, the headquarters of SIS, Colonel Dansey danced a metaphorical jig.[13] According to Professor Mackenzie – as we have seen – there was initially 'a tendency to throw the blame (for Caluire) on SOE through the instrumentality of Déricourt'.[14] And, by chance, it was on the same night that the Aubracs were rescued that Henri Déricourt was picked up for the last time by Lysander from a landing ground east of Tours and flown to London, having been recalled for MI5 interrogation. On arrival he was driven to Baker Street where he was immediately confronted with accusations of his treachery.[15]

And the wider political consequences in the London intelligence world were just as dramatic.

The double setback of PROSPER and Caluire sparked 'a blazing row' within SOE between two sections, F and the Gaullist R/F. An inquiry was opened[16] and this led to the future of SOE being reviewed by the Joint Intelligence Committee and the Allied Chiefs of Staff.[17] In a position paper, SIS took advantage of this opportunity to argue once again – strongly, though unsuccessfully – that SOE should be placed under its own direct control. Professor Foot described Caluire as 'the crowning disaster for the French resistance' since it 'disrupted the whole system for articulating a national uprising'.[18] But there is another way of looking at the event; because every one of Jean Moulin's achievements following his return to France in March 1943 could have been seen by allied policymakers as a problem and a challenge.

At a time when Roosevelt and Churchill were agreed that de Gaulle's power should be limited, his delegate in France had strengthened de Gaulle's position by recruiting the three southern resistance movements to the Gaullist cause. He had then sewn the three movements together into one Secret Army with a common command structure. He had next united the northern and southern resistance groups under his own control. And he had succeeded in welding the military and political arms of the Resistance into one body over which he presided.[19] In London's view all this made the Resistance dangerously vulnerable to penetration and was in direct opposition to allied policy. It also elevated de Gaulle to new heights, since he became the incarnation of the French state, which was precisely the role his political enemies in Washington, London and Vichy had been saying he aspired to play all along. Finally, 'Max' had quarrelled with the Communist resistance and cut off their funds, so threatening the efficiency of that component in the resistance movement that London regarded as the most promising in military terms.* [20]

---

* In January 1943 a Foreign Office memo answered an MI5 query about the arrival of a French Communist resistance delegate in London with, 'We have deliberately encouraged de Gaulle to seek the services of men of all parties from extreme left to extreme right in order to demonstrate the national character of his movement.'

The weakness in Moulin's position was that he was personally indispensable to his achievement. If he was 'eliminated' the whole structure fell to pieces – which is precisely what happened after his arrest. And following his disappearance London took over the tactical direction of the military Resistance. From July 1943 on, the Chiefs of Staff insisted that the Resistance should become decentralised. There were to be no national military delegates, and the organisation of all air movements, communications and military operations was to be devolved to local leaderships. Jean-Louis Crémieux-Brilhac, who was the secretary of the Gaullist propaganda committee, noted[21] that following Caluire, Jean Moulin's centralised military command was replaced by regional military delegates. These officers had their own direct radio links to London. From there they could be directed, following centralised plans, by the allied high command in preparation for D-Day.

And all this was achieved through the treachery of an SIS double agent, a connection that has been consistently overlooked.

PART V

THE SECRET WAR

17

The Remarkable Immunity of Madame Delettraz

> *It is absurd to subordinate a secret service to egalitarian*
> *morality . . .*
>
> Hugh Trevor-Roper, *The Secret World*[1]

Writing about his wartime years in SIS, the historian Hugh Trevor-Roper noted that, apart from the bitter struggle between rival intelligence agencies, there was a further division within the Intelligence Service itself between the 'professionals' and the 'amateurs'. The latter were wartime recruits such as himself. 'A natural distrust divided these two groups,' he wrote. 'The amateurs regarded the Service as existing to help win the war . . . the professionals sometimes regarded the war as a dangerous interruption of the Service.'[2]

Nonetheless, for much of the time, Trevor-Roper's amateurs and professionals worked together harmoniously in the interests of victory. Among the most determined and effective of these officers were the men charged with operating official deception, who worked beneath the umbrella of the LCS (the London Controlling Section). The LCS, as we have seen, had overall control of deception, but it had no executive duties or authority. As one might expect in the world of deception, a number of shadowy organisations were put in place, sprouting discreetly the better to conceal their own and each other's activities. One of them was the 'black propaganda' agency, the PWE (Political Warfare Executive). Another was the Twenty Committee (known as the 'XX' or Double-Cross Committee) which infiltrated the German espionage system in the United Kingdom. And behind these bodies there was another powerful presence that seems to have left no trace of its existence in the official records at all. This was the W board. In the words of

Professor Howard, the W board 'reported to no one, was responsible to no one and operated in total secrecy'.[3] It was initially composed of five men; the three directors of service intelligence and the directors of MI5 and SIS. SOE was not allowed anywhere near it, nor was the PWE, and it seems to have acted beyond the control of the Chiefs of Staff, the War Cabinet and the Supreme Allied Command – presumably reporting to the prime minister alone.

Commenting on its task Professor Howard wrote that the W board would have to do 'some odd things, of the kind that it was the job of Directors of Intelligence to authorise on their own responsibility'. Among the 'odd things' the W board could do was authorising the release of 'items of true information to be released to the enemy through double agents'.[4] Writing twenty years earlier, in 1971, J.C. Masterman, who had been chairman of the Twenty Committee, and thus worked under the nominal authority of the W board, made it clear that the LCS was deliberately kept in the dark about the work of double agents, and that even the W board did not have to approve of acts of sabotage.[5] Furthermore 'the control and running of double agents remained entirely in the hands of . . . two departments (MI5 and SIS).'[6] 'Of necessity,' Masterman added, 'the running of double-cross agents entailed not only the deception of the Germans but often and in many cases the deception of people on our own side.'[7] He continued, 'The basic idea of the deception policy of 1943 . . . was to "contain the maximum enemy forces in Western Europe and the Mediterranean area and thus discourage their transfer to the Russian front . . . The most important of these (operations) was Operation Starkey".'[8] Starkey, as we have seen, included a fictional invasion of northern France in the autumn of 1943. Double agents who had 'released genuine items of information to the enemy', in this case the Gestapo, were involved in the downfall of both 'Prosper' and 'Max'. And both Francis Suttill and Jean Moulin had been given the false impression just before setting off for France in the spring of 1943 that landings later in the year were likely, or at least possible.

In his entertaining reflection about the distinction between intelligence 'professionals' and 'amateurs', Professor Trevor-Roper may have been thinking about the man who was effectively the executive director of SIS, Claude Dansey – a consummate professional who spent much of his wartime service fighting a brisk private war against rival secret agencies. In 1939 Dansey was the most feared figure in the service. He was

ACSS (Assistant Chief of the Secret Service), being promoted in October 1942 to VCSS (Vice-Chief). Trevor-Roper once described him as 'an utter shit, corrupt, incompetent, but with a certain low cunning'.[9] Another wartime intelligence 'amateur' was the junior diplomat Patrick Reilly, later British ambassador in Paris and Moscow, who described Dansey as 'a wicked man', 'a flea in the folds of a diseased dog's ear',[10] and 'the only truly evil man I have ever met'.[11] Thanks to the arrangements set up for the operational control of double agents used for deception, this 'truly evil man' – Colonel Dansey – was a law unto himself. And curiously enough there is a direct line from Colonel Dansey's desk in Broadway to the doorstep of Dr Dugoujon in Caluire.

———

Claude Dansey had originally joined SIS in 1917. He came from a military family. His uncle and one of his cousins had won the Victoria Cross. He left SIS when the First World War ended and went to America. In 1936 – on the run from a US criminal bankruptcy charge following the collapse of his country club – he rejoined SIS and became responsible for the Z organisation.[12] This was a parallel network of secret agents largely funded by business interests, including oil companies. At a time when public funding was pinched it was an invaluable innovation.[13] Dansey ran it as his private empire. He deliberately kept Z isolated and nobody else in SIS knew the identity of his agents. In November 1939[14] SIS acquired a new chief, always known as C. The appointment of Colonel Stewart Menzies DSO, MC was greatly to Dansey's advantage. In the opinion of some observers, the new C deferred to his older deputy, who now had more or less free rein.* During the war, Menzies delegated most operational matters to Dansey, reserving only Enigma decrypts for his own attention.

On the outbreak of war Dansey decided to move the headquarters of Z from Bush House in the Strand in central London, to Switzerland,[15] where he installed Z men in six cities including Berne and Geneva. His explanation for this was plausible – Switzerland was the ideal base for spying on Germany. It was also an ideal listening post for anyone

---

* Stewart Menzies was appointed in November 1939, when the prime minister was Neville Chamberlain. When Chamberlain was succeeded by Dansey's old comrade-in-arms, Winston Churchill, in May 1940, Dansey's influence over Menzies may have increased.

interested in France. Z man Frank Nelson was sent to Berne. In Geneva, Dansey installed Victor Farrell, who had formerly been professor of English at the French military academy of St Cyr. Keith Jeffery's *MI6: The History of the Secret Intelligence Service 1909–1949* – a work in which SIS officers serving overseas are not generally named – records that the SIS station in Geneva already had a three-man staff in 1939 and continued to operate after the arrival of Dansey's Z men in November 1939.[16] And in London, Dansey was assisted by one of the first Zs he had recruited, Lieutenant Commander Kenneth Cohen RN, formerly a torpedo expert. Nelson, Farrell and Cohen all played a significant role in wartime British intelligence operations directed into or against France.

Throughout the war Dansey continued to use his Z men for 'private business'. So, in 1940, when SOE was launched, Dansey decided that since SIS could not close it down he could at least have some control over it. Frank Nelson was recalled from Berne to become the first head of SOE. And Dansey offered him the use of SIS's radio network and its forged document service. Then in 1941, when de Gaulle's BCRA began to complain about the activities and non-cooperation of SOE(F), it was Dansey who suggested[17] that the Gaullists should have their own section within SOE, known as 'RF'. It was clear that the Gaullists needed to cooperate closely with SIS and so Dansey appointed Lieutenant Commander Cohen as the BCRA-SIS liaison officer.*[18] Dansey very generously appointed himself as the overall SIS-SOE liaison officer[19] and thereby secured a desk for his personal use inside Baker Street.

In 1942 and 1943 Dansey maintained his special interest in Switzerland and France and worked at extending the secret networks he had installed in France.[20] What this meant in practice was that all other agencies, including any division of SIS that was outside his own control, were ruthlessly excluded from Switzerland. So Switzerland, 'the obvious danger spot of Europe', as it was described in August 1942 in an MI5 report, became 'a terra incognita' for Section V of SIS.[21]

---

* Colonel Passy, director of the BCRA, liked Dansey very much and got on well with Cohen, whose code name was 'Clam'; but he was sometimes rather confused about the exact role of the British officers he was dealing with. Passy always thought 'Clam' was an RAF wing commander, and since this would have involved Cohen in a promotion as well as a change of service, the naval officer may not have spent too much time correcting him.

In Switzerland, Dansey's unofficial operational base was Geneva, the neutral city on the frontier that had become a honeypot for spies and a centre of intrigue to rival Istanbul. Here Z man Victor Farrell's cover was as British vice-consul.[22] When Dansey learnt that another secret agency, MI9, had been set up to run escape routes for allied fugitives through German-occupied Europe, he offered to cooperate with this as well, and effectively became its operational head. One of the Geneva vice-consul's unpublicised tasks was facilitating the return of fugitive allied POWs. Escape lines across France to Spain had to be set up, and Farrell found the perfect ally in an exiled French intelligence officer, Colonel Georges Groussard. Farrell and Groussard were already acquainted; Groussard had been the commanding officer of the military academy at St Cyr when Farrell, already in SIS, had been working at the college as professor of English. Groussard was 'un personage sulfureux' (had a whiff of sulphur about him); one of the founders in 1936 of the anti-Communist terrorist conspiracy known as La Cagoule, he had been flown to England in June 1941[23] and had made contact with SIS, where he was given the code name 'Eric'. After returning to France he was arrested by the Vichy government but in November 1942 he managed to escape from French police custody and, once in Geneva, in collaboration with Farrell, he set up his own resistance network, codenamed GILBERT.[24] This was effectively an SIS circuit.

Using French citizens and SIS intelligence, Groussard linked up with MI9's 'PAT' line. When this was broken early in 1943 and its Belgian founder, Albert-Marie Guérisse, was arrested, one of its agents managed to escape from the Gestapo in Toulouse and made his way to Geneva where he reported to 'Victor'.[25] About Farrell's most secret tasks historians are necessarily silent but some of those operations would have been dependent on the continuing cooperation of Colonel Groussard.[26]

In all the turmoil about the betrayal of the meeting in the doctor's house at Caluire, and the obvious suspicion aroused by the contradictions and embroideries of Raymond and Lucie Aubrac, the falsifications of René Hardy, and the reckless or suspicious behaviour of Pierre Bénouville, one character has never really been scrutinised as thoroughly as she deserves, and that is the only resister who did *not* deny that she had been working for the Gestapo on that day – Edmée Delettraz.

In 1940 Delettraz, a resident of Geneva, had started to work for Victor

Farrell[27] and she subsequently became a courier for the PAT line. By the time this was broken early in 1943[28] she had been recruited by Groussard, and once inside the GILBERT network she reported to a young French infantry officer, André Devigny, who was Colonel Groussard's second-in-command (and son-in-law). On 16 April 1943 Edmée Delettraz called at the GILBERT letter box at the laundry in the rue Béchevelin in Lyons, where she was arrested by Robert Moog, 'K30', the *Abwehr* officer who had been seconded to the Gestapo. Moog was an accomplished actor who specialised in penetrating the GILBERT network by posing as an agent of SIS – which he called (in English) the 'Intelligence Service'. He searched Delettraz and found that she was carrying compromising papers. He took her to the Ecole de Santé Militaire, the Gestapo headquarters in Lyons, where – despite her commitment to resistance – she agreed, without being mistreated, to become a Gestapo 'double agent'. And on the following day she led her new employers to a rendezvous at Annemasse railway station, near the Swiss border. There they arrested her commander, André Devigny, who three days earlier had shot and killed the head of the Italian secret police in Nice.[29]

Impressed by this proof of her new allegiance, the Gestapo let Delettraz go free, on the understanding that she would report to their Lyons office whenever she was in the city. She then travelled to Geneva and told Colonel Groussard what had happened. Groussard instructed her to continue working for the Gestapo while maintaining contact with him.[30] This arrangement gave Colonel Groussard, and behind him Victor Farrell, a rather dubious double agent inside the Lyons Gestapo. In the course of the next two months Madame Delettraz worked efficiently with Barbie's unit and assisted in the arrest of several resisters.

Groussard had met Jean Moulin in 1941, before the latter's first journey to London. And he had two more recent links with him. The colonel's secretary (and mistress) Suzanne Kohn was the younger sister of Antoinette Sachs, who was one of 'Max's' couriers. Antoinette Sachs, who was not known for discretion, was in frequent touch with her sister. And Groussard was also in regular contact with Pierre Bénouville. Bénouville had called on the colonel shortly after his arrival in Geneva.[31] The two men had known each other since 1940[32] and both had contacts with SIS in Switzerland.[33]

Dansey took a professional interest in the internal political warfare of the Resistance – perhaps reminiscent for him of life in his native

Whitehall – and it was his duty to do so. Through his secret networks he could follow the bitter political struggle being waged for the future of France. He could keep tracks on Frenay and Bénouville through Victor Farrell's listening post in Geneva, and he could catch glimpses of 'Max' through Commander Cohen ('Clam') and Colonel Passy in London. And SIS continued to monitor all BCRA radio traffic.[34] Colonel Dansey, in London, would have had a ringside seat for '*l'Affaire Suisse*'.[35]

—

Meanwhile in the region of Lyons, throughout the spring and early summer of 1943, security police, assisted by their new recruit, continued their patient work. On 7 May Edmée Delettraz was present when the Gestapo arrested a resistance courier in Lyons who, without being harmed, supplied them with details of six letter boxes used by senior resistance leaders including Jean Moulin, Henri Aubry and René Hardy. Thenceforth these letter boxes were monitored by Barbie's staff; the correspondence was removed, photographed and replaced. By this time Delettraz had become the mistress of Robert Moog and on 28 May she led Klaus Barbie to the hotel in Mâcon, where he hoped to find Henri Frenay, the head of *Combat*.

While waiting for confirmation that he had a place on an early Lysander – the June moon lasted from the twelfth to the twenty-fourth – Frenay, with Berty Albrecht, his secretary, had taken refuge in the house of some friends who lived at Cluny, near Mâcon. Frenay had a letter box in the Hotel de Bourgogne in Mâcon. The Gestapo discovered this and used it to fix a meeting between Edmée Delettraz and Berty Albrecht. Madame Albrecht knew Delettraz and trusted her. The aim of the operation was to arrest Frenay. Once Delettrraz had identified Madame Albrecht, who was waiting in the hotel lobby, the police arrested her, beat her up in the street and found a note in her handbag containing an address in Cluny. The *kommando*, staffed by at least one Frenchman, called at Cluny that afternoon, but the leader of *Combat* was not there. He had just moved to Lyons, where he was staying in the empty apartment of Pierre Bénouville.* Berty Albrecht was transferred

---

* Bénouville was not at home; he was smuggling Berty Albrecht's teenage daughter into Switzerland.

to Fresnes Prison, where she died, probably from strangulation, within days of her arrival. She was buried in the prison cemetery on 7 June, while Frenay was still trying to discover her whereabouts.

In Geneva, Colonel Groussard took no steps – despite the loss of his son-in-law and the near arrest of the head of *Combat* – to terminate Edmée Delettraz's arrangements with the Lyons Gestapo.

———

161 Squadron conducted eight pick-up operations in France in June 1943 and Henri Frenay was on the second one out, Operation 'Knuckleduster', on 16 June. Arriving on the incoming flight was Claude Serreulles, formerly de Gaulle's aide-de-camp, now appointed as number two to 'Max'. He had been waiting for a passage to France since February,[36] but had been delayed, possibly by F section.[37] His arrival seemed to indicate that London was finally supporting de Gaulle's attempts to tighten his grip on the Resistance. The reception was organised in a field near Mâcon by RF's chief of air movements, Bruno Larat. It was to be Larat's last operation. Five days later he too would be arrested at Caluire.

At least three of the RAF's eight June operations were for SIS, three were for F and only one for RF. Frenay later complained that on arrival in London he had been greeted as 'an object of suspicion' rather than a friend and ally.[38] By the time his written denunciation of 'Max' and General Delestraint had reached the BCRA, Delestraint was on his way to Natzweiler and 'Max' was in a semi-comatose state in the custody of the Lyons Gestapo. Astier de la Vigerie and J.-P. Levy, the leaders of *Libération* and *Franc-Tireur*, eventually flew back to France on 24 July. Frenay, leader of the largest armed group in the Resistance, was never allowed to return.

———

On the morning of 21 June, Delettraz was summoned from the bed of 'K30' to the Hotel Terminus, another Gestapo office, and told that later that morning she was going to be introduced to 'a Frenchman who now understands'. He was referred to as 'Didot' (the Resistance code name of René Hardy). According to Delettraz, her task was to follow him to an address where he would be joining a resistance meeting that afternoon. She was then allowed to leave the Gestapo building and she said that before returning to be introduced to 'Didot' she had tried to warn those organising the Resistance meeting. She contacted two other resistance cells, one of them in the Lyons gendarmerie. But her warnings were too vague to be of use. So Delettraz duly followed 'Didot' up the funicular to his meeting point with Henri Aubry, and onto the 33 tram to the Place Castellane, where she watched him pass through Dr Dugoujon's front door. Then she returned to the rendezvous with Barbie and was picked up in a Gestapo car that she directed to the doctor's house. On the following morning she reported what had happened to her Geneva contact who passed her report on to Groussard,[39] and in due course he passed this account back to London.

After the war Delettraz's report, expertly redrafted by a PCF working party,[40] became the basis of the prosecution against René Hardy. And before she went into the witness box as the principal prosecution witness in Hardy's trial, she was coached by Antoinette Sachs.[41]

Despite the careful preparations and coaching, Madame Delettraz did not enjoy her days in court giving evidence against Hardy. His counsel, Maître Garçon, mounted a violent attack on her credibility and denounced her as the real traitor. The president of the court was outraged by her evidence and threatened at one point to order her immediate arrest on a charge of treason.[42] When Maître Garçon asked why she had been working for the Gestapo she stuck to her story, that she had been tricked into it and that she had promptly reported the fact to her superior officer in Geneva, Colonel Groussard. It was Groussard who had told her to continue working with the Gestapo as a double agent. After the war Colonel Groussard confirmed this. And Edmée Delettraz was never arrested, questioned or prosecuted. But a government prosecutor told Antoinette Sachs after Hardy's first acquittal that had he been found guilty both Edmée Delettraz and Colonel Groussard would have been arrested and charged with betraying Caluire.[43] This may explain why at Hardy's second trial the list of defence witnesses included a man only identified as from 'the Intelligence Service'.

In the years that followed the second Hardy trial his acquittal (and presumed guilt) became part of the French Communist Party's Cold War mythology. The political storm, which was reignited by the Communists whenever an opportunity occurred,[44] prevented any further light being thrown on the events of 21 June in Caluire.

But one of those personally connected to the Caluire affair did not let the matter drop. Mireille Albrecht, the girl who was being smuggled over the Swiss border on the day her mother was arrested in May 1943, grew up. And in 1986, one year before the Barbie trial, she decided to trace and confront Madame Delettraz, the woman who had led the Gestapo to the rendezvous in Mâcon with Berty Albrecht. During their meeting Mireille Albrecht was struck by the arrogant self-confidence of the older woman. And she concluded that Edmée Delettraz had played a far more important role in the GILBERT network than she had previously described.[45] She had not just been a courier. She had been one of the principal organisers of the network in France, and she had been protected from prosecution after the war by Colonel Groussard and his allies in British Intelligence. At the conclusion of their three-hour interview, when Edmée Delettraz realised that Mireille Albrecht had worked this out, she laughed in her face.

18

Setting History Ablaze!

Unless he or she is particularly ingenuous (or particularly arrogant)
the historian does not claim to attain absolute truth . . .
Javier Cercas, *The Impostor*[1]

If anything is perfectly clear from the official history of deception in the Second World War it is that deception is a continuing process and most of its triumphs and disasters will never be revealed. In the words of Dick White, quoted as the epigraph to this book, 'If the evidence can be hidden and the secrets kept, then history will record an inaccurate version.'

Churchill's notorious 'bodyguard of lies' – the means by which truth is protected in wartime – can be stood down in peacetime and replaced with a wall of silence. Barricaded behind that wall, deception shelters. The ongoing deception operation, the cover-up, has to start with the destruction of the evidence, and in the case of SOE this commenced with the fire that broke out in SOE's records department on 17 January 1946. The official line has always been that this was an accident. This is how Leo Marks, SOE's coding officer, described the event.

> Mindful perhaps of Churchill's injunction to 'Set Europe Ablaze!' parts of (the records department) went up in flames, and though 'immediate action was taken' to put them out, many important records were destroyed . . . I'd worked too long for SOE to believe it was accidental.[2]

Marks was transferred to SIS, where he did not stay long. He took SOE's wireless transmission records with him and handed them over for safe-keeping. He wrote that handing SOE's records over to SIS was 'like burying Hitler in Westminster Abbey' and noted that shortly after the handover 90 per cent of his W/T records had been destroyed. Among the losses were a 300-page report he had written on ciphering problems, and his detailed account of SOE's Dutch disaster.

In *The Secret History of SOE* W.J.M. Mackenzie explained that his narrative was 'based primarily on the departmental papers of SOE . . . [although] . . . after the dissolution of the department many of these were destroyed as unimportant'.[3] He added, 'Practically every section of SOE . . . produced a narrative of its work . . . they are all in a sense primary sources', and wrote that the agency's War Diary had been 'invaluable for reference'. Leo Marks had something to say on this subject as well. Of the War Diary, known in his department as the 'war diarrhoea', he wrote, 'Certain people in SOE, myself in particular, had wilfully misled it.' The officer who compiled it was 'the most lied-to officer in Baker Street, with the possible exception of the head of Finance'. Marks and other colleagues were simply too busy to bother with the War Diary – 'our preparations for D-Day had to be given slightly greater priority' – so they filled it with fabrications or shortened it with omissions. Marks was amused by the fact that these 'misrepresentations to the War Diary . . . would one day [be taken] . . . literally by certain professional historians in their erudite treatises'. Since he was writing two years before the publication of Mackenzie's *Secret History* this must have been a reference to Foot's *SOE in France*, which frequently quoted the War Diary.

The falsification of the record by straightforward destruction is a rather crude procedure, so now and again, as a distraction, an 'honourable' activity can be revealed. In the context of strategic deception, this happened in 1954 with the authorised publication of *The Man Who Never Was*, written by the deception officer in charge, Ewen Montagu. It was the true story of a corpse, disguised as a 'Royal Marine officer, Major Martin', whose body was washed up on a Spanish beach with a briefcase chained to his wrist. The briefcase contained top-secret information about an imaginary allied invasion of Greece. The major's body was released off the Spanish coast to drift ashore, the information – as intended – was passed by the Franco government to German Intelligence, and the 1st Panzer Division was sent on a fool's errand to defend Greece.[4] The operation was a XX Committee triumph and a model of deception. No one was hurt; indeed thousands of lives may have been saved.

But it is not always possible for such victories to be won so cheaply. And the dirty allegation that Professor Foot was hired to put to rest was that in the interests of strategic deception the British authorities had 'sold' a French Resistance network run by SOE to the Gestapo, and that as a result several hundred[*5] rank and file members of the Resistance had been deported and tortured or shot. This betrayal was supposedly perpetrated as part of a deception operation to mislead the German General Staff into the conviction that allied landings in northern France were imminent in the summer of 1943. This conviction would pin German divisions to the 'Atlantic Wall' and prevent them from being deployed in Italy or on the Eastern Front. The existence of the deception operation, Starkey, has been confirmed. That the PROSPER network was used as part of it has always been denied. But the allegations persisted, so where neither destruction nor distraction served, a third method had to be deployed, 'the cover-up'.

———

In his introduction to *SOE in France*, published in 1966, Professor Foot referred to the 'Starkey-PROSPER' connection as the 'conspiracy' theory and wrote, 'It is undoubtedly the case that no use was made of SOE's work in France for any purposes of deception then [*i.e. June 1943*] or later: no one trusted the agents enough for such delicate tasks.'[6] Foot wrote this even though he had been allowed to read W.J.M. Mackenzie's unpublished *The Secret History of SOE*, which stated[7] that 'SOE possessed unique facilities for deception: it could use its own men . . . as unconscious and convincing agents . . . But these opportunities were impaired by the danger of deceiving the Resistance as well as the Germans . . . *SOE therefore took no more than a subsidiary part [in] "Operation Starkey"* [my emphasis]. In other words Professor Foot must have known that Operation Starkey did involve SOE's operations in France and therefore provided some factual basis for the 'conspiracy' theory he had been hired to ridicule. He must also have understood that the reliability of SOE agents was irrelevant to the effectiveness of a deception operation, since they would not have been asked to operate the deception but would probably have been among those deceived. In his 'Notes on Sources' Foot further stated that he had seen 'no files on major strategic

---

* A precise figure is elusive. Some French estimates are as high as 1,500.

deceptions', making his confident contradiction of Professor Mackenzie, who had seen many more files than he had, even more mysterious.

When in 1958 Elizabeth Nicholas and J.O. Fuller, alerted by French suspicions, began to publish their barrage of awkward questions about SOE(F)'s performance in the summer of 1943, the official line was that defended by Professor Foot – SOE was never used for deception operations. At this stage a great deal of information about the war was still secret. The existence and activities of the GCCS (Government Code and Cypher School) at Bletchley, the XX (Twenty or Double-Cross) Committee and the LCS (London Controlling Section) remained top secret. The Official Secrets Act and the 'D' Notice system prevented the publication of any information about MI5 or SIS. The existence of SOE could be admitted since it had been abolished, but none of its records were open for inspection. This was the obscure stage on which Foot set to work.

Professor Foot's main argument against the suggestion that there was anything sinister in the breaking of PROSPER was – as we have seen – the chaotic state that Suttill had allowed his network to fall into by June 1943. 'The real wonder is not that Suttill and his friends were caught,' Foot wrote, 'but that it took so long for so many Germans to catch them.'[8] Much of the detailed evidence for this chaotic state of affairs was provided by one surviving member of the circuit, Armel Guerne. Guerne was an untrained local recruit who spoke fluent German. He was a Swiss national and a poet and translator who claimed, after the war, that Suttill had appointed him as deputy leader of PROSPER.

On 4 May 1944, one month before D-Day, MI5 sent a signal to three sections of SOE requiring assistance in the arrest of Armel Guerne, who was reported to be in France, having escaped from German custody, and who was required in England 'urgently for operational interrogation of the utmost importance'.[9] He was found in Spain already seeking passage to England, and was returned to London in secret[10] where his interrogation started on 14 May. Early on in the process he claimed to be having 'memory blanks' which his interrogator did not find very convincing.

A month later the British officers interrogating Guerne in London decided that the account he had given of his escape from German custody and his subsequent journey to England amounted to 'a carefully concocted cover story'. Furthermore, he had 'told a tissue of lies' and

MI5 considered that he had 'some pretty discreditable things to hide' in relation to the fall of PROSPER.*

Some of Guerne's statements had been deliberately misleading. It was Guerne who circulated the story about Suttill demonstrating the operation of a Sten gun in a Parisian nightclub.[11] Foot accepted this tale as fact, although it was he who added the detail about 'an interested mixed audience'.[12] This story surely demanded further investigation, and in fact Guerne's anecdote is nonsense. The club in question was not a nightclub, it was *Le Hot Club de France*, a jazz club in the rue Chaptal. It had been closed since 1940. There was a large room behind the deserted club with a separate entrance which Suttill used as a store. Occasional arms training took place in this room, which was hidden from the street.[13] There was no 'interested mixed audience', just the instructors and the Resistance trainees. Since Guerne claims to have been present he must have invented this story. The true nature of *Le Hot Club de France* was described in several French publications. Nonetheless, the fictional version survived into the French edition of Foot's book, published in 2008.

During his first interrogation[14] (which lasted from 14 to 20 May) Guerne said that he had first met 'Prosper' in this non-existent nightclub during this non-existent demonstration. The fact that Guerne had invented the occasion of his first meeting with the leader of a circuit that was subsequently betrayed would lead a suspicious mind to wonder what he was trying to conceal. Could Guerne's introduction have been arranged? Because Guerne did not bump into Suttill while the leader of PROSPER was 'stripping a Sten gun in a Montmartre night club'. As MI5 very quickly discovered,[15] he was introduced to 'Prosper' by Germaine Tambour, whose resistance identity and address had been known to the Gestapo since November 1942.[16] They were both members of CARTE. It is therefore entirely possible that it was the SD who arranged Guerne's original meeting with 'Prosper'. In which case Suttill's circuit was penetrated from the moment of his arrival in France.

---

* Foot made the original suggestion that these suspicions were aroused because MI5 had forgotten that Guerne was a poet and so did not express himself 'prosaically'. He next suggested, based on 'private information', that Guerne only appeared to be 'holding something back' because he did not want to disclose what he knew about the *Funkspiel* to MI5 and was unable to get through to SOE (Foot, *SOE in France*, p. 321). Since Guerne's MI5 interrogations lasted from May 1944 into August 1945, three months after the German surrender (TNA – HS9/631/5), this too seems improbable.

In another of Guerne's improbable stories, when 'Prosper' returned to France in May he informed his French colleagues that if the landings did not take place soon he intended to blackmail London into starting them by calling out the entire French Resistance in a premature insurrection. Foot[17] ridiculed this '*canard*' – but failed to point out that it was Guerne who had been spreading it. For a historian the interesting question, surely, should have been: 'Why was Guerne repeatedly inventing or embroidering stories that gave the impression that 'Prosper' was careless and irrational?'

––––––

After the war, Guerne was suspected of treachery by both the British and French authorities. He had been the last person to see Major Norman and Andrée Borrel before they were arrested. They had dined with him in his house that evening and could have been followed from there to the Boulevard Lannes where they were overpowered and taken into custody. Foot mentioned this link[18] in passing but did not mention another reason for being wary of Guerne. Because Guerne also knew that if the Gestapo wanted to arrest Norman they had to act quickly. Norman was about to be sent home on leave. Suttill had recognised that his number two was exhausted[19] and it was Guerne who had been instructed to organise the British officer's departure by Hudson from a field near Angers. Until then Guerne, who knew all eleven of the locations Norman used for transmitting, and also knew where he kept his wireless transmitters, was supposed to be finding him a convenient safe house.[20]

And it was not just MI5 that was suspicious of Guerne. Several other resisters were convinced that he had been involved in the arrest of Norman and Borrel, and the first SOE analysis, submitted to Buckmaster on 5 August 1943 by Miss Hudson and Miss Torr, argued that if Major Norman was a prisoner and if someone had his plans and was transmitting on one of his sets (which was the actual situation) then the most plausible conclusion was that 'Gaspard' (Guerne) was the traitor.[21] They were responding to a report received at the end of July from France Antelme, organiser of a different circuit. Antelme was also convinced that a note supposedly sent by 'Prosper' to a Normandy resister Georges Darling on 26 June, instructing him to surrender his arms to the German authorities,[22] was actually written by Armel Guerne. This was important as the note sent to Georges

Darling was the only direct evidence that 'Prosper' as well as Norman had agreed to cooperate with SS *Sturmbannführer* Josef Kieffer.*

Guerne was arrested by the Gestapo on 1 July.[23] They did not have to look too hard. He was lunching with his wife at a black-market restaurant in the rue Pergolèse, 300 metres from 82 Avenue Foch, just down the road from Déricourt's apartment. His wife was deported to Ravensbrück. Guerne himself was not questioned with much vigour in the Avenue Foch but nonetheless, urged on by Major Norman, he gave away several sub-circuits and arms dumps. He said that he was eventually loaded onto a deportation convoy from which he claimed to have escaped by cutting his way out of the heavily guarded train. Guerne's MI5 interrogator was not impressed by this anecdote. Under close questioning Guerne tended to become more inventive. He frequently said that he could not remember. He then explained his poor memory by his expert 'knowledge of psychology' which had enabled him within sixteen days of his arrest in Paris to hypnotise himself, and so forget everything he knew about PROSPER.[24] On 1 June 1944 – four days before D-Day – MI5 concluded that Guerne seemed to be lying on four points and that he should be 'held for further investigation'. Even Buckmaster regarded him as a 'self-confessed double agent' and he was in fact held in custody for another twelve months. In August 1945 Vera Atkins, F section's intelligence officer, noted that 'If Prosper's good faith is not in doubt, Guerne's must be'.[25] But on 14 May 1946, the Honourable Neville Lytton, identifying himself as 'a former officer in the Intelligence Service' (that is, SIS), wrote to tell him that, having been sworn to secrecy, he had been authorised to assure Guerne that he faced no further problems in England. The letter, which also advised him not to return to France, was sent to an address in Chelsea. From there it was forwarded to an address in Montparnasse. The warning came too late. On 26 February the *Deuxième Tribunal Militaire de Paris* had opened an investigation into Guerne on charges of endangering the security of the state, and Neville Lytton's letter ended up in the prosecution dossier.[26]

On 19 May 1947 the *Commissaire du Gouvernement de Cour de Justice de la Seine* [the government prosecutor in Paris], who was investigating Guerne,

---

* Guerne, incidentally, also claimed to have organised the failed attempt to rescue 'Jacqueline' from the hospital in Blois in June 1943. This was certainly untrue, although it was not picked up by MI5 at the time.

wrote to his opposite number in Orléans with an urgent enquiry: 'Were charges pending against Pierre Culioli, accused by "the German woman Mona Reimeringer"* of responsibility for the decimation of the French section and PROSPER in June 1943?' In France the prosecutions of Guerne, Culioli and Déricourt were linked. They were all part of the search to discover who had betrayed the resisters of the Sologne. And British Intelligence played an influential background role in all three cases. On 23 June 1947, the French authorities, having been assured that Culioli's prosecution could go ahead, dropped the charges against Guerne.

The last in the series of trials involving the Sologne Resistance was the second attempt to convict Pierre Culioli (this time on the combined evidence of a female Gestapo agent Mona Reimeringer and the SOE agent Raymond Flower). The attempt failed when Culioli was acquitted in March 1949. Armel Guerne gave evidence for the defence at both Culioli trials, but in the second trial he was allowed to give his testimony in camera. Curiously it was the prosecutor who requested this arrangement, even though Guerne was a witness for the defence. Whatever the reason, one can be confident that Guerne's testimony was different from the version he had given earlier in open court.[27] Guerne was certainly capable of some remarkably imaginative statements. During his original MI5 interrogation in 1944 he had invented a highly inaccurate account of the German ambush that trapped Pierre Culioli and 'Jacqueline' and then suggested that they could have been arrested because they had been betrayed by 'one of their own'. He justified this original suggestion by disclosing that 'Pierre has a foul temper and had not been making things easy for Prosper lately'.[28]

———

Leaving aside Foot's undue reliance on a suspicious character like Armel Guerne, his book contains many other inaccuracies. At least one F section field agent stated that 'virtually all the references to him were incorrect'.[29] Many of the errors in *SOE in France* could be explained by the crippling rules of engagement Foot had accepted. But this defence does not justify the more imaginative accounts he put together for his second book, *SOE: 1940–1946*, first published in 1984. Here Foot continued to polish his vivid impression of

---

* Reimeringer was French. She may have adopted a German identity to avoid being charged with treason. She had been born in Alsace under German rule and when she left school she spoke only German. She became a French citizen in November 1918.

the careless chatterboxes leading PROSPER. This time, 'Its members had formed an unfortunate friendship and a fatal habit. The friendship was with Henri Déricourt . . . [who] also worked hand in glove with the SD in Paris.'[30]

To describe the resisters' relationship with the German agent and SOE air movements officer Déricourt as 'a friendship' seems eccentric. Suttill distrusted Déricourt and avoided him wherever possible. Norman and Borrel were obliged to deal with him because that was part of their job. Had they known he was being paid by the SD they would probably have shot him out of hand. The 'fatal habit' was that they were 'meeting almost every day at a black-market restaurant near the Arc de Triomphe . . . and almost every evening at a café near the Sacré Coeur for cards; they did not always remember to talk French; and they forgot how many Paris waiters were in the Gestapo's pay.'[31]

Since the only member of this sociable group to survive the war was, once again, Armel Guerne, he must also have been the source for this more detailed version. This time the restaurant was not in the rue Pergolèse but in the rue Troyon, and once again it had been recommended to the PROSPER agents by Henri Déricourt.[32] There is certainly evidence that the network's security was slipping, but the idea that Suttill, Norman, Guerne and Andrée Borrel were chattering in English on a daily basis in a Parisian black-market restaurant, a meeting place that was notoriously popular with collaborators, seems far-fetched. Guerne's first language was French, Norman was bilingual, Suttill spoke fluent French, and Borrel, who was having an affair with Norman, understood very little English.[33]

In 2008 Foot used *SOE: 1940–1946* to issue a dignified rebuke to other authors who had trespassed on his private topic. 'Several books about . . . SOE . . . by authors who have not managed to get right inside their subject,' he wrote, 'fall back on deception when they can see no other explanation of some piece of apparent British incompetence.'[34] This was an unfortunate line of attack since his own second bite at the SOE cherry is studded with errors. His description of the Sologne arrests contains three factual errors in two lines.[35] In a later chapter, dealing with the arrests of General Delestraint, Jean Moulin and René Hardy, he scores fourteen mistakes in one page.

Turning to the affairs of 'RF' section, Foot, in *SOE: 1940–1946*, provided a picturesque account of General Delestraint's arrest in June 1943. In *SOE in France* he had already described how the general was 'so little skilled in the ways of clandestinity that when he reached a safe house in Paris but could not enter it, because he could not recall the password, he went off to a nearby hotel and took a room there in his real name: an incident that led directly to his arrest'.[36] In 1984 Foot improved this description, this time confiding that when the general reached the safehouse, 'A pretty girl answered his ring at the door . . . For the life of him he could not remember the password . . . Confused and unused to the secret life he went off to an hotel, registered in his own real name and was picked up without trouble next day while changing trains in the metro by the SD who had noticed his name in the morning police check of hotel registers. He died in Germany.' The amusing picture of the bumbling senior officer blushing at an unexpected meeting with a pretty girl is unfortunately unsourced in both books. But it appears to have originated with the account published in 1951 by Colonel Passy, who was in Paris on that evening in 1943 when the general forgot the password and who observed the aftermath of this incident.

In Passy's *Memoires* no mention is made of a pretty girl, or of the general signing into a hotel in his own name.[37] The incident did not occur in June. It occurred on 11 April. The general did not spend the night in the hotel because 'Max' moved him to a different address that same evening. And he was not 'picked up the next day' since his arrest actually took place two months later. So his misadventure did not 'lead directly' to his arrest. In fact it had nothing to do with it. General Delestraint was arrested in Paris on 10 June by two Gestapo agents who had arrived from Lyons that same morning. He was not 'changing trains' and he was not betrayed by his own incompetence. The time and place of the Paris rendezvous outside a metro station had been discovered in Lyons by the Resistance traitor Multon from an uncoded letter posted in the burnt letter box in the rue Bouteille by Henri Aubry.[38]

Otherwise Foot's anecdote is correct. The general 'died in Germany'.*

––––––

An important component in the original 'conspiracy theory' was that on his last visit to London in May 1943, Major Suttill had been summoned to a meeting with Winston Churchill during which the prime minister had

––––––

* Charles Delestraint was listed as 'NN' and sent to Natzweiler-Struthof Concentration Camp in Alsace, then transferred to Dachau where he was shot in the back of the neck on 19 April 1945, shortly before the camp was liberated by American troops. His memory is honoured today with a wall plaque in Natzweiler-Struthof.

misinformed him that France was about to be invaded. Foot referred to this rumour in a paper[39] co written in 2011 with Francis J. Suttill, son of the Major Suttill who had been 'Prosper'. This paper included a reference to the 'legend' [of the Churchill meeting] based on something that first appeared 'in a novel in 1985' and was then supported 'by the elderly Buckmaster, once head of F section'. Oddly, Foot himself had given some credence to this rumour in *SOE: 1940–1946*, when he wrote that the prime minister Winston Churchill may have 'seen individual agents on their way into the field, and mis-briefed them to suit a deception plan of which only he and Colonel Bevan held the key'.[40] However, Churchill was out of the country throughout the six days of Suttill's last London visit; so the suggested meeting between the prime minister and 'Prosper' could not have taken place. Furthermore, the legend of Suttill's meeting with Churchill did not spring from 'something that first appeared in a novel published in 1985'. It emerged from an error that first appeared in an official history. This rumour had sprung up because Professor Foot in *SOE in France* had mistakenly given Suttill's return date as 'about 12 June' (after Churchill's return to London) when it was in fact 20 May.

Foot was even less reliable when it came to the essential question of whether or not there had ever been any connection between deception operations and F section. His original categorical denial was repeated in 1986, in a letter published by the *Observer* on 11 May,[41] when Foot declared that Colonel Bevan, the wartime Controller of Deception (who had died in 1978), had personally assured him that he had never used SOE in deception. Then when W.J.M. Mackenzie's *The Secret History of SOE* was finally published in 2000 (after its author's death) Foot popped up again in the introduction with a modified view. Quite a lot more was known about Operation Starkey by this time and Foot corrected his earlier categorical denials, ruling that Colonel Bevan, Controller of the LCS, *did* use SOE for Operation Starkey. Then, in the 2004 edition of *SOE in France* (and in the French edition, *Des Anglais dans la Résistance*), Foot in the text[42] repeated his original assertion of 1966, that SOE was never used for deception, but with the addition of the words 'except in the case of Starkey', as the only necessary correction.[43] Foot's final communication on the matter came in the paper of 2011, in which he gave a different version of the 1978 conversation with Colonel Bevan; this time the colonel had told him that he *had* used SOE for deception three times, including Operation Starkey.*

---

* In the same paper F.J. Suttill reported that Sir Michael Howard had told him that

A cynical French reader, remembering Professor Foot's original brief, might have called it '*service après vente*'.

———

That Major Suttill never met Churchill in May 1943 does not alter the fact that he did return to France convinced that landings on the northern French coast within months were increasingly likely. Suttill's conviction followed meetings he had held in London with his commanding officer, Colonel Buckmaster. This was to some extent confirmed in 1958 with the publication of *They Fought Alone*, one of Buckmaster's wartime memoirs.

In the middle of 1943, Buckmaster wrote, 'we had had a top-secret message telling us that D-Day might be closer than we thought. This message had been tied up with international politics on a level far above our knowledge, and *we, of course had acted upon it without question* [my italics].'[44]

In *SOE in France* Foot imposed his own gloss on this perfectly clear recollection: 'His [Buckmaster's] orders as he remembered them many years afterwards, had been to accelerate his section's preparations to support an invasion, in case it turned out possible to mount one after all later in the year.'[45]

Foot's insinuation was that the elderly Buckmaster, 'many years afterwards', was either in a muddle or inventing a good story. In fact, there is no objective reason to challenge Buckmaster's memory. The former head of SOE(F) was aged fifty-six when the book in question was published, and he repeated the claim, and amplified it, in a memo to the Foreign Office in 1964 when he was aged sixty-two.[*]

Buckmaster's recollection shows that in the early summer of 1943 he gained exactly the same imprecise impression that Jean Moulin had received in March just before his final return to France – that allied landings in 1943 might well be possible. Some confirmation of this exists in Foot's own account of 1966 when he wrote, 'Suttill was sent back to Paris from London about 12 June [in fact 20 May] . . . with an "alert" signal, warning the whole circuit to stand by . . . [he returned] in the belief that an invasion was probably imminent.'[46]

Suttill had at least six meetings with Buckmaster during the six days of

———

Colonel Bevan had been 'deeply unhappy about the unintended consequences (of Operation Starkey) . . . for the resistance movements'.

[*] Foot was sixty-five when he published *SOE 1940–1946*.

his last visit to London.[47] They met in the SOE canteen, at hotels and restaurants, in Buckmaster's flat, and even in the office. Although we do not know what they discussed so thoroughly during this intensive period, any objective assessment of Buckmaster's memory and Suttill's conviction shows that they support each other. The director of SOE(F) and the leader of his principal network were both under the clear impression that landings on the northern French coast later that year were on the cards.

And the same suggestion is to be found implicit in briefings given to two other F section agents that spring. On 21 May France Antelme was parachuted back on the same flight as Major Suttill with clear instructions to build up food and money supplies for an invading force immediately.[48] And Claude de Baissac, who had returned to France in April, received the same briefing. De Baissac was the organiser of SCIENTIST, a circuit centred on Bordeaux. In March, when he was recalled to London for a break, he had reported that he had a force of 3,000 or 4,000 trained fighters in Gascony,[49] but very few weapons as he had received only nine air drops. He returned with a new mission. 'Our orders,' he recorded, 'are to cause the maximum damage and confusion in the shortest possible time. This will continue to apply *even if France is not the scene of actual hostilities during the next few months* [my emphasis], since we have been and must still be successful in pinning down a large number of troops who would otherwise be available for other sectors.'[50] So, on 1 April 1943, de Baissac was convinced that even if landings were not attempted that summer his growing network was under orders to carry out such operations as would deceive the enemy into thinking that such landings were about to take place. Between June and August SCIENTIST received 121 aircraft loads of arms and stores in almost 2,000 containers and was able to arm a force of about 8,000 men.[51]

Throughout the summer of 1943 the deception operation known as Cockade – of which Starkey was the most important component – ran on. There were repeated invasion warnings on the BBC that continued into the second half of August.[52] Foot noted[53] that 'broadcast warning messages [were sent] to every active SOE circuit in France, indicating that the invasion would come within a fortnight, but the action messages that should have followed were not sent'. He adds (confusingly) that 'this was part of a deception plan'. Another SOE officer commented, 'Evidently something powerful was building up.'[54] Foot also wrote: 'SCIENTIST . . . was snowballing too soon for safety.'[55] Shortly after that, disaster struck.

Foot blames what happened next to SCIENTIST on the unusual far-right/Communist political composition of the local recruits. It is far more likely that, as in the Sologne, the attention of the Gestapo was caught by the extraordinary profusion of night flights and air drops, and that this led to the mass arrests in the Bordeaux region in July.[56] In any event SCIENTIST was neutralised and for the second time a major F section circuit was destroyed during the 'Starkey' deception operation. The arming of SCIENTIST between July and August succeeded the fall of PROSPER in June.

In February 1945, in Paris, the Communist resister and poet Louis Aragon, talking to the British intelligence officer Eric Siepmann, recalled the disasters of 1943 – as Siepmann described in a letter to his future wife, the novelist Mary Wesley. 'Aragon talked all politics and no literature . . . He said nasty things about the BBC broadcasts in summer 1943, driving people to death . . . He said they [i.e. the Resistance] "hated us" when the landings were delayed.'[57]

Jean Moulin, Delestraint, Buckmaster, Suttill, Antelme and de Baissac were all convinced in the spring and early summer of 1943 that an allied landing in northern France later that year was anything from 'possible' to 'imminent'. Perhaps – as Foot suggests in Suttill's case – this conviction may have 'resulted from some misunderstanding between the section staff and himself about the probabilities of an early major allied landing'.[58] Or perhaps there was some other reason for this widespread and lethal delusion. In any event it was precisely the impression that Operation Starkey was designed to spread.

———

In an essay published in honour of M.R.D. Foot,[59] the historian Ralph White described him as 'a warrior historian, one of that generation of British scholars who served their country in the Second World War and later devoted their formidable talents to its academic study'.[60] Foot himself, in a lecture on SOE given in Paris in 1986, touched on the same point in more detail. Referring to the deliberate destruction of wartime records he said, 'As an historian I deplore [this]; though as a former intelligence officer I think [it was] quite right.'[61] A hint as to his preference if obliged to choose between those two activities appeared in another passage in the same paper where, dealing with the assassination of Admiral Darlan, he said: 'It does not seem likely – *it may not even be desirable* [my emphasis] – that this mystery should ever be unravelled entirely.' *SOE in France* carried great authority when it was published and is still a valid work of reference. It provides a readable and detailed account of the 'honourable' aspect of the secret war, the heroic actions of the agents who operated behind enemy lines. But its author's dual professional loyalties are confirmed by the way in which he dealt with the delicate question of the Gestapo/SOE double agent, Henri Déricourt.

In their joint paper of 2011, F.J. Suttill and Professor Foot stated[62] that 'there is no evidence that he [Déricourt] played any part in the arrests of Suttill, Norman and Borrel' since these started when Culioli and his passengers 'fell into a chance road control'. But that is a red herring, introducing and then denying an irrelevant allegation. Because Déricourt's treachery did not consist of giving information of Suttill's whereabouts.

It is correct that the road control in the Sologne led to the discovery of Suttill's address, and that this was not connected with Déricourt. But it was not a 'chance' roadblock. The ambush was put in place in response to the curiosity of a Luftwaffe colonel who had been alerted by the frantic pace of arms drops over a few days in that one small region.[63] Professor Mackenzie, writing unpublished in 1948, directly linked the delivery of 190 containers in ten days in June to the subsequent arrests. Attempts made by Pierre Culioli and 'Jacqueline' to arrange a pause in the RAF deliveries after one of the arms containers had exploded – because they feared, correctly, that German forces would be on the alert – were overruled by 'Prosper'. He overruled them because he had become convinced while in London that allied landings in northern France were imminent. His conviction, almost certainly based on conversations with Buckmaster (rather than Churchill), caused him to act with reckless disregard for normal security. Déricourt's responsibility in the matter came after the arrests, when the interrogations started and Suttill and Norman were presented with the devastating evidence that their circuit had long since been penetrated by a German agent apparently operating in London and inside SOE.

What would happen next in such a case was impossible to predict. The betrayed leader might commit suicide. Or he could remain silent, as happened with Agazarian, and probably happened in the case of 'Prosper'. Or he could talk, as happened with 'Archambaud'. It did not matter which path the resister chose. What mattered was that the arrests legitimised the information provided by the double agent, Boe.48. The SD could rely on the information he provided in future.

Years after his trial for treason before the *2e Tribunal Militaire Permanent* at Reuilly Barracks, Paris, in June 1948, when he had faced the death penalty, Déricourt told the author J.O. Fuller that in giving his evidence he had repeatedly lied. He had lied about the date of his 'arrest' by the Gestapo and he had lied about the Luftwaffe pilots taking him to the car. The obvious conclusion would be that his wartime contact with Karl Boemelburg had started as an extension of his original peacetime acquaintance. For both men, it promised to become a profitable relationship. Only the swift identification of Déricourt's secret purpose by SIS had blocked, and diverted, Boemelburg's scheme.

———

It remains an open question as to whether Professor Foot was duped by his SIS minders[*][64] or whether he was, as a solid ex-intelligence officer, happy to be led by the nose. There is a file in the SOE records held in the National Archives[65] labelled 'Legal correspondence concerning *SOE in France* by M.R.D. Foot'. The contents show the pressure Foot was under to toe the line. It records that Patrick Reilly, by then 'Sir Patrick' and British ambassador in Paris, was opposed to publication of Foot's history since it would be 'bound to re-open old wounds'.[66] The file also suggests that Foot himself suspected that someone in MI5, probably Colonel Sammy Lohan, was leaking his research to a rival author in an attempt to diminish the impact of his own book.

Perhaps this pressure explains why Professor Foot apparently stated conclusions for which he lacked evidence, wrote up inconclusive evidence to support a fragile conclusion and discounted evidence that went against it. In any event, the principal victim of the cover-up was history itself. It was history that suffered when, despite many of Déricourt's activities being known to Professor Foot, he continued to insist that PROSPER was broken through its leadership's mistakes. Of course, any admission that Déricourt's contacts with Karl Boemelburg might have played a part in the disaster would have opened the door to 'conspiracy theorists'. Nonetheless Foot's officially acceptable account left far too many questions unanswered.

———

* In particular Colonel Edward Boxshall.

Why was SOE unaware of Déricourt's one-night visit on 20/21 July? Why did Déricourt return on an SIS flight, an unprecedented arrangement in view of Claude Dansey's cast-iron security screen – unless Déricourt was in fact, as he later claimed,[67] recalled not by SOE but by 'another agency'. Why did Bodington scribble a note on an SOE file, in reply to criticism of Déricourt, 'We know he is in contact with the Germans and also how and why.'[68] Who did the 'we' in that note refer to? It did not include either Buckmaster – Bodington's direct superior – or Vera Atkins, F section's intelligence officer. If Déricourt's Gestapo contacts were known in London, why was the PROSPER network left to its fate instead of being warned? Had Déricourt been authorised to contact the Paris SD, and if so by whom, when and why? The MI5 interrogators at the Royal Victoria Patriotic School had every reason to feel dismayed. They had immediately picked out both Guerne and Déricourt as potential German agents. So why were their warnings in the latter case consistently ignored?

And then there is the most disturbing question of all. Why did 'a former British intelligence officer', Major Nicolas Bodington, travel to Paris three years after the war to give vital defence evidence on Déricourt's behalf? Unconvincing as Bodington's evidence was, with its feeble non sequitur – 'He can't have been a traitor because he did not betray me' – it was accepted by a French military court, unchallenged.

Only three facts about Déricourt's wartime activities are beyond dispute. First, he worked for SOE in France as an 'air movements officer', in charge of all secret air transport into and out of central France on behalf of F section. Second, soon after his first deployment in France, by parachute on 22 January 1943, he was in contact with a senior Gestapo officer in Paris, SS *Sturmbannführer* Karl Boemelburg. Third, Déricourt then became a double agent. The answer to the outstanding question, was he loyal to either of his known commanders, and if so to which, seems to be 'to neither'.

So if he had a third commander, as the French version of history suggests, who was it and what were the orders he followed?

19

The Last Mission of Jack Agazarian

Those who suppose that the papers were so long kept hidden because SOE had something exceptionally nasty to hide, are mistaken.

From *SOE: The Special Operations Executive 1940–1946*, M.R.D. Foot[1]

In order to dispel the 'uncertainty' surrounding Henri Déricourt[2] – as detected by Professor Foot – one has to examine the relationship he enjoyed with his good friend from pre-war Paris days, Nicolas Bodington. This relationship also provides the key to understanding the destruction of PROSPER. The pair of them were once described as 'two opportunist crooks propping each other up like drunken sailors',[3] but that description is unjust, and far too charitable.

Déricourt was born in 1909 in a small village in northern France on the edge of the Champagne region. He came from a humble background, the youngest of three brothers, the sons of the village postman. He was one of what Simenon called '*les petits gens*' – the little people who play no part in the world's affairs. At school he excelled in mathematics and in 1933, aged twenty-four, he was employed by Air France as a 'pilot-captain'. He became an outstanding technician who sometimes took part in air shows; he was known as a risk-taker and had survived at least one air crash. He spoke German and Air France employed him on the Paris–Cologne route, where he made friends with some of the Lufthansa pilots. At an aerobatics show Déricourt met an English journalist working for Reuters called Nicolas Bodington, and not long afterwards Bodington introduced him to Karl Boemelburg, a senior police officer stationed at that time at the German Embassy in Paris as a delegate to Interpol. The Interpol job was a cover; Boemelburg, who occupied a spacious villa in the fashionable suburb of Neuilly, was actually spying on German fugitives from Nazism and identifying pro-Nazi contacts.[4] Déricourt, Boemelburg and Bodington used to attend dirt-track motorcycle races, where they could drink and gamble. In this trio Déricourt was the essential link. Both Boemelburg and Bodington spoke their native tongue and excellent French. Déricourt spoke both German and English. In 1939, shortly before the outbreak of war, Boemelburg was declared *persona non grata* by the French government and expelled, and Déricourt was called up by the French Air Force.

When he first arrived in England, Déricourt explained his presence to MI5 as follows. He said that in 1941, following France's defeat, when he was once again a civilian pilot, he happened to be in Syria at the time of the surrender of Vichy forces. There he was contacted by an RAF officer who suggested that he should abandon Vichy and make his way to England. He got as far as Cairo, where he claimed that he had been offered a contract by BOAC. The RAF offered Déricourt a direct passage to England. But, pleading family reasons, he first returned to France where he stayed until August 1942, when he travelled to Marseilles and managed to join MI9's PAT escape line.[5] This entire story was a pack of lies. Déricourt had stolen another French pilot's genuine story.[6] He had never been to Syria or Cairo and he had never been offered a job by BOAC. In September 1942, MI5 put out a trace to check his account with the RAF and with BOAC in Cairo. But the reply, which was negative, only arrived *after 18 months*, in February 1944. No one in Cairo had ever heard of Déricourt, and he had never been seen in Syria.[7] The only correct part of the story he offered on his arrival in Glasgow on 8 September 1942, was that he had succeeded in joining an escape line in Marseilles in the late summer. He had travelled via Gibraltar.

Déricourt was interrogated at the London Reception Centre (LRC) and signed out on 23 September. He said that he wanted 'nothing to do with' the Gaullist 'Free French'. But he was not directed, as would have been usual, to SOE's F section. Instead he applied for the job allegedly promised by BOAC. At this point he ran into a problem. The MI5 officer who interviewed him at the LRC had immediately identified him as a possible German agent.

In Déricourt's security file[8] there is a correspondence between BOAC, MI5 and various civilian government agencies on the subject of whether or not he could be cleared to work for BOAC. There are occasional indignant interruptions from Déricourt himself. The correspondence lasts from September 1942 until 25 January 1943, and today it reads like the script of a dramatic farce. Towards the end of this correspondence an exasperated BOAC official says that the company has decided to stop the grounded pilot's pay, since they have heard that he is either going to America or 'is in prison'. Neither was the case. What the security file omits to mention is that while this bureaucratic struggle was going on Déricourt had been parachuted into France on the night of 22/23 January as an F section agent. On 16 November 1942, while MI5 was still stubbornly refusing to give him security clearance as a civilian pilot, he was resident at RAF Tempsford, where he joined Squadron Leader Hugh Verity who was training with 161 Squadron to fly Lysanders.[9] Déricourt was in army uniform and was being trained as an agent. He had to learn how to unload and reload a Lysander in less than three minutes, how to find suitable landing fields and how to guide the planes in at night.[10] He was there again on 15 December.

How Déricourt managed to get himself into SOE while he was still under suspicion in MI5 as a possible German agent is one of the engaging mysteries of his story. What is quite clear is that he was not passed to SOE by MI5. The official version is that he was recruited into SOE by André Simon, a conducting officer for the agency. If that was the case it is something of a coincidence that shortly after arriving in England for the first time he should have found himself in a highly secret organisation, SOE(F), whose deputy commander was his old friend, in fact the only English friend he is known to have had before the war, Nicolas, now Major, Bodington. It may also be relevant that André Simon worked for SIS as well as SOE,[11] and that SIS had been operating a 'spotter' system at the London Reception Centre since the spring of 1941, which was used to recruit potential agents.[12]

In 1942, before his departure for England, and in 1943, following his return to France, Déricourt was in contact with German security officers in Paris. He claimed that when he returned to France 'from Syria' in 1942 he moved under his own name into his pre-war Paris address at 58 rue Pergolèse in the 16th arrondissement and became the neighbour of an *Abwehr* agent, Hugo Bleicher (who had already penetrated F section circuits), who lived at No. 56, the house next to Déricourt's. In fact, Déricourt had never left Paris and never moved out. And MI5 eventually received information that he had been on friendly terms with German officers in Paris and Toulouse since the beginning of the Occupation.[13]

At his post-war trial in Paris, as explained in chapter 11, Déricourt stated that the first contact with German security came on 2 June 1943, and claimed that he had only given useless information to the Gestapo. In truth, the information Déricourt subsequently gave to Boemelburg and his deputy, SS *Sturmbannführer* Josef Kieffer, was far from 'useless' since it included details about his own work, the movements of SOE agents and their correspondence with Baker Street.

Déricourt had been parachuted 'blind'[14] into France during the January moon. The February moon made operations possible from the 13th to the 27th of the month, but Déricourt was inactive during this period, for reasons unknown. Presumably he was re-establishing himself in the rue Pergolèse after his five months in England and reporting back to Karl Boemelburg. He would certainly have made contact with Francis Suttill and with other agents already in place. The first operation Déricourt organised, nearly two months after his arrival, was a double Lysander landing on 18 March, near Poitiers. He received four agents and despatched three; among the latter was the forlorn figure of Raymond Flower, sent home by Suttill after a generally discredited posting. Had Boemelburg's men been watching this operation they would have appreciated the sight of the patriotic but over-cautious Flower being packed off by Flying Officer Henri Déricourt, alias 'Boe.48'. The field near Poitiers selected by Déricourt on this occasion was too bumpy for safety and this caused an engine fire in one of the planes. That was the only operation he organised during the seven clear nights of the March moon.

Déricourt's second operation was on 15 April with another double Lysander pick-up two miles north-east of Amboise. This time he placed the landing lights too close to the boundary so that one of the aircraft demolished a tree on its way in and very nearly crashed on its way home. The pilot was furious. The four passengers dropped off were also upset because Déricourt had failed to provide them with enough bicycles. On the following night, Déricourt's third operation – flown by Squadron Leader Hugh Verity, by now the CO of 161 Squadron – resulted in a damaged tail wheel, as the flare path was wrongly laid out. At that point he had been in France for nearly four months and had conducted just three chaotic landings. Verity therefore decided that Déricourt should be recalled and retrained, and until then the squadron would not use him again. Verity himself picked Déricourt up on 23 April from a field near Le Mans. He was given a rocket for sloppy work with the landing lights, retrained and parachuted back, once again 'blind', on 6 May, near Mer. He had been in England for over two weeks and after the war he claimed that during this period he was authorised in London by another intelligence agency to approach the Germans in France.* [15]

On 14 May Déricourt organised his fifth operation, another double Lysander, into a field near Azay-sur-Cher. Four passengers were dropped off and two picked up; one of the latter, as mentioned earlier, was Francis Suttill, who was returning at his own request partly because he had already become extremely worried about Henri Déricourt.

While Suttill was in London, Déricourt continued his unsupervised activities in France. Among the passengers who had been dropped off on 14 May – when Suttill was picked up – was Marcel Clech, on his second mission. In 1942 Clech had been sent out as Flower's wireless operator. This time he was due to join a new circuit in the Troyes-Nancy region and while making contact he deposited his codes and signals with Déricourt's number two, Marc Clement, for safekeeping. His plans were sabotaged when he returned to recover these essential documents only to find that they were no longer in his suitcase. Déricourt had removed them.† [16]

––––––

Nicolas Bodington, whose wartime career is almost as interesting and just as mysterious as Déricourt's, was born in 1904, the son of an English businessman and an American mother. He was raised and educated in France before going on to Cheltenham College and Lincoln College, Oxford. He spoke fluent French and always felt completely at home in France. As a Reuters correspondent in Paris in 1939, Bodington was also

––––––

* Referring to Déricourt's claim that another intelligence agency had instructed him to approach the Germans in Paris, Foot commented, 'Nothing in the files of any British service bears this out.' Given that Professor Foot was not allowed to consult the files of other intelligence services, it is not clear how he could be sure of this.

† Foot mentions this incident in his account of Déricourt's record but attributes it to a muddle in London, although the correct account had been published twelve years earlier in the memoirs of the *Abwehr* officer Hugo Bleicher.

soon in uniform, as a war correspondent. As a resident correspondent he would have relied on the help of the press attaché in the British Embassy, Sir Charles Mendl. Mendl had been *en poste* since the 1920s.[17] He was a member of a wealthy and influential Romanian Jewish family, had been knighted after the previous war for services to British Intelligence, and in 1939 he was still in SIS – the post of 'press attaché in the Paris embassy being an SIS cover. At this time Bodington may also have met and perhaps passed some convivial hours with *The Times* war correspondent, a charming and quietly spoken figure called Kim Philby, who was on assignment in France from November 1939 to May 1940.

During that winter Bodington decided that he had had enough of journalism and took a step that Philby was also considering – he applied to join SIS. His application would have passed across the desk of Sir Charles Mendl and may have been seen by Leslie Humphreys, another SIS officer stationed in Paris. Humphreys, who was 'a specialist in clandestine communications'[18] acted in Paris as the representative of Section D, the department in SIS that was responsible for irregular activities which could never be disclosed, such as sabotage, assassination and infiltration. In any event, Bodington's application was turned down.[19] Sir Charles Mendl would have known of Bodington's reputation for drinking, gambling and not repaying his debts. Shortly after this, in April 1940, a month before the German attacks on Holland, Belgium and France, Bodington's accreditation as a war correspondent was withdrawn by the French authorities on the grounds that he had '*un mauvais esprit*' and Mendl had to supervise his departure. Bodington returned to London where he made a second application to join SIS. He was interviewed and turned away once again but this time he was directed towards a new government service that was recruiting – and by 7 October 1940 Bodington was working as an adviser in SOE's planning department.[20] In December he was transferred to the new agency's French section, under Leslie Humphreys. Section D had been cut out of SIS, much to the surprise of its officers, who were only informed after they had become the nucleus of SOE. And Humphreys, who had been evacuated in haste from France as the Germans approached Paris, was the first head of SOE (F).[21]

When SOE was set up, Dansey, as mentioned in chapter 4, had managed to get one of his Z men, Frank Nelson, appointed as its first executive director, or CD. It is not known whether Humphreys was also a Z man but, given Claude Dansey's close interest in France, he would have known of Humphreys when the latter was stationed in Paris. F was destined to become SOE's most important country section and Dansey had a lively interest in penetrating it. Bodington would have been the ideal man for the job. Six months later Dansey's influence within SOE increased when a 'big gun', Air Commodore A.R. Boyle, previously Director of (Air) Intelligence, became SOE's Director of Intelligence and Security. Boyle and Dansey already knew each other well[22] and were in charge of all information passed between SIS and SOE throughout the war.

Bodington's SOE personal file[23] shows that he signed the Official Secrets Act on 18 December 1940 and was accorded the rank of second lieutenant. A week later, on Christmas Day, he received a handsome present, being jumped up three ranks to temporary major. This was linked to his appointment as deputy head of F section, an appointment made by his CO, Leslie Humphreys. The 'inexactitudes' in his CV start almost at once. Bodington claimed to be able to run the 100 yards in ten seconds and listed 'parachute jumping' among his hobbies. This was unwise as he was shortly afterwards sent on a parachute course and promptly failed as 'a potential casualty' who had taken little exercise for fifteen years. One jump from a training tower had left him 'too stiff and bruised to continue'. The training reports stand out in SOE records because, unlike so much else, they are brisk, accurate and verified. But these qualities in a world of evasions, half-truths and lethal deceit did not always increase their influence. The hint that there might be something unreliable about Bodington was not taken – an error for which at least one F section radio operator would eventually pay with his life.

———

Although Bodington and Déricourt both worked for SIS (unknown to their colleagues in SOE), there is no record that they were in direct contact between January and the summer of 1943. Then, following the destruction of PROSPER, with Déricourt continuing to act as F's air movements officer in central France, Bodington decided to undertake a personal tour of investigation. This was against all the rules. As deputy head of F, Bodington knew far too much to be allowed to go into the field. But he seems to have undertaken his apparently reckless journey to Paris on 23 July with higher approval, although without the knowledge of his CO, Colonel Buckmaster.

Just before Bodington set out, Déricourt made a one-night visit to

London, according to Foot on his own initiative.[24] He arrived on 20 July on an SOE flight, as normal, but he departed on 21 July in a highly unusual arrangement, on an SIS flight. One curious aspect of this flying visit by Déricourt is that no trace of it appeared in SOE records. He did not go to Baker Street and it may be that no one in SOE, apart from Bodington and the second SIS 'sleeper' André Simon, was aware of it. Déricourt spent the night in Simon's flat off Oxford Street.

Concerning this mysterious visit Foot wrote: 'He (Déricourt) probably said as little as he could about PROSPER's troubles, of which he can hardly have failed to know; a taciturnity little to his credit with the British.'[25] This is one of the most disingenuous of all Foot's comments on Déricourt. Suttill had by then been under arrest and torture in the Avenue Foch (or Berlin) for four weeks. Was Foot hinting that Déricourt bore some responsibility for Suttill's arrest? In which case why place so much emphasis on PROSPER's lack of security? And if he was so hinting, why write that Déricourt's alleged 'taciturnity' was little to his 'credit'? A Gestapo double agent would hardly start boasting of his successful activities while visiting London.

Foot continued, 'Of what passed between the visitor and his staff . . . no record remains . . . In all likelihood, most of his few hours in London went on sleep and on essential discussions about pick-up techniques.'[26]

Since Déricourt's one-night flying visit preceded the arrival in France of the deputy head of F section on a three-week tour to investigate the total destruction of his service's most important circuit, 'pick-up techniques' were 'in all likelihood' at the very bottom of the probable list of topics discussed. The record of those discussions between Henri Déricourt and Major Nicolas Bodington would have been among the most interesting of F section records to have been made available after the war. Unfortunately, they were among the seven-eighths of SOE records that did not survive the custodianship of SIS. In fact, they were probably among the first to be destroyed. In his second volume, *SOE: 1940–46*, Foot revealed that the original 1946 fire consumed 'several bunches of files bearing on circuits penetrated by the enemy'. He then added, in reference to the files he had not seen, another confident if under-evidenced assertion: 'Those who suppose that the papers were so long kept hidden because SOE had something exceptionally nasty to hide, are mistaken.'[27] In response to which one can only wonder, again, how could he be certain?

For his trip to France in July 1943 Bodington needed to take a radio operator with him. This would have embarrassed a more sensitive man because the officer selected was Jack Agazarian. Agazarian had just returned from France and at his debriefing on 23 June had reported Suttill's continuing concern about Déricourt.[28] Now he was supposed to be enjoying a much-needed break at home with his wife. Instead, at Bodington's request, he agreed to re-enter the field and place his life in the hands of a man he knew to be under suspicion. What Agazarian did not know was that Bodington was not just 'aware of' allegations against Déricourt. He actually *knew* that the agent who would be organising their arrival and departure was in contact with the Gestapo. Foot asserts that Bodington was unaware of this contact,[29] but on 23 June, the day of Agazarian's debriefing, Bodington had left a note recording his personal knowledge of the real situation on Déricourt's file.[30] The two men were dropped off from an SOE Lysander on the night following Déricourt's return, and were met by Déricourt. Agazarian's feelings on coming face to face with the suspected double agent can only be imagined. Déricourt escorted them to Paris and lodged them, separately, near his own apartment.

Bodington's first task was to find out what had happened to Major Norman, who had disappeared four weeks earlier. Norman's wireless was still transmitting and there were hopes in London that he might still be free. (The wireless was of course being played by the Gestapo in the Avenue Foch as part of a *Funkspiel*.) So Déricourt gave Bodington the address in the rue de Rome that Norman had last used. Since the address was clearly unsafe Bodington said that he and Agazarian tossed up to decide who should go there, and Agazarian lost. Agazarian then went to the address where he was immediately arrested, taken to the Avenue Foch, beaten up and tortured. Despite this, Agazarian refused to talk and did not reveal Bodington's whereabouts. His arrest, following that of Suttill, meant that the two F section officers who were most suspicious of Déricourt had fallen into German hands. From Déricourt's point of view, this must have come as a relief.

Bodington, now without a radio operator, continued his ineffectual enquiries and finally managed to contact Noor Inayat Khan, who had been isolated and without a network since her arrival on 17 June. Bodington asked her to continue working in the Paris region, since she was one of the few radio operators still at liberty in central France.[31] Khan, who was exceptionally conscientious and brave, was subsequently ordered to return to London by Buckmaster. She declined to do so until her replacement had been sent out. She was eventually arrested on 13 October, when she returned to an address that she knew the Gestapo had already identified.[32] After her arrest Dr Goetz in the Avenue Foch started another *Funkspiel* on her set. Khan, like Major Norman, sent the prearranged warning, omitting her true check, on 18 October. This was immediately picked up by Leo Marks – but Buckmaster was unpersuaded and once again decided to act as though nothing was amiss.[33] In February seven SOE agents were dropped by arrangement with Dr Goetz, using Khan's radio. They were all arrested on landing.[34] Khan's circuit was finally closed down in March 1944, five months after her arrest.*

Bodington terminated his trip to Paris at the first opportunity, leaving on the third night of the August moon, his departure supervised again by Déricourt. On his return to London he was sent on indefinite leave. His visit had been almost as much of a fiasco as his earlier mission to investigate CARTE. His story – that he and Agazarian had tossed up to decide who would check Major Norman's old address – was widely disbelieved within SOE. The standard procedure in such a case was to pay a passer-by, someone who had no connection with resistance, to go ahead and check out the suspicious location.

On returning from Paris unharmed in August 1943 Bodington added a note to Agazarian's personal file. This gave a self-serving and mislead-ing account of the way in which he had sent Agazarian into a Gestapo trap and claimed that Agazarian had subsequently received such a beat-ing in the Avenue Foch that an SD interrogator had been given fifteen days' prison for it. This information, Bodington continued, came from 'a French source' (presumably Déricourt). Bodington then recom-mended Agazarian for an MC.[†] In his own personal file Bodington gave a similar account of events and continued to conceal what had happened.

---

*Noor Inayat Khan attempted to escape from Avenue Foch. She was eventually tortured in Dachau by a guard called Ruppert and executed in September 1944.

†In a separate citation Major General Sir Colin Gubbins noted that Agazarian had volunteered for this last mission 'even though he knew that the Gestapo had his photograph'.

And in another report he stated that Agazarian had been arrested at 'a contact given by Major Norman',[35] omitting to mention that it was actually Déricourt who had given him the address.

At his trial in Paris in 1948 Henri Déricourt was asked about the episode which led to Agazarian's arrest. The prosecutor wanted to know why Déricourt had not warned Bodington and Agazarian that Norman had already been arrested. He replied that he had warned them against going to Norman's address and told them that the concierge had informed him that Norman had been arrested. The prosecutor then asked him why he had not told them that it was the Gestapo, not the concierge, who had told him of Norman's arrest. 'It would have been of no use,' said Déricourt. 'It is futile to try to convince a British officer that he is mistaken.' This ridiculous reply passed without comment.

———

In May 1945, shortly before leaving SOE, Bodington asked for permission to attend an investiture as he was to be decorated with a military MBE. CD (the abbreviated title of the chief of SOE, Major General Sir Colin Gubbins) comments, 'There have been one or two insinuations against this officer. Are you certain they have been investigated and the officer cleared?' Major Frank Soskice of MI5 reassured him. In fact, MI5 had opened a file on Bodington three months earlier[36] as he was by then under serious suspicion of being a German agent. His chief accusers were the former BCRA, soon to become DST, the French Security Service. Their suspicions were mainly based on his uncompromising rejection, over a period of eighteen months, of all the accusations that had been made against Henri Déricourt.

Bodington's personal file closes with a characteristic intervention from Bodington in person. It is a newspaper cutting; his MBE had been gazetted in July and he felt safe from further investigation. When he was signed out, in August 1945, he celebrated his departure by contributing a paragraph to the *Daily Express*, his old newspaper. The information he supplied was about himself.

> Nicholas [sic] Bodington, reporter, late of the Resistance, is just back from Paris. He went to the Grand Prix at Longchamp racecourse, and went to the same race two years ago, when the Germans were strutting around the course . . . 'That's the way we had in the Resistance,' he said.

This item gave a pleasing symmetry to the file, since it was about as reliable as his opening claim to be able to run the 100 yards in ten seconds. The 1943 *Grand Prix de Paris* was not run at Longchamp, which was too close to the Renault factory at Boulogne-Billancourt, a prime target for Bomber Command, so the race was moved outside the city. Apart from which, if you were the deputy head of F section in hiding from the Gestapo in Paris and were anxious to avoid an SS-*Sturmbannführer* who loved racing and gambling, you probably would not have gone to the races in the summer of 1943. In fact, according to his security file, Bodington understandably spent most of his three weeks in Paris inactive and out of sight.[37]

Since André Simon as well as Bodington worked for SIS, 'conspiracy' theorists – in M.R.D. Foot's phrase[38] – also lean towards the conclusion that SIS may have had something to do with Déricourt's SOE career. There are only two references in 161 Squadron's records to F section agents being flown into France before the arrival of Déricourt, and one of those flights was onto a regular runway. Until the deployment of the French pilot, F was relying on parachutes. Henri Déricourt was F's first air movements officer, and as such he was essential to their ability to operate. He was the gift Buckmaster could not afford to refuse.

———

If one sets aside the uncertainties of Professor Foot it is possible to assemble a brisk and coherent account of the true story of Henri Déricourt.

He had been living in France throughout the Occupation and had made contact with old German friends from the early days. One of them was Karl Boemelburg. Boemelburg had recruited him, offered him a lucrative contract as 'Boe.48' and persuaded him to make his way to England. The SD sent him to Marseilles, where they had already penetrated, and would shortly break, the PAT line which was being run by Captain Ian Garrow of the Black Watch, a brother officer, and fellow escaper, of Bill Bradford. There Déricourt was accepted as a genuine resister and sent on to Gourock via Gibraltar. Since he came through MI9 he was first interviewed by SIS. Dansey used MI9 as part of his personal intelligence service, 'and frequently gave the impression that his engagement was as much to deny any other government department the opportunity to meddle on the Continent as it was to rescue British personnel'.[39] An SIS 'spotter'[40] at the LRC quickly identified Déricourt as a German agent and turned him. His previous connection with Bodington was established and he was introduced into SOE (as Bodington had been) possibly by Air Commodore Boyle or possibly by André Simon. He was only passed on to MI5 after he had been recruited by SIS. MI5 were kept in the dark, which was why they were still refusing to clear him for BOAC when he was about to be dropped into France on his first mission for SOE. Once inside SOE, Déricourt was run by Bodington. Buckmaster and Vera Atkins were as much in the dark as MI5. The deft manoeuvring has the fingerprints of 'Uncle' Claude – as he was sometimes known – all over it.

In the autumn of 1942, when Déricourt arrived in England, the LCS and the W board were working on a strategic deception plan to cover Operation Torch, the allied landings in French North Africa.[41] The necessity for similar plans to cover fictional landings in northern France was already foreseeable and work started on those in January 1943. In this area of operations, remembering J.C. Masterman's comment that 'the control and running of double agents remained entirely in the hands of . . . two departments (MI5 and SIS)', Dansey was able to manoeuvre unsupervised. With Déricourt parachuted back into France on 23 January as an undisclosed SIS agent working for SOE – and once more in touch with Boemelburg – he had the outline of his own scheme.

We have the evidence of Harry Sporborg, the vice-chief of SOE, for what happened next. He said that around the middle of May 1943 he, CD (Major General Gubbins) and Air Commodore Boyle were informed by SIS that PROSPER had been penetrated and a decision had been taken to exploit the situation.[42] The leaders of F section were not to be informed. What Buckmaster was told instead, and what he relayed to Suttill, was that landings on the French coast might take place sooner than previously expected. PROSPER was to be sacrificed for reasons of strategic deception.

For such an operation to be mounted Claude Dansey would have had to be involved in the execution of deception operations, and would have had to be free to act unsupervised – which he was, on both counts. A note from MI5 to the W board in October 1941 read: 'The Security Service and MI6 (i.e. MI5 and SIS) remain normally the best judges as to how the machine under their control can be put into motion to the best advantage.'[43] And Masterman emphasised that neither the LCS, nor the

W board, nor the Twenty Committee ever 'questioned or adversely criticised the practical control and running of the (double) agents by MI5 or MI6'.[44]

A month later, on the ground in France, events followed the pre-ordained course. The date of the arrest of Pierre Culioli and 'Jacqueline', 21 June, was fortuitous. But the huge increase in arms deliveries to the Sologne in preparation for a non-existent paratroop invasion was actu-ally intended to attract German attention and to precipitate the eventual discovery of the arms dumps. And as an operation in strategic deception it was well timed: it took place two weeks before von Manstein's Panzers launched their assault on the Soviet salient at Kursk.

In Paris, Boemelburg and Kieffer, with help from Déricourt, had gathered enough information to arrest the leaders of PROSPER when they wished. The impending departure of Major Norman to London, known to Armel Guerne, precipitated the decision. Norman and Borrel could have been followed from Guerne's house to the Boulevard Lannes on the night of 23 June, or information in Culioli's briefcase could have provided that address. Suttill's new address, unknown to Culioli and the Laurents, could have been obtained from the false identity cards spread out on the kitchen table in the Boulevard Lannes when the Gestapo broke in. The information supplied over six months by Déricourt would have enabled Kieffer during his interrogation to persuade Suttill and Norman that further resistance was futile since he already knew so much about both PROSPER and F section. Kieffer's claim to have an informer in Baker Street would have seemed plausible. Suttill still said nothing and was deported to Germany. Norman broke when Buckmaster reprimanded him for omitting his true check – confirmation for Norman that he had indeed been betrayed from inside SOE. Norman then decided that there was nothing to be lost in accepting Kieffer's 'deal'. So he instructed Culioli and Couffrant to give up the arms on the promise of immunity for the wives and children of the resisters.

In the Avenue Foch, the success of the operation confirmed Déricourt's invaluable status as 'Boe.48'. He had delivered the 'leader-ship of the Intelligence Service' in France,[45] and had betrayed a huge resistance network that was holding a vast arsenal of arms and explo-sives. Information he passed in future, in particular about the date of the invasion, could be trusted. From Dansey's point of view the operation was a brilliant success. Déricourt could stay in the field, protected against allegations of treachery by Bodington and Boyle, and providing SIS with a reservoir of future deception possibilities.

It is a reasonable and convincing version of history that fits in with the known facts, but of course in the absence of any documentary support one has to agree with Professor Foot that it remains a 'conspiracy theory'.

20

Colonel Dansey's Private War

*The evidence of eyewitnesses, as every criminal lawyer learns
to his cost, cannot always be taken as gospel . . . But written
evidence can be just as untrustworthy. The word 'document'
often lends a spurious authority. 'Memoirs' written long after
the event are generally scarred lapses of memory. . . . Still
more dangerous are distortions motivated by politics. The
highest degree of caution should be reserved for information
provided by a secret service.*

Hans Magnus Enzensberger,
Hammerstein, ou l'Intransigeance[1]

There is ample evidence that from the day of his arrival in Glasgow on 8
September 1942 Henri Déricourt was regarded as a suspicious character.
Throughout 1943, MI5 continued to express concern about Déricourt's
activities. Foot dates the first warning as 23 June 1943.[2] In fact, the first
adverse report about Déricourt reached MI5 six months earlier than that,
on 5 December 1942. MI5 did not pass this on to SOE because at that time
Déricourt was still thought to be applying for a job with BOAC. The
information came from the Gaullists, marked '*TRES SECRET*' and said
that Déricourt, who was known to have been associating with Germans
in Paris and Toulouse from just after the Armistice, was now in London
and claiming to be on the point of departure for France on behalf of '*un
service britannique*'.[3] Seven weeks later he was parachuted into France.[4]

By the end of January 1943, MI5 had discovered two facts about
Déricourt. One was that he was reported to have joined SOE; the other
was that he was talking openly about leaving for the United States. This
was passed on to SOE. F section thanked MI5 for the information

without mentioning that Déricourt was actually on an RAF station waiting to be flown out on his first mission. By the end of April, MI5 had discovered that Déricourt was an agent in the field and passed on two further warnings about 'your agent Déricourt'. No alarm bells rang. SOE's reaction was to say that the information had 'been noted'.[5]

Then on 10 June the BCRA deposited what should have been a bombshell on the desk of Captain Beaumont of MI5's B1b division (intelligence analysis). The report said that:

> Henri Déricourt, who recently departed _en mission_ for France on behalf of a British agency, is behaving in a particularly imprudent manner. All of his friends who knew of his departure for London, now know of his return to France. The Gestapo know this too, and they are looking for him. They have asked to be put in touch with him <u>not in order to arrest but to make use of him</u> . . . This man should not be employed as an agent.[6]

Beaumont passed this report to SOE with a covering memo. 'Here is a further report from the French about the indiscretions of this man . . . In view of the seriousness of the allegations you may like to consider the advisability of employing him as an agent.'

On 23 June, the day before the Gestapo arrested 'Archambaud', 'Denise' and 'Prosper', at 75 Boulevard Lannes, Major Bodington in Baker Street scribbled a note on a summary of this warning: 'We know he is in contact with the Germans and also how and why.'[7] Professor Foot, barking – yet again – up the wrong tree, suggested that this note could have been written in August, _after_ Bodington's journey to Paris. This seems most unlikely in view of the reply to Captain Beaumont's warning sent on 28 June by Flight Lieutenant Parke of SOE. This read, with reference to the BCRA's allegations, 'I am most obliged to you for this information which has been noted. _We were not unaware of the fact that the Gestapo were interested in him_ . . . [my emphasis].'[8] Parke, coached by Bodington (or possibly Boyle), remained sanguine.

In the second half of 1943, other returning SOE agents continued to complain about Déricourt's reliability. Major Francis Suttill had been among the first to have doubts about him. Having first complained about Déricourt in May, he told his wireless operator, Jack Agazarian, early in June that he was worried about the air movements officer's security.

Agazarian reported this on his return to Baker Street on 23 June, and added his own concerns.[9] Another organiser, France Antelme, reported on 23 July that Déricourt knew 'hundreds of Germans'.[10] Then in August, when Bodington was still in Paris, yet another organiser, Henri Frager (codename 'Louba'), told Bodington that he believed that Déricourt was in contact with the SD. He had direct evidence from a source inside the *Abwehr* of Déricourt's contacts with the Avenue Foch. His suspicion was supported by a report from R/F which suggested that Déricourt had been responsible for the arrest of three agents who were caught shortly after they were landed in August.[11] MI5 became increasingly concerned and dismissed Buckmaster's reasoning for trusting Déricourt – 'He never once let any of our boys down' – by pointing out that the Gestapo might just be biding its time before acting.[12] When nothing was done by October, Henri Frager travelled to London with the 'primary object' of having Déricourt recalled and interrogated. On the night of his departure he had a violent argument with Déricourt on the landing strip. At one point he grasped the revolver in his pocket, and was ready to pull the trigger.

———

In Professor Foot's work, *SOE in France*, 'Dansey, Sir C.' rates only two entries in the index. On page 22 he has evaporated altogether, while on pages 354–5 he survives as an unidentified surname in banal conversation with Colonel Passy. Commenting in 1992 on the theory that Henri Déricourt may have been working for SIS, the intelligence specialist Nigel West wrote, 'The evidence for this is thin to the point of being non-existent, apart from a few ambiguous remarks attributed to Déricourt.' He added, 'The evidence of Déricourt's connections with SIS is . . . entirely circumstantial . . . Whilst one might wonder about his involvement in the collapse of PROSPER or the exact nature of his relationship with the SD nothing of substance has ever emerged to tie him in with Dansey or SIS's French sections . . . Nor is there any evidence that the two men . . . even knew each other.'[13] And this is the line that has been followed by many other authors writing about SOE.*

Arguing that because there is no 'evidence' in the official records of an unavowable deception plan therefore no such plan exists is, of course,

———

* See, for example, Rita Kramer, *Flames in the Field* (1995); Sarah Helm, *A Life in Secrets* (2005); and Francis J. Suttill, *Shadows in the Fog* (2014).

tendentious. But without access to Secret Service records, theories sometimes have to take the place of facts. Fortunately, during the 1990s, the tattered remnants of the SOE archive were finally prised out of SIS's iron grip and deposited in the National Archives at Kew. An additional group of heavily censored files was released in 2002.

Among the files now available at Kew is KV2/1131, which is Henri Déricourt's security file, largely stocked by MI5. Even today, seventy-five years after the war ended, it remains heavily redacted. Sheet after sheet bears the neat little stamp in red ink – '*This is a Copy. Original Document Retained in Department under Section 3 (4) of the Public Records Act 1958*', and then the date – '*March 2002*'. In every case that I noticed, these redactions related to correspondence involving SIS. One cannot forget, of course, that this is a corrupted file. It has not been released for general inspection in the interests of accurate history. The information it contains has been carefully selected to lead nowhere – or to mislead.

But the most conscientious censor can make the occasional slip, so I waded through KV2/1131 hoping that something would emerge. And then, on the second or third trawl through its torn and crumpled pages, something actually did. I was startled to find that I was reading what even an official historian would have to accept as documentary evidence of an indisputable tie between the SOE-Gestapo double agent Henri Déricourt and Colonel Claude Dansey, Vice-Chief of SIS.

To Major G.P. Wethered, MI5, London
From Commander John Senter, RNVR, SOE
SECRET AND PERSONAL

18 February 1944
Dear Geoffrey,

I refer to yours of 6th December and (mine) of the 15th instant and conversations I have since had with you and with BLANK [name redacted] . . .

I confirm that from what you heard it appeared that this SIS agent was still in this country, that Cowgill* had the papers, and that Dansey was said to be dealing with the matter on a high level with us. It later

---

* Lieutenant Colonel Felix Cowgill, head of Section V.

appeared that the SIS agent has since gone abroad, that Cowgill had not the papers, and as regards Sir Claude Dansey's interest in the matter, I have so far been unable to identify that, either with your help or with that of Liversidge,* who rang me about it.

The present position is that SIS are sending a message to their agent asking if he can amplify the accusations against Déricourt but I understand no great hope is entertained on that score, and that BLANK [name redacted] will try and find out Sir Claude Dansey's interest in the matter . . .

Yours sincerely,

John

Here at last was the documentary proof that tied Déricourt in with SIS and with Dansey. The agent who had been making accusations against Déricourt (codenamed 'Cub Minor')[14] had done so at 'the LRC', that is the London Reception Centre run by MI5, where all foreign nationals entering the United Kingdom from enemy territory were taken for debriefing and interrogation – even if they were loyal secret agents returning from the field.

Apart from the fact that this short letter from John Senter, SOE's director of security (and ex-MI5), to Geoffrey Wethered of MI5's B1b division, revealed that there was indeed some sort of connection between Déricourt and Dansey, it seemed to suggest that an SIS Section V agent, operating in France, had reported that SOE's air movements officer was a dubious character – and that Cowgill's superior officer, Colonel Dansey, who had no responsibility for Section V, had nonetheless intervened in the enquiry 'at a high level'. A 'high level' for Dansey, the vice-chief of SIS, could have meant CD, Brigadier Colin Gubbins, SOE's chief, or his deputy, V/CD Harry Sporborg, his opposite number. Another possibility would have been A/CD, that is Air Commodore A.R. Boyle, who was responsible within SOE for delicate inter-service matters such as liaison with the PWE (Political Warfare Executive). Air Commodore Boyle was John Senter's boss. The advantage to Dansey of contacting Boyle would have been that the two men had already worked together. Before joining SOE, Air Commodore Boyle had been, as we have seen, Director of (Air) Intelligence, and as such a member of the

---

* Major Keith Liversidge, section V officer responsible for the LRC.

W board,[15] which authorised deception operations such as Operation Starkey. SIS's representative on the W board had been C himself, Sir Stewart Menzies, but when he had been unavailable, Dansey may have deputised. In any event, Dansey and Boyle worked hand in glove throughout the war.[16]

One curious aspect of John Senter's letter was that MI5 had apparently had some trouble in getting him to write it. More than two months had passed between Major Wethered's December communication and Senter's initial reply. In the first paragraph Senter's letter referred to previous correspondence, and this could be traced through the 'Minute Sheet' at the front of KV2/1131. I wondered if any of it would give a hint of what had caused Dansey to break cover in this uncharacteristic fashion. An answer was quickly suggested by the first MI5 letter of 6 December. This, it turned out, was simply a copy of the 'bombshell' warning from the BCRA that MI5 had originally forwarded to SOE on 18 June,[17] the warning that Bodington had brushed aside with his scribbled note, before setting off for Paris. I followed the paper trail of correspondence back through the Minute Sheets and found that the story started with the arrival in London of Henri Frager on 21 October 1943. It was Frager who had finally succeeded in opening a full investigation into Henri Déricourt.

———

In the Resistance, Henri Frager was a loose cannon – and a nightmare for anyone trying to use F section as part of a deception operation. He was an anti-Gaullist army officer and a survivor of CARTE, who had succeeded in transferring to SOE.

The evidence he had against Déricourt came from a German source, a man calling himself 'Colonel Heinrich', who was in reality Sergeant Hugo Bleicher the *Abwehr*'s master spy catcher. The 'colonel' had contacted Frager and introduced himself as an anti-Nazi whose main ambition in life was to get to England. He had said that there was 'a struggle to the death' between the Gestapo and the *Abwehr*, and he provided evidence that he himself was engaged in a personal feud with Josef Kieffer of the Paris SD. Bleicher had told Frager that '*l'homme qui fait le pick-up*', a British agent who 'was in charge of receptions in the Lyons area' (i.e. F's air movements officer) was in German pay. He also told Frager that the SD had been aware of Bodington's presence in Paris in July and August, but had not arrested him because they regarded '*l'homme qui fait le pick-up*' (Déricourt) as more valuable than Bodington, and wanted to protect his cover. F section, unsurprisingly, discounted Frager's allegations, but the report nonetheless reached MI5 and as a result a meeting was held at Baker Street on the evening of 18 November 1943, to discuss 'Louba's (Frager's) denunciation of 'Gilbert' (Déricourt). This was an inter-agency discussion, attended by representatives of MI5, SIS and SOE, and for SOE at least this was a rather unusual event. Major Wethered of MI5 wrote up the notes.

At this meeting were the following: -
From SOE: Commander Senter [director of intelligence]
                   Colonel Buckmaster [head of F section]
                   Major Warden
                   Fl/Lt. Miller
From MI5:   Major Wethered
                   Miss Sample [of the LRC]
From Section V: BLANK [name redacted].

Proceedings had kicked off with the usual assurance from Colonel Buckmaster who, unsurprisingly, 'was inclined to regard "Gilbert" as genuine'.[18] Déricourt was OK. He had been in charge of receptions for nearly nine months. There had not been a single failure. He had been responsible for important people. Buckmaster waffled on, mentioning that among the important people 'Gilbert' had been responsible for in France was Major Bodington, his own deputy in F section. And, as a clincher, Buckmaster confided that, until 'Louba's' report arrived, there had been a move to 'have "Gilbert" decorated'.

Buckmaster then cautioned against listening to 'Louba'. He suggested that one reason to be wary of 'Louba' was that he was 'a difficult man to get on with and had already quarrelled bitterly with Carte'. Even by Buckmaster's standards this was quite an intervention. 'Carte' (André Girard) was the fantasist whose insecure record-keeping had delivered the addresses of several hundred resisters to the Gestapo. Henri Frager had quarrelled with Girard when he realised that CARTE as a resistance network did not exist. Buckmaster was thereby advancing Frager's justified anger with Girard as a reason to distrust Frager. At this point BLANK intervened in the discussion for the first time and was revealed, according to the typescript, to hold the rank of Major. His four recorded interventions on the subject of 'Gilbert' were always tactful and generally non-committal – although he did tend to discount the strength of the evidence against him. He seemed to be, if anything, slightly pro-Déricourt.

The meeting reached no definitive conclusions but Major Wethered continued his enquiries and on 30 November he sent a grateful memo to Captain Osborne, MI5's man at the LRC; he had received the new report from the 'SIS accredited agent' accusing 'Gilbert' of working for the Germans, and appreciated the fact that this had been sent to him *without SIS knowledge or approval, in breach of agreed procedures.* In return he was sending Captain Osborne the full MI5 file on 'Gilbert'. 'Various SOE officers,' he wrote, 'are inclined to regard him as reliable.' It was the further denunciation of Déricourt that Wethered had received, illicitly, from the LRC that led to his letter of 6 December to SOE. While waiting for a reply to that letter Wethered carried out an exercise known as 'look-ups'. He trawled through all the back files looking for any 'adverse traces' in previous reports on Déricourt, and on 22 December he wrote to BLANK of SIS noting that 'SIS is listed as having further information' about this man. When no response to either the letter or the 'look-ups' had been received six weeks later, MI5 had had enough. They had been registering objections and suspicions about Déricourt for twelve months and might as well have been talking to a brick wall. On 14 February Major Wethered, aiming his guns at SOE, issued his 'L.397/FRANCE/11(B.1.B)'.

Major Wethered opened this three-page letter to John Senter, which he sent by hand, with the information that he had already 'shown it to Guy Liddell, who agrees with its terms'. Liddell was MI5's head of counter-espionage and his approval meant that this was an ultimatum. Major Wethered then weighed the case against 'Gilbert' (Henri Déricourt), and pointed out that the damaging evidence came from two dedicated and quite separate sources; he also noted that the SOE agent 'Louba' (Henri Frager) who had denounced 'Gilbert' (Déricourt) was considered so reliable that he was soon to be returned to France.* [19]

---

* Henri Frager was arrested in Paris on 8 August 1944, two weeks before the city was liberated. He was deported to Buchenwald where he was executed on 6 September. His work for the Resistance was partly summarised by Professor Foot as follows: 'He lived in Paris . . . engaging in the incessant conversations that represented for many Parisians the sum total of their resistance activity.'

Major Wethered concluded that the likelihood was that 'Gilbert' was 'an enemy agent of a very high grade'.

Major Wethered's finger then moved towards the nuclear button. 'If by any chance,' he said in his last paragraph, 'your organisation proposed to use "Gilbert" for any D-Day activities ... or ... in respect of missions in connection with invasion operations ... I am sure you will agree that it would be essential for the Chiefs of Staff to be informed of the position.'[20]

This letter, wrote Guy Liddell in his diary that week, 'created a tremendous upheaval in SOE'. MI5's nuclear threat – intended to terminate SOE's infatuation with Henri Déricourt – had instead unearthed Colonel Dansey, who appeared to be no less protective. Little wonder that Major Wethered was taken aback. But here at last was the explanation for Dansey's unexpected appearance above the parapet, as revealed in John Senter's response of 18 February.

Attracting the hostile attention of the Chiefs of Staff was the last thing a seasoned Whitehall assassin like 'Uncle Claude' was prepared to risk. And his swift reaction suggested that MI5's suspicions were correct. Dansey *was*, apparently, intending to use 'Gilbert' in exactly the way they suspected. Déricourt evidently had a role to play in what the ex-Nanteuil pupil Robert Cecil (who had succeeded Patrick Reilly as C's personal assistant in October 1943) called 'the secret networks "Uncle Claude" was developing in France in anticipation of D-Day'.[21]

At first, F section plugged on. Buckmaster agreed to summon Déricourt to London on the understanding that, once cleared, he would be returned to the field.[22] And he continued to prejudge the enquiry. On 15 February, in the midst of further reassurances,[23] Buckmaster included what looks like a brazen lie, claiming that 'no breath of suspicion' had reached F section about Déricourt 'until the return of "Louba" in October'[24] (the real date had been 30 April). These reassurances did not work. MI5's threat to involve the Chiefs of Staff was no longer a threat. On 16 February, Alanbrooke's Diary (which almost never mentions SOE) complains of a 'fairly long CoS (Chiefs of Staff meeting) with shipping and SOE problems'.[25]

Despite the enquiries supposedly mounted by John Senter, the mystery of Colonel Dansey's interest was never solved – at least not in what was left of KV2/1131 – because SOE were just as horrified as Dansey by the involvement of the Chiefs of Staff. The Chiefs of Staff had very nearly abolished SOE and amalgamated it with the Secret

Intelligence Service five months earlier, after the raid on Caluire. So, on 19 February, SOE finally threw in the towel. Harry Sporborg – who knew a great deal more about what had been going on than F section had ever been told – informed CD[26] that Henri Déricourt, who had been recalled from France as a suspected German agent, would not be returning.[27] MI5 were copied in.

Déricourt organised his own departure from a meadow somewhere 'east of Tours'.[28] Buckmaster, lucid to the end, strongly opposed the decision to recall Déricourt and put him up for the DSO. Harry Sporborg, several ranks higher than Buckmaster as vice-chief of SOE, presided over the subsequent inquiry into the French pilot's record. In 1983 Sporborg said[29] that although he had found no proof he had become convinced that Déricourt had been an agent of SIS, and that SIS had effectively blocked a thorough investigation. Throughout Déricourt's thirteen months in the field his fiercest defender had been Nicolas Bodington.[30] Indeed Bodington – who knew that Déricourt was in contact with the SD – was still trying to persuade MI5 that he should be returned to France on 21 April, six weeks before D-Day.[31] In 2005, one official estimate calculated that twenty-seven F section agents who had been flown into France to a Déricourt reception had been arrested on landing.[32]

Déricourt's final Lysander landed early in the morning of 9 February 1944. He was expected to arrive alone, but he turned up with his wife, thus leaving no hostage for Boemelburg. When Karl Boemelburg heard that Déricourt had gone to England and that he had taken his wife with him, he said: 'Oh well, that's our four million francs down the drain.'[33] Meanwhile in London, while the inter-agency struggle was being fought out in the bombproof basements of Whitehall, Henri and Madame Déricourt were lodged in a suite in the Savoy Hotel, overlooking the Thames. Their telephone was tapped by Special Branch. The police sergeant listening in reported that Madame Déricourt was negotiating to buy a very expensive fur coat.[34]

———

So what exactly was Colonel Dansey's unexpected interest in Henri Déricourt? Déricourt was of course a classic candidate for a deception operation, a Gestapo agent unmasked on arrival in England and sent back into France to work within and betray a circuit that was already 'vulnerable'. We know from post-war interrogation and evidence given in the French treason trials that, following the destruction of PROSPER, the SD in Paris trusted Déricourt and were counting on him to give them advance warning about D-Day. His deception potential had always been outstanding. Dansey had apparently been the first to notice this, but it was still unclear what exactly he had done about it. Putting aside Déricourt's security file, I switched to his personal file and there I found a second copy of Commander Senter's letter to Major Wethered which, interestingly, had been redacted by a different censor with stricter views.[35] Here it was not just BLANK who was missing, it was the whole of paragraph 2, which effectively meant that while Dansey and Déricourt remained locked together in paragraph 3, Dansey's 'high level' approach had disappeared, as had Felix Cowgill, Liversidge and Section V. Logically it would seem that the second censor was hiding not just the identity of BLANK but his connection with Section V, SIS's counter-espionage section. For the researcher in redacted archives, this was a rare and delightful experience – *because it was the censored material that revealed what it was supposed to hide*.

The chief remaining interest in this document was the identity of BLANK of Section V. The letter identified Colonel Dansey, Vice Chief of SIS, and Lieutenant Colonel Felix Cowgill, the head of SIS's Section V, its counter-espionage division, intervening in a matter in which they could have no evident legitimate interest. Their names were published. So what other name could possibly have been so sensitive, even in 2002, that it had to be redacted? And what could that excision be hiding? Would it be possible to discover more about Dansey's precise interest in Déricourt if one could identify BLANK? I searched through the Minute Sheets in the weeks following Henri Frager's arrival, looking for any references to the passage through the London Reception Centre of the 'SIS agent' whose accusation had terminated Déricourt's lucrative relations with the Gestapo. There was one relevant entry. In Major Wethered's memo thanking Captain Osborne for the information passed on without SIS approval he also mentioned that there had already been a meeting with SOE about 'Gilbert', *and that BLANK had been present at it*. The meeting he referred to was the inter-agency conference of 18 November. So the BLANK who was pursuing enquiries into Dansey was the representative of Section V, who had been considering the charges laid by Henri Frager, known as 'Louba', and who had seemed to be mildly pro-Déricourt.

And though this 'Major' did not have a name in Geoffrey Wethered's record of that meeting, he did have a number of letters to his name. In the days of the typewriter every letter occupied an equal space – the carriage moved for the same distance whether one was typing ',' or 'i' or 'W'. In the case of BLANK, by counting off the number of carriage movements against the lines above and below his redacted name one could see that it moved twelve times. At least two of those spaces would have been empty. In the example '*Major BLANK said*' the typewriter carriage would have printed '*Major_1234567890_said*'. So his name must have had a maximum of ten letters. It could of course have been shorter had he also used his Christian name or his initials; or it could have been double-barrelled.

By November 1943, Section V, under the overall command of Lieutenant Colonel Felix Cowgill, was divided into a number of geographical sections, several of which were commanded by a major. The officer sent across to Baker Street should logically have been the major in command of Vb, which was the west European sub-section of V and included France. I looked through the Minute Sheets again to see if there had been any trace of a response from SIS to Major Wethered's three-pager. There were five responses, and on each occasion where there was the redaction of a name there were the correct number of spaces for Major 'ten Letters in my Name' BLANK.

Then I noticed that on BLANK's letters out there was not just a blanked-out signature, there was also a heading with a personal internal reference. Within SIS, officers never used their names in written records. They all had numbers.[36] Could it be that outside SIS they used the internal ID reference but enclosed their surname within the reference? So, for external communications Major Blank's letter reference became

$$CX/_____/E/27$$
$$Vb$$

'CX' was the prefix routinely used to identify reports from SIS agents in the field. According to Professor Peter Hennessy, CX reports remain protected to this day by 'the very highest classification levels'.[37] Vb indicated the head of sub-section B of Section V. BLANK now had a job. As Vb he was the commander of that sub-section; the i.d. of his deputy would have been Vb1, then Vb2 and so on. And in his correspondence reference his typed name would have been reduced from ten to six spaces. No initials, just a surname of six letters. D-A-N-S-E-Y has six letters of course, but he was a colonel and had already been identified by name. 'P-H-I-L-B-Y' is another name with six letters, and he was also an officer in Section V.[38] The addition of his correct initials H.A.R. would have added too many spaces to the redacted name. But Philby often used the initials 'K.M.',[39] a reference to his nickname.

And Philby's was the obvious Section V name that would have remained sensitive in 2002. Whose name could possibly have been a bigger secret than the names of Dansey and Cowgill, unless that officer's name was Philby?*[40] He was a civilian officer, but sometimes appeared in the office in uniform.[41] Philby held a formal commission[42] and with the addition of his rank, which had been that of an honorary major since September 1943,[43] 'Major K.M. Philby' fitted the space in the Wethered report.

For years Philby had been Vd, head of the Iberian sub-section. But by November 1943 he had become Vk. There was no K sub-section. The K stood for Kim. At the same time Cowgill had put several regional sub-sections under his command and he had effectively become deputy head of Section V. As Vk he still had final responsibility for Iberia (Vd), but he was also in charge of Italy (Vt) and France, which was part of Vb.[44] With D-Day approaching, Iberia and Italy were of marginal interest. But France, six months before D-Day, was more than ever critical.

If a delicate matter involving a Dansey double agent, planted in France, had suddenly become a potential embarrassment, who better than Philby to sort it out? He would have been the ideal man to attend the meeting in Baker Street, where he appeared under his own name but representing the whole of Section V. As Vk he could identify himself as Vb whenever he chose. And who better to beard Dansey on behalf of the puzzled senior officers of MI5 and SOE? Dansey quite liked Philby and respected him. Philby got on with absolutely

---

* John Cairncross, 'the Fifth Man', has a ten-letter surname and he transferred into Section V from Bletchley Park in July 1943. But his rank was captain and he worked in the German section editing *Abwehr* intelligence traffic.

everyone and had a perfectly correct relationship with Dansey. I went back to the start of my quest and consulted the anonymous major's riddles, looking for possible references to Philby.

> The curious goings-on at Cliveden . . . the conference room at Rastenburg, a man called Stuelpnagel and the history of the cross of Lorraine . . .

Rastenburg was the 'Wolf's Lair' where Hitler awaited news from the battlefield of Kursk, and where he was nearly assassinated on 20 July 1944. General Heinrich von Stuelpnagel was the military governor of France at the time of that near-assassination, and one of the anti-Hitler plotters.

The chain from Cliveden to Rastenburg connected the pre-war (and anti-war) British appeasers and the anti-Nazi German resistance of 1944. It evoked the friendship between 'the men of Munich', such as Lord Lothian, our ambassador in Washington in 1940, and Adam von Trott – the Anglophile intellect of the 20 July attempt to assassinate Hitler. Late in 1942, and in 1943, anti-Nazi emissaries travelled to Madrid and Lisbon and attempted to contact C, the director of SIS, hoping to open negotiations on behalf of the post-Nazi German government that would be installed once Hitler was dead. These overtures came to nothing – partly because the dossier landed on the desk of the head of the Iberian sub-section of Section V, at that time still Philby, who was implacably opposed to a separate peace with Germany. He dismissed the envoys as 'unreliable' and refused to pass the information on.[45] As a link to Philby it seemed rather far-fetched. Furthermore I could find no references to Philby identifying himself while on duty as a major. So the identity of BLANK remained uncertain.

———

I returned to the anonymous major's riddles, but this time enlisted the help of a friend who has spent a lifetime decoding far more obscure riddles than any of those in the anonymous letter.*

---

* George Huxley, sometime Professor of Greek at Queen's University, Belfast, honorary Professor of Greek at Trinity College, Dublin.

The Ordre Martiniste-Synarchique, the frankly weird Otto Rahn, the conference room at Rastenburg, a man called Stuelpnagel and the history of the cross of Lorraine . . .

The cross of Lorraine was the symbol of the Free French, chosen by de Gaulle. After the war Churchill once said that 'of all the crosses he had had to bear, the heaviest was the cross of Lorraine'.

But it was Professor Huxley who pointed out that with its two cross bars the 'cross of Lorraine' was a clear reference to the 'Double-Cross' (Twenty or XX) Committee. This was confirmed, he suggested, by the introduction of the *Ordre Martiniste-Synarchique*. 'Martiniste' was a reference to 'Major Martin', the name given to 'the Man Who Never Was' – the dead body in a Royal Marines uniform, floated off the Spanish coast to mislead the German High Command before the landings in Sicily in July 1943. It had been one of the XX Committee's most successful deception operations. 'Synarchique', George continued, was of considerable interest to a philologist being – as he assured me – a most unusual Greek derivation. And this reconfirmed the reference since Major Martin's briefcase had contained information disclosing the false information that the landings would be in the Peloponnese, not Sicily. In other words, the paragraph indicated that the connection between PROSPER and Caluire was not Dansey alone, it was the XX Committee.

At this point Professor Huxley seemed to go slightly off-piste, his excitement about the abstruse nature of 'Synarchique' (and its relevance in patristics to certain texts of the Church Fathers) recalibrating his focus away from events in the mid-twentieth century into a far deeper past, and leaving me several thousand years out of my depth. So I looked up the *Ordre Martiniste-Synarchique*[46] and found that it was an occult movement popular among members of the extreme right in France in the 1930s and that this 'mysterious' Dr Martin had been the intelligence officer of the *Cagoule*. Both Colonel Groussard, the SIS agent in Geneva working with Victor Farrell, and his young colleague Pierre Bénouville – who sent René Hardy to Caluire, knowing that he had been in the hands of the Gestapo – were ex-*cagoulards*. Major X seemed to be working the *Ordre Martiniste-Synarchique* clue impressively hard.

By coincidence Professor Huxley's suggestion that the riddles were pointing towards the XX Committee came the day after my final visit to the National Archives at Kew. As the loudspeakers announced that the reading room would be closing at 7 p.m. until further notice, because of COVID-19, I was working through a newly discovered file, KV4/120, which was headed 'Proposals for the Union of Section V of SIS and B Division of the Security Service [MI5], 1942'.

Of course, nothing came of these 'proposals'. Hostilities broke out in March and MI5 was routed in October. SIS regarded the move as a blatant takeover bid of their counter-espionage section by MI5. The MI5 team was led by Sir David Petrie, the Director General, and Dick White, the deputy director of B Division. SIS was represented by C, Sir Stewart Menzies and yet another BLANK. Through a further slip in the redaction I was able to see that this new BLANK was C's personal hatchet man David Boyle – who had started his career as an intelligence officer in the Black and Tans, when he had served with such enthusiasm that even that brutal regiment had found him an embarrassment; in 1921 he had been deported from Dublin and returned to London. (Philby said he rather liked him.)

I had hoped that this MI5 file would contain some additional information about SIS, which it did. On 5 June 1942, Petrie sent a rather blunt message to Menzies: 'Is it not a fact that both SIS and SOE have for months past been suffering serious losses of agents . . . through constant penetration . . . by the German SS?' KV4/120 revealed that one of the most aggressive SIS negotiators in response had been the head of Section Vd (Iberia), 'K.M. Philby'. At one point Philby had outraged MI5 by suggesting that one of their officers was so incompetent that he should be stripped of his commission. C seemed to approve. He mentioned that were he to lose sole control of Section V he would probably hive off a large part of the section and keep it in the SIS building under an independent director, BLANK (ten spaces) – possibly once again 'Mr (four plus six spaces) Philby'. The MI5 report made special mention of Philby, noting that he had 'made a deliberate attempt to render [his Iberian sub-section] self-contained'.

The MI5 investigation of Section V also disclosed that SIS had a problem with one of their own senior officers, a certain Colonel 'Dansie' [*sic*]. This officer was preventing Section V from having 'any direct liaison with SOE', and the section was 'forced to do the best they could through Colonel Dansie'. Furthermore, one of the sub-sections of V, (Vpa, responsible for Switzerland) was 'not a section at all' because

Switzerland was 'Colonel Dansie's pet' and he would 'not allow any requests or questions from Section V to be passed to agents in the territory'. In other words, in Switzerland Uncle Claude could do as he pleased. The MI5 officer added: 'It is ironical that this territory which . . . is the obvious danger spot of Europe should be a *terra incognita* for the purposes of Section V'.

And then KV4/120 introduced an alternative candidate for the original BLANK of KV2/1131. It identified a sub-section Vx, devoted to 'Special Agents and Deception Plans'. 'Special agents' was code for double agents.[47] At the head of Vx was a 'Major F.E. Foley'. Major Foley had complicated responsibilities. At one point, like Z man Victor Farrell in Geneva, he was building escape lines, linking Switzerland through France to Spain.[48] Separately, as Vx he worked in Section V, side by side with Philby, running double agents. But he also worked with Colonel Dansey and ran the colonel's A section, where he was 'charged with rebuilding networks in occupied Europe' and presided over a sub-section devoted to the Free French.[49] And then, in March 1942, he became the SIS representative on the XX Committee.[50] If 'Major BLANK' was indeed Major Foley, then the tactfully non-committal representative of Section V at the inter-agency meeting called to sit in judgement on Henri Frager's denunciation of Déricourt on 18 November 1943 was not just a close associate of Colonel Dansey, he was also the unidentified representative of the top-secret committee that was running 'doubles'.

I returned to counting the movements of the MI5 typewriter carriage. Foley did not fit the CX reference, which would have had to revert to being a symbol. But 'Major (F.E. FOLEY)' covered ten spaces. Frank Foley flew to Lisbon on XX Committee business on 10 November 1943.[51] If he had returned to London by the evening of 18 November, he fitted the report of that meeting like a glove.

In any case, whoever represented Section V at that meeting in Baker Street, it was increasingly clear that throughout 1943 Déricourt had been run as a XX Committee double agent by SIS as part of the agency's contribution to what became known as Operation Starkey.

———

Before leaving Kew, I decided to take another look at HS9/421, Déricourt's personal file. Originally it had seemed to contain rather trivial information. Following D-Day, SOE had stopped paying for the Déricourts' suite at the Savoy and packed them off to the Swan's Nest Hotel in Stratford-upon-Avon. Madame Déricourt was furious and Henri was not amused. He regarded his exile in Stratford as 'a material and moral punishment' and added that his 'sentiments had been profoundly wounded'. His rather optimistic request to be given a job as a delivery pilot was turned down and it was clear that the War Office no longer knew what to do with him. In June 1945 he was allowed to return to France, where, as we have seen, a judicial prosecution for treason was announced in 1946.

The last file I consulted at Kew before the National Archive closed was KV2/1132, the second volume of Déricourt's security file. And here the penultimate entry was a reference to that prosecution. It was a pasted-in press cutting from the *Sunday Empire News* of 1 December 1946. 'British secret service witnesses,' it read:

> may go to Paris to testify at the trial of 'Captain Gilbert', Henry Alfred Eugene Déricourt, who is charged with treason. Signed statements have been taken from British agents who were associated with Captain Gilbert when he was famous in MI5 ... German documents left in Gestapo HQ disclose that he was working for the enemy in 1943.

Beneath the yellowing clipping was a neat pencilled note to 'B2b from B4'.

> GILBERT was well-known to this officer during the war. If you are required to take any action would you bear in mind that I can provide you with a valuable source of information which will greatly supplement what appears on our files. T.A.R.

'Tar' was the nickname, and initialled signature, of Thomas Argyll Robertson, who founded the XX Committee and ran its agents from 1941 to 1944. Here was final confirmation that in February 1944, after twelve months of dedicated security work, Major Geoffrey Wethered, of MI5's B1b division, in recalling Déricourt, had succeeded in blowing up one of our own double agents.

21

The Depths of Deception

> *Counter espionage is nothing to do with catching spies, or collecting information. Its target is the enemy's intelligence service. Its purpose is to make the enemy's intelligence service an extension of one's own. The classic technique is penetration.*
>
> Patrick Seale and Maureen McConville,
> *Philby: The Long Road to Moscow*

Sir Claude Dansey, the 'pantomime villain' of SIS – who had been 'showing signs of wear' according to Robert Cecil – retired in 1946 and died a year later, but the mess he left behind him took much longer to clear up. Concealing any British intelligence link with Caluire would not have been a problem, the bitter struggle between rival Resistance factions provided the best possible distraction. But the French authorities could not be so easily diverted in their search for the traitor who was responsible for the destruction of the hundreds of resisters who had been sucked into PROSPER. There were two obvious suspects, Bodington and Déricourt.

By the spring of 1945, MI5 was already running investigations into both members of F section. The officer investigating Bodington was at a loss to know what the deputy head of F had achieved by going to Paris in July 1943, unless it was to 'renew contact with the Germans'.[1] MI5 also noted that since Bodington was 'responsible for checking the work of SOE agents in France', he was 'admirably placed for calming any doubts which might arise in London about the bona fides of any double agent'[2] – the prime suspect being Déricourt.

Meanwhile the BCRA, working along parallel lines, wrote to MI5 raising the possibility of '*une trahison éventuelle de Major Bodington*' (a

possible betrayal by Major Bodington).[3] Captain Vaudreuil described
his enquiry as '*une matière aussi délicate*' (such a delicate matter), and
regretted that the BCRA had not been allowed to see the SOE files on
PROSPER. A principal piece of evidence against both officers was the
way in which Jack Agazarian, Bodington's radio operator, had been
directed into a known Gestapo trap. There was a technical complication when it came to Déricourt. He was French on French territory,
and under French law only the French could interrogate him. But
most of the relevant information was in Baker Street. Eventually on
14 February the BCRA and MI5 did a deal.[4] It was agreed that the
investigation into Déricourt should be decided in France. SOE undertook to supply all relevant records* and to assist fully with the French
enquiry. The French, in turn, would drop the case of Bodington.

The MI5 case officer investigating Bodington eventually reached the
conclusion that there was a circumstantial case against him, largely because
of his behaviour in Paris.[5] MI5 thought it particularly suspicious that
Bodington had gone on trusting Déricourt even though he knew that
Déricourt was in contact with the SD[6] and had told the Germans of
Bodington's presence in Paris. The alternative explanation, that Bodington
and Déricourt were engaged in a separate operation, following different
orders, does not seem to have occurred to anyone involved in the MI5
investigation – which was finally shelved as 'inconclusive'. Although
Bodington's superior officers frequently expressed serious doubts about
his motivation and ability, none of them recorded a suspicion that he
might have been reporting to Claude Dansey. It was only in 1994 that one
of those colleagues, Vera Atkins, F section's intelligence officer, broke
many years of discreet silence by giving voice to a long-standing conviction. 'Nick,' she told a French journalist, 'probably worked for SIS.'[7]
Bodington's last duty as an SIS mole was to attend Déricourt's trial in
Paris in June 1948 and double-cross the French prosecutors by securing
Déricourt's acquittal. This was the crowning absurdity. Two F section
officers were suspected of treason by both the British and French security
agencies. When one of the suspects finally came to trial he was acquitted
on the evidence of the other.

---

* T.A. Robertson's reference to unfiled information about Déricourt (see p. 284) shows
that MI5's 'relevant records' were irrelevant. The deal was designed to mislead the
BCRA.

Some months after this exploit Bodington met Vera Atkins in the street and greeted her warmly. 'I no longer know you Nick,' she said, and walked on.[8] Miss Atkins had been in a bad mood for several years. Starting in September 1944 she had launched a personal investigation into the fate of the F section agents who had not come home. She was particularly concerned about the women agents.* Miss Atkins spent months travelling to France and eventually to Germany, interrogating SD personnel, but – as Sarah Helm has revealed in her biography of Vera Atkins – her enquiries were consistently blocked by SOE's 'security director', John Senter. Vera Atkins, who had no knowledge of wartime deception operations, was infuriated by this patronising reaction, not realising that Senter was still engaged in an extensive cover-up, designed to keep F section officers permanently in the dark. She eventually managed to interrogate her principal target, Josef Kieffer, who was in British custody awaiting trial.[9] Kieffer knew what had really happened inside No. 84. He knew the truth about 'the pact' and he knew the whole story of Déricourt's treachery. Miss Atkins was convinced that his evidence would ensure the air movements officer's conviction. But by the time Déricourt came to trial in June 1948, Kieffer himself had been tried and hanged. He was convicted of war crimes by a British court. In the summer of 1944, shortly after D-Day, he had received an order from Kopkow in Berlin to execute a group of uniformed British POWs who were in the SAS, and he had carried it out. By the time Kieffer was hanged, Kopkow – who had issued the criminal order – was safe in Berlin and working for MI5.

In 1965, before the publication of *SOE in France*, one of the government lawyers employed to vet the book noted that 'the now impecunious Bodington' might sue Professor Foot for hinting that the temporary acting major had not been authorised to allow Déricourt to remain in contact with the Paris SD. The lawyer, who had clearly never worked in wartime deception, added: 'It is beyond doubt that Bodington had never been given any authority to make such a statement.'[10] Bodington died in 1974. At the time of his death he was in the process of suing both the Crown and Professor Foot for libel.[11] Nicolas Bodington had no money and could never have afforded a High Court

---

* Of the fifty-four women sent to France by SOE(F) one in three were caught and of those caught 78 per cent were killed, frequently in humiliating or brutal circumstances.

libel action. He was going for a fat settlement, and had he lived he
might well have received one.

Commander John Senter's '*Secret and Personal*' letter to Major Wethered
of 18 February 1944 had provided the evidence missing from the
'conspiracy theory'. Déricourt was London's man and had been all
along. And that discovery answered so many of the questions previously unresolved. It explained why SOE were unaware of Déricourt's
one-night visit on 20/21 July, and why he had returned to France on an
SIS flight in apparent breach of Dansey's security screen. It explained
why Bodington had left a note on the file, just before setting off for
Paris – 'We know he is in contact with the Germans and also how and
why.' And it also provided a chilling explanation as to why the resisters
of the PROSPER network had been left to their fate instead of being
warned. This was the thread that led out of the labyrinth. The destiny
of Nanteuil's *Réseau Adolphe* had been settled at one level or another by
the deception planners of Whitehall. When Dansey waltzed into Patrick
Reilly's office at the end of June 1943, chanting 'Great News! . . . One
of the SOE networks in France has just blown up!'[12] he was not just
gloating; he was celebrating an encouraging development in that
summer's most important deception, one in which he had operational
control. The breaking of PROSPER had been part of Operation
Starkey. But where was the evidence – as suggested in the anonymous
letter – of a connection to Caluire? And why should London have been
involved in the arrest of 'Max'? An answer to those questions might be
found by reconsidering allied strategy in 1943, the part deception played
in it, and its impact on German Intelligence.

'Deception' has been defined by the professionals as a proposition that
'induces belief that something false is true', it conceals falsehood. This is
distinct from 'cover' which 'induces belief that something true is false'
and conceals truth.[13] The British deception operations of 1943 were
central to overall allied strategy, the need to avoid defeat and manage an
eventual victory. The most urgent priority for Britain and the United
States, in the absence of a Second Front, was to keep the Soviet Union
in the battle. 'The basic idea of the deception policy of 1943,' in the

words of J.C. Masterman '[. . . was to] contain the maximum enemy forces in western Europe and the Mediterranean area and thus discourage their transfer to the Russian front.'[14] The matter became even more urgent on 2 July, when Stalin recalled his ambassador Ivan Maisky. Maisky, who enjoyed excellent relations with Churchill, left London saying that since there was to be no Second Front that year his mission was pointless.[15] In Washington, Roosevelt had a secondary aim, entirely compatible with the first. He intended to eliminate de Gaulle politically and prepare for an Allied Military Government in France, once German forces had been driven out. In the elimination of de Gaulle's influence, at least, he was supported by Churchill.

'The most important of [our deception] operations,' Masterman continued, 'was Operation Starkey.'[16] The critical period for Starkey was from 28 February – when the Red Army's advance in the Ukraine, following the victory at Stalingrad, was brought to a halt by von Manstein on the Donetz River – to 10 July, when allied forces landed in Sicily. During those four months the major concern was the need to support Soviet forces in the Ukraine, as they regrouped and awaited the German counter-attack. It was then that every effort had to be made to pin German divisions in the west by passing false information that the Allies were planning large-scale cross-Channel operations before the autumn of 1943.

On 11 April, Field Marshal von Manstein signalled to Hitler that he was ready to launch Operation Citadel. This was the assault on the Soviet salient outside Kursk that was designed to destroy the armoured capacity of the Red Army. This signal was decoded at Bletchley and on 26 April, General Morgan, COSSAC (Chief of Staff to the Supreme Allied Commander), was ordered to prepare a deception plan that would last over the whole of the summer.[17] Morgan delegated this task to the appropriate body, the LCS. But the blueprint for such a plan already existed. On 29 January, following the Casablanca Conference, the Chiefs of Staff had instructed the LCS to prepare general strategic deception plans for three amphibious operations against the French coast. These plans, as we have seen, were to include real raids to provoke real air battles, an imaginary bridgehead on either side of Boulogne and imaginary landings of a larger force on the Cotentin Peninsula. The plans had been approved by the Chiefs of Staff on 9 February and were already in operation. In April they were updated.

In mid-June, two weeks before Kursk, and three weeks before the Sicily landings, when reliance on the success of Starkey was at its peak, the Gestapo in France had a significant run of success. They arrested the French general commanding the Secret Army, captured a huge cache of arms and explosives as well as several hundred resisters, and eliminated the leaders of both the British and French Resistance organisations.[18] For the deception to have its maximum impact on German plans all the components of those Gestapo triumphs were essential. In July the situation changed because the Sicily landings forced Hitler to fight on a real second front, and this took some of the pressure off the deception staffs.*[19] But Operation Starkey ran its crooked course throughout the summer. It was described as a failure in London since it did not succeed in pinning German divisions to the 'Atlantic Wall'. But Starkey was not a complete failure, it can also be seen as a partial success. It supported the idea that the allied invasion plans of 1943 had been genuine – and had only been cancelled thanks to the brilliance of the Paris SD, whose judgement Hitler was thenceforth more likely to trust. And Starkey made a powerful impression on Field Marshal von Rundstedt, the German commander-in-chief in France. Von Rundstedt continued to believe that a cross-Channel invasion was imminent until the arrival of the 1943 autumn gales.[20]

And Starkey offered one further advantage. It established the reliability of the double agents involved in circulating the information that led to the arrest of 'Max' and 'Prosper', agents such as Henri Déricourt and Edmée Delettraz. That is why Dansey and Bodington continued to protect Déricourt throughout 1943 and why Bodington was still arguing in favour of Déricourt's return right up to the month before D-Day. Starkey had been a useful dry run for Operation Fortitude, the celebrated deception operation mounted by the XX Committee to cover the Normandy landings. Until those landings took place Henri Déricourt had useful work to do.

————

Professor Huxley had been intrigued by the reference to John the Baptist in Major X's anonymous letter, which, as he pointed out, falls

---

* Forty-three *Wehrmacht* divisions were sent from northern Europe and the Eastern Front to Italy in July 1943.

on 24 June – '. . . *The feast day of John the Baptist – there now I've virtually handed it to you on a plate . . .*'. So I looked at the calendar again. The raids in the Sologne and Caluire had taken place on 21 June. But it was not until 24 June that Francis Suttill had been arrested in Paris. And it was on that same day that 'Max' was identified in Lyons.[21] What had been 'handed to me on a plate' seemed to be another irrelevant coincidence between the two operations. But what looks like a coincidence today would not have looked that way to the SD in June 1943.

For it was only on 24 June that the Gestapo in the Avenue Foch realised what they had achieved. Only then could Boemelburg and Kieffer have made the connection and understood that in catching 'Prosper' and 'Max' they had trapped both the leadership of French resistance and the ringleaders of the British agency sent to organise it. In Lyons, on that day,[22] Barbie, having uncovered the true identity of 'Jacques Martel', started to give him the treatment. In Paris, Kieffer, using more intelligent methods, was attempting to persuade Suttill and Major Norman that they should cooperate because he had a spy in Baker Street. On 27 June Colonel Buckmaster made his memorable intervention, accusing Major Norman of committing '*a serious breach of security which must not, repeat must not, happen again*'. At which point Gilbert Norman, convinced by now that he *had* been betrayed in London, threw in the towel and started to sing to Kieffer's tune. Once Norman started to cooperate, Suttill – who had remained silent – was sent to Berlin. By the following day, 28 June, Barbie in Lyons realised that either through zeal or carelessness he had made it impossible to extract any information from the political head of the French Resistance. So 'Max' was driven up to Paris and Boemelburg discovered what had happened. He was reported to have been very angry at the desperate condition Barbie's prisoner was in.[23] But Berlin urgently needed a report and Boemelburg had to supply one.

On 29 June, the day after Barbie delivered a moribund prisoner to his villa outside Paris, Boemelburg sent an account of events to Kaltenbrunner in Berlin, which was forwarded to Himmler, and then shown to Hitler. It described the Caluire affair and the importance of the arrests carried out, but stated that 'Max, de Gaulle's delegate to the Resistance, had been expected at the meeting *but had unfortunately not been present* [my emphasis].'[24] The Paris SD were presumably still trying to work out how to explain the fact that although they had arrested

'Max', he was past interrogating. And while Boemelburg was working on that problem, Kieffer, assisted by Norman and Culioli, was constructing a solution. Arms raids in the Sologne were launched on 1 July. By 6 July it was clear to the Blois Gestapo that they had made 'the most important seizures of arms and explosives since 1940'. And Boemelburg finally had a way out of his difficulty. Because on 5 July, on the Eastern Front, a massive German tank offensive opened the Battle of Kursk.

So, on 7 July, with the Sologne arms depots in his grasp, Boemelburg owned up and put 'Max' – correctly identified as 'Jean Moulin, a former prefect' – on a train to Germany. Jean Moulin died that night, reportedly from a heart attack, before the train reached the frontier. By which time, as the Paris SD would have calculated, Kaltenbrunner and Himmler had other preoccupations.

In the case of both PROSPER and Caluire, the Gestapo's principal quarry would have been desperate to conceal the same misleading 'fact' – that landings in northern France in 1943 formed part of allied strategy. Had Kieffer or Barbie been able to persuade 'Prosper' or 'Max' to talk, the information gleaned from those arrests would have dovetailed, and led the Gestapo to the same desired conclusion. The arrest of 'Max' would have doubled the impact of the arrest of 'Prosper', and so reinforced the deception.

Starkey may even have 'failed' because 'Max', 'Vidal' and 'Prosper' – the agents primed to hand over misleading information – refused to cooperate with the Gestapo.

———

The wartime structure of British deception was so complex and obscure that it eventually defeated even Michael Howard, its refreshingly frank official historian. But that structure had not been cobbled together by chance. It was deliberately designed to maximise security and minimise accountability, to bolster what intelligence professionals value so highly, 'deniability'.[25]

At the top of the chain was the War Cabinet, all-powerful, but unconcerned with deception. Below them were the Chiefs of Staff, who knew that deception was in hand, and insisted on its use but wanted nothing to do with it. Then there was the Joint Intelligence Sub-Committee, a wartime regulator and review body, and below that the London Controlling Section. The LCS was designed to screen deception operations from those above, an entirely sensible precaution. It identified strategic objectives and was directed by the Controller of Deception, who had no executive powers, and who in turn purposely excluded himself from knowledge of specific operations. Supervision of these was delegated to the W Board which was manned by the three heads of service intelligence and the directors of MI5 and SIS. But they too were more than happy to be kept in the dark. Below, or parallel to the W Board responsibility becomes opaque and circular. The W Board had a sub-committee, the XX Committee, which specialised in devising schemes to misinform German Intelligence through the use of double agents. The work of the XX Committee has become legendary[26] but it too delegated responsibility because the double agents were 'run' by just two of its members, the directors of MI5 and SIS.[27] These two men, Sir Stewart Menzies and Sir David Petrie, C and DGSS, were already members of the W Board, and they were far too busy to get involved in the operational details. So they in turn appointed their own delegates; which is how one reaches the murky depths of extreme secrecy that are the natural feeding ground of operators like Colonel Groussard, and 'Uncle Claude' and K.M. Philby.

That is the hierarchy that can be reconstructed from the works of Professor Howard, J.C. Masterman and General Frederick Morgan. But according to the files of the NKVD (later KGB), some of which were published in London in 2009, there was a further body, the 'inter-departmental committee for deception', which was not mentioned by any of the above authorities. It was known as TWIST.[28] And TWIST is of particular interest for two reasons. Firstly, although it depended directly from the LCS it was – to quote the NKVD – 'an executive organisation'. And secondly because its ten-man board included Colonel T.A. Robertson; Ewen Montagu, who invented, and wrote, *The Man Who Never Was*; Major Frank Foley; and the 'assistant to the deputy director of B Division of MI5' – a 'Major [Anthony] Blunt'. Blunt's official duty was to spread rumours, via foreign diplomats and the foreign press. He passed genuine information to his controller, Anatoli Gorski, who passed it on to Moscow Centre in the diplomatic bag.* Blunt targeted TWIST and went to some trouble to join it,

---

* This was totally secure as the MI5 officer responsible for checking diplomatic bags was called Anthony Blunt.

realising the misuse he might make of a knowledge of deception operations. He approached T.A. Robertson, who disliked Blunt because of
his homosexuality, but nonetheless sponsored his application.[29]

Major Foley's single duty at TWIST, according to the NKVD (i.e.
Anthony Blunt), was 'the transmission of disinformation to the enemy
through double agents of the Secret Intelligence Service abroad',[30] and
regular meetings were held with operational agencies such as SIS and
SOE.[31] Presumably it was to one such meeting, in May 1943, that the
leaders of SOE – Gubbins, Sporborg and Boyle – were summoned to be
informed 'by SIS' that 'PROSPER had been penetrated and a decision
had been taken to exploit the situation.'[32] SIS in this case would have
been the SIS emissary from TWIST, possibly Major Foley.

Double agents who had penetrated German Intelligence and were
working within deception operations were primed to 'release genuine
items of information to the enemy',[33] and double agents working in
France during this period were involved in the downfall of both 'Max'
and 'Prosper'. Furthermore, three 'loyal' agents, Jean Moulin and
Charles Delestraint in March and Francis Suttill in May, had been
given the false impression while in London, just before setting off for
France, that landings later in the year still formed part of allied plans.
To have confided that information in good faith, to the general in
command of the Secret Army, on the eve of his departure for France,
would have been an act of incredible recklessness. But imparted as an
element of deception – suggesting that something false was true – it
made sense.

The arrival of Blunt in the story was unexpected. No sooner had
Philby slipped away amid the clatter of SIS typewriter keys than he was
replaced by the willowy but solidly documented alternative of Major
Blunt. Blunt and Philby sometimes cooperated during the war in their
espionage activities[34], and they were both openly and officially involved
in the organisation of deception. So if there is a connection between
Broadway and Caluire, it had two hypothetical pathways – one through
Geneva, and the other via Moscow.

––––––

Following the Geneva road, one could start by asking when it might
first have occurred to Colonel Dansey that the PROSPER component
of Starkey could be strengthened by the additional sacrifice of 'Max'?

A possible date is 10 June, when the news reached London that 'Vidal' had been arrested on the previous day in Paris.[35] With the arrest of General Delestraint, Max's operations in France, amputated of their military significance, lost much of their already limited value from London's point of view. Delestraint was known and liked in London, whereas Max was an obscure functionary, building up an unauthorised and unwelcome political structure so that, in Roosevelt's words, de Gaulle can 'run a one-party state in France after the war'. Even the BCRA in London was increasingly critical of his strategy.[36] And with the loss of 'Vidal', 'Max's' authority within the already divided Resistance, was weakened. Since all SOE(RF) communications were sent via the British Embassy in Berne or the consulate in Barcelona,[37] and Gaullist radio traffic was also monitored, news of this loss of authority would have been immediately apparent to the SIS officers running Starkey.

Dansey certainly had the means to take Jean Moulin out of the game. In referring to the *Cagoule*'s intelligence service, my anonymous correspondent, Major X, was suggesting that Dansey worked through Geneva, via Victor Farrell and Colonel Groussard. The final link in that chain to Caluire would have been Dansey's double agent inside the Lyons Gestapo, Edmée Delettraz. In Delettraz, and in her commander Colonel Groussard, Dansey had collaborators who were every bit as ruthless as he was. And Groussard's man in Lyons, Pierre Bénouville, who ordered René Hardy to force his way into the meeting at Caluire, did so[38] in the knowledge that Hardy had recently been in Gestapo hands.

Having set the trap, and checked that it had worked, Bénouville fled the city. After hearing of the arrest of 'Max' he took the night train to Toulouse,[39] subsequently explaining that he had decided to get married. Delettraz was left to face the music. But she was protected by British Intelligence after the war; as one resistance leader put it, 'she remained miraculously untroubled'.[40] She knew that, despite all the help she had given the Lyons Gestapo, she would never face prosecution. She had been instructed to continue working for Barbie, and she had done so. When 'Max' paid the price, de Gaulle's control of the Resistance was dismantled and allied policy was served.

After Hardy's first trial, when the judge threatened to arrest Delettraz in the witness box, French prosecutors said that had Hardy been found guilty, both Delettraz and Colonel Groussard would have been charged with treason.[41] It was a situation worthy of a trial by the King and Queen of Hearts. If Hardy was innocent, then Delettraz, who claimed to be working for the Gestapo, was lying – and could not be punished for her self-proclaimed treason. Whereas if Hardy was guilty, then the Gestapo agent Delettraz was telling the truth, and could be shot. One could go further and argue that if she was telling the truth, and Hardy was guilty, then she was acting as a loyal Gestapo double agent for Colonel Groussard. Whereas if she was lying, and Hardy was innocent, she had been forced into the witness box, as a Communist Party stooge, to conceal another man's guilt.

———

When records are destroyed and the wells have been poisoned there is no history, there are just official myths, which are at least as damaging as 'conspiracy theories'. In the words of another Oxford historian, A.J.P. Taylor, 'Secrecy, as so often happens, injures those whom it is supposed to protect.'[42] But the pattern left by deception in redacted files leaves an outline that can be traced, like the invisible letters left by the spacing of a typewriter carriage. The shape is further defined by another void, the gap between official explanations and awkward facts. The redacted shreds of KV2/1131 provide an example, for they strongly suggest that something very unpleasant is still being concealed. It could be clear evidence of the Geneva link. Or, if 'CX/ _____ /E/27' does conceal the identity of P.H.I.L.B.Y., it could be the Moscow pathway to the same destination.

The Moscow pathway would start in the autumn of 1942, during the weeks leading up to Operation Torch, when Philby as head of the Iberian section was invited to take a closer interest in Tangier, where – under the International Convention of 1923 – there was a joint Franco-Spanish police presence. After those landings he had been instructed by Felix Cowgill, head of Section V, to extend his interest to include French North Africa. Later, as Vk, and acting deputy head of Section V, he acquired overall responsibility for counter-espionage in France. Here he had to penetrate the Dansey 'exclusion zone', as described in the previous chapter. Since – in the words of a former SIS case officer who witnessed the wreckage caused by Philby – he was a master at 'getting his nose under the wire of all sorts of operations he had no business to know about', this may not have posed too much of a challenge. Where Philby was concerned 'all thoughts of "compartmentalisation" disappeared'.[43]

MI5 ran double agents on British territory. In Spain and Portugal the 'specials' were controlled by SIS. And K.M. Philby, head of Section Vd, had 'oversight and overall management of all the communications between [special agents, such as] Garbo and the Germans'.[44] Garbo, one of the most celebrated of our double agents, and Agent Popov were both deployed in support of Starkey.[45] When it came to France, the 'specials' were also controlled by SIS, in the event by Major Foley of Section V and the XX Committee, and by Colonel Dansey, who had an independent intelligence network running through Geneva. Major Foley sometimes worked directly under Dansey[46] and was also responsible for keeping tabs on the Free French. The areas of intervention overlapped like a folding fan, and the possibilities of penetration were enhanced. Both Dansey and the XX Committee knew that Déricourt was giving information about PROSPER to the Paris SD. Their response was to 'exploit the situation' and F section was not to be informed.

Sir Claude Dansey always said that he despised counter-espionage – although he seems to have been happy to indulge in it when the 'enemy' target was SOE. With Bodington and André Simon he certainly penetrated F in classic counter-espionage style. And, in Air Commodore Boyle and Commander John Senter, he had close allies inside SOE – who were well above Buckmaster's head. Both officers worked with Major Foley of the XX Committee, who was reporting directly to Colonel Dansey. Since Philby was nominally Foley's superior, he might have found a means to persuade the latter to copy him into Starkey. Or he could have alerted Major Blunt, Foley's colleague on the TWIST committee. Or he could simply have used his old technique of working late in the filing cabinets.[47] In 1943 Philby and Blunt were both reporting, via Gorski, to Moscow Centre.[48] And Moscow Centre was well connected[49] through Toulouse to the FTP, the French Communist Resistance.

Philby's ultimate interest in France was of course quite different to Dansey's. Claude Dansey's interest in pre-liberation France was to gain control of the Resistance, and limit or eliminate the influence of de Gaulle. Philby's interest, in the course of 1943, was to extend the influence of the Communist Resistance, in anticipation of the post-liberation power struggle. But 'pre-liberation' these programmes were complementary, and both were greatly assisted by the raid on Caluire. For 'Max' was an obstacle to both these designs. Following his arrest, General de Gaulle's control of the military resistance was permanently eliminated[50] – and replaced by Communist domination. And it was soon noticed in London that the only segments of the great PROSPER network to survive more or less unscathed, were the Communist circuits.[51] 'Moscou–Londres, même combat'.

Revealing the penetration by Kim Philby or Anthony Blunt of the 1943 French deception operation would have opened a can of very large worms in 2002 when KV2/1131 was redacted and released – as it would today. In such a case the last link in the Caluire chain would have been Aubrac, not Madame Delettraz. Both the Aubracs worked secretly to infiltrate the non-Communist Resistance movements, and modify their policy towards the PCF line.[52] And if Aubrac had betrayed the meeting that could answer a different set of questions. The expectation that the meeting would be raided would explain the late arrival of 'Max' and Aubrac. The diversion into the waiting room and the mysterious letter from the doctor in Nice could have been arranged by Aubrac for 'Max'. The torn fragments that my anonymous reader, Major X, had posted to me in his second package had referred to the letter 'Max' had supposedly received from 'the doctor in Nice'.

And the Moscow link could explain the eventual identification of 'Max' – and the survival of Aubrac. All the time that Barbie was dislocating Henri Aubry's shoulder and putting him before four simulated firing squads, he would already have known the real identity of 'Jacques Martel'. But since Barbie needed to conceal his source he could only summon 'Max' after three days, when Aubry had cracked. QED.

But I had found no documentary evidence to complete the circumstantial Moscow chain. And QED is not history, it's a parlour game.

––––––

The ingenious triumphs of the XX Committee in the use of double agents have become justly celebrated. But it would be naïve to suppose that these well-publicised 'avowable' operations were the end of the story. In the shadow war and the pursuit of victory, there were nice calculations to be made and lists to be drawn up – decisions as to who would be saved and who would be let go. Jean Moulin has long since been transformed into a legend of national heroism and suffering. But we should not forget those others, the people who were expendable and who died in the labyrinth, in the shades of successful deception.

They include Jack Agazarian, who was sent into a Gestapo trap in order to protect the role of an agile double agent, Déricourt, and the safety of his commander, Bodington; Andrée Borrel, who was thrown into a Natzweiler incinerator while still alive, and described post-war, in the official history, as one who socialised too much in Paris cafés; Francis Suttill, who built the largest armed resistance network in France, and who went to his death refusing to play the Gestapo game, convinced that he was protecting a parachute invasion that was never going to take place; Gilbert Norman, formerly of the Durham Light Infantry, who was vilified after the war because – through his commanding officer's incompetence – he had been broken in the belief that the Gestapo had infiltrated SOE HQ in Baker Street; and Yvonne Rudellat, who died slowly and alone with a bullet in her head, in Belsen, two weeks after the camp had been liberated, unidentified because she was still so terrified of being recognised as an SOE agent.

And there were the hundreds of resisters, men and women of the Sologne, *les petits gens* who never came back, or returned in broken health. They all played their part in what the inventive officers of the XX Committee sometimes called 'the Great Game'. They too deserve to be remembered 'in the truth', like the soldiers who fought and died on the beaches of Normandy.

Perhaps it is also worth recording how the SIS double agent Henri Déricourt passed the time in France during the crucial week of 21 June 1943. He was due to conduct a pick-up near Amboise that night, but he never turned up, possibly having been tipped off about the German military operations in the Sologne. The pick-up was rescheduled for the Feast Day of John the Baptist, 24 June. Déricourt did turn up on that occasion and escorted the two incoming agents to the Paris train. It was the morning when Francis Suttill, Gilbert Norman and Andrée Borrel were facing Josef Kieffer in the Avenue Foch for the first time. On the train Déricourt was seen walking up and down the corridor peering into compartments. One of his charges, Colonel Bonoteaux, was arrested by the Gestapo shortly after arriving at the Gare d'Austerlitz. He later died in Dachau. His fellow agent, who escaped, said after the war that he was sure Déricourt had pointed out Colonel Bonoteaux to the German police.[53]

Afterword: The Level Sands

Remorse is the knife that probes far deeper than the wound . . .
It is the feelings that are killed . . . and the effects lie like
bleached bones on the level sands . . .

Wordsworth by Herbert Read

In 1973 I received a letter from Nanny, who had been visiting friends in England over Christmas.

Nanteuil January 5,

My dear Patrick,

I am sorry I missed you when you came to Nanteuil. I would so love to see you again and hope before long you will come back. Thank you so very much for the tea, it saves my life at times and I do need it more often than I should . . .

I am at Betty's but have lunch with Moune. The big house is too cold for me. I don't know how Moune lives in it. She is still unsettled and still doesn't know when she will be able to move, she will have so much to do when she does, she is taking on a lot. So [are] Serge and Betty taking on Nanteuil, they will need a lot of courage and patience . . .

Here we have Frédéric very ill. I should say he has brain fever. He has been very ill for three weeks, at first he was unable to sleep, he was so worn and delirious at times . . . He sleeps most of the day now. For three days and nights Serge never left him, he has been wonderful with him . . . There is some talk of him going to a hospital in Paris. At these times I long for a Doctor that speaks English that I can understand . . .

I still miss Madame de Bernard and since I lost my friend in England
I feel so alone, which is the fault of old age . . .

All my love to you. Come back to see us soon.

Yours,

Nanny

The last time I saw Souris she was sitting in her sunny alcove overlooking the courtyard, surrounded by the leather-bound works of
Victor Hugo, and drinking a cup of Nanny's English tea. She had the
same slightly hesitant smile that I remembered, and she apologised for
being too tired to come downstairs. She died in February 1971. She
had been confused for some weeks, thinking she was back in
Ravensbrück, with Dorothea Binz, Vera, Carmen, Irma – and all
those others. There were 546 *Aufseherinnen* guarding the camp, who
competed for the approval of the 1008 male SS. For Souris, time had
levelled the sands, and the bones of the shadow land had emerged: the
land of unimaginable cruelty where the hospital was run by doctors
who carried out surgical experiments without anaesthetic, where
nurses beat you with clubs and poisoned their patients, and where
new-born babies were drowned in a bucket of water before their
mothers' eyes – a procedure that could take twenty minutes or more.[1]
Of the 11,000 French women registered at Ravensbrück, 8,000 never
returned, a mortality rate of 72 per cent, comparable to that of the
sappers on the D-Day beaches. But the women who died in
Ravensbrück did not die quickly, or in the heat of battle, or with the
RAMC to back them up and help them through.

Most of those who died, died slowly. They were worked or beaten
or starved to death. In January 1945, three months before the Swedish
Red Cross was able to rescue 300 French prisoners – including Souris –
Himmler had ordered the SS Guards at Ravensbrück to raise the death
rate in the camp to 2,000 women a month.[2] At that point there were
about 46,000 surviving prisoners and a gas chamber was installed. One
month later Souris was among those marched away along frozen winter
tracks to the nearby camp of Rechlin. The women in Rechlin were
worked day and night, their already wretched food ration was halved,
and they were provided with no blankets at night.[3] The prisoners called
it 'the extermination camp'.

After her mother's death Moune continued to work as a volunteer

with the *Comité d'Histoire de la 2e. Guerre Mondiale* recording[4] and analys-
ing the fate of the deportees. She tried to keep the language school
going but it became too much for her and so Betty, who had married
Serge Théry, the younger brother of Pierre, bought her out. She left
Nanteuil in March and signed the Visitor's Book '*Moune Gardnor-Beard
Watson 28.6.1922 – 3.3.1973*'. With Moune's departure, teaching at
Nanteuil came to an end and the Visitor's Book fell into disuse. In 1975,
Betty's son Frédéric, who had trained as a professional chef, agreed to
keep the house going, first as a restaurant and then as a hotel. It was, as
Nanny said, a lot to take on. An Australian traveller recorded her discov-
ery of the new arrangement in 1984.

When pouring rain interrupted our summer camping trip . . . we saw
a sign to the Château de Nanteuil Hotel outside Blois. We followed its
arrow along the winding lane bordering the Cosson River with only
faint hope.

We drove over an old lichen-covered stone bridge, through a
pillared gateway, into a courtyard of pebbles, roses and weeds, and
pulled up in front of a gracious 18th century château. In the damp
heavy air only the cooing sounds from a dovecote and the rushing of
a stream broke the silence.

A search for the *maître d'hôtel* discovered him fast asleep on a
four-poster bed in the coach house, looking like the hero in a
Zeffirelli film. But, yes, there was a room vacant, if we didn't mind
one without a bath; the Blue Room (in which both the Duke of
Wellington and Dick Seaman had slept) on the second floor, whose
dormer windows looked out on a terrace by a stream overhung
with ash and sycamore trees, and an old mossy footbridge over the
weir . . .

Along the passage a huge antique porcelain bowl collected rain
which occasionally dripped through the ceiling; the rods on the wide
staircase were of solid brass, some were loose and others missing, the
carpet seldom vacuumed; a suit of armour presided over the entrance
hall; the panelled dining room was furnished with carved chairs and
tables, and dominated by an immense fireplace.

Frédéric, our sleeping hero, is a descendant of the original owners.
With quiet desperation he holds on to the château, trying to make
ends meet and get repairs completed through summer tourists. He is

encouraged by Nanny – a true survivor – who had looked after the family since 1918 and who remained at the château throughout the war after Frédéric's grandparents were sent to concentration camps. During those lean years she and the cook cared for the children, grew vegetables and fought off starvation.

Now, each morning and evening, Nanny strides out with her two dogs and an ebony walking stick with a carved silver handle – a present from the Empress Eugenie – to relive memories of a bygone era, in the woods along the river, when hunting parties and balls were the way of life . . .[5]

Frédéric was nearly defeated by the task of reinventing Nanteuil and one day, tracked by the banks and French bureaucracy and running out of money, he told Nanny that he thought he would have to sell up and do something else. Nanny would have none of it.

'Frédéric,' she said. 'Your grandmother never had any money. And you . . . *Work*'.

He kept going.

———

The Gestapo took the Nanteuil Visitors' Book with them to Orléans when they arrested Bébert. It was returned to Nanteuil some months later. It shows that there were no visitors to Nanteuil in 1945 and the first pupils arrived in August 1946 with a school master from Stowe. Before that there had been just two visitors. Ingrid Brilioth was from Sweden, possibly one of the Red Cross nurses who had saved Souris' life a year earlier. Before her there was a solitary English name, 'Oscar Watson, St Pancras Rectory, Chichester – March 1946'. He stayed for three months.

Oscar's real name was Owen and he arrived at Nanteuil as a 23-year-old French literature student who was researching a dissertation on the wartime Resistance movement in the Sologne. He was the first of *les jeunes anglais* to return after the war and he had to get special permission from the French Embassy to enter France. He had been told about Nanteuil by his tutor at Corpus Christi College, Cambridge, who had sent students to Souris in the 1930s. Owen had left school in 1940 after winning three scholarships to Corpus. His studies had been interrupted by the war, on which he did not look back fondly. He had been

seventeen when it broke out, staying with a friendly German family
called Schöttl who had a son called Walter. One evening his host,
Colonel Schöttl, Walter's father, told Owen to pack his suitcase and
say his goodbyes, they were leaving immediately. The colonel had just
received orders to lead his battalion to the Polish frontier, which they
were to attack on the following day. He realised that if Owen were
still in Germany when war was declared he would probably be interned
– or worse – for the duration. So, disobeying his orders and risking a
court-martial – or worse – the colonel drove his house guest to the
Dutch border and waited until he was safely across. It was an extraordinary act of courtesy for which Owen remained grateful for the rest
of his life.

––––

In Ravensbrück the French deportees found that the camp was run
along nationalist lines. The French women were crowded together
into a separate block and the friendships they formed became a vital
assistance to survival. Like all prisoners Souris was stamped with a
number on arrival. Her five-figure tattoo began with 27, the number
of her convoy of 938 women deported by their own government from
the Vichy internment camp at Romainville. The friends she made
included Germaine Tillion and Geneviève de Gaulle, the general's
niece, who had both been in the Musée de l'Homme group, one of the
first Resistance *réseaux* to be formed. Both survived and pursued
successful careers after the war. In 2015, the ashes of Germaine Tillion
and Geneviève de Gaulle were moved to the Pantheon, the highest
posthumous honour the Republic offers its citizens. Another of
Souris' friends was Maisie Renault, sister of 'Colonel Rémy'.* She,
like Germaine Tillion, wrote an account of life in the camp. Souris is
mentioned in both those books as someone to whom others turned for
help. Another survivor of the Sologne Resistance, Marguerite
Flamencourt, the widow of the chicken farmer from Meung-sur-
Loire (whose husband had died in a German camp), paid tribute to

–––––––––––

* 'Colonel Rémy' (Gilbert Renault) was the first Gaullist secret agent to enter occupied France. In 1940 he founded an enormous network, the *Confrérie Notre-Dame*,
which was active along the Atlantic coast, from Bordeaux northwards as far as
Brittany.

Souris at her funeral and talked about her 'incredible vitality and strength of character' and how she had never given way. Marguerite Flamencourt said that she could still see Souris at the interminable roll calls, standing straight, always ready to fight back, so that her friends often had to calm her with a gentle squeeze of the arm, lest she become the target of a fatal punishment beating.

The few women who returned from Rechlin were often driven directly to Ravensbrück's gas chamber,[6] which was designed to accommodate 150 women at a time. Those who were sent back to the main camp were a frightening sight, often unrecognisable, their skin burnt black, their bodies shaking with fatigue and pain, a 'wild, hunted' expression in their eyes. On the night Souris returned, Germaine Tillion saw her and noticed that several of her companions in the queue waiting to enter the de-lousing showers had already died. Marguerite Flamencourt recalled seeing her on the following morning in a freezing dawn, still queuing and on her feet, but 'so thin, so weak, that the breeze blew her around like a reed'.

Before she was sent to Rechlin, Souris' main concern had been looking after 'Jacqueline', who arrived one day in August 1944 at Ravensbrück on the last convoy out of France. 'Jacqueline' still had a bullet in her head, which gave her a great deal of pain. Because her papers were marked 'NN' she was sent to Block 17 where she made no friends because she was so frightened of being identified as an SOE agent that she pretended to have lost her memory.[7] Whenever Souris was able to evade the guards she would visit 'Jacqueline' and take her a treat, a piece of bread, a raw carrot, or a clove of garlic. They had heard that Paris had been liberated and they would talk of what they were going to do when they were free. 'Jacqueline' wanted to see the lights of Piccadilly. She said that because her father had been English and her mother French she had two countries, and she did not know which she loved more.

When Souris returned from Rechlin she went in search of 'Jacqueline', who had disappeared, and she was told that she had been sent to the gas chamber. In fact, she had been sent to Belsen. There she died of typhus on 23 April 1945, eight days after the camp was liberated by units of the British Second Army. No one in Belsen knew that she was a British agent or knew anything about her at all. 'We don't know who will live and who will die,' she once told

Souris. '*C'est peut-être vous, c'est peut-être moi. Celle qui restera, finira le Job.*' (Perhaps it will be you, perhaps it will be me. The one who remains alive will finish the Job). 'Finishing the Job', Souris explained in a newspaper tribute she wrote in memory of her friend after the war, meant 'finishing off the collaborators'.[8] It was anger that had kept Souris alive in Ravensbrück and some of it remained with her for the rest of her life.

———

I first met 'Oscar', as Nanny always called Owen Watson, in 1962 when he came to lunch at Nanteuil. His student dissertation on the Sologne Resistance had won the Corpus Christi College Cowell Prize. He had interrupted his undergraduate studies at Cambridge for three years and once said that he had fought in the war, although he never talked of exactly what he had done. He eventually graduated with a 1st in Modern Languages in June 1947 – he said that he 'had lived in Dante for a year'. After that he went to India with the Royal Artillery. On his return he joined the Cambridge University Press. By then Moune had an apartment in the Latin Quarter on the Rue du Temple. They married in 1954 and settled in Cambridge. They lived in Martin Ryle's house. Professor Ryle had a small telescope in the attic and one day he came downstairs and told Oscar and Moune that there was something very odd going on in the Milky Way. He sat up all night and by morning had mapped the trajectory of the first Sputnik. There were about 300 journalists outside the front door within half an hour, and Ryle had to escape through the back and move into a hotel. That was the high point of Moune's life in Cambridge. She could find nothing to do there. Oscar said she still suffered from the typhoid she had caught during the war. She kept to her room and became very depressed and one day she told Oscar that she was terribly worried about her mother and that she was returning to Nanteuil to look after her, and they never lived together again.

At around this time Oscar inserted in the proofs of a CUP catalogue details of a forthcoming volume by S. Frogsbaum and O. Wede. The title was '*Some Spodulitic Tendencies of the Trundary, including a minute analysis of the acerotoid annetion of the bastic urena, crenotic evulsions and the goin in the common toad. It dissects Wyandotteau's classic work "Pondactillicus Majus" and proves that its author's position has been thoroughly undermined'*. When he was reprimanded for this pleasantry, he thought that the time might have come for a change so he moved to Paris and became the editor of the English edition of the *Larousse Illustrated Dictionary*. Then he moved into a ruined hut in a wood near Chaumont, half an hour's drive from Nanteuil. It was up a dirt track that was impassable in winter by car; the local *paysans* still used bullock carts. He always hoped that he and Moune could start again. He came to her funeral in 1989 but he did not return to the house for lunch.

———

In October 1949 Souris and Pierre received a visit from General de Gaulle, who was accompanied by his wife and by Jacques Baumel ('*Z'Oreilles*)', one of the leading survivors of *Combat* who had been in Lyons at the time of Caluire. The local paper described the general's arrival in Nanteuil as '*Une reception entourée de Mystère*' and it was certainly highly unusual for de Gaulle to acknowledge the patriotism of resisters who had been working for his bête-noire, SOE (F). There is no other record of the visit or of what was said during dinner. In 2012 Betty, the last survivor of that occasion, said that it had been Madame de Gaulle who kept the conversation going while Camille rattled the dishes. It was not unusual for de Gaulle to remain silent. During the war he had never seemed to understand that 'resisters' were an elite, since he looked on 'resistance' as every citizen's simple duty. Perhaps, glancing round the dining room that evening he thought of Souris and his niece Geneviève in Ravensbrück, and reflected on the gap between his wartime illusions and reality. True resisters frequently had their lives destroyed.

The general's signed photograph arrived some weeks later and took its place beside the rather blurred, framed snapshot of the woman Souris always called 'Jacqueline', the only name by which she had ever known Yvonne Rudellat. The two portraits then sat side by side on the chimney piece in the dining room. They overlooked the table at which both had been entertained, six years apart. On the left the enormous statesman, who as a young officer had been bayonetted in hand-to-hand fighting at Verdun and whose voice had previously only been heard on Nanny's wartime radio. On the right the tiny grandmother from London who borrowed English books from Souris' library when she was not blowing up German troop trains. It was the room where she had last been seen, gay and carefree, on that Sunday in June, the day before she was shot in the head.

————

Souris was given the Légion d'Honneur in 1955, another detail that was never mentioned in front of her English guests. With other survivors of the *Réseau Adolphe* she founded an *Amicale* in the 1950s and held an annual reunion, usually on 21 June and often in the Le Meurs' hotel at Chambord. They toasted the memory of '*les absents*' and 'Jacqueline'. She and Pierre de Bernard remained on good terms with Pierre Culioli and they sometimes talked about Déricourt and Gilbert Norman. While they tried to uncover the truth about what had happened to them in the summer of 1943 the secret committees of Whitehall continued to bury it. One theory was that Norman had betrayed the Bernards in September because he needed to keep giving information and was running out of names. Culioli was indignant that whereas Déricourt had been defended at his trial by a British intelligence officer, the only witness sent from London to his trial had appeared for the prosecution.[9] The question of what had happened was never settled. It was hard for the survivors to accept, but Déricourt was one of those who had got away. He had turned out to be useful, like Kopkow, Barbie and Mona-la-Blonde.

After he was saved from a well-deserved firing squad – by an SIS 'sleeper' – Déricourt went into exile and was said to have found work as a pilot in Laos, trading gold and guns for opium. The *Amicale* could picture him in Vientiane, sitting on a café terrace, watching a blood-red sun setting over the Mekong River, brooding about which nightclub to distract himself in that night. We have no idea whether, like 'Multon from the Poitou', he believed in God. He certainly believed in money, and his belief served him well. Looking back on it all, as he sipped his pernod and France's colonial empire collapsed around his ears, Henri Déricourt must have congratulated himself on having had a good war.

The news that he had been killed when his plane ran out of fuel over the Laotian highlands in November 1962 was greeted with some scepticism in the Sologne, because his body was never recovered. Gradually over the years there was a growing presumption that the PROSPER network had become part of a complex deception operation intended to safeguard the D-Day landings. Pierre de Bernard, who had never been fully cured of Buchenwald, died in 1959. By the time Moune died in 1989, Jeanne de Tristan had become convinced that the betrayal of PROSPER had been organised in London.[10]

———

Nanny died in 1992, aged 93. She asked for her ashes to be scattered in the park, under the oak with the divided trunk, two trees united in one she said, like the two countries in her heart. I lost touch with Oscar until the day, about ten years later, when Frédéric suggested we should visit him. By then he was an internationally famous potter. He had abandoned publishing and his pots quickly becoming celebrated for the beauty of his wood ash glazes. He started to attract pupils. He had built a kiln on the slope behind his little stone house; it took fifty hours of firing the kiln to produce enough heat to fire pots for five hours. He said the pupils did all the work, and at the age of seventy in 1992 he had added metal sculpture to his crafts. He opened his workshop to customers at 2 o'clock every afternoon and one day sold a pot to Mick Jagger, who was a neighbour. There were chickens scratching up the lawn and several dozen peacocks in the surrounding undergrowth, he thought there were about 150 of them. He vaguely remembered me from the 1960s. When Frédéric mentioned that I was about to publish a biography of Jean Moulin there was a vigorous and hostile reaction. '*Une biographie de Jean Moulin! Encore un tas de mensonge?*' (A biography of Jean Moulin! Another heap of lies?). For a moment I had the impression that a complete stranger had replaced the courteous, scholarly gentleman. It was as though a mask had slipped. That was about a month before the publication of the book.

Ten more years passed before I saw Oscar again. He was still living in the woods by his kiln, but at the age of ninety he had given up pottery. His eyesight was failing and a recent operation had not been a success. The trouble with pottery, he said, was that 'sooner or later pots always break'. 'The kiln does all the work,' he added. 'It's all given to you.' I asked him how he had become interested in pottery and he explained that it had started in his childhood, when he and his older brother lived with their father, the Revd Basil Watson, who was the Vicar of St Pancras, Chichester. He said that throughout his childhood in Chichester his mother had been confined to a chaise longue.

She had been paralysed at his birth. So, to make her happy, he had gone out each morning into the rectory garden to pick flowers. Choosing the right vase had become part of the present. Oscar was still living alone, but with the company of nine feral cats. He was down to his last twelve peacocks. He said the cats all slept on his bed at night so that 'there's hardly room for me'. His great pleasure was listening to Schubert *Lieder*, preferably sung by Matthias Goerne. He listened to them every night before going to sleep.

He spoke impeccable French but with a marked English accent. His English, which he hardly used, was pleasantly antique. 'Who in the world is this?' he exclaimed, when a stranger came through the unlocked door. Looking at the weather – it was raining, the trees dripped, the roof leaked, the peacocks were sodden – he said, 'You wouldn't imagine there was so much wet around. *Sad*. I hate a grey light.' He lived in one room that was a bit of a shambles. There was a wood fire in the grate every day of the year. It was the only way of keeping the damp at bay. He said that he had been to England only once in the previous fifty-seven years, and that was to bury his brother. As a boy he had hero-worshipped his brother, who had once saved his life when he panicked climbing a cliff. He had heard that his brother's widow had recently died at the age of ninety-nine. 'So at least she did not have to face all the rejoicings of being one hundred.'

It took me some time to get him to talk about the house by the river. 'I don't live in the past,' he insisted. Eventually he showed me some photographs of Moune and told me to keep them. 'She lived in the truth,' he said. 'There was no artifice in her, she never wore makeup. She treated men as equals. Or less than equals. When her mother was dying she slept in the same bedroom for weeks, and was up three times every night. She once told me she was so tired that she thought she would die first.'

'Providence has played a part in my life,' he said. 'I've saved an old house, and I've lived my own life, like the people round here. They don't have their lives dished out to them by the administration.' Not so long before, a tax inspector had called on Oscar to impose the dreaded ordeal of '*un contrôle fiscal*'. This had caused a great deal of amusement in the village. From the administration's point of view it had not been time well spent.

I asked him about his first visit, in 1946, but all he would say was

that Pierre de Bernard's Buchenwald tattoo had been on his shoulder.
So I recalled his prize-winning dissertation and told him that it could
be very interesting from my point of view to see what was being said
in the Sologne so soon after the war. But he dismissed the idea. He no
longer had a copy of it. I suggested that since it had won the prize
there might be a copy in the college archives. And he looked at me
and suddenly stopped smiling and said, 'I can see that one really has
to be quite careful with people like you.' And it was the same look,
the same tone of voice, the same exact contempt, as he had shown ten
years earlier with *'Une biographie de Jean Moulin! Encore un tas de
mensonge!'* It made me all the more curious to know what he had
discovered in 1946 and to wonder about the missing years in his CV.
Could he have been in Intelligence during the war? He had the right
profile, fluent French, some German and Italian. And it was not easy
to get permission to enter France in March 1946, unless you were on
official duties. I asked the archivist in Cambridge whether Corpus
still held a copy of Oscar's essay, but although there was a record of
his residence and achievements their copy of the Cowell Prize Essay
for 1947 was missing.

It was on that last visit that Oscar told me the story of Colonel
Schöttl, and again there was something in his voice, a sense of gratitude
and respect, a total rejection of the conventional post-war point of
view. And it brought back the echo of another voice with a similar intonation, a voice that I had read but never heard.

Will you forgive me for supplying neither my name nor my address?
In the first place I've no taste for pointless debate – and such really
would be pointless as I'm quite sure I would move you as little as you
are likely to move me . . . You don't know who I am, you don't know
where I am: . . . It's pleasing to offer you the position of 'ghost'.

And anyway, you've had your say, really, haven't you – over two
hundred very public pages of it, and this little handful of piffling
querulous old-man whingeing's is hardly the stuff of serious debate.
Indeed, I hardly know why I bother to write it at all.

Maybe it's because of Karl. Karl Boemelburg and the post-war
indoctrinated all-Nazis-were-unthinking-sadists approach which, I
confess, has finally got to me. Funny, after all these years, that it
should be suddenly so. But it is so . . . Karl was discretion itself and

most definitely by his heroic silence saved his friends. From the *épura-tion*, that is, not from the baby-gobbling Germans.

Oscar died in 2014, and so I never managed to plunder his memories. They were too well concealed, like the w/t transmitter in the pool in the Cosson. When I mentioned this book to him, and outlined my plans, he looked thoughtful. Then he looked away and said, 'We make the history that we need.'

———

Souris was buried in the village cemetery of Huisseau-sur-Cosson. Both her husbands lie there too. She chose to be with Pierre. The foot of their grave is marked with a small, chipped plastic plate. It reads:

In Memoriam – Royal Air Force Escaping Society.

Postscript

The truth about some of 'Uncle Claude's' imaginative (and unsupervised) deception ploys became known to a select group of insiders in the post-war years, but nothing was said in public. Nobody wanted to believe it, and Sir Claude Dansey (knighted 1944) died in 1947. By then SIS – still under the direction of Sir Stewart Menzies – was well into the process of acquiring and systematically destroying the bulk of SOE's records.

The most eloquent denunciation of this procedure was provided by Leo Marks. He received permission to publish his recollections of SOE, *Between Silk and Cyanide*, in 1998 – although it had been completed many years earlier. In the year of publication Marks attended a conference held at the Imperial War Museum, under the aegis of SIS, to mark the release of what remained of the SOE archive (87 per cent of which had by then been destroyed). After a number of speeches by various officials Marks managed to get permission to say a few words, and it was evident from his intervention that the passage of fifty years had done nothing to diminish his rage over the treatment of his precious records. He made it clear that even during that day's proceedings SIS continued to deceive historians about what had happened, and he flatly contradicted the SIS convenor – while congratulating him on the 'brilliant' way he had muddied the waters.[1]

Leo Marks then recalled that in 1946, when SOE was wound up, he had been invited by C, Sir Stewart Menzies, to identify the most important operations – 'the cream of our signals activities' – so that, as he subsequently realised, C could prioritise their destruction. Among the records that SIS destroyed he gave two examples. The first was his detailed account of the catastrophe that had overtaken the Dutch Resistance (see p. 177); and the second was the 'back traffic' – the double game played by SOE with the Gestapo – that followed the downfall of

PROSPER. Every single one of those signals was destroyed, as was the record of Vera Atkins' subsequent efforts to discover the truth. Marks' insistence that Baker Street had quickly realised what had happened to 'Archambaud' (Gilbert Norman) made Nicolas Bodington's explanation for the arrest of Jack Agazarian during their mysterious journey to Paris in July 1943 even less convincing.

Following publication of *War in the Shadows* several readers have supplied additional evidence that Henri Déricourt's systematic betrayal of F section agents was known to British Intelligence.

One of those agents was Erwin Deman, a veteran French officer, an ex-Foreign Legionnaire of Hungarian Jewish descent, who carried out several successful missions for SOE and MI9. On 20 August 1943 he was flown to a chaotic Déricourt reception near Angers. After the war he told his son, Michael Deman, that he believed he had narrowly avoided a German trap by absconding from the landing ground on Déricourt's bicycle. Deman eventually escaped across the Pyrenées. Before his death Erwin Deman lodged a statement in the archives of the Imperial War Museum recording his conviction that he had been sent into France as 'expendable', by an intelligence officer who knew the landing ground was a trap.[2]

Deman's landing took place on the very same ground Déricourt had chosen two months earlier to receive three women agents – Noor Inayat Khan, Cecily Lefort and Diana Rowden. Déricourt used this location regularly, and his nearby safe houses were all under joint SD-Abwehr observation. By the time Deman arrived all three women were being trailed by the Gestapo, and by November they had all been arrested. Noor Khan's radio was then taken to the Avenue Foch and played by Dr Goetz for more than four months. The situation was quickly detected by Leo Marks (see p. 261) but he was once again overruled by Buckmaster.

Among the agents welcomed by German police via Khan's radio was France Antelme, who is mentioned in chapter 18. His parachute drop had been organised on Khan's radio, even though F section officers had been convinced for several months that this was under enemy control. He was warned that the arrangements were suspicious but in view of his enthusiasm was allowed to take the chance. He was arrested as he landed in February 1944 and immediately shouted out that he had been betrayed. According to one account of Antelme's interrogation he described those in London who had sent him as 'no better than murderers'. France Antelme refused to cooperate and was executed in Gross Rosen camp in the late summer of 1944. One of his grandsons has told me that the Antelme family are divided today between those who still deny he was deliberately betrayed and those who accept it.

I am grateful to Dr Antony Percy for referring me to an extremely detailed paper that he and Professor Anthony Glees published on the website Coldspur in July 2020.[3]

Based on research in the National Archives, this confirms the importance of Claude Dansey's covert Geneva operation and the prominent role played in it by the former 'Z' man, Victor Farrell. Farrell's cover was 'passport control officer' at the Geneva consulate. In the summer of 1940, Dansey instructed Farrell to facilitate the passage from Switzerland to England of a known enemy agent, Ursula Kuczynski. Her code name was 'Sonya' and she was an experienced Communist spy working for the GRU (Soviet military intelligence), the Soviet Union being at that time an ally of Nazi Germany. A sham marriage was arranged in Switzerland between 'Sonya' and a British citizen named Len Beurton who was one of Dansey's informers. 'Sonya' thereby acquired a fraudulent British passport and she and her 'husband' travelled to Liverpool, via Lisbon, in record time, thanks to Victor Farrell.

Dr Percy suggests that Dansey's intention may have been to use 'Sonya' to penetrate Soviet intelligence. (An alternative explanation is that he wanted to use her to feed disguised Enigma decrypts to Moscow.[4]) In either case the operation was a security catastrophe. Unknown to Dansey, 'Sonya', once safely in England, became the GRU's contact with fellow Soviet agent Klaus Fuchs, the German Communist scientist who supplied Moscow with the secrets of the British and American atomic bombs.

Victor Farrell and Claude Dansey were still in contact with Len Beurton and Sonya Kuczynski, and thereby with Soviet intelligence, in June 1943 when German police were led to the house in Caluire to arrest Jean Moulin – possibly evidence of what I have described as 'the Moscow Pathway' (see p. 296).

Finally, I would like to thank Jérôme Tillette de Mautort, who referred me to a document at Kew which is in a collection of 'Lord Selborne's Correspondence'.

This is entitled *SOE Activities: Summary for the Prime Minister: Quarter – April to June 1943* and is part of a regular series of reports by the minister responsible for SOE covering the whole range of SOE operations throughout Europe and the Near East. In France the period in question follows the departure from London of 'Vidal' (General Delestraint) and 'Max' (Jean Moulin), and the subsequent visit of 'Prosper' (Major Suttill). It also covers the downfall of the PROSPER network and the raid on Caluire. These events are briefly referred to in Lord Selborne's report, as follows.

> The Germans made an attempted round up of the leaders of the Resistance groups in June, apparently under the impression that an Allied invasion of France was imminent. They succeeded in capturing some important men and a very few British officers. The work of the Resistance groups has been injured, though not to any fatal extent; but the incident shows once more the chronic French incapacity in security.[5]

Mr Churchill read Lord Selborne's summary some weeks after it was sent and made his customary 'jottings' in the margin. The only mark he made in the French section was to ring the words 'a very few' (British officers) with the laconic comment, 'what happened to them?'

The passage quoted clearly refers to events in both the Sologne and Lyons. And it is valuable evidence for two reasons. It associates the Gestapo actions against 'Prosper' and 'Max' *as part of the same German operation*, one that had been triggered by a conviction that invasion was imminent.[6] And it reveals a curious hiatus in the prime minister's curiosity. He fails to ask a question that obviously demands an answer; Mr Churchill has no interest in discovering why Lord Selborne thinks that the Germans were 'apparently under the impression' that an Allied invasion was 'imminent'. One can take it that he did not ask that question because he already knew the answer. The deception operation he had authorised was having precisely the effect intended.

Instead, Mr Churchill asks another question, which is even stranger, because it is one to which the answer is obvious. Mr Churchill knew exactly what had happened to the 'very few' British officers who had been captured in civilian clothes on enemy territory. They had been interrogated, would quite possibly be tortured, and eventually executed.

But perhaps Mr Churchill asked the question anyway, because the answer troubled him. It may have troubled him because he knew why those officers had been arrested. It was one of the unavoidable risks of Operation Starkey.

The prime minister made no enquiries as to the fate of the 'important' French Resistance leaders who, according to Lord Selborne, had been captured due to their 'chronic incapacity in security'. He may have been encouraged by the thought that following their loss 'Resistance security' in France would be tightened, and de Gaulle's hold over the Resistance loosened, as he had requested on 19 June.

Casualty List

Réseau Adolphe – Deported and died in the camps

Sylvain Beignet
Fernand Bernier
Maxime Bigot
Maurice Buhler
Marius Caillard
Henri Canard
Maurice Corbeau
Auguste Cordelet
Gilbert Cordelet
Henri Daguet
Guy Dutemps
Jean Dutemps
Joseph Galliot
Armand Goleau
André Habert
Prosper Legourd
Robert Mandard
Albert Mercier
Guy Mercier
Julien Nadau
Paul Sausset
Jean Sidney
Marcel Thénot
Pierre Théry

———

Meung-sur-Loire
Jean Bordier
Edouard Flamencourt
Jean Flamencourt
Alain de Robien

SOE PROSPER – Deported and executed

Francis Suttill
Gilbert Norman
Jack Agazarian
France Antelme
Andrée Borrel
Marcel Clech
Paul Frager
Noor Inayat Khan
Nicolas Laurent
Ken Macalister
Frank Pickersgill
Yvonne Rudellat (died in Belsen)
Edouard Wilkinson

SOE(RF) / RESISTANCE – Deported and executed

Berty Albrecht (died in Fresnes Prison)
Charles Delestraint

———

Jean Moulin (died after torture)
Bruno Larat
Emile Schwartzfeld

Réseau Adolphe – Deported and survived

Anne-Marie de Bernard
Pierre de Bernard
René Boucher
René Bouton
André Brasseur
Georges Brault
Roger Couffrant
Pierre Culioli
Michel Drunat
Pierre Fouquet
André Habert
Gerard Oury
Marcel Petit
André Rabier

———

Meung-sur-Loire
Marguerite Flamencourt
Marie de Robien
Maurice Lequeux

PROSPER – Deported and survived

Maude Laurent
Marcel Rousset
Germaine Tambour
Yvonne Wilkinson

SOE(RF) / RESISTANCE –
Deported and survived

André Lassagne

Released
Albert Lacaze
Henri Aubry

———

Frédéric Dugoujon

Escaped
René Hardy
Raymond Aubrac

Sources

Archives Départmentales, Loir-et-Cher; Lucien Jardel et Raymond Casas, *La Résistance en Loir-et-Cher* (Vendôme: Vendôme Impressions, 1964); The National Archives, Kew.

Bibliography

Archives

The National Archives at Kew
Archives nationales, Pierrefitte-sur-Seine
Service historique de la Défense, Vincennes
Archives départementales de Loir-et-Cher, Blois

Publications

Alain-Fournier, *The Lost Domain*, translated from the French by Frank Davison (London: OUP, 1959)

Field Marshal Lord Alanbrooke, *War Diaries: 1939–1945*, ed. Alex Danchev and Daniel Todman (London: Weidenfeld & Nicolson, 2001)

Eric Alary, *L'Exode: Un drame oublié* (Paris: Perrin, 2000)

Sebastien Albertelli, *Les Services Secrets du général de Gaulle. Le BCRA 1940–1944* (Paris: Perrin, 2009)

Mireille Albrecht, *Berty* (Paris: Laffont, 1986)

Henri Alleg, *La Question* (Paris: Éditions de Minuit, 1958)

Henri Amoretti, *Lyon Capitale: 1940–44* (Paris: Eds. France-Empire, 1964)

Christopher Andrew, *The Defence of the Realm: The Authorized History of MI5* (London: Allen Lane, 2009)

—, *Secret Service* (London: Heinemann, 1985)

Christopher Andrew and Vasili Mitrokhin (eds.), *The Mitrokhin Archive*, (London: Allen Lane, 1999)

Geoff Andrews, *Agent Molière: the Life of John Cairncross* (London: I.B. Tauris, 2020)

Lucie Aubrac, *Ils partiront dans l'ivresse* (Paris: Seuil, 1984)

Raymond Aubrac, *Ou la mémoire s'attarde* (Paris: Odile Jacob, 1996)

Bernard Aulas, *Vie et Mort des Lyonnais en Guerre: 1939–1945* (Roanne: Horvath, 1974)

Jean-Pierre Azéma (ed.), *Jean Moulin: Face à l'Histoire* (Paris: Flammarion, 2000)

Shrabani Basu, *The Life of Noor Inayat Khan* (Stroud, Glos.: The History Press, 2008)

Jacques Baumel, *Résister* (Paris: Albin Michel, 1999)

Jacques Baynac, *Les secrets de l'affaire Jean Moulin* (Paris: Le Seuil, 1998)

Antony Beevor and Artemis Cooper, *Paris after the Liberation* (London: Hamish Hamilton, 1994)

J.G. Beevor, *SOE: 1940–1945* (London: Bodley Head, 1981)

Charles Bendfredj, *L'Affaire Jean Moulin* (Paris: Albin Michel, 1990)

Gill Bennett, *Churchill's Man of Mystery: Desmond Morton and the world of Intelligence* (London: Routledge, 2007)

Guillain de Bénouville, *Le Sacrifice du matin* (Paris: Robert Laffont, 1970)

Marc Bloch, *L'Etrange Défaite* (Paris: Gallimard, 1946)

—, *The Historian's Craft*, translated from the French by Peter Putnam (Manchester: Manchester University Press, 1954)

Philipp von Boeselager, *Valkyrie: The Plot to Kill Hitler*, trans. Steven Randall, (London: Weidenfeld & Nicolson, 2009)

Genrikh Borovik (ed.), *The Philby Files* (London: Little, Brown, 1994)

Philippe Bourdrel, *L'épuration sauvage 1944–1945: Vol. I* (Paris: Perrin, 1988)

Robert Bourne-Patterson, *SOE in France, 1941–1945* (London: Frontline Books, 2016)

Tom Bower, *The Perfect English Spy, Sir Dick White and the Secret Way: 1935–90* (London: William Heinemann, 1995)

Andrew Bradford, *Escape from Saint Valéry-en-Caux, The Adventures of Capt. B.C. Bradford* (Stroud, Glos.: The History Press, 2009)

Alain Brossat, *Libération, fête folle* (Paris: Éditions Autrement, 1994)

Anthony Cave Brown, *Bodyguard of Lies* (London: W.H. Allen, 1976)

—, *Philby Père et Fils: La Trahison dans le Sang* (Paris: Pygmalion, 1997)

Jacques Bureau, *Un soldat menteur* (Paris: Robert Laffont, 1992)

Jimmy Burns, *Papa Spy* (London: Bloomsbury, 2009)

Philippe Burrin, *La France a l'heure allemande: 1940–44* (Paris: Eds. du Seuil, 1995)

Henri Calef, *Jean Moulin: Une vie* (Paris: Plon, 1980)

Charles Carter, The Private Diary of Charles Carter (unpublished)

Miranda Carter, *Anthony Blunt: His Lives* (London: Macmillan, 2001)

Gérard Chauvy, *Lyon des Années Bleues* (Paris: Plon, 1987)

—, *Aubrac Lyon 1943* (Paris: Albin Michel, 1997)

E.H. Cookeridge, *Inside SOE* (London: Arthur Barker, 1966)

Daniel Cordier, *Jean Moulin: L'Inconnu du Panthéon Vol. I* (Paris: Editions J.C. Lattès, 1989)

—, *Jean Moulin: La République des Catacombes* (Paris: Gallimard, 1999)

Jacques de Bayac, *Histoire de la Milice: 1918–1945* (Paris: Fayard, 1969)

Ladislas De Hoyos, *Barbie* (Paris: Laffont, 1987)

Francois Delpla, *Aubrac: les faits et la calomnie* (Paris: Le Temps des Cerises, 1997)

André Devigny, *A Man Escaped*, translated from the French by Peter Green (New York: Berkley Books, 1959)

François-Georges Dreyfus, *Histoire de la Résistance* (Paris: Fallois, 1996)

Georgette Elgey, *La fenêtre ouverte*, translated by J.A. Underwood (London: Woburn Press, 1974)

Hans Magnus Enzensberger, *Hammerstein ou l'intransigeance* (Paris: Gallimard, 2010)

Roger Faligot et Remi Kauffer, *Les Résistants* (Paris: Fayard, 1989)

Jean-Louis Faure, *Catalogue Irraisonné* (Paris: Eds. de Fallois, 2014)

Jacqueline Fleury-Marié, *Résistante* (Paris: Calmann-Lévy, 2019)

M.R.D. Foot, *SOE in France* (London: HMSO, 1966)

—, *SOE: The Special Operations Executive, 1940–1946* (London: Pimlico, 1999)

—, *Memories of an SOE Historian* (Barnsley: Pen and Sword Military, 2008)

M.R.D. Foot and J.M. Langley, *MI9* (London: Bodley Head 1979)

Henri Frenay, *L'Énigme Jean Moulin* (Paris: Robert Laffont, 1990)

Jean Overton Fuller, *Déricourt: The Chequered Spy* (London: Michael Russell, 1989)

Max Gallo, *1940: De l'abîme à l'espérance* (Paris: XO Editions, 2010)

Jean Galtier-Boissière, *Mémoires d'un Parisien* (Paris: Quai Voltaire, 1994)

David Garnett, *The Secret History of PWE: The Political Warfare Executive 1939–1945* (London: St Ermin's Press, 2002)

Charles de Gaulle, *Mémoires de Guerre: Vols. I–III* (Paris: Plon, 1954)

Martin Gilbert, *Winston S. Churchill, Vol. VII* (London: Heinemann, 1986)

Robert Gildea, *Marianne in Chains* (London: Macmillan, 2002)

Gabriel Gorodetsky (ed.), *The Maisky Diaries* (New Haven: Yale University Press, 2016)

Peter Grose, *Gentleman Spy: The Life of Allen Dulles* (London: André Deutsch, 1995)

Georges Groussard, *Services Secret: 1940–45* (Paris: La Table Ronde, 1964)

Paul Guillaume, *La Sologne au temps de l'héroïsme et de la trahison* (Orléans: Imprimerie Nouvelle, 1950)

Claude Guy, *En écoutant de Gaulle* (Paris: Grasset, 1996)

René Hardy, *Derniers Mots* (Paris: Fayard, 1984)

Max Hastings, *The Secret War: 1939–45* (London: William Collins, 2015)

Edward Harrison, *The Young Kim Philby: Soviet Spy and British Intelligence Officer* (Exeter: University of Exeter Press, 2012)

Sarah Helm, *A Life in Secrets: The Story of Vera Atkins* (London: Little, Brown, 2005)

Roger Hesketh, *Fortitude* (London: St Ermin's Press, 1999)

Peter Hoffmann, *Stauffenberg: A Family History, 1905–1944* (Cambridge: CUP, 1995)

Alistair Horne, *To Lose a Battle: France 1940* (London: Macmillan, 1969)

—, *A Savage War of Peace: Algeria 1954–1962* (London: Macmillan, 1977)

Michael Howard, *British Intelligence in World War II: Vol. V* (London: HMSO, 1990)

Agnès Humbert, *Notre guerre* (Paris: Frères Paul, 1946), translated, with notes by Barbara Mellor and published as *Résistance: Memoirs of Occupied France* (London: Bloomsbury, 2008)

Julian Jackson, *A Certain Idea of France: The Life of Charles de Gaulle* (London: Allen Lane, 2018)

Lucien Jardel et Raymond Casas, *La Résistance en Loir-et-Cher* (Vendôme: Vendôme Impressions, 1964)

Keith Jeffery, *MI6: The History of the Secret Intelligence Service 1909–1949* (London: Bloomsbury, 2010)

Ray Jenkins, *Pacifist at War: The Life of Francis Cammaerts* (London: Hutchinson, 2009)

Liane Jones, *A Quiet Courage* (London: Bantam Press, 1990)

John Keegan, *The Second World War* (London: Pimlico, 1989)

—, *Intelligence in War* (London: Hutchinson, 2003)

David M. Kennedy, *Freedom From Fear: The American People in Depression and War, 1929–1945* (New York: Oxford University Press, 1999)

François Kersaudy, *Churchill and De Gaulle* (London: Fontana Press, 1990)

Ian Kershaw, *Making Friends with Hitler* (London: Allen Lane, 2004)

Stella King, *Jacqueline* (London: Arms and Armour Press, 1989)

Rita Kramer, *Flames in the Field* (London: Michael Joseph, 1995)

Jean Lacouture, *De Gaulle, Vol. I – Le Rebelle* (Paris: Le Seuil, 1984)

Richard Lamb, *Churchill as War Leader* (London: Bloomsbury, 1991)

Marghanita Laski, *Little Boy Lost* (London: Persephone Books, 2001)

Pierre Lefranc, *La France dans la Guerre 1940–1945* (Paris: Plon, 1990)

Jean-Pierre Levy, *Mémoires d'un Franc-Tireur, 1940–44* (Brussels: Editions Complexes, 1998)

Libération, 'Les Aubracs et les historiens' (Paris, 9 juillet 1997)

Magnus Linklater, Isabel Hilton and Neal Ascherson, *The Fourth Reich: Klaus Barbie and the Neo-Fascist Connection* (London: Hodder & Stoughton, 1984)

Helen Long, *Safe Houses are Dangerous* (London: William Kimber, 1985)

Andrew Lownie, *Stalin's Englishman: The Lives of Guy Burgess* (London: Hodder & Stoughton, 2015)

Ben Macintyre, *Double Cross: The True Story of the D-Day Spies* (London: Bloomsbury, 2012)

W.J.M. Mackenzie, *The Secret History of SOE* (London: St Ermin's, 2000)

Leo Marks, *Between Silk and Cyanide: A Code Maker's War 1941–45* (London: HarperCollins, 1998)

J. Manson, *Leçons de ténèbres: résistants et déportés* (Paris: Plon, 1995)

Patrick Marnham, *Jean Moulin: Biography of a Ghost* (London: John Murray, 2000), paperback edition (London: Pimlico, 2001)

—, *Army of the Night: The Life and Death of Jean Moulin, Legend of the French Resistance* (London: Tauris Parke, 2015)

—, (ed.), *Darling Pol: The Letters of Mary Wesley and Eric Siepmann* (London: Harvill Secker, 2017)

M.R. Marrus and R.O. Paxton, *Vichy France and the Jews* (New York: Basic Books, 1981)

Robert Marshall, *All the King's Men* (London: Collins, 1988)

J.C. Masterman, *The Double-Cross System* (London: Granada, 1979)

Evan Mawdsley, *The War for the Seas* (New Haven: Yale University Press, 2019)

Tim Milne, *Kim Philby* (London: Biteback, 2014)

Youri Ivanovitch Modine, *Mes Camarades de Cambridge* (Paris: Robert Laffont, 1994)

Ewen Montagu, *The Man Who Never Was* (London: Evans Brothers, 1953)

Simon Sebag Montefiore, *Stalin: The Court of the Red Tsar* (London: Weidenfeld & Nicolson, 2003)

Frederick Morgan, *Overture to Overlord* (London: Hodder & Stoughton, 1950)

Jean Moulin, *Premier Combat* (Paris: Editions de Minuit, 1946)

Laure Moulin, *Jean Moulin* (Presses de la Cité, 1982)

Henri Noguères, *Histoire de la Resistance en France, 1940–45 Vols. I–V* (Paris: Robert Laffont, 1967–1981)

Lynne Olson, *Madame Fourcade's Secret War* (London: Scribe, 2019)

Colonel Passy, *Mémoires du chef des services secrets de la France libre* (Paris: Odile Jacob, 2000)

Pierre Péan, *Vies et Morts de Jean Moulin* (Paris: Fayard, 1998)

Gilles Perrault, *Les Jardins de l'Observatoire* (Paris: Fayard, 1995)

Edward Peters, *Torture* (Oxford: Basil Blackwell, 1985)

Alain Peyrefitte, *C'était de Gaulle* (Paris: Editions de Fallois, 1994)

Kim Philby, *My Silent War* (London: Panther 1969)

Roland Philipps, *A Spy Named Orphan: the Enigma of Donald Maclean* (London: Bodley Head, 2018)

Thomas Rabino, *Laure Moulin: Résistante et soeur de héros* (Paris: Perrin, 2021)

Philippe Ragueneau, *Humeurs et Humour du Général* (Paris: Jacques Grancher, 1990)

Anthony Read and John Fisher, *Operation Lucy* (London: Hodder & Stoughton, 1980)

—, *Colonel Z* (London: Hodder & Stoughton, 1984)

Maisie Renault, *La Grande Misère* (Pontivy: Imprimerie Auffret, 1948)

David Reynolds, *In Command of History: Churchill Fighting and Writing the Second World War* (London: Allen Lane, 2004)

David Reynolds and Vladimir Pechatnov (eds.), *The Kremlin Letters* (New Haven: Yale University Press, 2018)

Brooks Richards, *Secret Flotillas* (London: HMSO, 1996)

Andrew Roberts, *Churchill* (London: Allan Lane, 2018)

K.G. Robertson (ed.), *War, Resistance and Intelligence* (London: Leo Cooper, 1999)

David Rousset, *L'Univers Concentrationnaire* (Paris: Éditions de Minuit, 1965)

Marcel Ruby, *La Contre-Résistance à Lyon 1940–44* (Lyon: Hermes, 1981)

Patrick Seale and Maureen McConville, *Philby: The Long Road to Moscow* (London: Hamish Hamilton, 1973)

Pavel Soudoplatov, *Missions Spéciales* (Paris: Seuil, 1984)

David Stafford, *Britain and European Resistance, 1940–1945* (London: Macmillan, 1980)

—, *Secret Agent: the True Story of the SOE* (London: BBC, 2000)

Francis J. Suttill, *Shadows in the Fog* (Stroud, Glos.: The History Press, 2014)

Francis J. Suttill and M.R.D. Foot, *SOE's 'Prosper' Disaster of 1943* (London: Intelligence and National Security, DOI, 28 March 2011)

Matthew Sweet, *The West End Front* (London: Faber & Faber, 2011)

A.J.P. Taylor, *English History 1914–1945* (London: OUP, 1965)

J.-M. Theolleyre, *Procès d'après guerre* (Paris: La Découverte, 1985)

Germaine Tillion, *Ravensbrück* (Paris: Le Seuil, 1973)

Hugh Trevor-Roper, *The Last Days of Hitler* (London: Macmillan Press, 1947)

—, *The Philby Affair* (London: William Kimber, 1968)

—, *The Secret World* (London: I.B. Tauris, 2014)

Roger Vailland, *Drôle de Jeu* (Paris: Phebus, 2009)

Jean-Marc Varaut, *Le Procès Petain* (Paris: Perrin, 1995)

'Missie' Vassiltchikov, *Journal d'une jeune fille russe à Berlin, 1940–45* (Paris: Phebus 1991)

Vercors, *Le Silence de la Mer* (Paris: Editions de Minuit, 1942)

Hugh Verity, *We Landed by Moonlight* (Shepperton: Ian Allan Ltd, 1978)

Laurie Vernay, *Lyon des Restrictions* (Grenoble: Éditions de terre et de mer, 1982)

Anthony Verrier, *Assassination in Algiers* (New York: W.W. Norton, 1990)

Pierre Vidal-Naquet, *Le trait empoisonné* (Paris: La Découverte, 1993)

Calder Walton, *Empire of Secrets: British Intelligence, the Cold War and the Twilight of Empire* (London: Harper Press, 2013)

Léon Werth, *Déposition: Journal 1940–1944* (Paris: Viviane Hamy, 1992)

—, *33 Jours* (Paris, Viviane Hamy, 1992)

Nigel West, *MI6: British Secret Intelligence Service Operations 1909-45* (London: Weidenfeld & Nicolson, 1983)

—, *Secret War: The Story of SOE* (London: Hodder & Stoughton, 1992)

—, (ed.), *The Guy Liddell Diaries: Vol. II* (London: Routledge, 2005)

Nigel West and Oleg Tsarev (eds.), *Triplex: Secrets from the Cambridge Spies* (New Haven: Yale University Press, 2009)

Olivier Wieviorka, *Histoire de la Résistance 1940–1945* (Paris: Perrin, 2013)

—, (ed.), *Nous entrerons dans la carrière: De la Résistance a l'exercise du pouvoir* (Paris: Seuil, 1994)

Peter Wilkinson and J.B. Astley, *Gubbins and SOE* (London: Leo Cooper, 1993)

Francis Zamponi, Nelly Bouveret and Daniel Allary, *Jean Moulin: Mémoires d'un homme sans voix* (Paris: Editions du Chêne, 1999)

Notes

KEY to archive sources

TNA   National Archives at Kew: TNA – followed by file no.
AN   Archives nationales, Pierrefitte-sur-Seine
SHD   Service historique de la Défense, Vincennes
AD   Archives départmentales de Loir-et-Cher, Blois
FBS   *Franco-British Studies : Journal of the British Institute in Paris* (2/
        Autumn 1986; 7/Spring 1989)

Introduction: An Anonymous Letter

1 Sarah Helm, *A Life in Secrets: The Story of Vera Atkins* (London: Little, Brown, 2005), pp. 347–8.
2 *Libération*, 9 July, 1997, p. 17.

1 Summer of '62

1 Alain-Fournier, *The Lost Domain*, translated from the French by Frank Davison (Oxford: OUP, 1959), p. 145.
2 Alistair Horne, *A Savage War of Peace* (London: Macmillan, 1977), p. 543.

3 The Fugitive

1 Andrew Bradford, *Escape from Saint Valéry-en-Caux: The Adventures of Capt. B.C. Bradford* (Stroud, Glos.: The History Press, 2009), p. 53.
2 Ibid., p. 53.
3 Ibid., p. 58.
4 The private diary of Charles Carter (unpublished, no page numbers).
5 Max Gallo, *1940: de l'abîme à l'espérance* (Paris: XO Editions, 2010), p. 150.
6 Eric Alary, *L'Exode: Un drame oublié* (Paris: Perrin, 2000); Christian Couppé, *Blois des Bombes et des Ruines* (Blois: J. Rollin, 1990).

7 Carter, op. cit.

8 Bradford, op. cit., p. 97.

9 Ibid., p. 100.

4 'Setting Whitehall Ablaze'

1 Alistair Horne, *To Lose a Battle* (London: Macmillan, 1969), p. 159.

2 W.J.M. Mackenzie, *The Secret History of SOE* (London: HMSO, 2000), pp. 3–5.

3 Keith Jeffery, *MI6: The History of the Secret Intelligence Service 1909–1949* (London: Bloomsbury, 2010), pp. 353, 361.

4 Mackenzie, op. cit., p. 337.

5 Jean Overton Fuller, *Déricourt: The Chequered Spy* (London: Michael Russell, 1989), pp. 17, 20.

6 Mackenzie, op. cit., p. 80.

7 Brooks Richards, *Secret Flotillas* (London: HMSO, 1996), p. 194.

8 Jeffery, op. cit., p. 392.

9 Richards, op. cit., pp. 24–9.

10 Ibid., p. 239.

11 M.R.D. Foot, *SOE in France* (London: HMSO, 1966), p. 162.

12 Leo Marks, *Between Silk and Cyanide* (London: HarperCollins, 1998), p. 40; Jeffery, op. cit., p. 356.

13 Peter Wilkinson and J.B. Astley, *Gubbins and SOE* (London: Leo Cooper, 1993), pp. 77, 99, 113–15.

14 Wilkinson, op. cit., p. 114, paraphrasing TNA – PRO CAB80/62.

15 TNA – HS9/171/1.

16 Jean Lacouture, *De Gaulle, Vol. 1 – Le Rebelle* (Paris: Seuil, 1984), pp. 309–15.

17 François Kersaudy, *Churchill and De Gaulle* (London: Fontana Press, 1990), p. 53.

18 Pierre Lefranc, *La France dans la Guerre: 1940–1945* (Paris: Plon, 1990), p. 25 (Author's translation). See also Julian Jackson, *A Certain Idea of France: The Life of Charles de Gaulle* (London: Allen Lane, 2018), p. 127.

19 Lacouture, op. cit., pp. 369–72.

20 Lefranc, op. cit., p. 39.

21 Horne, op. cit., p. 229.

22 Lacouture, op. cit., p. 371.

23 Olivier Wieviorka, *Histoire de la Résistance: 1940–1945* (Paris: Perrin, 2013), p. 21.

24 Jean Galtier-Boissière, *Mémoires d'un Parisien* (Paris: Quai Voltaire, 1994), p. 779.

25 Léon Werth, *Déposition: Journal 1940–1944* (Paris: Viviane Hamy, 1992), pp. 39–40.

26 Mackenzie, op. cit., p. 230.

27 Ibid., p. 230.

28 Colonel Passy, *Mémoires du Chef des Services Secrets de la France Libre* (Paris: Editions Odile Jacob, 2000), pp. 176, 306.

29 Ibid., p. 176.
30 Ruth Kramer, *Flames in the Field* (London: Michael Joseph, 1995), pp. 289–91.

5 *The Swamps and the Forest*

1 Hugh Trevor-Roper, *The Last Days of Hitler* (London: Pan, 1947), p. 34.
2 Michael Howard, *Peace and War, the Fifth Athenaeum Lecture* (London: The Athenaeum, 2002), p. 9.
3 Lucien Jardel et Raymond Casas, *La Résistance en Loir-et-Cher* (Vendôme: Vendôme Impressions, 1964), pp. 125–6.
4 Andrew Bradford, *Escape from Saint Valéry-en-Caux: The Adventures of Capt. B.C. Bradford* (Stroud, Glos.: The History Press, 2009), p. 200.
5 Jardel et Casas, op. cit., p. 20.
6 Stella King, *Jacqueline* (London: Arms and Armour Press, 1989), p. 222.
7 AD – 1J 104/2 (*Déclarations faites par M. et Mme. de Bernard à Nanteuil 17/5/49*).
8 'NANNY' – unpublished account of the life of Nesta Cox by Elizabeth Gicquel, pp. 33–4.
9 Francis J. Suttill, *Shadows in the Fog* (Stroud, Glos.: The History Press, 2014), pp. 18–22.

6 *A Network Called* Adolphe

1 Gilles Perrault, *Les Jardins de l'Observatoire* (Paris: Fayard, 1995), Chapter 12.
2 M.R.D. Foot, *SOE in France* (London: HMSO, 1966), p. 196.
3 Francis J. Suttill, *Shadows in the Fog* (Stroud, Glos. The History Press, 2014), p. 32.
4 Foot, op. cit., p. 196.
5 Stella King, *Jacqueline* (London: Arms and Armour, 1989), pp. 239–40, *pace* Foot, op. cit., pp. 198–9.
6 Suttill, op. cit., p. 42.
7 K.G. Robertson (ed.), *War, Resistance and Intelligence* (London: Leo Cooper, 1999), p. 169.
8 AD – 1J 104/2 (*Déclarations faites par M. et Mme. de Bernard à Nanteuil 17/5/49*).
9 *La Nouvelle République du Centre-Ouest*, 1945.
10 AD – 1J 104/2 (*Declaration de Madame Julien Nadau 22/9/49*).
11 Foot, op. cit., p. 195.
12 Shrabani Basu, *The Life of Noor Inayat Khan* (Stroud, Glos.: The History Press, 2008), p. 107.
13 Interview with Madame Béatrice Théry, 19 October 2012.
14 'NANNY' – unpublished account of the life of Nesta Cox, by Elizabeth Gicquel, p. 33.
15 Suttill, op. cit., p. 141.
16 Lucien Jardel et Raymond Casas, *La Résistance en Loir-et-Cher* (Vendôme: Vendôme Impressions, 1964), p. 107.
17 AD – 1J 104/2 (*Déclarations faites par M. et Mme. de Bernard à Nanteuil 17/5/49, p. 2b*).

18 AD – 1J 104/2 (*Déclarations faîtes par M. et Mme. de Bernard à Nanteuil 17/5/49, p. 2b*). *Notes de Culioli.*

19 TNA – HS9/43; Suttill, op. cit., p. 68.

20 Paul Guillaume, *La Sologne au temps de l' héroïsme et de la trahison* (Orléans, Imprimerie Nouvelle, 1950), pp. 38–9.

21 Ibid., p. 50.

22 AD – 1J 104/2 (*Déclarations faîtes par M. et Mme. de Bernard à Nanteuil 17/5/49, p. 2b*).

23 TNA – HS9/183.

24 Suttill, op. cit., p. 106, quoting AD – Loiret, Orléans 1221/W11.

7 Dreaming up a Second Front

1 Lieutenant General Sir Frederick Morgan, *Overture to Overlord* (London: Hodder & Stoughton, 1950), p. 109.

2 Martin Gilbert, *Winston S. Churchill, Vol. VII* (London: Heinemann, 1986), p. 267–8.

3 Simon Sebag Montefiore, *Stalin: The Court of the Red Tsar* (London, Weidenfeld & Nicolson, 2003), pp. 387, 399.

4 Andrew Roberts, *Churchill* (London: Allen Lane, 2018), pp. 753, 756, 783.

5 David Reynolds and Vladimir Pechatnov, *The Kremlin Letters* (New Haven: Yale University Press, 2018), p. 129.

6 Reynolds and Pechatnov, op. cit., p. 142.

7 Roberts, op. cit., pp. 756–7.

8 Gabriel Gorodetsky (ed.), *The Maisky Diaries* (New Haven: Yale University Press, 2016), p. 463.

9 John Keegan, *The Second World War* (London: Pimlico, 1989), pp. 262–3.

10 Reynolds and Pechatnov, op. cit., p. 212; Martin Gilbert, *Winston S. Churchill, Vol. VII* (London: Heinemann, 1986), pp. 339–40.

11 Richard Lamb, *Churchill as War Leader* (London: Bloomsbury, 1991), pp. 221–2.

12 Reynolds and Pechatnov, op. cit., p. 193.

13 Gilbert, op. cit., p. 310.

14 Ibid., p. 228.

15 Michael Howard, *British Intelligence in World War II: Vol. V* (London: HMSO, 1990), p. 72.

16 Gorodetsky, op. cit., p. 479.

17 John Keegan, op. cit., p. 385.

18 Anthony Read and John Fisher, *Colonel Z* (London: Hodder & Stoughton, 1984), p. 148.

19 Gilbert, op. cit., p. 364.

20 Anthony Read and John Fisher, *Operation Lucy* (London, Hodder & Stoughton 1980), p. 151.

21 Gorodetsky, op. cit., p. 499; Gilbert op. cit., pp. 362–3.

22 Reynolds and Pechatnov, op. cit., p. 216.

23 Gilbert, op. cit., pp. 383–4.

24 Gorodetsky, op. cit., p. 509.

25 Ibid., pp. 506, 509–10; Montefiore, op. cit., pp. 340–1.

26 Reynolds and Pechatnov, op. cit., p. 239.

27 Gilbert, op. cit., p. 383.

28 J.C. Masterman, *The Double-Cross System* (London, Granada, 1979), p. 62; Howard, op. cit., pp. 7, 10, 27.

29 Howard, op. cit., p. 32.

30 Ibid., p. 243.

31 Roger Hesketh, *Fortitude* (London: St Ermin's Press, 1999), p. 1.

32 Morgan, op. cit., p. 92.

33 Ibid., p. 109.

34 Jean Overton Fuller, *Déricourt: The Chequered Spy* (London: Michael Russell, 1989), p. 279; David Stafford, *Britain and European Resistance, 1940–1945* (London: Macmillan, 1980), p. 254.

35 Francis J. Suttill, *Shadows in the Fog* (Stroud, Glos.: The History Press, 2014), p. 90.

8 'That Jeanne d'Arc in Trousers'

1   W.J.M. Mackenzie, *The Secret History of SOE* (London: HMSO, 2000), p. 229.

2   Julian Jackson, *A Certain Idea of France: The Life of Charles de Gaulle* (London: Allen Lane, 2018), pp. 174–80.

3   Ibid., p. 211.

4   Mackenzie, op. cit., p. 290.

5   Field Marshal Lord Alanbrooke, *War Diaries: 1939–1945*, eds. Alex Danchev and Daniel Todman (London: Weidenfeld & Nicolson, 2001), p. 278.

6   Ibid., p. 326.

7   Jackson, op. cit., p. 240.

8   Brooke, op. cit., p. 326.

9   Mackenzie, op. cit., p. 252.

10 Jacques Baynac, *Les Secrets de l'Affaire Jean Moulin* (Paris: Seuil, 1998), pp. 176–82.

11 Mackenzie, op. cit., p. 566.

12 FBS 7, p. 115.

13 FBS 7, pp. 115–6; AN – 171/MI/1.

14 Jean-Louis Crémieux-Brilhac, interview with author, 8 November 2014.

15 M.R.D. Foot, *SOE in France* (London: HMSO, 1966), pp. 205–6.

16 Evan Mawdsley, *The War for the Seas* (New Haven: Yale University Press, 2019), p. 284.

17 Anthony Verrier, *Assassination in Algiers* (New York: W.W. Norton, 1990), pp. 197, 214–5.

18 Gilbert, op. cit., p. 249.

19 FBS 7, p. 87.

20 Gilbert, op. cit., pp. 277–8.

21 Charles Williams, *The Last Great Frenchman* (London: Little Brown, 1993), p. 204.

22 Pierre Lefranc, *La France dans la Guerre: 1940–1945* (Paris: Plon, 1990), p. 304.

23 Jean Lacouture, *De Gaulle, Vol. 1 – Le Rebelle* (Paris: Seuil, 1984), pp. 622–4.

24 Verrier, op. cit., p. 246.

25 Colonel Passy, *Mémoires du Chef des Services Secrets de la France Libre* (Paris: Editions Odile Jacob, 2000), p. 447.

26 TNA – HS9/183.

27 *Sunday Times Magazine*, 15 March 2009, p. 21.

28 Passy, op. cit., p. 20.

29 Ibid.

30 Ibid., p. 366.

31 M.R.D. Foot, *SOE in France* (London: HMSO, 1966), p. 137.

32 TNA – F.O. 660/178; Liddell, op. cit., p. 206.

33 Liddell, op. cit., p. 206.

34 Anthony Read and David Fisher, *Colonel Z* (London: Hodder, 1984), p. 327.

35 TNA-FO 660/178.

36 Gilbert, op. cit., p. 336.

37 Gorodetsky, op. cit., p. 483.

38 Daniel Cordier, *Jean Moulin: L'Inconnu du Panthéon Vol. I* (Paris: Editions J.C. Lattès, 1989), pp. 142–5.

39 Passy, op. cit., p. 509.

40 Brooke, op. cit., pp. 386–7.

41 Martin Gilbert, *Winston S. Churchill, Vol. VII* (London: Heinemann, 1986), p. 346.

42 Julian Jackson, *A Certain Idea of France: The Life of Charles de Gaulle* (London: Allen Lane, 2018), p. 263.

43 Cordier, op. cit., p. 145.

44 Mémorandum pour l'Amiral Stark, 11 mars 1943 – *AN 3 AG 2 1*; Daniel Cordier *Jean Moulin: La République des Catacombes* (Paris: Gallimard, 1999), pp. 320–3, 913.

45 Michael Howard, *British Intelligence in World War II: Vol. V* (London: HMSO, 1990), p. 72; Gilbert, op. cit., p. 311.

46 Jean-Pierre Azéma (ed.), *Jean Moulin face a l'Histoire* (Paris: Flammarion, 2000), pp. 123, 199.

47 AN–171/MI/48Mi2, 18 March 1942.

48 David Reynolds and Vladimir Pechatnov, *The Kremlin Letters* (New Haven: Yale University Press, 2018), pp. 265–6.

49 Brooke, op. cit., pp. 422, 424; David Reynolds, *In Command of History: Churchill Fighting and Writing the Second World War* (London: Allen Lane, 2004), p. 331.

50 Jackson, op. cit., p. 274.

51 J.G. Beevor, *SOE: 1940–1945* (London: Bodley Head, 1981), p. 148.

52 Gilbert, op. cit., p. 78.

53 Azéma, op. cit., p. 197.

54 Ibid., pp. 201, 401.

55 Cordier, op. cit., p. 501.

56 Brooke, op. cit., p. 422 ; Gill Bennett, *Churchill's Man of Mystery: Desmond Morton and the World of Intelligence* (London: Routledge, 2007), p. 192..

9 The Fall of PROSPER

1 Jacques de Bayac, *Histoire de la Milice: 1918–1945* (Paris: Fayard, 1969), pp. 378–9.

2 AD55J3.

3 Lucien Jardel et Raymond Casas, *La Résistance en Loir-et-Cher* (Vendôme: Vendôme Impressions, 1964), p. 96.

4 Francis J. Suttill, *Shadows in the Fog* (Stroud, Glos.: The History Press, 2014), p. 123.

5 Stella King, *Jacqueline* (London: Arms and Armour, 1989), p. 302; Suttill, op.cit., p. 106.

6 Suttill, op. cit., pp. 90, 140–1.

7 Daniel Cordier, *Jean Moulin: La République des Catacombes* (Paris: Gallimard, 1999), p. 333.

8 *Nouvel Observateur*. November 2013, p. 42.

9 Suttill, op. cit., p. 119.

10 AD55J4 – letter to Culioli from FCO, 17 September 1984.

11 Suttill, op. cit., pp. 144–7.

12 Muriel Watson, post-war memorandum.

13 AD IJ/104/2 Cote 14, Dossier Culioli.

14 Paul Guillaume, *La Sologne au temps de l'héroïsme et de la trahison* (Orléans: Imprimerie Nouvelle, 1950), p. 66.

15 Suttill, op. cit., p. 147.

16 Ibid.

17 Lucien Jardel et Raymond Casas, *La Résistance en Loir-et-Cher* (Vendôme: Vendôme Impressions, 1964), pp. 97–8.

18 M.R.D. Foot, *SOE in France* (London: HMSO, 1966), p. 315.

19 Jardel et Casas, op. cit., p. 109.

20 Gérard Chauvy, *Aubrac Lyon 1943* (Paris: Albin Michel, 1997), p. 161.

21 Guillaume, op. cit., p. 10.

22 AD – IJ/104/2 Cote 14.

23 Shrabani Basu, *The Life of Noor Inayat Khan* (Stroud, Glos.: The History Press, 2008), p. 163, *pace* Foot, op. cit., p. 316.

24 TNA – HS9/1430/6.

25 Suttill, op. cit., pp. 152, 201. Archives départmentales de Loiret, Orléans. AD 1221/W/11.

26 Suttill, op. cit., pp. 143, 151–2.

27 Suttill, op. cit., 152.

28 The French army officer, Colonel Bonoteaux, was carrying orders from General Giraud for the ORA – the Resistance organisation of officers serving in France's post-armistice army who did not recognise General de Gaulle as their leader. Hugh Verity, *We Landed by Moonlight* (Shepperton: Ian Allan Ltd., 1978), pp. 100, 166.

29 E.H. Cookeridge, *Inside SOE* (London: Arthur Barker, 1966), p. 240.

30 Suttill, op. cit., pp. 148–9; AD 1375W70.

31 AD – IJ/104/2 Cote 22.
32 Dossier of 2e Tribunal Militaire, 12 March 1948 (AD IJ104/1–8). Déposition de Knochen.
33 J.G. Beevor, *SOE: 1940–1945* (London: Bodley Head, 1981), p. 156.
34 Foot, op. cit., p. 233.
35 AD – 1J 104/2 (*Déclarations faîtes par M. et Mme. de Bernard à Nanteuil 17/5/49, p. 2b*).
36 Comte Henri de Bernard, AD – 1J 104/2 (*Déclarations faîtes par M. et Mme. de Bernard à Nanteuil 17/5/49, p. 2b*).

10 *The Purge*

1   Jean Galtier-Boissière. *Mémoires d'un Parisien* (Paris : Quai Voltaire, 1994), p. 850.
2   Lucien Jardel et Raymond Casas, *La Résistance en Loir-et-Cher* (Vendôme: Vendôme Impressions, 1964), p. 167.
3   Galtier-Boissière, op. cit., pp. 829–30; Pierre Lefranc, *La France dans la Guerre: 1940–1945* (Paris : Plon, 1990), p. 487.
4   Christian Couppé, *Blois des Bombes et des Ruines* (Blois: J. Rollin, 1990).
5   Philippe Bourdrel, *L'Epuration Sauvage 1944–1945: Vol. I* (Paris: Perrin, 1988), pp. 406–7 ; Henri Amoretti, *Lyon Capitale 1940–1944* (Paris: Eds France-Empire, 1964), p. 369.
6   Bernard Aulas, *Vie et Mort des Lyonnais en Guerre: 1939–1945* (Roanne: Editions Horvath, 1974), p. 96.
7   Jean-Louis Faure, *Catalogue Irraisonné* (Paris: Eds. de Fallois, 2014), p. 93.
8   Léon Werth, *Déposition: Journal 1940–1944* (Paris: Viviane Hamy, 1992), p. 726.
9   Boissière, op. cit., p. 830.
10 *La Marseillaise*, 21 September 1944.
11 Details about events in the Sologne during this period come from AD – 55/J/7–11. Jardel, op. cit., pp. 278–9.
12 Maisie Renault, *La Grande Misère* (Pontivy: Imprimerie Auffret, 1948), pp. 168, 171.
13 Stella King, *Jacqueline* (London: Arms and Armour, 1989), p. 398.

11 *The Jurors of Honour*

1   Jean Overton Fuller, *Déricourt: The Chequered Spy* (London: Michael Russell, 1989), p. 47.
2   AD 55 – J-2.
3   Francis J. Suttill, *Shadows in the Fog* (Stroud, Glos.: The History Press, 2014), pp. 277–85.
4   Marghanita Laski, *Little Boy Lost* (London: Persephone, 2008), pp. 29–32.
5   AD/IJ-104/1/1074.
6   AD 55J4/1794.
7   Ibid.

8 Ibid.

9 SHD – GR/P/16364747.

10 Suttill, op. cit., p. 168.

11 TNA – HS 9/1430/6.

12 Suttill, op. cit., p. 149.

13 Hugh Verity, *We Landed by Moonlight* (Shepperton: Ian Allan Ltd., 1978), p. 165.

14 TNA – HS9/421.

15 TNA – HS9/421.

16 Robert Marshall, *All the King's Men* (London: Collins, 1988), p. 101.

17 Jean Overton Fuller, *Déricourt: The Chequered Spy* (London: Michael Russell, 1989), p. 47.

18 Paul Guillaume, *La Sologne au temps de l'heroisme et de la trahison* (Orléans: Imprimerie Nouvelle, 1950), p. 151.

19 AN – Dossier 2e Tribunal Militaire 12 March 1948. *Deposition Mona Reimeringer 8 August 1946. Cote 14.*

20 Suttill, op. cit., p. 242.

21 AD – 1J 104/2 (*Déclarations faîtes par M. et Mme. de Bernard à Nanteuil 17/5/49, p. 2b*).

22 Ibid., *p. 3b.*

23 AD-IJ:104/2; (*Déclarations faîtes par M. et Mme. de Bernard à Nanteuil, 17/5/49, 10/6/49, 28/8/49*).

24 Following Culioli's acquittal the vendetta continued. In 1952 the British government awarded Culioli the King's Medal for Courage, but in February 1960 he was still trying to ruin Maurice Lequeux. Meanwhile, he himself continued to suffer from the story of Raymond Flower's poison pill, which was re-published in a satirical Parisian weekly, *Le Crapouillot.* Jean Galtier-Boissière, *Mémoires d'un Parisien* (Paris: Quai Voltaire, 1994), pp. 1059–62.

12 Questions in Parliament

1 Anthony Cave Brown, *Bodyguard of Lies* (London: W.H. Allen, 1976), pp. 270, 860; interview with Colonel John Bevan.

2 Paul Guillaume, *La Sologne au temps de l'héroïsme et de la trahison* (Orléans: Imprimerie Nouvelle, 1950). See Chapters 3 to 6.

3 Henri Noguères ed. *Histoire de la résistance en France* (Paris: Robert Laffont 1967–1981), Vol. III, p. 487.

4 Sarah Helm, *A Life in Secrets: The Story of Vera Atkins* (London: Little, Brown, 2005), p. 367.

5 Jacques Bureau interview, *Journal de la Sologne*, April 1993, p. 53.

6 Leo Marks, *Between Silk and Cyanide* (London: HarperCollins, 1998), p. 311.

7 M.R.D. Foot, *SOE in France* (London: HMSO, 1966), p. 337.

8 Helm, op. cit. p. 191.

9 Shrabani Basu, *The Life of Noor Inayat Khan* (Stroud, Glos.: The History Press, 2008), pp. 232–3.

10 Rita Kramer, *Flames in the Field* (London: Michael Joseph, 1995), p. 225.

11 Foot, op. cit., p. 4.

12 Hansard, 6 March 1945.

13 Foot, op. cit., p. 48.

14 Ibid., p. 293.

15 Ibid., p. 293.

16 Ibid., p. 303.

17 TNA – KV2/1131.

18 Foot, op. cit., p. 348.

19 Ibid., pp. 309–11, 322.

20 Ibid., p. 198.

21 Ibid., p. 310.

22 Ibid., pp. 310, 314.

23 Ibid., p. 307.

24 Ibid., p. 348.

25 Ibid., p. 348.

26 Ibid., p. 348.

27 See Jones (1990); West (1992); Kramer (1995); Helm (2005); Basu (2006) and F.J. Suttill (2014).

28 Foot, op. cit., p. 348.

29 AD – 1375W70.

13 *Inside 84 Avenue Foch*

1 W.J.M. Mackenzie, *The Secret History of SOE* (London: HMSO, 2000), p. 303.

2 Nigel West, *Secret War: The Story of SOE* (London: Hodder & Stoughton, 1992), p. 94.

3 Leo Marks, *Between Silk and Cyanide* (London: HarperCollins, 1998), pp. 98–9.

4 Mackenzie, op. cit., pp. 303–5.

5 Carl Schmitt, *New York Review of Books,* 24 September 2015, p. 8.

6 Edward Peters, *Torture* (Oxford: Basil Blackwell, 1985), p. 124.

7 Ibid., p. 125.

8 Francis J. Suttill, *Shadows in the Fog* (Stroud, Glos.: The History Press, 2014), pp. 220, 225.

9 SHD – GR/P/16/364747.

10 Suttill, op. cit., pp. 153–6.

11 SHD – GR/P/16/364747. P.V. Ernst Vogt. (DST, 29 March 1949).

12 Ibid., p. 153.

13 Sarah Helm, *A Life in Secrets: The Story of Vera Atkins* (London: Little, Brown, 2005), p. 285.

14 Marks, op. cit., p. 326.

15 Suttill, op. cit., p. 217; M.R.D. Foot, *SOE in France* (London: HMSO, 1966), p. 335.

16 Gilles Perrault *Les Jardins de l'Observatoire* (Paris: Fayard, 1995), p. 40.

17 Gérard Chauvy, *Aubrac Lyon 1943* (Paris: Albin Michel, 1997), p. 78.

18 Olivier Wieviorka, *Histoire de la Résistance 1940–1945* (Paris: Perrin, 2013), p. 154.

19 Daniel Cordier, *Jean Moulin: L'Inconnu du Panthéon Vol. I* (Paris: Editions J.C. Lattès, 1989), p. 207.

20 Peter Grose, *Gentleman Spy: the Life of Allen Dulles* (London: André Deutsch, 1995), p. 168.

21 Cordier, op. cit., p. 217.

22 Pierre Lefranc, *La France dans la Guerre 1940–1945* (Paris: Plon, 1990), p. 348.

23 Cordier, op. cit., pp. 241–7.

24 Ibid. (report dated 27 May 1943), p. 247.

25 Ibid., pp. 244–7.

26 Ibid., p. 215.

27 Ibid., p. 241.

28 Ibid., p. 218.

29 Lefranc, op. cit., p. 359; Daniel Cordier *Jean Moulin: La République des Catacombes* (Paris: Gallimard, 1999), pp. 392–3.

30 Jean-Louis Crémieux-Brilhac in *Jean Moulin: Face a l'Histoire*, ed. Jean-Pierre Azéma (Paris: Flammarion, 2000), p. 196.

31 Cordier, *La République*, p. 393.

32 Ibid., pp. 435–8.

33 Ibid., p. 393.

34 Ibid., p. 447.

14 *The House of Doctor Dugoujon*

1 Daniel Cordier, *Jean Moulin: La République des Catacombes* (Paris: Gallimard, 1999), p. 453.

2 Daniel Cordier, *Jean Moulin: L'Inconnu du Panthéon Vol. I* (Paris: Editions J.C. Lattès, 1989), pp. 249–51.

3 Cordier, *La République*, p. 460.

4 Ibid., p. 466.

5 Ibid., p. 473.

6 Gérard Chauvy, *Aubrac Lyon 1943* (Paris: Albin Michel, 1997), p. 177.

7 Cordier, *La République*, pp. 466–7, 470–2.

8 Ibid., pp. 472–3.

9 Ladislas De Hoyos, *Barbie* (Paris: Robert Laffont, 1987), p. 193.

10 See Henri Calef, *Jean Moulin: Une Vie* (Paris: Plon, 1980), p. 384.

11 Calef, op. cit., p. 386.

12 Chauvy, op. cit., p. 162.

13 Jacques Baynac, *Les Secrets de l'Affaire Jean Moulin* (Paris: Seuil, 1998), p. 374; Calef, op. cit., p. 386.

14 Baynac, op. cit., pp. 374–5.

15 *A Resistance Legend Is Born*

1 Hugh Verity, *We Landed by Moonlight* (Shepperton: Ian Allan Ltd., 1978), p. 169.
2 *Libération*, 9 July 1997, p. 17.
3 Gérard Chauvy, *Aubrac Lyon 1943* (Paris: Albin Michel, 1997), p. 322.
4 Ibid., p. 323.
5 Ibid., pp. 264–5.
6 Christopher Andrew and Vasili Mitrokhin (eds.), *The Mitrokhin Archive* (London: Allen Lane, 1999), p. 197.
7 Daniel Cordier, *Jean Moulin: La République des Catacombes* (Paris: Gallimard, 1999), p. 734.
8 Ibid., pp. 727–8, 952.
9 Ibid., p. 732.
10 Pierre Péan, *Vies et Morts de Jean Moulin* (Paris: Fayard, 1998), p. 634.
11 *Le Monde*, 15 April 1987.

16 *The Trial of Commissioner Aubrac*

1 *Libération*, 9 July 1997, p. 16.
2 Claude Guy, *En écoutant de Gaulle* (Paris: Grasset, 1996), p. 237.
3 Daniel Cordier, *Jean Moulin: La République des Catacombes* (Paris: Gallimard, 1999), pp. 453–5; Henri Calef, *Jean Moulin: Une Vie* (Paris: Plon, 1980), pp. 381–5.
4 Cordier, op. cit., p. 455.
5 AN CJ 244(2); Cordier, op. cit., pp. 452, 926.
6 *Libération*, op. cit., p. 18, col. 1.
7 Jacques Baumel, *Résister* (Paris: Albin Michel, 1999), p. 161.
8 Cordier, op. cit., p. 759.
9 Ibid., p. 402.
10 Colonel Passy, *Mémoires du Chef des Services Secrets de la France Libre* (Paris: Editions Odile Jacob, 2000), p. 616.
11 Daniel Cordier, *Jean Moulin: L'Inconnu du Panthéon Vol. I* (Paris: Editions J.C. Lattès, 1989), p. 241.
12 Ibid., p. 289.
13 Unpublished Papers of Sir Patrick Reilly, held in the Bodleian Library, Oxford.
14 W.J.M. Mackenzie, *The Secret History of SOE* (London: HMSO, 2000), p. 590.
15 Hugh Verity, *We Landed by Moonlight* (Shepperton: Ian Allan Ltd., 1978), pp. 163, 165, 168–70.
16 TNA – JIC(43)325(O) of 1 August 1943.
17 Peter Wilkinson and J.B. Astley, *Gubbins and SOE* (London: Leo Cooper, 1993), p. 123.
18 M.R.D. Foot, *SOE in France* (London: HMSO, 1966), pp. 348–9.

19 Daniel Cordier, *Jean Moulin: La République des Catacombes* (Paris: Gallimard, 1999), pp. 479–80. Also Jean-Louis Crémieux-Brilhac in *Jean Moulin: Face a l'Histoire*, ed. Jean-Pierre Azéma (Paris: Flammarion 2000), p. 200.

20 TNA – FO 371/36004, 26 January 43; quoted in Jean-Pierre Azéma (ed.), *Jean Moulin: Face a l'Histoire* (Paris: Flammarion, 2000), p. 175. TNA – HS9/42 of 23 July 1943; Cordier, op.cit., p. 277; Mackenzie, op. cit., pp. 572–3.

21 Azéma, op. cit., p. 203.

17 *The Remarkable Immunity of Madame Delettraz*

1   Hugh Trevor-Roper, *The Secret World* (London: I.B. Tauris, 2014), p. 166.

2   Ibid., p. 39.

3   Michael Howard, *British Intelligence in World War II: Vol.V* (London: HMSO, 1990), p. 7.

4   Ibid., pp. 7–10.

5   J.C. Masterman, *The Double-Cross System* (London: Granada, 1979), p. 63.

6   Ibid., p. 64.

7   Ibid., p. 70.

8   Ibid., p. 130.

9   *Encounter*, April 1968, quoted in Hugh Trevor-Roper, *The Secret World*, p. 206.

10 Trevor-Roper, op. cit., p. 206.

11 Robert Marshall, *All the King's Men* (London: Collins, 1988), p. 193. See also unpublished Papers of Sir Patrick Reilly, held in the Bodleian Library, Oxford.

12 Keith Jeffery, *MI6: The History of the Secret Intelligence Service 1909–1949* (London: Bloomsbury, 2010), pp. 314–6.

13 Ibid., p. xiii.

14 Ibid., p. 330.

15 Ibid., p. 378.

16 Ibid., pp. 378–80.

17 Colonel Passy, *Mémoires du Chef des Services Secrets de la France Libre* (Paris: Editions Odile Jacob, 2000), pp. 175–8.

18 Ibid., p. 80.

19 Jeffery, op. cit., p. 354.

20 Ibid., p. 476.

21 TNA – KV4/120.

22 Christopher Andrew, *Secret Service* (London: Heinemann, 1985), p. 381.

23 Pierre Lefranc, *La France dans la Guerre 1940–1945* (Paris: Plon, 1990), p. 142; Olivier Wieviorka, *Histoire de la Résistance 1940–1945* (Paris: Perrin, 2013), pp. 39, 97; Nigel West, *MI6: British Secret Intelligence Service Operations, 1909–45* (London: Weidenfeld & Nicolson 1983), p. 148.

24 Passy, op. cit., p. 171.

25 M.R.D. Foot and J.M. Langley, *MI9* (London: Bodley Head, 1979), p. 141; Jeffery, op. cit., p. 410.

26 Daniel Cordier, *Jean Moulin: La République des Catacombes* (Paris: Gallimard, 1999), p. 435.

27 Jacques Baynac, *Les Secrets de l'Affaire Jean Moulin* (Paris: Seuil, 1998), p. 216.

28 Foot and Langley, op. cit., p. 141.

29 André Devigny, *A Man Escaped* (New York: Berkley Books, 1959), p. 9.

30 Baynac, op. cit., p. 217.

31 Pierre Péan, *Vies et Morts de Jean Moulin* (Paris: Fayard, 1998), pp. 424–7.

32 Baynac, op. cit., p. 163.

33 Daniel Cordier, *Jean Moulin: L'Inconnu du Panthéon Vol. I* (Paris: Editions J.C. Lattès, Paris 1989), pp. 206–8.

34 Cordier, *La République*, pp. 276–7.

35 Ibid. p. 337.

36 François-Georges Dreyfus, *Histoire de la Résistance* (Paris: Editions de Fallois, 1996), p. 259.

37 AN 171/MI/1: meeting between Passy and Sporborg, 14 November 1942.

38 Cordier, *L'Inconnu*, p. 238.

39 Cordier, *La République*, p. 720.

40 Ibid., p. 733.

41 Péan, op. cit., p. 613; Cordier, *La République*, p. 733.

42 Péan, op. cit., p. 635.

43 Ibid., pp. 621–2, 634.

44 Cordier, *La République*, p. 784.

45 Mireille Albrecht, *Berty* (Paris: Editions Robert Laffont, 1986), pp. 340–6.

18 *Setting History Ablaze!*

1 Javier Cercas, *The Impostor*, translated from the Spanish by Frank Wynne (London: MacLehose Press, 2017), pp. 274–5.

2 Leo Marks, *Between Silk and Cyanide* (London: HarperCollins, 1998), p. 593.

3 W.J.M. Mackenzie, *The Secret History of SOE* (London: HMSO, 2000), pp. xxviii–xxix.

4 Nigel West (ed.), *The Guy Liddell Diaries: Vol. II* (London: Routledge, 2005), p. 78.

5 Nigel West, *Secret War: The Story of SOE* (London: Hodder & Stoughton, 1992), p. 106.

6 M.R.D. Foot, *SOE in France* (London: HMSO, 1966), p. 308.

7 Mackenzie, op. cit., pp. 614–5.

8 Foot, op. cit., p. 310.

9 TNA – HS/9/631/5.

10 TNA – HS9/631/5: 6 May 1944.

11 TNA – HS9/631/5.

12 Foot, op. cit., p. 198.

13 Jacques Bureau, *Un soldat menteur* (Paris: Robert Laffont, 1992), pp. 106–7.

14 Foot, op. cit., p. 198.

15 TNA – HS9/631/5.

16 TNA – KV2/830, p. 8; Pean, p. 424.

17 Foot, op. cit., p. 309.

18 Ibid., p. 316.

19 TNA – HS9/1430/6.

20 TNA – HS9/1110/5.

21 TNA – HS9/1110/5.

22 Francis J. Suttill, *Shadows in the Fog* (Stroud, Glos.: The History Press, 2014), pp. 159–161.

23 Foot, op. cit., p. 319.

24 TNA – HS9/631/5.

25 TNA – HS9/631/5.

26 AN – Z/6NL/707/17339.

27 Ibid.

28 TNA – HS9/631/5, par. 32.

29 West, op. cit., p. 4.

30 Foot, op. cit., p. 190.

31 Foot, op. cit., p. 310; M.R.D. Foot, *SOE: The Special Operations Executive 1940–1946* (London: Pimlico, 1999), p. 190; Rita Kramer, *Flames in the Field* (London: Michael Joseph, 1995), p. 202.

32 Kramer, op. cit., p. 202.

33 TNA – HS9/183.

34 Foot, op. cit., p. 221.

35 Ibid., p. 189.

36 M.R.D. Foot, *SOE: Special Operations Executive 1940–46*, p. 314; *SOE in France* (London: HMSO, 1966), pp. 237, 240.

37 Colonel Passy, *Mémoires du Chef des Services Secrets de la France Libre* (Paris: Editions Odile Jacob, 2000), p. 562.

38 *Rapport Gegauf, dossier Hardy*; Gérard Chauvy, *Aubrac Lyon 1943* (Paris: Albin Michel, 1997), pp. 106–8.

39 Francis J. Suttill and M.R.D. Foot (2011) 'SOE's 'Prosper' Disaster of 1943', *Intelligence and National Security*, 26: 1, pp. 99–105, DOI.

40 M.R.D. Foot *SOE: The Special Operations Executive 1940–1946* (London: Pimlico, 1999), p. 221.

41 Jean Overton Fuller, *Déricourt: The Chequered Spy* (London: Michael Russell, 1989), pp. 341, 349.

42 M.R.D. Foot, *SOE in France* (London: HMSO, 1966), p. 308.

43 Michael R.D. Foot *Des Anglais dans la Résistance*, traduit de l'Anglais par Rachel Bouyssou (Paris: Tallandier, 2008), p. 429.

44 Foot, *SOE in France*, p. 308.

45 Ibid.

46 Ibid., pp. 308–9.

47 Francis J. Suttill, *Shadows in the Fog* (Stroud, Glos.: The History Press, 2014), p. 90.

48 Suttill, op. cit., p. 202; TNA – HS9/42.

49   Foot, op. cit., p. 278.

50   Suttill, op. cit., p. 86; TNA – HS9/75.

51   Foot, op. cit., p. 278.

52   *Daily Telegraph*, 21 August 1943.

53   Foot, op. cit., p. 278.

54   Ibid.

55   Ibid.

56   Foot, op. cit., p. 279.

57   Patrick Marnham (ed.), *Darling Pol: The Letters of Mary Wesley and Eric Siepmann* (London: Harvill Secker, 2017), pp. 30–1.

58   Foot, op. cit., p. 309.

59   K.G. Robertson (ed.), *War, Resistance and Intelligence* (London: Leo Cooper, 1999).

60   Ibid., p. 105.

61   FBS 2, 1986, p. 25.

62   Intelligence and National Security, 26: 1, 102, DOI.

63   Paul Guillaume, *La Sologne au temps de l'heroisme et de la trahison* (Orléans: Imprimerie Nouvelle, 1950), p. 66.

64   Nigel West, *MI6: British Secret Intelligence Service Operations, 1909–45* (London: Weidenfeld & Nicolson, 1983), p. 4.

65   TNA – TS58/1156.

66   TNA – TS58/1156: Patrick Reilly to Foreign Office, 5 May 1965.

67   Robert Marshall, *All the King's Men* (London: Collins, 1988), p. 101.

68   Foot, op. cit., p. 303.

19 The Last Mission of Jack Agazarian

1   M.R.D. Foot, *SOE: The Special Operations Executive 1940–1946* (London: Pimlico, 1999), p. 364.

2   M.R.D. Foot, *SOE in France* (London: HMSO, 1966), pp. 290, 303.

3   Jean Overton Fuller, *Déricourt: The Chequered Spy* (London: Michael Russell, 1989), p. 273.

4   Fuller, op. cit., p. 62; Robert Marshall, *All the King's Men* (London: Collins, 1988), p. 25.

5   M.R.D. Foot, *SOE in France* (London: HMSO, 1966), p. 291.

6   TNA – KV2/1131: 18a. Situation of French pilot Léon Doulet.

7   TNA – KV2/1131: 24c.

8   TNA – KV2/1131.

9   Hugh Verity, *We Landed by Moonlight* (Shepperton: Ian Allan Ltd., 1978), pp. 13–8.

10   M.R.D. Foot, *SOE: The Special Operations Executive 1940–1946* (London: Pimlico, 1999), p. 142.

11   K.G. Robertson (ed.), *War, Resistance and Intelligence* (London: Leo Cooper, 1999), pp. 172, 175.

12 Keith Jeffery, *MI6: The History of the Secret Intelligence Service 1909–1949* (London: Bloomsbury, 2010), p. 366.

13 TNA – KV2/1131: BCRA to MI5, 7 December 1942.

14 M.R.D. Foot, *SOE in France* (London: HMSO, 1966), pp. 291–2.

15 Ibid., p. 292.

16 Foot, *SOE in France*, p.299; Francis J. Suttill, *Shadows in the Fog* (Stroud, Glos.: The History Press, 2014), pp. 11, 212, 214.

17 Sarah Helm, *A Life in Secrets: The Story of Vera Atkins* (London: Little, Brown, 2005), pp. 173–4.

18 Brooks Richards, *Secret Flotillas* (London: HMSO, 1996), p. 104.

19 Helm, op. cit., p. 41.

20 David Garnett, *The Secret History of PWE: The Political Warfare Executive 1939–1945* (London: St Ermin's Press, 2002), p. 52.

21 TNA – HS9/171/1; Foot, op. cit., p. 20.

22 Jeffery, op. cit., pp. 354–5.

23 TNA – HS9/171/1.

24 M.R.D. Foot, *SOE in France* (London: HMSO, 1966), p. 293.

25 Ibid.

26 Ibid.

27 M.R.D. Foot, *SOE: The Special Operations Executive 1940–1946* (London: Pimlico, 1999), p. 364.

28 TNA – HS9/11/1; M.R.D. Foot, *SOE in France* (London: HMSO, 1966), p. 299.

29 Foot, op. cit., p. 313.

30 M.R.D. Foot, *SOE in France* (London: HMSO, 1966), pp. 303, 305.

31 Foot, op. cit., pp. 324, 338.

32 Shrabani Basu, *The Life of Noor Inayat Khan* (Stroud, Glos.: The History Press, 2008), p. 192.

33 Basu, op. cit., pp. 191, 199; Leo Marks, *Between Silk and Cyanide* (London: HarperCollins, 1998), pp. 399, 511.

34 Foot, op. cit., pp. 341–2; Foot, *SOE: The Special Operations Executive 1940–46*, p. 193. (The agents arrested included France Antelme, who had denounced Déricourt in 1943.)

35 TNA – HS9/171/1.

36 TNA – KV2/830.

37 TNA – KV2/830.

38 Foot, op. cit., p. 308.

39 Jeffery, op. cit., pp. 409–10.

40 Ibid., p. 366.

41 Martin Gilbert, *Winston S. Churchill: Vol. VII* (London: Heinemann, 1986), p. 228.

42 Marshall, op. cit., p. 153.

43 J.C. Masterman, *The Double-Cross System* (London: Granada, 1979), p. 64.

44 Ibid., p. 65.

45 AN – Dossier 2e Tribunal Militaire 12 March 1948. *Déposition Helmut Knochen, 18 November 1946*. Cote 22.

20 Colonel Dansey's Private War

1 Hans Magnus Enzensberger, *Hammerstein, ou l'Intransigeance* (Paris: Gallimard, 2011). (Author's translation.)

2 M.R.D. Foot, *SOE in France* (London: HMSO, 1966), p. 299.

3 TNA – KV2/1131.

4 Foot, op. cit., p. 291.

5 TNA – KV2/1131: 7 May 1943.

6 TNA – KV2/1131: 10 June 1943.

7 Foot, op. cit., pp. 303, 305.

8 TNA – KV2/1131.

9 TNA – HS9/11/1.

10 TNA – HS9/42.

11 Foot, op. cit., p. 300.

12 Ibid., pp. 301–2.

13 Nigel West, *Secret War: The Story of SOE* (London: Hodder & Stoughton, 1992), pp. 125, 251–2.

14 TNA – KV2/1131: 49a.

15 J.C. Masterman, *The Double-Cross System* (London: Granada, 1979), pp. 61–2; Michael Howard, *British Intelligence in World War II: Vol. V* (London: HMSO, 1990), pp. 7–8; Thaddeus Holt, *The Deceivers: Allied Military Deception in the Second World War* (London: Weidenfeld & Nicolson, 2004), p. 148.

16 Keith Jeffery, *MI6: The History of the Secret Intelligence Service 1909–1949* (London: Bloomsbury, 2010), p. 355.

17 TNA – HS9/423; Vol. III.

18 TNA – KV2/1131: 6a.

19 Foot, op. cit., p. 371.

20 TNA – KV2/1131: 32a; West (ed.), *The Guy Liddell Diaries: Vol. II* (London: Routledge, 2005), p. 175.

21 Keith Jeffery, op. cit., p. 301.

22 TNA – HS9/421, 29 January 1944.

23 TNA – HS9/421.

24 TNA – KV2/1131: MI5 memo dated 17 February 1944.

25 Lord Alanbrooke, *War Diaries: 1939–1945* (London: Weidenfeld & Nicolson, 2001), 16 February 1944.

26 TNA – KV2/1131: 19 February 1944.

27 TNA – HS9/421.

28 Hugh Verity, *We Landed by Moonlight* (Shepperton: Ian Allan Ltd., 1978), p. 165.

29 Rita Kramer, *Flames in the Field* (London: Michael Joseph 1995), p. 274.

30 TNA – HS9/171/1, 13 February 1945; TNA – KV2/830.

31 TNA – KV2/1131: 76a.

32 Sarah Helm, *A Life in Secrets: The Story of Vera Atkins* (London: Little, Brown, 2005), p. 434.

33 Foot, op.cit., p. 305.

34 TNA – HS9/421.

35 TNA – HS9/421.

36 Tim Milne, *Kim Philby* (London: Biteback, 2014), p. 66.

37 K.G. Robertson (ed.), *War, Resistance and Intelligence* (London: Leo Cooper, 1999), pp. 230, 238.

38 Anthony Cave Brown, *Philby Père et Fils: La Trahison dans le Sang* (Paris: Pygmalion, 1997)), pp. 289, 291.

39 TNA – KV4/120, 13 October 1942.

40 Geoff Andrews, *Agent Molière* (London: I.B. Tauris, 2020), pp. 128, 139–41.

41 Malcolm Muggeridge, *Tread Softly for You Tread on my Jokes* (London: William Collins, 1966), p. 183

42 Brown, op. cit., pp. 289, 291. And see Edward Harrison, *The Young Kim Philby: Soviet Spy and British Intelligence Officer* (Exeter: University of Exeter Press, 2012), p. 81; Tim Milne, *Kim Philby* (London: Biteback, 2014), pp. 124–5.

43 Tim Milne, op. cit., p. 125.

44 Ibid., pp. 125–30; Harrison, op. cit., p. 152; TNA – KV4/120, 13 October 1942.

45 Hugh Trevor-Roper, *Secret World* (London: I.B. Tauris, 2014), pp. 106, 193–4, 225–6.

46 Pierre Péan, *Le mysterieux Docteur Martin* (Paris: Fayard, 1993).

47 Christopher Andrew, *The Defence of the Realm: The Authorized History of MI5* (London: Allen Lane, 2009), p. 315.

48 Jeffery, op. cit., p. 403.

49 Ibid. p. 361.

50 Ibid., p. 760.

51 Ben Macintyre, *Double Cross* (London: Bloomsbury, 2012), p. 210.

21 *The Depths of Deception*

1 TNA – KV/2/830.

2 Ibid.

3 Ibid. Letter from Capitaine J. Vaudreuil (BCRA) to Monsieur Marriott (MI5), 9 February 1945.

4 Memo dated 15 February 1945, from Hugh Astor of MI5, B.1.A, TNA – KV2/830.

5 TNA – KV/2/830.

6 TNA – KV2/1131/41c.

7 *Nouvel Observateur*, 2 June 1994.

8 Sarah Helm, *A Life in Secrets: The Story of Vera Atkins* (London: Little, Brown, 2005), p. 346.

9 Ibid., pp. 66–7, 77, 85–7, 334–46.

10 TNA – TS58/1156.

11 Nigel West, *Secret War: The Story of SOE* (London: Hodder & Stoughton 1992), pp. 3–4.

12 Sir Patrick Reilly, September 1986: see Robert Marshall, *All the King's Men* (London: Collins, 1988), p. 193.

13 Thaddeus Holt, *The Deceivers: Allied Military Deception in the Second World War* (London: Weidenfeld & Nicolson, 2004), p. 53.

14 J.C. Masterman, *The Double-Cross System* (London: Granada, 1979), p. 130.

15 Gabriel Gorodetsky (ed.), *The Maisky Diaries* (New Haven: Yale University Press, 2016), p. 528.

16 Masterman, op. cit., p. 130.

17 Roger Hesketh, *Fortitude* (London: St Ermin's Press, 1999), p. 1.

18 Daniel Cordier, *Jean Moulin: La République des Catacombes* (Paris: Gallimard, 1999), pp. 426–7, 922.

19 John Keegan, *The Second World War* (London: Pimlico, 1989), p. 394.

20 Holt, op. cit., p. 492.

21 Pierre Péan, *Vies et Morts de Jean Moulin* (Paris: Fyard, 1998), p. 598; Gérard Chauvy, *Aubrac Lyon 1943* (Paris: Albin Michel, 1997), p. 167.

22 Cordier, op. cit., p. 470.

23 Péan, op. cit., p. 569.

24 Gérard Chauvy, op. cit., pp. 161–2.

25 Keith Jeffery, *MI6: The History of the Secret Intelligence Service 1909–1949* (London: Bloomsbury, 2010), p. 314.

26 See Masterman, op. cit., and Ben Macintyre, *Double Cross* (London: Bloomsbury, 2012).

27 J.C. Masterman, *The Double-Cross System* (London: Granada, 1979), p. 65.

28 Nigel West and Oleg Tsarev (eds.), *Triplex: Secrets from the Cambridge Spies* (New Haven: Yale University Press, 2009), pp. 274–8.

29 Miranda Carter, *Anthony Blunt: His Lives* (London: Macmillan, 2001), pp. 284–5, 286.

30 West and Tsarev, op. cit., p. 276.

31 Holt, op. cit., pp. 201, 478; West and Tsarev, op. cit., p. 293.

32 Robert Marshall, *All the King's Men* (London: Collins, 1988) p. 153.

33 Michael Howard, *British Intelligence in World War II: Vol. V* (London: HMSO, 1990), p. 7.

34 Edward Harrison, *The Young Kim Philby: Soviet Spy and British Intelligence Officer* (Exeter: University of Exeter Press, 2012), pp. 130–1.

35 Olivier Wieviorka, *Histoire de la Résistance 1940–1945* (Paris: Perrin, 2013), p. 293; Cordier, op. cit., p. 442.

36 Jean-Pierre Azéma (ed.), *Jean Moulin: Face à l'Histoire* (Paris: Flammarion, 2000), pp. 158, 202.

37 Daniel Cordier, *Jean Moulin: L'Inconnu du Panthéon Vol. I* (Paris: Editions J.C. Lattès, 1989), pp. 276–7, 337; Jean-Pierre Azéma (ed.), *Jean Moulin: Face à l'Histoire* (Paris: Flammarion, 2000), p. 203.

38 Daniel Cordier, *Jean Moulin: La République des Catacombes* (Paris: Gallimard, 1999), p. 448.

39 Ibid., p. 466.

40 Jacques Baumel, *Résister* (Paris: Albin Michel, 1999), p. 326.

41 Péan, op. cit., pp. 621–2, 634.

42 A.J.P. Taylor, *English History 1914–1945* (London: OUP, 1965), p. 483.

43 Private information.

44 Jimmy Burns, *Papa Spy* (London: Bloomsbury, 2009), pp. 295–6, 374.

45 Howard, op. cit., pp. 231–4; Macintyre, op. cit., pp. 147–9.

46 Jeffery, op. cit., p. 359–61.

47 Kim Philby, *My Silent War* (London: Panther, 1969), p. 67.

48 Edward Harrison, *The Young Kim Philby* (Exeter: University of Exeter Press, 2012), pp. 154, 157.

49 Christopher Andrew and Vasili Mitrokhin (eds.), *The Mitrokhin Archive* (London: Allen Lane, 1999), p. 197.

50 Patrick Marnham, *Army of the Night: The Life and Death of Jean Moulin, Legend of the French Resistance* (London: Tauris Parke Paperbacks, 2015), pp. 193 5; Claude Guy, *En écoutant de Gaulle* (Paris: Grasset, 1996), p. 240.

51 W.J.M. Mackenzie, *The Secret History of SOE* (London: St Ermin's, 2000), pp. 572–3.

52 Olivier Wieviorka, *Histoire de la Résistance 1940–1945* (Paris: Perrin, 2013), pp. 164, 265–7.

53 Hugh Verity, *We Landed by Moonlight* (Shepperton: Ian Allan Ltd, 1978), pp. 165–6.

Afterword: The Level Sands

1 Germaine Tillion, *Ravensbrück* (Paris: Seuil,1973), pp. 114, 123, 199.

2 Ibid., p. 91.

3 Ibid., p. 355.

4 AD55J2.

5 Anne Annear, *The West Australian*, 18 August 1984.

6 Tillion, op. cit., p. 341.

7 Stella King, *Jacqueline* (London: Arms and Armour, 1989), pp. 365–6.

8 *La Nouvelle République du Centre-Ouest 1945*; King, op. cit., p. 407.

9 King, op. cit., p. 407.

10 Jeanne de Tristan, interview with the author, 22 October 2012.

Postscript

1 The proceedings of the conference were recorded and can be followed on an audio tape in the National Archives, Accession number IWM 18610/ 80017672. https://www.iwm.org.uk/collections/item/object/80017672.

2 Private recording (reel 5 of 5), deposited at the Imperial War Museum.

3 http://www.coldspur.com/sonia-mi6s-hidden-hand.

4 See *Operation Lucy* by Anthony Read and John Fisher (London: Hodder & Stoughton 1984).

5 TNA – HS 8-899-9.

6 This link was confirmed by Col. Knochen's evidence at a 1946 treason trial (ADII/133/Cote22).

Acknowledgements

My thanks are due to Frédéric Théry of Château Nanteuil, the grandson of Anne-Marie de Bernard, who made this book possible by allowing me to consult his family papers and the records of his house and offered me so much generous hospitality over the years. I am also grateful for the assistance offered by his brother Christophe and to Vicky Read, a descendant of the Irelands, the family that first introduced Nesta Cox to Nanteuil. The story I have told is that of the previous generation of Frédéric's family, of his mother Béatrice, *née* Gardnor-Beard, his aunt Muriel, always known as 'Moune' and of his uncles, Pierre Théry and Owen Watson.

In the Sologne, I am particularly grateful to Madame Elizabeth Gicquel of Vineuil, who assembled a long account of the extraordinary life of her friend Nesta Cox, which I have drawn on heavily in chapters 2 and 10. I have also been helped by the late Madame Jeanne Dambrine, *née* de Tristan, of Bracieux, formerly of the *Réseau Adolphe*, and Madame Françoise Clerget of Nanteuil.

I was able to interview or correspond with two *anciens élèves* of the 1930s, the late Jeremy Hutchinson QC (Lord Hutchinson of Lullington) and the late Valerian Wellesley (8th Duke of Wellington). Among other former students of Nanteuil I would like to remember David Pinckney, Annabel Farrell (1957) and Patrick Brooks, and salute my fellow pupils of the summer of 1962, Neil Pike, Angela Toller and Elizabeth Shaw, with whom I have long since lost touch. Nor do I forget our neighbour of those days, Chantal de Froberville.

In Paris I was generously entertained by the late Pierre Braillard and assisted by Jean-Pierre Pujes, Jean-Louis Crémieux-Brilhac, Jean-Louis Faure and Gilles Perrault and also by Jean-Pierre Villemer. In Brussels, Manu Riche was a generous host and one of the first to encourage my interest in the story of Nanteuil; he also invested his time and money in a proposal to film it. In addition, I was encouraged by Kathleen de Bethune and advised by Philippe Van Meerbeeck. I would also like to thank Mrs Brenda Hope, niece of the late Corporal Charles Carter for permission to quote from her uncle's diary, and Andrew Bradford, the elder son of the late Brigadier B.C. Bradford of the 2nd Battalion, Black Watch.

I have not forgotten the role played many years ago in this project by my sometime publisher Liz Calder, with whom I have had so many years of friendship, and I remain grateful to Nicola Solomon, chief executive of the Society of Authors, for her professional advice which was of invaluable help during a difficult episode.

Steve Hawes was kind enough to read and comment on much of the first draft. William Théry, of Nanteuil, great-grandson of Anne-Marie de Bernard, undertook additional research in the departmental archives. Professor George Huxley decoded part of an anonymous letter. At Corpus Christi College, Cambridge, Dr Anne McLaughlin, Head Librarian, and Dr Lucy Hughes, Archivist, were most generous with their time and Dr James Howard-Johnston granted me regular access to the library of my old college, Corpus Christi College, Oxford.

I would like to thank the staff of the Bodleian Library at Oxford, and the librarians of the London Library in St James's Square, as well as the staff of the National Archives at Kew, the Archives nationales at Pierrefitte-sur-Seine, the Service historique de la Défense at Vincennes, the Archives départmentales de Loir-et-Cher at Blois and the Musée de la Résistance in Blois.

This book is not always uncritical of the official history of secret intelligence, so I should acknowledge the considerable debt I nonetheless owe to a number of distinguished practitioners in this field. They include Christopher Andrew, the late Sir Michael Howard and the late Keith Jeffery. I should also mention David Reynolds, David Stafford, Thaddeus Holt and Edward Harrison. I could not have proceeded with my own research without a close study of their work and I hope I have adequately recorded my debt in the bibliography and in the source notes. I have also been enthused by Julian Jackson's remarkable biography of Charles de Gaulle, and among French authorities I would mention Daniel Cordier MBE, the late Jean-Louis Crémieux-Brilhac, Jean-Pierre Azéma and Olivier Wieviorka.

Other authors working in this field whose work I have found

particularly helpful include Nigel West, Jimmy Burns, Sarah Helm and Francis J. Suttill. I am also grateful to Tom Bower, biographer of Sir Dick White, who succeeded in extracting the quote that became this book's epigraph.

I owe a great deal to my agent Veronique Baxter of David Higham and to my editor at Oneworld, Bill Swainson, for his patient and painstaking criticism, and for shepherding *War in the Shadows* through the pandemic lock-down crisis of 2020. I of course remain entirely responsible for any errors outstanding.

Finally, this book was written with the assistance of a grant from the Authors' Foundation, a fund administered by the Society of Authors. The support of the Foundation's trustees in 2012 enabled me to undertake months of additional research in Paris and Blois. My greatest debt, once again, is to my wife, Chantal.

Patrick Marnham, Woodstock, May 2021

Index

About the Author

PATRICK MARNHAM lived and worked in France for many years. He has been a staff writer for *Private Eye*, a BBC script writer, Literary Editor of the *Spectator* and Paris correspondent of the *Independent* and the *Evening Standard*. His biographies include lives of the Resistance leader Jean Moulin, as well as Georges Simenon and Mary Wesley. His most recent travel book is *Snake Dance: Journeys Beneath a Nuclear Sky*.